W9-AFS-544

POLITICS IN ENGLISH
ROMANTIC POETRY

POLITICS IN ENGLISH
ROMANTIC POETRY

Carl Woodring

Cambridge, Massachusetts
Harvard University Press
1970

Distributed in Great Britain by Oxford University Press, London

Publication of this book has been aided by a grant from the
Hyder Edward Rollins Fund

Library of Congress Catalog Card Number 74-111490

SBN 674-68882-1

Printed in the United States of America

TO SAN

PREFACE

The subject of politics in the poetry of the romantic period in England has not been adequately explored. It is perhaps difficult to regard as neglected a subject that has received extensive treatment from Edward Dowden, Georg Brandes, A. E. Hancock, Charles Cestre, Walter Graham, and Crane Brinton, and sporadic treatment from many others. Even the standard work, however, Crane Brinton's survey in *The Political Ideas of the English Romanticists*, relies on statements in prose more than on the configurations of diction and metaphor in the poems. It seemed to me in 1952, as a professional student of poetry, that there was room for a book on the different guises of politics in the poetry itself. I was curious also about the oddity that almost all students of English literature equated romanticism with revolt and that almost all social scientists equated romanticism with conservative reaction. That particular contradiction has since eased, but it has not disappeared.

It is still necessary to declare that politics is more pervasive in the poetry of 1789–1832 than has of late been generally acknowledged. Romantic poems involve political theory, political convictions, and practical politics, as well as many traditions and conventions of political writing.

Notably, since the present study was begun, dozens of critics have helped clarify the nature of the romantic enterprise. David V. Erd-

Preface

man has provided the narrower field with *Blake: Prophet against Empire*. In 1957 F. M. Todd published *Politics and the Poet: A Study of Wordsworth*. I treated separately, as *Politics in the Poetry of Coleridge,* details that took too much unraveling for a single chapter. The present work was promised in my Preface of 1961 as "a less detailed examination of politics in the poetry of Wordsworth, Byron, Shelley, and poets associated with them." Revision has consisted largely of reducing detail and eliminating the inconclusive results of several lines of research. One effect is that numerous older books on such subjects as "The French Revolution in English History," which influenced the study at early stages, have been replaced in the documentation by fewer and more recent books that acknowledge indebtedness to the same studies I have used. The reduction of documentation is probably a gain. American scholars have fallen into the habit of excessive citation, and of chain citation from one study to another, just at the time when our bibliographies, indexes, and concordances are well organized to eliminate the need for expensive repetition of bibliographic detail. I have tried to document all citations from unique or rare material. For the poets closely followed, I have tried to be exact in reference where it was convenient on the page, as in blocked quotations, and wherever my use of phrases is interpretative or admittedly debatable.

My obligations to teachers, students, colleagues, and librarians are too numerous to name unless in a list that would reduce benefactors to sardines. I have indicated a few special obligations in the footnotes. For eliminating errors from specific sections of the work at various stages, I am grateful to Professors William H. Young, David V. Erdman, Leslie A. Marchand, Kenneth Neill Cameron, and Jerome H. Buckley. Former students Ruth Aldrich, Thomas Lombardi Ashton, Carl Dawson, Ellen Gahtan, Stephen L. Goldstein, Robert Hartley, June Q. Koch, Eve Leoff, Robert M. Maniquis, Anne T. Kostelanetz Mellor, and Brian Wilkie have influenced my interpretation of particular works.

I am especially conscious of the mouse brought forth when I reflect that this work has absorbed portions of generous grants from the John Simon Guggenheim Memorial Foundation, the American Council of Learned Societies, the Fund for the Advancement of Edu-

Preface

cation (Ford Foundation), and the Research Committee of the Graduate School, University of Wisconsin. Funds from the Dean of Graduate Faculties, Columbia University, secured the expert typing of Mrs. Diana Beddoe Blaikie. I am grateful to the Clarendon Press, Oxford, for permission to quote from *The Poems and Songs of Robert Burns*, edited by James Kinsley; *The Poetical Works of John Keats*, edited by H. W. Garrod; *The Letters of Percy Bysshe Shelley*, edited by Frederick L. Jones; *The Poetical Works of William Wordsworth* and *The Prelude*, both edited by Ernest de Selincourt, revised by Helen Darbishire, and to Oxford University Press for brief quotations from several other editions; to Doubleday & Company, Inc., for permission to quote from *The Poetry and Prose of William Blake*, edited by David V. Erdman; to the University of Illinois Press for quotations from *Shelley's "The Triumph of Life": A Critical Study*, by Donald H. Reiman; and to Alfred A. Knopf, Inc., and Faber & Faber Ltd. for quotations from P. B. Shelley, *The Esdaile Notebook*, edited by Kenneth Neill Cameron, © The Carl and Lily Pforzheimer Foundation, Inc.

C.W.

Columbia University

CONTENTS

ILLUSTRATIONS

Illustrations

Edmund Burke "the swinish multitude" and therefore sardonically represented here, as in Shelley's *Swellfoot the Tyrant,* as pigs. Among the stricken advocates of peace, the heavily bearded man wearing a cap of liberty is Charles James Fox. The imp kissing Pitt's buttocks is the Prince of Wales, later George IV. For further identifications see M. Dorothy George, *Catalogue of Political and Personal Satires . . . in the British Museum,* VII (1942), 179-180. It is implied, as in the earliest political poems by Coleridge, that the abominations of Pitt are divine evidence of a blissful millennium to come. Meanwhile, the ministers are Wordsworth's "vermin working out of reach."

BYRON IN A HELMET OF HIS OWN DESIGN *page 151*
"Drawn from a Sketch in Possession of the Compte Demitrie Deladezima, in Cephalonia; corrected & Published in London Feb^r 1825, by A. Friedel, Publisher of Portraits of all the principal Greek Chiefs." From September through December 1823, at Metaxata, where Byron reportedly designed the helmet, Count Delladecima acted as interpreter and intermediary between Byron and emissaries from Missolonghi and other strongholds of the Greek leaders. (By courtesy of the City Librarian of Nottingham and Curator of Newstead Abbey.)

DOCTOR SOUTHEY'S NEW VISION *page 192*
By George Cruikshank, a fold-out engraving at page 46 of *A Slap at Slop.* Robert Southey, dressed as a jester and wearing on his head emblems of his Jacobin past, plays music from a cask of wine representing simultaneously his annual stipend as Poet Laureate and the barrel-organ tone of his poem *A Vision of Judgment.* George IV, as Apollo and *roi-soleil,* rises above the peg leg of John Sewell, president of the Constitutional Association ("the Bridge-Street Gang"), who is immersed in a pail of slop (representing the Tory *New Times,* edited by John Stoddart, Hazlitt's brother-in-law, whom the radicals called "Dr. Slop"). Leigh Hunt had gone to prison for deriding Tory praise of the Prince Regent as an Adonis; here in 1822 the same monarch is a fat Apollo wearing spurs made of peacock feathers. See M. D. George, *Catalogue,* X (1952), 238-239. This plate accompanied a parody of Southey's poem by William Hone.

Illustrations

Illustrations

Aquatint caricature by James Gillray, 9 June 1792. No. 8105 in
M. D. George, *Catalogue,* VI (1938), 916-917. The subject, Queen
Charlotte's protection of Pitt against Lord Chancellor Thurlow, is too
early for all the romantics except Blake, but the print splendidly
illustrates the iconographical method of aligning Milton (or Shakespeare
or another classic), a design from a prominent painter (here William
Hogarth), venal intermediaries (here the publisher John Boydell and the
artist Henry Fuseli, both in 1792 promoting elaborate editions of
Milton), and the immediate political target. Of all the romantic
emulations of the allegorical encounter of Satan, Sin, and Death in
Paradise Lost (II.648–889), the most strikingly original is Shelley's
in "Lines Written among the Euganean Hills."

POLITICS IN ENGLISH
ROMANTIC POETRY

ABBREVIATIONS

BL S. T. Coleridge, *Biographia Literaria,* ed. J. Shawcross. 2 vols. Oxford University Press, 1907.

BWP *The Works of Lord Byron: Poetry,* ed. E. H. Coleridge. 7 vols. London: John Murray, 1898–1905, corr. to 1924.

CPW *The Complete Poetical Works of Samuel Taylor Coleridge,* ed. E. H. Coleridge. 2 vols. Oxford University Press, 1912.

EN P. B. Shelley, *The Esdaile Notebook,* ed. K. N. Cameron. New York: Alfred A. Knopf, 1964.

LJ *The Works of Lord Byron: Letters and Journals,* ed. R. E. Prothero. 6 vols. London: John Murray, 1898–1901.

SL *The Letters of Percy Bysshe Shelley,* ed. F. L. Jones. 2 vols. Oxford: Clarendon Press, 1964.

SP *The Complete Poetical Works of Percy Bysshe Shelley,* ed. Thomas Hutchinson. Oxford University Press, 1952.

SW *The Complete Works of Percy Bysshe Shelley.* ed. Roger Ingpen and W. E. Peck. 10 vols. London and New York: Julian Editions, 1926–1930.

WPW *The Poetical Works of William Wordsworth,* ed. E. de Selincourt and H. Darbishire. 5 vols. Oxford: Clarendon Press, 1947–1954.

I

INTRODUCTION

Poems contain ideas. In turn, housed by long tenure in most words, ideas have consequences for poetry. However grossly the ideological tenants misbehave by changing identities, taking in cousins, or carelessly subletting to foreign ideas, poems can never keep their words vacant. "Jug, jug" may cease to sound like a nightingale's song, but it can never escape the sort of connotation that all words invite. Every poem has been influenced by the ideas of the poet and by the preconceptions of his time. The physical theory that climate affects or determines cultural products, taken with increasing seriousness from Montesquieu to Taine, vaulted into easier acceptance through Alfred North Whitehead's revival of a supple phrase, "climate of opinion." The English poets of the period 1789–1832, we say, wrote in a climate of revolution, reaction, and reform. Born into such a climate, a poet could enlist or defy, but he could not ignore, for "not to choose is choosing," and withdrawal was reaction. At a time when most poems were read in the light of political principles and reviewed with a partisan puff or a partisan hatchet, it is not surprising that most poets responded to ideas and events with the deepest profundity they were individually capable of.

Concerning general movements of thought or society there will always be debate. Many of the adjectives applied by the poets to the events of their era, and retained for historical shading in Chapter

Politics in English Romantic Poetry

II below, on "The Climate," have been much discussed and frequently rejected in historical writing of recent years. They have been questioned especially by the revisionist disciples of Sir Lewis Namier and the statisticians who have refined Sir John Clapham's *Economic History of Modern Britain*. Many historians have replaced the term Agricultural Revolution with the idea of acceleration in a long process of mechanization and enclosure.[1] The term Industrial Revolution is now assigned to a period after 1830, when mass production spread statistically from the manufacture of textiles to all other industry. Scholarship always requires qualification, but it seems worth while to say what the poets thought they saw: "One only master grasps the whole domain." Near this domain, enclosed for agricultural efficiency and the pleasures of the hunt, the landscape is interrupted by the smokestack of a dark Satanic mill. Aware that an acceleration to eight miles an hour is less than what is scientifically possible, we can nonetheless respond to the joy and terror of acceleration caught by De Quincey in "The Glory of Motion" and "The Vision of Sudden Death" in *The English Mail-Coach*. In reordering experience, poems sometimes create ordered history and sometimes disorder events for literary ends. The present investigation, treating poems as final, self-authenticating objects of study and admiration, takes as its point of beginning the poetic responses to an age of acceleration. Little attention can be given here to developments that seem much more important to historians today than they seemed to Wordsworth and his fellow poets. For understanding their poetry, I take it as more pertinent to review the grounds of the romantic attack on Malthus than to speculate on the possible reasons for the poets' failure to take seriously enough the doubling of the population in Britain between 1751 and 1821—a development that the economic historian Phyllis Deane could treat in 1965 as the acceleration underlying all the other accelerations.[2]

The operative thesis of the present study is that political concern is more important as a generative force and an argumentative presence in the romantic movement in England, and in major poems of that movement, than one could gather from most criticism of the last fifty years. I wish to explore also a subsidiary proposition; namely, that the discrepancies between the rationalistic, empirical,

Introduction

and utilitarian bases of liberalism and the romantic intuitions of organicism and the unifying imagination created a crisis, and usually remained as a dilemma, in the political beliefs of each of the major English romantic poets.

Rationalistic, external changes in the responses of Helen Maria Williams, who resided in France throughout the Revolutionary and Napoleonic years, provide a convenient paradigm for the internal, emotional changes in the major poets. When she witnessed in Paris the ceremony of the Federation of 1790, "it required but the common feelings of humanity to become in that moment a citizen of the world." A few days later, she repeated with all her heart and soul, "Vive la nation!" In this short span she epitomized the change occurring in France and anticipated the first stage in the spiritual journey of the English romantic poets. After telling the story of a friend tormented through the tyrannical use of a *lettre de cachet* (a story similar to Wordsworth's "Vaudracour and Julia"), she asked: "What, indeed, but friendship, could have led my attention from the annals of imagination to the records of politics; from the poetry to the prose of human life?" She asked because the hostility of the French to Shakespeare reminded her that Shakespeare "was not only the glory of England, but of human nature." She tried to believe that the leaders of the Revolution had "not trusted merely to the force of reason," but had studied also "the most powerful passions of human nature."[3] And so they had. For Miss Williams, as for Byron's Don Juan, it took a physical storm during her return by sea "to exclude every idea but that of preparation to die with composure"; for greater poets, equally biased toward liberty but troubled over rational arguments for progress, the storm to come in France heralded a storm within. Miss Williams would speak for them in her sequel of 1816: "All the noble promises of liberty had proved faithless, all its altars had been profaned."[4] With scorn she could dismiss Napoleon as a betrayer and coward; Byron felt Napoleon's betrayal and cowardice too deeply for the simple response of scorn.

Although the French Revolution brought to the deprived and the young in England a sudden joyful sense of apocalypse, neither the events nor their rationale could sustain the sense of expectancy or the substance of the expectations. Literary history pits the poets when young against the Augustan age of Pope, but the poets themselves did not think of their dissent as the revolt of one generation against another. At an inconvenient point in time Newton and Locke had provided instruments that were then used in the period from Pope to William Paley for false measurements of man, but the false ways of measuring continued after Paley, Adam Smith, and Joseph Priestley in the writings of Thomas Robert Malthus, James Mackintosh, Jeremy Bentham, Francis Jeffrey, and countless imitators of these. By "the Spirit of the Age" Hazlitt means especially the meanness he saw about him: the classical economists, the minds bound by a utilitarian psychology, the living practitioners of "one idea." Initially the spirit of the new age was liberty, but in fact the age has continued the suppression of liberty. So, to arms![5]

Whatever their trust in original genius, however great their dissatisfaction with the restraints of decorum, the romantic poets gave much greater exercise to genres from the traditional store than the Augustans had. They sought liberty in the narrow cell of the Miltonic sonnet. So often did they pillage Milton's ode "On the Morning of Christ's Nativity" for political apocalypse that the ode itself has come to be considered political. Emulation of great models led them typically to the higher aspiration of remodeling those models. The subjectivity of their search for the grounds of knowledge undermined all walls.

New varieties of lyric poetry resulted. The symbolic concentration of protest in Blake's "London"; the obliquity of Wordsworth's addresses to the daisy ("Thou unassuming Common-place"); the synthesis of irony, simplicity, symbol, and argument in "Michael"; the scalding blasts in the midst of irresolute commentary in *Don Juan;* the ideological lyricism of "Ode to the West Wind"—none of these ways of harnessing political impulse had been known before. *Prometheus Unbound* is as innovative and inimitable as the works of Lewis Carroll.

Lyric novelties derived in part from tensions common to the political thought of all the major poets. Although the search for resolution took each poet in his own direction, the more each (except Byron) softened his initially radical position, the more he sought nonpolitical

Introduction

solutions to problems he had once deemed political. The difficulty was not created solely by political thought. The conflict between advocacy of reform and faith in the imagination was not merely a conflict over what to say in verse addressed to all men. The problem began in the discrepancy between the rationalistic doctrine of abstract rights and a faith in the affections of the individual as basic to human society, but the dilemma did not end there. The deeper problem was to say through the instruments of the imagination—organic unity, symbol, and myth—something admissible when expressed in language other than that of the instruments. If the imagination is divine or autonomous, then a poem can say nothing that is simultaneously true and logical. Poetry contains ideas, but clear and distinct ideas are another matter.

The older poets, Wordsworth and Coleridge if not Blake, retracted their claims for the autonomy of poetic genius. Despite his ardent desire to prove the human mind deeper than dreams and generative of its own "plastic stress," Coleridge's movement toward an increasingly severe Christian idealism led from belief in natural law as *ordo ordinans,* "ordering order," to advocacy of tradition, making law (the terms are from Hugo Grotius) *ordo ordinatus,* "ordered order."

Wordsworth revised passages of *The Prelude* to say that the mind of man, though it grows like harmony in music, is made of dust and kindred to the worm. He thereby acknowledged the need of the individual not only to kneel before his maker but also to accept the ordering power of the state. Wordsworth's whole canon testifies that his political passion was an incurable but life-enhancing habit. His expressions of compassion, however, return after about 1804 to the poetic cellar of mere statements. The statements become increasingly social and less and less political. In this respect Wordsworth's poetry, like Byron's *Don Juan,* was on its way to the Victorian novel.

For the younger poets the French Revolution had funneled into one leader. Napoleon, who soured Blake's regard for Leviathans of energy, challenged the younger poets as well to define the basis of faith in liberty. From his earliest poems to his last, Shelley sought to mediate the dichotomy between love and revolution. Although

5

imagination meant for him what action meant for Byron, neither poet could respect an art free of political concern. Shelley converted the law of Necessity into the law of Love. Social revolution must occur, but only after the oppressed have forgiven their oppressors. Liberty, imagination, and love are nearly synonymous.

The generation of the 1770's learned to revere the organic state. The younger men looked for a Bolivar who would not shrink to a Napoleon. In the debate of historians over the relative importance of the American and French Revolutions for the subsequent world, English romantic poetry inevitably serves the partisans of the French, but it shows clearly enough that the recurring presence of Napoleon forced a return to Jefferson and especially Washington as heroic models. In poems of 1804 Tom Moore had predicted a quick end to the North American republic, tainted as it was with "foul Philosophy" from France—the "Gallic dross" among "slaving blacks and democratic whites." After Waterloo, Byron and Shelley needed a different view. Columbia, coarse but united under representative government, afforded a grotto to which the hopes of man could retire if revolutions elsewhere failed.

Of the major poets, Byron most nearly avoided the dichotomy between political and aesthetic inclinations. The others faced the problem as a continuing dilemma. To be a democrat, as Wordsworth thought he was, one needs either to trust man as he is or to favor a system of reform that might make man more trustworthy in the future. As a poet, Wordsworth, like Blake, was in retreat, knew it, and resented it. Coleridge, who early abandoned the possibility of democratic equality as inconsistent with reality, assimilated more completely than Wordsworth the political doctrines shaped by Transcendentalists and Romantics in Germany to their own aesthetic and religious needs. Shelley, pushing his readers into poetic pleasure and political action, kept the deep truth imageless.

Critics from Aristotle on have declared poetry to be closer to philosophy than to history. Byron, for his part, was determined not to be misled by imagination into an abandonment of history and experience. After a fierce but brief struggle, he accepted the failure of reconciliation. In *Don Juan* he achieved a live organism by bring-

Introduction

ing together his dreams, his observation of political and social circumstance, and his deflation of both what he dreamed and what he observed. Ironic deflation did not eliminate the symbolic action and progress of his stanzas. This action, like his logistic preparations in Greece, was based on a fusion of private dream and public experience.

The paradox of imaginative commitment to public affairs made the younger men practice, although it kept them from saying in verse, what Tennyson was to say in the stanzas beginning "You ask me why, tho' ill at ease." "Should banded unions persecute Opinion," he complains, then he will abandon England to its folly: "I seek a warmer sky." The romantic poets crossed the Channel, but they aimed at English hearts. The period before the collapse of the Chartists in 1848 saw a tremendous increase in the pressure of public opinion on political action. Poetry, although it did not greatly accelerate this growth in the power of opinion, served it. Our subject is politics in poetry, not poetry in politics, but the utility of the poems, along with the Sunday papers, tracts, essays like Hazlitt's, and political caricatures, helps to validate the subject. Since the new force was popular and largely radical, Byron and Shelley fed the course of legislation more directly than Wordsworth and Coleridge. Even though the severe prophet at Rydal Mount was respected more widely than the atheistic imp of Pisa, and read more evenly through the social strata, Shelley employed the right rhetoric, as Wordsworth did not, for cheap distribution through the artisans' libraries and other societies of the workers who had begun their thrust toward the Reform Bills of 1867 and 1884.

The limitation of the romantics is not what Arnold thought it was, a failure of intellect or idea. They limit their art most seriously by their rejection of social objectivity, their reluctance to separate personal feeling from the perception of order among phenomena. Always mindful of the process of creation itself, they produced little poetry of action and almost none of proportioned acts. They refused to please the geometric side of the moralist in each of us, and yet they surrounded myth with rhetoric and supported symbol with assertion. The result was not an extreme either of explicit doctrine

7

or of verbal symbol, nor was it a compromise. The result was a poetry of search, of excited leaps suspended in tentative assertion, skeptical in essence but seldom in manner.

These limitations and difficulties in the poetry of the romantics came largely from their unprecedented virtue of defining man in terms of his consciousness. Man is conscious, according to the empiricists, only as an individual. As complex as the poetic uses of politics were in the years shared by Wordsworth, Blake, and Hazlitt, it may not be wrong to identify passionate individualism as the true voice of the era. When John Clare cries, "I am the self-consumer of my woes," or one of the Brontë sisters insists, "I'll walk where my own nature would be leading," we label the voice romantic. "The tygers of wrath are wiser," *The Marriage of Heaven and Hell* tells us, "than the horses of instruction"; likewise, "One Law for the Lion & Ox is Oppression."

There was reverence for original genius and the energetic hero. Yet the valid objection against a movement that produced Wordsworth's poems on beggars, vagrants, and derelict mothers cannot be its inattention to ordinary individuals. The divine energy is in every man. Coleridge and Wordsworth admired Sir Henry Vane the younger, James Harrington, and Algernon Sydney; they did not choose Oliver Cromwell. Shelley hoped to convert and to love the polluting multitude. Unable to accept the view of Locke's disciples that the individual is a self-interested entity isolated from other individuals, the romantics nevertheless sought ways of maintaining the individuality of the common man within a vast organic universe. Each poet, attempting in his own way to relate the creative imagination to the philosophic bases of the French Revolution, attempted also to relate the individual to society and the vital universe.

The interest of Coleridge, Wordsworth, Byron, and Shelley in political theory—"politics" in the Aristotelian sense—is easily documented. It is not unduly hard to demonstrate the earnest concern of these poets, and even the concern of Keats and Lamb, for current political events. It is reasonably safe to assert that great poetry came from these poets. The quality of their concern with politics, as reflected directly in the poetry, is more difficult to assess. None of the

Introduction

English poets made the transition from republican to royalist with the metaphysical precision of Friedrich Schlegel; and perhaps no Englishman combined artistry and keenness of intellect as magnificently as Leopardi in satiric escape from the political dilemma posed by Napoleon. But it can be argued that several used their crisis more nobly than he for affective poetry of affirmation. One of their most distinctive forms is passionate political and social prophecy, practiced by Coleridge even more rashly than by Shelley. The basic requirement of such prophecy is not that it prove true, but that it excite belief in the possibility of influencing political change.

The major poets took no pleasure from working old veins of political satire such as "instructions to a painter" or the mocking "character" of a politician or a mere ode on the new year, even though those conventional forms were still employed by satirists of their day.[6] Byron and Shelley, as we shall see, as well as Coleridge, did nevertheless make innovations within several forms having a tradition of political utility. Blake and Shelley forged anew from crudely keen songs of the people, such as the medieval distich, "When Adam delved and Eve span, / Who was then the gentleman?" or a less famous one of 1391: "The ax was sharp, the stock was hard, / In the thirteenth year of King Richard."[7] Shelley or Blake could have raised to purity and dignity "The patriotic gore / That floods the streets of Baltimore." The English did not, like Chateaubriand and (later) Hugo, hold public office, but neither did they interest themselves in "the permanent politics of human nature" to the exclusion of "local and temporary affairs."

Drawn toward fundamental political propositions, the romantics felt with an opposite pull that poetry should not make statements. Yet fundamental propositions were diffused throughout lyrics like the "Ode to the West Wind" and through lyric adaptations of reflective, dramatic, and narrative genres, especially through the imagery of these. Byron's tyrant-defying Prometheus and Napoleonic eagles advertise themselves. Shelley's lyre, sleeping as if drugged by Castlereagh, prays for the awakening wind that will bring social regeneration. The symbols of stirring breeze and Aeolian harp, the first in Wordsworth and the second in Coleridge and Shelley, are primarily psychological and religious; but if breeze and harp only

9

Politics in English Romantic Poetry

secondarily stir a political leaf or a string of social harmony, other persistent metaphors and symbols bind the lyric and reflective poems of the senior poets to their sonnets on political heroes. The hope of sunrise in Coleridge's early poems is that revolution which was subsequently fixed in the coat of arms of each Soviet.

Unlike Chaucer's *Parliament of Fowls,* or the secular moralities of the early Renaissance, or *Paradise Lost,* or the novels of Disraeli, romantic poetry seldom reveals political activity from the inside. The romantic accomplishment was in drenching political attitudes with emotion and imagery drawn from deep wells of nonpolitical and quasi-political experience. Some of the images lie dead or deathly weak. Getting back to nature, the poets of lakes and heaths wrote inevitably of oaken statesmen, sheepish patriots, and frosty parliaments. Few of them were so engrossed in politics as to write explicitly of statesmanlike oaks, patriotic sheep, or parliamentary frosts. Byron is rare among them, and among English poets generally, in using political activities metaphorically as the vehicle to make more pungent the tenor of his thought.

Separated from their original social context, many tendentious poems seem now hardly political, or not at all. In his *Poems* of 1797 Robert Southey published sapphics entitled "The Widow." The widow, "a poor wanderer," way-sore for lack of shelter, called out for pity. "Worn out with anguish, toil and cold and hunger," she died. The editors of the *Anti-Jacobin* recognized the implied processes of thought, and in their issue of 27 November 1797 they made Southey's argument explicit. Where there is poverty, there is "a graduated scale of violence and cruelty." Where there is a widow, there was recently a married soldier. Southey had aided identification to the extent of juxtaposing dactylics entitled "The Soldier's Wife."[8] A dead soldier suggests violence, and reminds the reader of sordid impressment, war on French liberty, loans to despotic allies, soaring taxes, Pitt's aggressions against civil liberties, and unreformed Parliament. Editors George Canning and John Hookham Frere composed a parody, "The Friend of Humanity and the Knife-Grinder," to reveal what they found on Southey's mind. Therein the Southey-figure asks, "Did some rich man tyrannically use you?"—was he squire? covetous parson? roguish lawyer?—then "Have you not read

10

Introduction

the Rights of Man, by TOM PAINE?" Finding the contented, reprobate grinder indifferent to politics, the Friend of Humanity kicks
him, but departs undaunted, "in a transport of republican enthusiasm and universal philanthropy." The historical scholar today follows with no hesitation the implications recognized by Canning and
Frere in Southey's sapphics, but he has come to similar poems by
Wordsworth and Coleridge as a critic judging their place in the
stream of great English poetry, and thus has often overlooked or
underestimated their original revolutionary or reactionary tendency
and impact. Coleridge wrote to Humphry Davy in 1800 that he
had much at heart an essay on poetry. Its title would be "an Essay
on the Elements of Poetry," but "it would in reality be a *disguised*
System of Morals & Politics—." His point can be applied equally
well to his poems.

It is not different political beliefs so much as different attitudes
toward political belief that are likely to affect the quality of specific
poems. There is not necessarily any difference aesthetically between
a poem that asserts a political doctrine and a poem that denies
it. For one reason, a partisan poet is inclined to answer an opponent
in kind. A sonnet on Cromwell often evokes a sonnet on Charles.
Belief that a poet can and should influence moral, social, and political evolution offers a large scope for poetical enthusiasm; reasoned
beliefs in the existing status, and in a poet's duty to serve its preservation, ought to lend themselves more readily to a verse of ordered
calm. But do they?

I find it personally hard to assert that the French Revolution
exerted pressure for a renovation in prosody, although a new freedom
entered English prosody with the romantic generation, a freedom
that brought relaxation, if not revolution, as in the free substitution
of trisyllabic feet within a basic iambic meter. The new freedom
cracked the regular prosody of the Popian couplet, broke open
the Bastille of the closed couplet itself, gave new life to stanzaic forms
that had not been exercised for a century, and created (for example,
in *Prometheus Unbound*) a great variety of new stanzaic forms.

The thrust of the Revolution cannot be altogether extricated
from other revolts. Wordsworth attacks poetic abstractions, which
are rational, passionless; he attacks poetic diction, which is aristo

cratic and privileged; he attacks sophisticated periphrasis, which avoids the simplicity of speech used by the common man; he attacks urbane generalizations about the rustic poor, who are actually individual farmers, shepherds, cottagers, discharged soldiers, paupers, peddlers, beggars, fathers, sons, and brothers, speaking and acting at particular times from unique combinations of human feelings. Leigh Hunt, and for a time Keats, practiced feminine caesura, hiatus, stress failure, and other devices nearly as debilitating, because their rigid predecessors did not practice them. This was not empty license; these abominations required conscious effort.

Whether or not poetry influences or accompanies political or intellectual change in a way to legislate for mankind is of little moment for the chapters that follow, for ours is the opposite topic, politics in poetry. A stanza is not necessarily the worse for encouraging some of its readers to action, but here we are to ask how the deeds of public figures may have affected the final form of certain poems. If we take delight in some of these poems, what have the political interests of the poet contributed to our delight? The poet's "intention," implied in this question, although it involves chronological probability, does not give to chronology the bedrock of a Newtonian absolute and does not require us to believe the poet fully conscious of his aim or his creative processes. If we have taken delight, and even more if we have not, how and why does the poem differ in constitution and spirit from what we find impressive in the spirit of our own day? It may be that the centripetal force in poetry is language, so defined as to minimize thought. Yet the basic stuff of a literary work that leaves a powerful residue when translated into other languages would seem to be something for which language is no more than a fleshly covering. It would seem to be an ethos or pathos of story or argument or condition, not in a general way that suffers unimportant loss when transmogrified into another medium, such as sculpture or music, but in its proportion and detail of rise, curve, and fall, like the essence of an inked line of beauty translated in pencil on a different surface. Within the poems here studied, much of the reference and connotation along the rise and fall can be accounted political.

II

THE CLIMATE

The relation between romantic poetry and the reactions of the poet to political theory and opinion is debatable, and it must be debated here. Concerning the political events to which the poets reacted there is fortunately little debate. For nearly every believer in Anglo-Saxon liberties, the fall of the Bastille in July 1789 symbolized the commencement of a Glorious Revolution in feudal France. A century or more late, but finally, Frenchmen were to enjoy some of the liberties that their best writers had discovered with approval in England. Edmund Burke's *Reflections on the Revolution in France,* 1790, which condemned the revolution on philosophic grounds but in passionate language, served at first largely to create a stronger reaction in favor of the French. Several answering pamphleteers charged Burke with hysteric fear of revolution in England. Even the declarations of war at the beginning of 1793 did not bring the whole people into loyalty. Under Scottish law, dissidents were quickly condemned for treasonous utterance, but similar charges brought by George III's government in 1794 found no jury willing to render a verdict of guilty. There were serious mutinies at Spithead, and elsewhere in the Channel Fleet, as late as 1797. Yet the English, as a seafaring nation, took pride in the metaphor of the ship of state. They liked to believe that their hearts and their leaders were of the same oak as their vessels. Gradually they turned in patriotic

13

pride against the enemy. Believers in constitutional reform, including the poets, sought excuses for France, even for the Jacobin left ("the Mountain") that gained control of the National Convention (1792–1795) and for its chief instrument of terror, the Committee of Public Safety; but English reformers found inexcusable the ritualistic worship of Reason, the monotonous excess of public executions, the emphasis upon equality rather than upon liberty, and the evidence of imperial longings, soon inflamed by Bonaparte. The rise of geographic and cultural nationalism, divorced from dynastic monarchy at first gradually and then in 1789 abruptly, contributed to the rise of the Corsican; it contributed also to the fervor of British opposition when the Corsican swallowed other nations besides France.

Burke believed the Revolution to contain seeds of inevitable despotism and imperial expansion. Charles James Fox and his steadily diminishing followers argued that the allied monarchs were driving peacefully inclined revolutionists into desperate extremes. It took both the excesses of the Jacobins and the fearful victories of Bonaparte to swing the popular press from Fox to Burke. When General Bonaparte not only drove the Austrians out of northern Italy but subjugated Switzerland, pulverized the Turks (even after the destruction of his fleet by Nelson at the battle of the Nile, August 1798), and replaced the Directory (1795–1799) with himself as monarch (under the euphemism of "first consul"), George III recovered a degree of personal popularity. But George's ministers were required to answer for sins other than their own military defeats, treaties with lethargic allies, and suppression of civil liberties at home. Under the same king, before "the young helmsman" Pitt took over in 1783, the regime had upheld the King's cause against his subjects in America; by losing the Colonies, they had lost the argument, and thereby lost the preliminary of a more basic debate over inalienable rights and popular sovereignty. The open immorality of the King's sons in time of war, satirized daily in public caricatures and the columns of opposition newspapers, thoroughly shocked the compound of prudery and snobbish respectability that would come to be called Victorianism but is evident in the journalism of Leigh Hunt and the bowdlerized work of Scott, Lamb, and Keats, as well as in reactions against Byron and the royal sons.

To observers prone to hostility it seemed clear enough that the rural cottager had been dispossessed and pauperized by the "improving landlords" whom Farmer George had permitted to enclose common land; it seemed equally clear that the dispossessed were now being huddled into black, despotic mills and mines. Samuel Jackson Pratt thus annotated in sentimental hostility his humanitarian poem, *Bread, or the Poor:* "The various manufacturing towns which the Author of the Poem attentively examined, are so replete with filth, poverty, and disease, in the lanes, alleys, lofts and cellars, where the weaving-trades are carried on; their places of labour so close, their beds so ragged in furniture, and so loaded with promiscuous bodies, that one miserable wretch becomes the nuisance of another."[1] The shifts of population, through the alliance of agricultural and industrial change, aggravated day by day the inequalities of representation in an unreformed Parliament earlier denounced by Pitt himself. Wartime ministers laid taxation more heavily upon the middle classes without making any adjustments to reduce the political power of the lords temporal and spiritual—who came to the upper house, according to Leigh Hunt's *Examiner,* only to pass stricter laws against poaching. The politics of class arose out of the war and its aftermath. Upon the poor the recruiting officers practiced chicaneries for impressment into foreign, and often disastrous, service for the King. And yet military service was the more disastrous because impressment failed to meet the challenge from new French methods of national conscription.

Courts—if we remain with the hostile observer—seemed hardly more kind than recruiting sergeants. In 1688 a member of the errant poor could be put to death for some fifty crimes; by 1819 his chances of capital felony had risen to an indeterminate height by the addition of 187 new capital statutes, each literally fascistic; that is, each was a bundle of rods designed to punish a variety of new capital offenses.[2] The thief often escaped hanging, but he saw that his life was valued less than coin or other property. Meanwhile, Wordsworth learned from Cesare Beccaria, as Jeremy Bentham did, that penal

15

institutions should have the purpose of aiding society, not of punishing the errant. Ministers did not hold office in order to please Bentham, and, says Richard Pares in *King George and the Politicians,* "not in order to legislate, but in order to govern: to maintain order, to wage war, and, above all, to conduct foreign affairs." I have been using the metaphors and language of the contemporary caricatures and their captions, but the facts once freely summarized as "oppression" are confirmed by conservative historians.

Not only the politics of class, but the system of two-party discipline of most members of Parliament also grew out of the war, with its dramatic increases in governmental borrowing to finance the hostilities and the consequent reliance on public opinion, rather than on a few bankers as formerly, for successful financing.

Although the Opposition throughout the era lacked the disciplined unity of Parliamentary parties today, the Whigs had some coherence and a remarkable degree of continuity. Disarray increased inevitably with the death of the charismatic Charles James Fox in 1806, yet Charles Grey (Viscount Howick in 1806, Earl Grey from 1807) remained the party leader for Parliamentary Reform from 1792 until victory in the Reform Bill of 1832. Grey declined to press for Reform while Napoleon threatened, and he acted often with the conservative Grenville family, "the crypto-Tory Grenvilles," who had defected to Pitt in 1790. It seemed natural for William Wyndham, Baron Grenville (1759–1834), to be premier of the short-lived coalition ministry of 1806–1807 known as "All the Talents." Comfortably conservative Whigs, mildly encouraged (not led) by the Dukes of Devonshire, recruited for the party through invitations to Devonshire House, where the ladies had formed the chief attraction since 1784, when Georgiana, the then Duchess, had campaigned for Fox. Fox's nephew, the third Baron Holland (1773–1840), near the middle of the party, entertained moderates at Holland House, where Lady Holland tyrannized over such party aides and wits as the founding editors of the *Edinburgh Review,* Henry Brougham, Francis Jeffrey, and Sydney Smith. Brougham, energetic and independent, earned the distrust of the party leaders, but he served the Opposition, as distinguished from the Whig party, by continuous debate against the slave trade (abolished in 1807) and then against

The Climate

slavery; by defending the Princess of Wales during the "delicate investigation" of her marital conduct and at her trial in 1820; and less dramatically by his various labors for popular education.

The left edge of the party (the Duke of Bedford, the legal reformer Sir Samuel Romilly, Samuel Whitbread, and a handful of others, known as the Radical Whigs or "the Mountain") joined often with the Westminster Radicals, who were led publicly by Lord Cochrane and Sir Francis Burdett and urged on by the pamphleteering Major John Cartwright, the utilitarian philosopher Jeremy Bentham, the bootmaker Thomas Hardy, and the tailor Francis Place. Few Whigs supported Burdett when he was committed to the Tower (after noisy resistance) in 1810: he had charged the House of Commons with abusing its privileges to the point of suppressing free speech.[3]

Of the Tory ministers opposed by Coleridge, Wordsworth, and Southey for subverting civil liberties in the 1790's, Pitt died in 1806; Henry Dundas, Viscount Melville (1742–1811), fell into disrepute even among his colleagues; lesser figures faded; but Robert Stewart, Viscount Castlereagh (1769–1822), achieved enough power as Foreign Secretary to scorn abuse from the radical press and the younger romantics. His fellows in crime, as Byron, Shelley, Hazlitt, and Leigh Hunt viewed the ministries of Portland (1807–1809), Perceval (1809–1812), and Liverpool (1812–1827), were Henry Addington (Viscount Sidmouth from 1805, Home Secretary, in charge of spies and other such instruments of domestic suppression, from 1812 to 1821); John Scott (Lord Eldon from 1799, earl from 1821, "on the woolsack" as Lord Chancellor from 1801 to 1827); and Edward Law (Baron Ellenborough from 1802, Lord Chief Justice of England from 1802 to 1818).

A drumbeat of opposition came from William Cobbett's *Register* (with varying title from 1802 to 1835); John and Leigh Hunt's *Examiner,* founded in 1808; various periodicals, notably the *Republican,* edited by the freethinker Richard Carlile (1790–1843); a steady shower of leaflets and other publications by William Hone (1780–1842), usually illustrated by George Cruikshank; Thomas J. Wooler's *Black Dwarf,* 1817–1824; dozens of ephemeral periodicals, usually "unstamped" in evasion of the government's "tax on

17

Politics in English Romantic Poetry

knowledge," like *The Cap of Liberty*, 1819–1820; and the "public prints" by such caricaturists as James Gillray (1756–1815) and Thomas Rowlandson (1756–1827). The iconography of the caricaturists often passed into the literary satires of the day, including those of Coleridge, Byron, Shelley, and Keats.

Recent currents of thought and feeling aided the propagandists for change. When the energy of John Wesley's Methodism sped outward, and by way of Evangelical clergymen upward through the wealthy and the educated classes, the predominant liberalism from John Locke became surprisingly emotional. The flowering of humanitarian altruism, epitomized by John Howard's reports on prisons, was nourished by the whole society, while novelists, poets, painters, and illustrators reacted to the dryly rational by appealing to pity and tears. Even the skeptic Hume signalized the philosophic and psychological movement from reason to sympathy. Although mild in comparison with Continental rigor, British methods of dealing with the criminal and the pauper, symbolized in the gibbet and the workhouse, looked ugly to newly softened eyes. Intellectual and social progress, as well as some kind of biological evolution, was increasingly sensed as a law of nature.

Such nonparliamentary movements as these aided in making Pitt's wartime budgets and emergency legislation uncomfortable for the educated merchant, especially if he had attended a Dissenting academy and graduated into exclusion from professional and political life. Newspapers of the Opposition encouraged the taxed tradesmen of London and Westminster to resent the subsidies frequently granted (usually with attempted secrecy) to Britain's chief Continental allies, the despots of Prussia, Russia, and Austria. Nor were the granting Ministers themselves without resentment, as their private correspondence reveals. To Ministers as well as to caricaturists, the despots seemed to spend most of their occasional energy in planning partitions of Poland, and the rest in alternating unsuccessful military campaigns against France with separate treaties of peace and neutrality, while Pitt sweated and Britons bled.

By restrictive acts the Government drove poets and other wielders of language and thought toward sympathy with malcontents and the laboring classes. In a common, indeed notorious metaphor of

The Climate

the day, Pitt and Burke opposed all repairs to the political roof while the French threatened the house with fire and flood. Reminding all who listened or read that the British Constitution was perfect and therefore unimprovable, Lord Justice Braxfield sentenced the reformers who came before him at Edinburgh between 1793 and 1795—Muir, Palmer, Skirving, Gerrald, and Margarot—to transportation (Botany Bay) for various nuances of political crime. Habeas Corpus was suspended in 1794, as it would be again in 1799 and in the troubled years after Waterloo. Societies formed to enforce the limitations on the monarchy won in the Glorious Revolution of 1689, such as The Friends of the People (1792), were eclipsed by egalitarian societies formed to correspond with each other, and with Jacobins and Girondins in France, on the new cries of liberty, fraternity, and the rights of man. In May 1794 the government charged officers and friends of the most suspect of these organizations, the London Corresponding Society, with an accumulation of small seditious acts amounting to "constructive treason," but abandoned the prosecutions soon after acquittal of the first two defendants, Thomas Hardy and John Horne Tooke. At the end of 1795, after an open attempt on the life of the King, the Ministers sought by a Treasonable Practices Act and a Seditious Meetings Act to forestall further violence by catching treason somewhere between the mind and the lips. Gracelessly the Ministers brought to pass in 1799 an act to suppress completely such societies as those represented by the "acquitted felons." Further restraints met with some success in limiting that part of the public press not more directly controlled by the Government.

The Combination Acts of 1799–1800 drove underground the incipient unionization of labor, and made possible such prosecutions as that of James Watson at the Lancashire assizes in September 1819, when the jury "almost instantly found a verdict of *guilty*": he was sentenced to twelve months' imprisonment "for a conspiracy to raise the wages of those employed in the art, craft, or mystery of weaving" at Blackburn. So the *Times*, 15 September 1819. National statistics for wages, and even regional and occupational statistics, are hard to come by and even harder to interpret, but scarcity and famine made the price of bread fluctuate more wildly than

19

wages. In the early years of the war, the middle classes supported the Government reluctantly from fear of revolution. Pamphleteers, but also experience, told the poor that they were exploited in new ways.

Only when the brief ministry of Addington tested Bonaparte with the Peace of Amiens in 1802, and thereby confirmed the Pitt and Grenville view of him as deceitful and insatiable, did the nationalism of the British gather itself into a single force. Even then, when Napoleon's decrees against British commerce in 1806 were answered by the Orders in Council of 1807, which claimed to forbid trade with the King's enemies by any vessel anywhere, the poets stood in wait for a better cause.

The Peninsular War against Napoleon, 1808–1814, interpreted by the older poets as a rising of the Spanish and Portuguese peoples in guerrilla warfare against a foreign tyrant and his local functionaries, provided the first cause in international politics, since the French Revolution had tumbled into expediency and terror, to which a poet could give unstinted moral fervor. Even then, the poets' fervor began in what they took to be a betrayal of the Portuguese by Arthur Wellesley and other British representatives in the Convention of Cintra (August 1808), whereby the French were evacuated in English vessels. Wellesley was made Viscount Wellington for Talavera and other Peninsular victories in 1809, but none of the poets ever admired or trusted him.

After the defeat of Napoleon, the older poets had little interest in international affairs. They seldom looked further away than Ireland, where continuing unrest was interpreted by Coleridge, Southey, and Wordsworth as a threat to the security of the Church of England. These middle-aged poets took up positions within the range of "sentimental Toryism," which was broad enough in its humanitarian conservatism to attract Sir Francis Burdett as well as the young Benjamin Disraeli.

The second generation of poets, Byron, Shelley, and Keats, started nearly where Blake, Wordsworth, Southey, and Coleridge had started. Too young for the moral shocks sent through their quivering elders by Robespierre and Napoleon, they rebounded like the earlier enthusiasts from a cold monarchic and "exclusive" aristocratic wall. For their elders, Irish unrest had been treasonous support of Bonaparte; the war at an end, the new generation could sympathize fully with the pleas of Irish Catholics. During famine and economic crisis, the government of Liverpool, Addington (now Viscount Sidmouth), Castlereagh, and Eldon imitated Pitt's alarmist policy of shaming and intimidating reformers by a program of secret committees and Parliamentary acts against treason and sedition, particularly in 1812, 1817-18 and 1819-20. The radical journalists William Cobbett, Richard Carlile, Thomas Wooler, and William Hone, about whom it is still argued whether they inflamed the masses by demagoguery or calmed and organized them for peaceful reform, had helped bring about a democratic spirit somewhat more social than the theoretic republicanism that had flourished at Cambridge in the youth of Wordsworth and Coleridge, when the moderate Girondins had hopes of ruling France.

Population, trade, and employment had greatly increased during the war; after Waterloo trade declined suddenly, unemployment seemed to leap up, harvests failed, and the Corn Law of 1815, with further protection of rents in the following decade, increased the evils of inflation. The Poor Laws were reducing almost to the level of agricultural laborers the independent farmers now crushed under the burden of poor rates in lieu of adequate wages. Classes consequently hated and feared each other. Luddite smashing of machinery and less purposeful rioting of the poor encountered new suspensions of habeas corpus. In addition, the Six Acts of 1819 restricted public meetings and—by taxation—the circulation of radical newspapers; forbade seditious literature and unauthorized drilling or marching; and liberalized methods of arrest without warrant and confinement without trial. In August 1819 local magistrates employed cavalry to disperse a mass meeting in Manchester thereafter known as "Peterloo," about equal to the Boston Massacre in bad management, small loss of life, and explosive consequences. On specific issues and events the younger poets took the side of the radicals more often than one of them, Lord Byron, could comfortably admit.

As one focus for satire, there was the "green bag" episode of 1817, when Secret Committees of each House examined the bulky evidence of revolutionary plots that Sidmouth had solicited from

21

George Cruikshank, "Victory of Peterloo"

The Climate

magistrates and spies. As another focus, memory of the sale of commissions in wartime by the Duke of York's mistress. Mary Anne Clarke, paled under the scandalous glare of the Prince Regent's attempts to divorce Caroline, attempts which she countered vigorously for fourteen years. The liberal hopes that died with Princess Charlotte in 1817 tried to revive when Caroline, her mother, returned from vulgar displays on the Continent in a final desperate attempt to achieve enthronement at George IV's side in 1820-21. Another green bag brought in the secret evidence against Caroline. These ministerial and royal absurdities were apt for Keats's Elfinan and Hum in "The Cap and Bells," Shelley's Swellfoot the Tyrant, and many digressive stanzas of Byron's *Don Juan*. J. Steven Watson sees a turning point at 1809, when Mrs. Clarke's sale of commissions revived the Pitt-suppressed movement for electoral reform.[4] To the extent that Keats, Shelley, and Byron perceived the revival, they credited Leigh Hunt, rather than Bentham or any independent member of Parliament, with the initiating power of exposure.

After 1815, under the firm guidance of Metternich and with strong assistance from Castlereagh, Europe refixed legitimacy, the principle of hereditary rule, which had been unsettled by Napoleon. Castlereagh tightened Britain's alliances with strong monarchies determined to restrain the nationalism not only of upstart peoples in central Europe but also of Italians and Greeks, who were especially sacred to poets nourished on either Latin and Greek or Chapman's Homer and Cary's Dante. Byron especially, but also Shelley, composed verses against the monarchic congresses: Treaty of Paris, 1814; Congress of Vienna, 1815; a conference at Aix-la-Chapelle in 1818 to admit the King of France to the Alliance; the Carlsbad Conference of German princes, 1819; meeting of the Crown Prince of Prussia with the Emperors of Russia and Austria at Troppau, 1820; meeting of Ferdinand of Naples with the Holy Alliance, Laybach, 1821; Congress of Verona, 1822. From prospects of trade, English merchants forced the Ministers to act more favorably toward the struggling new nations of South America. To Byron, Shelley, and Hunt, Castlereagh represented the chief link between the despotic and imperial force of the Holy Alliance and the oppressive domestic measures that he supported in Parliament. A vast expedition has gone out to rescue the most industrious of foreign ministers from romantic opprobrium; but the romantics did not misjudge the evidence as Castlereagh allowed them to see it, and their course of action as universal poets conformed to moral duty as nearly as his actions in the role of national statesman.[5]

Few of the meliorative acts of Parliament from 1819 to 1829 greatly interested the major poets. They could ignore partial resumption of payment in specie, for they had left attacks on paper money largely to Cobbett and Tom Moore. After four years of debate, and with some help from Coleridge's prose, Parliament passed in 1819 the bill of Sir Robert Peel (the elder) that restricted juvenile cotton-spinners to a working day of twelve hours. Francis Place, a self-educated tailor, worked successfully for repeal of the Combination Acts in 1824, and struggled to keep them repealed. Despite Wordsworth's warnings that property-owners would be exterminated one by one, the unreformed Parliament reduced capital punishment by the repeal of four statutes in 1820, when pressed hard by Sir James Mackintosh and by a maturing dragon, public opinion; and Parliament under the leadership of the younger Peel consolidated about three hundred statutes (although for the purpose of reducing the sentimental discrepancy between convictions and executions).[6] Byron and Shelley were pleased to foresee the success of several national revolutions. They would have rejoiced to read Metternich's assurances to his wife that the world had been in perfect health in 1789 compared to what it was by 1819. The younger poets had the delight of these favorable developments abroad; but they had left England, and had died, before the last convulsive opposition to the moderate Reform Bill of 1832. Byron missed by five years the Catholic Emancipation of 1829.

II

Those English poets of the period 1789–1832 who said harsh things against what they took to be the established regimes in politics, literature, and the academies are often casually called "romantic" because the speaker or writer equates romanticism with revolt, and thus with liberty, fraternity, and equality. The reaction against romanticism, conceived as "romantic revolt," was led in France by

The Climate

Charles Maurras (propagandist for the fascistic Action Française), from whom it passed to T. E. Hulme in England. Hulme, in turn, along with Irving Babbitt, Paul Elmer More, and other "New Humanists," helped shape the antiromantic views of T. S. Eliot. According to Babbitt, More, and many after, romanticism is a loosening of the inner check, escape from responsibility, revolt against law. Paul Roubiczek says that its flight from reality, with its erroneous belief that the human ego is omnipotent, has led to a general misinterpretation of man. Already proved by Carl Schmitt to be "subjective occasionalism," romanticism has been variously defined as the denial of science, a riot of unreason, and the revolt of the unconscious.[7] In sum, it is egoistic *revolt* in headlong *flight*. For those who equated romanticism with revolt, Wordsworth simply ceased to be a romantic when and because he came to believe in the reality of evil, the prevalence of sin, and the eternal rightness of such classical staples as episcopacy, the House of Lords, duty, and decorum in poetic diction.

Attacks on the "romantic temperament" and on romantic ideals for society were subtly immersed in attacks on romantic literary techniques. Only a small portion of T. S. Eliot's admirers followed him in his trinitarian credo as classicist in art, royalist in politics, and Anglo-Catholic in religion, but a host accepted his description of tradition as somehow combining these three. For convenience we give the name "romanticism" to a conglomeration of impulses that modified most, or all, Western traditions. Whatever it was that swept through the arts in various countries at various times in the nineteenth century, we may as well refer to it as romanticism as by any other name. Whether the cultural development to which Eliot's poetry belongs has begun a successful revolution against romanticism or whether, like realism and naturalism, it is a further modification—a reform—of romanticism, the increase in emotion said to begin with Rousseau forms that part of the poetic tradition which Eliot could not escape, even though his theory of tradition treated the years between Rousseau and Ezra Pound as time out. More recently it has not been the avowed Neo-Romantics who have seemed most "romantic."

Among students of literature, the linking of romanticism with

Politics in English Romantic Poetry

Fascism is a special aberration that grew partly out of the self-contradictory identification of romanticism with political revolt and escapist withdrawal. Clearly we need to disperse the conflicting connotations of revolt and escape if we are to designate any characteristics common to English poets of the early nineteenth century. First, however, we should deal with a still harsher contradiction, for in circles outside the arts romanticism does not always mean either revolt or escape.

Just as most literary historians continue to associate romanticism with liberalism and revolt, by a linkage already popular when Babbitt and Hulme made it a focus of attack, so with a flip of the coin social scientists, with large obligations to European and especially German thought, currently associate romanticism with conservatism, reaction, or the totalitarian State. Among students of the English movement, Alfred Cobban's grouping of Southey, Wordsworth, and Coleridge with Burke has been the most influential. Twentieth-century admirers of Burke have interpreted the conflict of Coleridge's day as one between mechanistic liberalism and romantic conservatism. But the delimitation of romanticism to its conservative phases awkwardly excludes not only the later romantics in France but also Blake, Shelley, and Byron, most of the notable poetry of Coleridge, and the early poems of Wordsworth and Southey. For students of English verse, this definition admits comfortably only Scott and the later Wordsworth; it leaves scarcely two dozen lines of major poetry from the romantic period in England. Its proponents talk about poets, but quote only their prose. Students of literature who seek a workable definition of romantic tendencies will not find it in Russell Kirk's "Romantic conservativism." Nor will they receive adequate help in this area from the conservative liberalism of David P. Calleo's *Coleridge and the Idea of the Modern State.*

Where, then, will they find it? If romanticism is not revolt and is not Christian reaction, is it anything? Fortunately, literary critics who are also scholars have come more and more to describe it not as escape, not as the opposite of realism, but as a collection of tendencies opposite to the tendencies of classicism. To aid this distinction, W. J. Bate, in *From Classic to Romantic,*[8] drew up a list of the contrary emphases in both theory and practice between the

26

romantics and their eighteenth-century predecessors. These emphases, slightly altered for our purpose, are romantic imagination against Augustan reason, the particular against the general, the individual against the universal, the "real" against the "ideal," the strange against the familiar, the original against the conventional, emotional expression over against external form, gusto against clarity. Where Pope, Handel, and Watteau emphasized decorum (defined by Professor Bate as "the glorification and preservation of the type"), Byron, Beethoven, Blake, and Delacroix paid homage to energy, as in Napoleon. These distinctions between the Apollonian and the Dionysiac, like Fritz Strich's antithesis between Classic pursuit of perfection and Romantic yearning for the infinite, remain useful so long as they are not taken as infinitely or perfectly applicable.

Not at all fixed characteristics of every romantic, such qualities as emotion, particularity, energy, and novelty are tendencies at most. They can be found in isolation only among minor artists. Abhorrence of *An Essay on the Principle of Population,* issued by T. R. Malthus in 1798 as a counterfoil to William Godwin's optimism, was almost the only matter on which the major poets were firmly united. Nor had the qualities they emphasized been entirely suppressed from the work of Racine, Pope, or Fragonard. To distinguish the romantics too sharply from their predecessors is to make Beethoven's delicate first symphony cross Mozart's last in a no-man's-land with Watteau's *Embarkation for Cythera* and Géricault's *Horse Held by Slaves*—a wasteland where literary historians used to put the so-called "Pre-Romantics," who were neither coldly correct nor egotistically impassioned. A sharp distinction must ignore altogether such "Jacobin" poets as Robert Merry, Erasmus Darwin, and Richard Payne Knight, who used obsolescent poetic techniques to glorify sentiment and universal love.[9] The editors of the *Anti-Jacobin* recognized no significant differences among Payne Knight, Della Cruscans like Merry, and "Coleridge and Southey, Lloyd, and Lambe and Co.," who were equally in "sweet accord of harmony and love."[10] Differences between the Della Cruscans and the early Coleridge are mainly in talent.

Characteristics, then, were unsorted, and part of the vital change was gradual.

27

Politics in English Romantic Poetry

Whether or not there were as many romanticisms as Arthur Lovejoy thought, romanticism is no one thing, and no one artist of the nineteenth century was ever merely "romantic." Definitions of romanticism should nonetheless be attempted, for a major change of taste did occur. The major writers of the early nineteenth century we can call *romantics* for convenience, whether they were "romantic" or not. The word *romanticism* I would reserve for what was new in the literature and arts of the period. The problem, of course, is to define what was new.

Better definitions mitigate the damage done by poorer definitions. A common view, for example, not only takes "romantic revolt" to be inseparable from primitivism, or the belief that man should return to an idyllic simplicity of precivilized Nature, but takes it at the same time to be equally inseparable from a conviction of progress, or the belief that man should (and will) continually improve society in a movement ever onward and upward into universal fraternity. Since the complexity of human life had obviously increased between Adam and Louis XIV, a belief in linear progress could hardly include a belief in progressive simplification. On the other hand, the idea of progress began with increased control over nature from increase of knowledge. To believe in progressive complexity would therefore be to endorse to some extent the growth of industrial smudge. Joseph Priestley could give up simplification in favor of progress; Wordsworth could not. Undoubtedly, quite as many persons in the romantic period as in the previous quarter-century believed simultaneously, from time to time, in aspects of both primitivism and progress, but this contradiction is not the romanticism in them.

The definitions of romanticism most widely accepted at present among students of English literature insist upon a movement toward organicism: beginning in revolt against the concept of reality as a mechanistic arrangement of matter perceptible to the understanding, with the understanding aided only by the physical senses, romanticism moves to a positive belief in an organic universe perceptible to the imagination.[11] For the full-blown romantic, the creative mind has an organic interrelationship with the physical universe. The undertsanding analyzes data. Imagination is the process of unifica-

28

tion in the mind that modifies physical nature by giving it, for man, the organic synthesis imperceptible to the rational understanding. Imagination, or what romantics sometimes meant by the word *reason,* is forever opposed to what Friedrich Schlegel called "der vernunftig denkenden Vernunft," the rationally thinking reason (more nearly Kant's *Verstand*).[12] With some justice, pragmatists and philosophers of science say that the romantics called "reason" what we should call "intuition"; the romantics answered in advance that reason as they comprehended it, or *divined* it, had been so impoverished under the logic of the *philosophes* that their own nourishment of the concept was necessary for the rational survival of man: they did not wish to overthrow narrow understandings of the mental and neural system, but merely to subsume them in a larger comprehension of the positive, expansive, creative processes of man's mind. Scientific advances have not rendered us incapable, I think, of distinguishing between reason and wisdom, and this is roughly the distinction that the English romantics sought to illuminate and make prevail.

By typical romantic argument, mind and physical nature grow as interdependent branches from one divine trunk. The imagining mind and growing nature form one organism, which the understanding would murder to dissect. This "organism" is not physical; or, more precisely, man can know that it exists, but cannot know that it has a physical existence. By the age of seventeen, according to the earlier version of *The Prelude,* Wordsworth "saw one life and felt that it was joy." Only a comprehensive, unified soul could perceive its own union with the vital *other,* the rest of life. According to Blake, the poetic imagination looks with full vision, not *to* nature, but *through* nature, not *with* the eye, as Wordsworth would have it, but *through* the eye, in order to perceive the spiritual wholeness of the single divine form of all humanity. If we follow the lines of René Wellek's definition of romanticism, the romantic perceives, by way of the creative imagination, an organic relationship of man and nature, which he communicates in mythic and symbolic art.[13] We may recognize these perceptions and procedures as common among the poets and artists we call romantic.

The organic unity is as much moral as metaphysical. And here

29

we may note that the coming of vitalistic and organic analogy was not as sudden as some of the poets believed it to be. Baron d'Holbach, at the culmination of mechanistic rationalism in France, depicts a universe of sentient, fraternal beings imbued by one Spirit of Nature. Rousseau, as a Deist, had perceived a conformity between his own immortal nature and the constitution of the world, between the physical order and the correspondent moral order. This is late Rousseau, *Les Rêveries du promeneur solitaire* of 1782. Although the English poets resemble Rousseau less than Montaigne in the uncertainties and undulations of their search, they resemble Rousseau in the twists of agony. Their search, like his, is moral, spiritual, and emotional. The English poet discovers self, and seeks social community, in the process of exploring the reality in or beyond nature. To be is to be perceived, if not for Berkeley's reasons, then for unreasoned reasons. The mind and nature make one whole by interchange of values. Their union exists in the imagination, for to imagine is to perceive fully. Men are capable of perceiving alike, if not because Berkeley's God of the Jews and Christians has created a world of arbitrary symbols, then because a divine unity seems to lie within the self and beyond nature. In this union the poets felt an analogy with the community of men.

Strong suspicion that spirit and body are one, in the universe as well as in man, teased the romantic individualists and particularizers into a search for the universal amid the political intrigues, as well as the violent revolutions, of their own day. In consequence of uncertainties in the search, they surrounded the symbols that partake of universal reality, as in Shelley's *Prometheus Unbound* and quite differently in the Ismail canto of Byron's *Don Juan,* with generalized argument about politics and war in their historical contexts.

Despite this conjunction of universal particulars with generalized argument about politics, the organicism of romantic art is to be distinguished from its counterparts in political theory, as their separation in England makes clear. In a return to medieval analogy, J. G. Fichte as early as *Der geschlossene Handelstaat,* 1800, and even more Fichte's followers in political theory, described metaphysically a body politic that had head, arms, and legs each performing the function required for the health of the whole. Friedrich Schlegel, in opposing the democratic voice-lottery that results when the whole decomposed population has the destructive privilege of atomistic balloting to secure further unit-votes in a strictly confined legislature, set over against this lottery the vital maintenance and forward evolution of the nation-state, the historical life of the nation formed into an organic whole through the life of its organic members, that is, of its several estates or essential corporations ("in den organischen Gliedern eines Ganzen, und den einzelnen Ständen, oder wesentlichen Corporationen").[14] Blake employs the image of the universal human body to an entirely different end. The other English poets thought of the analogy only in terms of living tissue in the body politic: if you cut one member, the blood of the whole body is affected. No class of individuals need represent the foot.

The English were not in bondage to Fichte's anthropomorphic State, yet the dilemma of the English poets can be seen precisely in these analogies of the organic as opposed to the mechanistic. In a time of scientific change from the static Newtonian sciences of physics and mathematics to the organic sciences of geology, chemistry, and biology—the sciences of life, change, and growth—each poet except Byron came quickly to believe in the unifying imagination and in the organic unity of a work of art: a poem is made of living tissue. (Even a weak poem has sap in it. If you cut the living tissue of a great poem, it bleeds.) In this general movement from the static and mechanistic to the dynamic and the organic, the only political philosophers utilizing organic analogy were the conservatives who opposed revolution and democracy. The philosophy of democratic reform, which each poet espoused in youth, was rooted in an epistemology and aesthetic that even Byron felt an impulse, and the others felt a compulsion, to reject. If a poet believed in the vitalistic principles of organic growth, how was he to believe in radical politics, which would uproot the living organism and sever the future from the past?

The English poets agreed among themselves on little more than the inadequacy of describing human association without reference to emotion and growth. It is as one consequence of this agreement that they confronted mechanism with images of the organic and vitalistic. They instinctively chose symbolic rather than logical presentations of their alternatives to a mechanical universe viewed logically. Negatively, all the romantics made common cause. They distrusted the "clear and distinct ideas" declared sovereign by Descartes and Locke. De Quincey interrupted his essay on *Macbeth* at the end of the first paragraph to give warning: "Here I pause for one moment to exhort the reader never to pay any attention to his understanding when it stands in opposition to any other faculty of his mind. The mere understanding, however useful and indispensable, is the meanest faculty in the human mind and the most to be distrusted. . . ."

In literature this opposition to the mechanical understanding accompanied such changes as looser, less mechanical structure; resuscitation of the past, with an indwelling upon the fluidity of time; and a closer examination of nature, other than human nature acting in society. From the foreground of landscapes, human figures disappeared. Even in cloud-gazing Wordsworth and Constable, however, study of nature was never amoral or dehumanizing. The romantic artist or poet did not continue the old way of generalizing the typical social patterns of courting, drinking, or fighting; but his new way was not to depict in objective detail the political show at the hustings. Representatively, the romantic caught the moment when the daisy in the grass spoke to him of the solitude of an individual performing the humane labor of Pericles, or of Newton, or of a girl sewing for a soldier of Charlemagne. Daisy, Pericles, and girl belonged to one life.

III

Two complexities have made it easier for some students to associate English romanticism with revolt and for others to associate it with the conservatism of Burke. First, the two strands of abstract rationalism, with its emphasis on natural law, and empiricism, with its reliance on individual experience, were intertwined throughout the previous century. They are intertwined in the revolutionary slogan, "the rights of man." Secondly, each of the poets favored in youth the mixture of rational and empirical sanctions underlying the French Revolution, and wrote verses based on that set of sanctions, before he began to commit his faith to imagination and organic wholeness.

It is clear that the romantics were not in combat against the predominant literary practices of William Collins, Bishop Percy, Mark Akenside, the Wartons, Chatterton, Cowper, Sterne, or Henry Mackenzie, author of *The Man of Feeling*—to take some obvious examples from the age of Johnson. They found their belief in imagination at odds with interpretations of man argued or implicit in political, social, and economic tracts issued steadily by both liberals and conservatives of their own day. The theoretical, imaginative, and intuitive justifications of the new literary methods contradicted the available justifications of the Revolution.

Concerning the diversity of reactions to this contradiction, it is my argument that none of the philosophical bases and justifications of liberalism available to the English poets of 1789–1832 could be harmonized with the convictions that motivated their poetic practice. Revolutionary abstractions looked at first like total revolt from convention, but romantic introspection found the new abstractness to be only a film on the top of a century's emotional timidity. Creating for all the poets an intellectual crux, the disharmony between liberal tenets and belief in imaginative perception of organic interchange drove each toward a crisis in either political allegiance or poetic method, sometimes in both. No English poet seemed ready to declare, as Victor Hugo would declare, that political freedom was one with artistic freedom, and innovation in politics essential to innovation in literature. Nor had anyone yet proposed a wave-and-quantum theory of gradual change through a series of revolutions, although this is the theory that Shelley tried to work out for himself. In the absence of a philosophic or a general solution, a means of escape from the crisis, if escape was to come, had to be personally discovered and individually appropriate.

The poets grew up in an environment of democratic ideas: the natural goodness of man as opposed to the doctrine of original sin, natural rights derived from natural law, the universality of individual freedom and equality, social contract, mixed government in an ideal commonwealth, tolerance for every sect and individual (or isolated "mental substance," as F. S. C. Northrop unsympathetically puts it for Locke),[15] and the greatest good for the greatest number. All these ideas descended into the romantic period from or through the eighteenth-century rational *philosophes*. Fraternity, equality, and associated ideals of the French Revolution derived from a belief in the possession of reason by all men, or, what is near it, the fundamental equality of men, because all are equally capable of reason, and the associated Protestant—especially Puritan—insistence upon the inalienable right of the individual to free inquiry for the salvation of his soul. To be made in the image of God meant to possess reason. Such propensities the romantics inherited.

The chief founder of this inheritance was John Locke. Romantic objection to him began in psychology, in that blank, idly receptive slate that Locke attributed to every man at birth. The empirical argument of Locke and his followers against ultimate ideas can be seen very well in Hume's attempt to praise imagination, in *An Enquiry concerning Human Understanding:* "Nothing is more free than the imagination of man, and though it cannot exceed that original stock of ideas furnished by the internal and external senses, it has unlimited power of mixing, compounding, separating, and dividing all the varieties of fiction and vision" (sec. V, pt. ii). For Coleridge, who may be taken as the theorist of English romanticism, such a statement offended both by repudiating all sources of wisdom or knowledge except through the bodily senses and by making the human mind a passive mirror.

Opponents and disciples of Locke have alike regretted the lack of continuity between his general philosophy and his treatises on government. But his theories of human understanding and his theories of civil government have a common flaw for the romantic. They neglect human and social originality, growth, and variety. Government for Locke was not only passive but negative, a necessary evil, "the proper remedy for the inconveniences of the state of Nature." By this remedy, in each known state, a governor had contracted to protect the lives, labor, and other property of those who consented to be thus protected and governed. Locke's theory of contract serves rather well a nation with a written, virtually unchangeable constitution, but not a nation with legislative sovereignty or other mechanism (or organism) for change. Must all members of the society agree to the contract? No, only the majority. After the contract is formed, my "consent" means merely that I submit, that I do not move to another country. Perhaps Rousseau's doctrine of the General Will leads too easily to totalitarianism, as experience has made it fashionable to say, but the theory of majority rule needs some such doctrine as his for avoiding tyranny of the majority over individuals constituting the minority. Rousseau tried to provide the majority with some rule of self-restraint other than expediency. Romantics felt that the state, as the official being of the society, was a moral entity, where Locke's mere arithmetic addition of individuals, each seeking his own happiness, could be an amoral accumulation at best. Where each person has only indefeasible rights, there can be little sense of duty to or within the community.

The individual, as considered by Locke either psychologically or politically, is an abstraction on the page. Locke allows nothing for the extent to which the individual is formed by the society he grows in and re-formed by any society he lingers in. Even from Locke's psychological premises, one can conclude that our individual needs of personal liberty, our very definitions of individuality, come always in part from the society that surrounds, evaluates, and silently invades us. Coleridge and his peers found Locke's independent persons isolated, static abstractions not to be found in human society. English psychology between Locke and Coleridge neglected the originating force of human imagination and ignored individual differences.[16] Political theory after Locke ignored the difference between one individual added to himself a million times and a society of a million people.

Most of the rationalists of eighteenth-century France ignored as completely as their empirical English master what Wordsworth called "the blood & vital juices of our minds."[17] As a reader of Wordsworth, Coleridge, or Southey sees readily enough, the tide turned against liberal ideas in England partly because they were "French ideas," a poisonous weapon of the enemy. Meanwhile the doctrines of reason and equality had indeed returned to England, for the use of the poets, in the dogmas of William Godwin.

The energy of Godwin's opposition to institutions and establish-

35

ments, the strength of his hope, the similarity of his egalitarianism to the poets' fervent belief in benevolence based upon emotional sympathy, and similar affinities drew Southey, Coleridge, and Shelley in collegiate immaturity, and Wordsworth as a fresh graduate, to the rationalistic doctrines of his *Enquiry concerning Political Justice,* first published in 1793 (revised 1796). From the initial dubious premise of man's rationality and a second premise of mechanistic though not materialistic determinism, Godwin erected a logical system: equality, or the duty of doing exact justice to every man for the benefit of all, leads to "perfectibility," or the infinite improvement of society, already made inevitable by the law of Necessity. The whole program seemed easily practicable by the equalization of property and privilege, with the consequent extermination of envy, theft, and violence. Reason required the abolition of oaths and of such oath-making and contract-writing institutions as marriage and government, which limit future decisions and frustrate sole reliance on justice as prescribed *ad hoc* by reason. The perfectibilitarian future would avoid such nonreasonable devices as the secret ballot. Godwin's conclusions, even before Coleridge helped convert him to belief in the affections, suggest that his rationalistic premises had encountered the sentimentalizing influence of Rousseau, but he keeps before him the dispassionate tone of Helvétius, Holbach, and (for his second edition) Condorcet.[18] He does not subscribe to "the rights of man." Although *Political Justice* leaves man no appeal except to his own inner voice, Godwin by no means allows self-direction as a right. Like the Rousseau of *Le Contrat social,* he denies rights and insists upon duties. For Godwin in 1793, the individual has the duty at all times, under all circumstances whatsoever, to obey the voice of reason. How, except by the rational power within himself, may a man recognize the rationality and justice of an external appeal?

Coleridge and Shelley could agree with Godwin on the duty of obeying the inner voice, without any question of right, but they could not accept the narrow standard of logic. By the principle of rational justice Godwin calls upon you, when certain death awaits either Archbishop Fénelon or your own mediocre sister or father, to save the invaluable statesman and forget your "own." Wordsworth and Coleridge saw quickly—Coleridge perhaps at once—an erroneous elevation of mechanistic understanding above human affections. We achieve universal benevolence, said the romantic, not by dry reason but by act of will enlarging the range of our sympathetic associations. Hazlitt believed that his chief contribution to human salvation was his explanation that we love ourselves and our sisters and aunts more than we love the coolie in Shantung not because of natural egoism but because our impression of ourselves and those near to us is much more intense than our impression of the distant Chinese. Coleridge's wayward pupil Charles Lloyd, in the "Advertisement" to *Edmund Oliver*, 1798, explained that he had written the novel to counteract the "generalizing spirit" of the Godwinians, with its "indefinite benevolence," which, "by means of annihilating all the dear 'charities of father, son, and brother,' would at last lead to a callousness that spurns at all affections, to a mad spirit of experiment, that would eradicate all the valuable feelings of man's nature." Coleridge himself subscribed to a sentiment that he quoted back to its author, John Thelwall: "He who thinks & *feels* will be virtuous . . ." All in all, *Political Justice* gave the poets an exemplary show of reason dehumanized, even better than they could have got by reading the works of Bentham, who (to paraphrase Oliver Elton) reduced the cool insanities of a Godwin or a Condorcet to common sense detailed and codified.

Historians of political theory and historians of cultural change have seen that rationalism was crossed and undermined in the eighteenth century by empirical utilitarianism, that both the materialism and the *bon sens* of the Enlightenment actively combated its doctrinaire rationalism.[19] Denis Diderot, in *Pensées sur l'interpretation de la nature*, 1754, asked thinkers to serve man by turning from mathematical logic to observation. Without being altogether friendly toward empiricism, the romantics found its psychology and its respect for experience less incompatible with their needs than the arid logic of neoclassical rationalism. Romantic art is "scientific" in its insistence upon experience and its observation of particulars. Do not number the streaks of the tulip, advised Dr. Johnson; to generalize is to be an idiot, answered Blake. In Wordsworth's metaphoric line "We murder to dissect," the vehicle for expression, the figurative example, is botanical and biological experiment, but the object of attack is rational analysis. The life of the organism escapes, Wordsworth is saying, when we classify into sapless abstractions only those parts of the living whole that logical understanding can perceive.

An effort to discriminate between the romantics' use of experience and their distrust of rational analysis—which they also used, of course, however furtively—should not leave unstated their dissatisfaction with mere experience, mere observation, pure description. Of any detail, they wished to know the meaning for the whole. They deplored the detachment of observation from moral purpose. In "A Poet's Epitaph," Wordsworth ordered away from the poet's grave not only the rational philosopher with "smooth-rubbed soul" but also the dry, empirical "fingering slave," the botanizing physician. Experiment must have a moral direction.

If the romantics were inexact and therefore unjust when they transferred to Godwinian rationalism the materialistic assumptions of experimental science, they were more accurate when they opposed the union between acceptance of matter and meanness of ends in the dogma of utility. They were especially distressed by the utilitarian doctrine of enlightened selfishness, as it can be found in Bernard Mandeville's aphorism, private vices, public benefits; in Hume's essay *Of the Original Contract,* where he explains how the moral obligation that we attribute to the duty of allegiance actually derives from the interest we each have in peace and public order; or in Adam Smith's assumption that enlightened selfishness is basic to "the nature and causes of the wealth of nations." Every luxury, answers Godwin, adds a burden, for the only wealth is labor.

Not merely in Edmund Burke's sense of the word *interest* as "privilege attaching to family or estate," but in all senses of the word except one, it was a contemptible noun to the romantics. The only legitimate *interest* was "the excitement of the feelings." Poetry should be especially defended in the nineteenth century, said Shelley, because poetry would disown the worst inclination bequeathed by the Enlightenment, "an excess of the selfish and calculating principle." Despite this passion against utility, the Tory failure to reform Parliament had to be attacked, to the confusion of the poets, on the grounds of its irrationality. They based their attack on the illogic of unequal representation, on the inutility of having landowners

The Climate

represent tradesmen, and on the system's failure to provide the greatest happiness or fullest avoidance of pain. Nobody produced a new, vitalistic, or "romantic" argument for direct rather than virtual representation.

Born to end a period when the shibboleths had been reason, general nature, universal citizenship, happiness (or pleasure), and utility, and finding these doctrines still entrenched in their own day, the romantics discovered a deeper satisfaction in emotion and feeling, the individual, the particular group, and the moral unity of life. Concerning the relations between politics and several of these satisfactions, notably romantic individualism, collectivism, and the sense of organic moral unity, something more needs to be said.

IV

Biographical accounts of Byron, as of Berlioz and most of the energetic among their contemporaries, have more often than not been case histories of egotism. In the adolescence of each romantic champion of energy, according to the cautious as well as the popular biographies, unconscious drives exploded against society. Jean-Jacques Rousseau, formerly accused of egoistic individualism and recently charged with totalitarian collectivism, "originated," says George Sabine, "the romantic cult of the group." Hippolyte Taine was apparently the first—and the author of *The Open Society and Its Enemies*, Karl Popper, probably the fiercest—in declaring that Rousseau originated romantic collectivism out of his monstrous egoism.[20]

Both the individualism and a kind of collectivism were present in the romantic movement. For better or worse, the popularity gained by romantic literature and art increased the social freedom of individualists, dissentients, and eccentrics. But eccentricity was always to be valued for its Promethean service to the human spirit. In 1793 a major committee of the London Corresponding Society began its declaration of principles: "1st. That all men are by nature free, equal and independent of each other."[21] When the individual sacrifices self, the group can tyrannize, as John Stuart Mill was to discover (partly through reading Coleridge and Wordsworth).

39

Politics in English Romantic Poetry

Byron and Shelley followed the *philosophes* and the London Corresponding Society in supporting the individual against oligarchy, monopoly, and public opinion. They opposed the family when it seemed to serve as an instrument conserving the social, religious, and political institutions of the past against the claims of the individual.

When Jacques Barzun first published *Romanticism and the Modern Ego* in 1943, he needed to mount a defense of romanticism not only against the charge of excessive individualism but also against the charge then current that the romantics had fathered twentieth-century Fascism. In 1961, when the latter charge came infrequently, Mr. Barzun's book appeared in a second revision under the more neutral title of *Classic, Romantic, and Modern.* But the charges he originally answered still recur, and it is impossible to deny that the apologists for Fascism held tenets in common with the romantics and drew heavily on the language of Herder, Fichte, and Friedrich Schlegel.

The authoritarianism of the Fascists, like the individualism of the romantics, in an exaltation of emotion and intuition over what we normally call reason, emphasized "the importance of the particular over the general, of national over international society, of personality over humanity."[22] But the absence of individual freedom from the Fascist emphasis makes all the difference.

Failure to emphasize individual freedom makes easier a call for the leadership of "commanding spirits," especially if the vitalistic premises of nationalism are also taken to encourage aspirations for a super race. Among the English, although Blake and Byron revered energy, the concept of commanding spirits, which Coleridge took momentarily from Schiller, received lasting support only from Carlyle, who restated it in the lectures published as *On Heroes, Hero-Worship, and the Heroic in History* (1841) and darkened it through the years to language not unlike that of the Nazi propagandists.

Even in the time of the English romantics, German apologists tried to reconcile their collectivism with the claims of the individual in the idea of "community," as a cooperative association of free individuals, in distinction from the more strictly binding "society" and "state."[23] Such an idea of community can be easily reconciled with

The Climate

the populist views that allowed Wordsworth in his later years to consider himself still a democrat.

Some have been less troubled over the encouragement romantic egoism gave to collectivism and commanding spirits than over its relation to the deistic idea of natural goodness. Again, the link is individualism. The belief that every individual is born naturally good—associated in the Christian West since the fifth century with Pelagius—spread wide over Europe during the Enlightenment. Equality in the eyes of God came to mean equality of reason, of responsibility, and of right to justice. Men were no longer born bad, but were made so by bad government. The romantics did not correct this heresy. In general, however, they should be thought of not as believers in natural goodness but in something far more dangerous. They believed in the mysterious capacity of the human individual, perhaps an infinite capacity, for good or evil.

It is this excited sense of potentiality for evil as well as for good that gives peculiar force to romantic irony. It invited in not only the "romantic agony" of Baudelaire, but even the pretentious agonies of Huysmans, Wilde, and D'Annunzio. The socialist Robert Owen, a secular son of the Enlightenment, set out to rescue "poor traduced and degraded human nature" from "the ridiculous and absurd mystery with which it has been hitherto enveloped by the ignorance of preceding times."[24] For Owen's romantic contemporaries, the Augustinian and Calvinistic traditions had traduced human nature with their emphasis upon original sin, but oversimplifying deism had of late traduced it more deplorably; followers of Locke had been ridiculously ignorant of the human mystery. Shelley has a fairy remind us as early as *Queen Mab* (III.16–17): "Thou knowest how great is man, / Thou knowest his imbecility." But the romantics looked higher, into fairyland itself.

In a literary context closely allied to the political, I use the term "Jacobin" as a blanket to include those writers at the end of the era of individual taste, "moral sense," and sensibility who expressed new social concerns, often stridently, and widened the subject matter previously restrained by neoclassical decorum, but employed poetic techniques that had become desiccated conventions in the course of the eighteenth century. Contemporaneous with Macpherson, Beattie, and Cowper, who had based their pieces on individual taste in beauty, sublimity, the picturesque, the grotesque, or the droll, the Jacobins fell into new codifications. In genres considered appropriate to a given effort, they were satirical, sentimental, expostulatory, and expository. Erasmus Darwin, for one, exploited simile and allegory for biological and political exposition.

The romantics created a body of literature still more personal and subjective than anything in the era of individual taste. If a poet turned from the doings at Vauxhall Gardens to trace the growth of a mind, what mind could he trace except his own? It is to be noted, moreover, that the epistemological questions shared by the audience as well as by the poets encouraged both an actual subjectivity and an apparent subjectivity in the treatment. Egoism, not merely temperamental, was partly modal. If the cultural situation encouraged actual egoism, it also encouraged egoistic modes to display "subjective" interests. The exploitation of the egoistic mode, which reaches its fullest complexity in Lamb's essays and Wordsworth's "Tintern Abbey" and "The Solitary Reaper," was naively stated by Coleridge's walking companion, Joseph Hucks, at the beginning of *A Pedestrian Tour through North Wales,* 1795:

> He claims the indulgence of his readers for the tautology and egotism, almost inseparable from works of such a description; but he has, as much as possible, endeavoured to avoid a repetition of names, and for this reason, has, in most cases, spoken of himself as being the only spectator; at the same time, in justice to those who accompanied him, he takes this opportunity of acknowledging himself, upon many occasions, greatly indebted to them for many interesting remarks and useful information, which otherwise he could not have had the means of acquiring.

In a cultural climate where every man is an important potential source of social good, the poet may stress his own importance as a representative man, solitary but unusually equipped to communicate.

The Jacobins exulted over the natural goodness of man. The romantics knelt in awe of the great potentiality compressed in every soul. It is not the doctrine of natural goodness, but that of infinite

The Climate

potentiality for progress, that explains Coleridge's optimistic remark to John Thelwall: "We are but frail beings at present." The doctrine likewise best explains the antidemocratic republicanism typical of the poets: men must and will be lifted up, as individuals. (Wordsworth calls this democratic antirepublicanism.)

Byron and Hazlitt could the more easily admire the individualism, the energy, and the audacity of a Bonaparte because, without making it a part of their creed, they lived in an atmosphere where will was ascendant. Coleridge and Shelley sought to depose analytic understanding, or "consecutive reasoning,"[25] and enthroned instead the sovereign imagination. In the actuality around them, reason subsided under the growing supremacy of will. The old Renaissance belief in man's freedom, immortality, and reason became less prudently belief in man's freedom, creative imagination, and illimitable power of will. Man is a paradox, as the Christian humanists had believed, but he is a paradox of infinities, as illustrated beyond Hamlet in Marlowe's overreaching protagonists. The new aim was to overreach with love.

Romantic belief in will has often been described as refusal to accept reality. John Morley found this weakness central to the French Revolution: "Men thought that they had only to will the freedom and happiness of a world, and all nature and society would be plastic before their daring . . . They could only conceive of failure as another expression for inadequate will."[26] John Bowle found a faith in will expressed politically, with and without system, from Rousseau and Burke to Mazzini and T. H. Green.[27] Herder, and especially Hegel, erected systems to replace the view of man as psychologically fixed by immutable laws of conscious reason. The effect of the new respect for irrationality in fields outside politics need not be stressed in any study undertaken subsequent to Baudelaire, Schopenhauer, and Freud.

To recognize that the romantics redefined reason and respected will is not necessarily to describe them as groping in a world from which all traditional bases of order had sunk away. Some recent critics have discovered in romantic poetry an anguished, Arnoldian suspension between a dead world and one powerless to be born. Others have thought to flatter the romantics by finding in them the bleak modernity of existentialist despair. Fear, even among men given more to emotion than to reason, is not the only cause of doubt, nor despair its only possible end. The poet of *The Prelude* was fostered *alike* "by beauty and by fear" (1805, I.306). Strong doubts become apparent in Wordsworth, Byron, and Shelley when, in their desire to annihilate the false security of confidence in simple order, they hesitate before accepting a preferable vision. In the vision of a unified, vital universe, depending for its life upon a power known to, immanent in, and so far dependent upon, the human imagination, they acknowledge the possibility of solipsistic illusion. They recognize in limitless aspiration the possibility of limitless evil. The romantic thus risked far graver consequences from error than any risked by Pope, Thomson, or Akenside. The romantic exerted the will to hope.

Faith in the power of will strengthened romantic insistence on morality in politics. Public morality had to feed and refresh the souls of a unified populace.[28] Keith Feiling has summarized what Southey, Wordsworth, and Coleridge concluded—that "the statesman must substitute morals for rights, obedience for will, and character for expediency."[29] Among the many who say that poetry and politics do not mix, some are so wrong as to believe that Wordsworth referred to Lady Hamilton when he said that Nelson's "public life" was "stained with one great crime." The moral poet referred to Nelson's violation of the character of the true warrior by his annulment of Captain Foote's treaty in Lady Hamilton's Bay of Naples in 1799.[30] Nelson had crushed Neapolitan liberty. If the older poets found a justification for Nelson's crushing of Armed Neutrality at Copenhagen in 1801, the younger poets (and Blake) found only disgrace in Canning's promptness to crush Denmark's "unarmed neutrality" in 1807. Yet the poets emphasized the necessity of virtue in the whole people even more than the necessity of virtue in their leaders. Tyranny, they thought, steamed up from "the self-murdered Virtue and inner freedom of the People, i.e. the Majority of the Citizens of the State."[31]

Romantic faith in will strengthened the insistence on political morality; it did not invent its maxims. Belief that freedom depends on virtue is one of the Roman elements in Elizabethan tragedies

The Climate

and histories. It was the Ciceronian center of British education. It became the ruggedness of Rugby, the point of the playing fields of Eton. Dominant in the English republican tradition from Rome, the coupling of freedom and virtue was voiced equally from both sides of the House of Commons. The social lessons of the Old Testament, with their moral imperative of national virtue, confirmed classical tradition. And "Romantic Hellenism" retained Cicero beside Plutarch.

From this moral base the poets rose to prophecy and to patriotic agony. To the altruistic liberal who loves his home, finds a scarcity of virtue there, and believes that there can be no freedom without virtue, there comes the painful disease of patriot's agony. Shelley could have the fury of a patriot against those who lived by principles or attitudes different from his own; yet he, like the other romantics, transferred from the individual to the society the excruciating sense of infinite potentiality.

Emphasis upon the collective virtue of a people fitted well with the burgeoning nationalism. Both the philosophic foundation of the French Revolution and the flying buttresses of its oratory were international. All men should join in equal fraternity. Much of the momentum of the Revolution, however, and especially the momentum whose push through Europe survived Waterloo, was nationalistic: a novel separation of unified land and people from the claims of a particular dynasty. Dante could think of Italy as formed by the boundaries of sea and Alps, language, common customs, even civilization, but not by the characteristics of a state. His political loyalty was to Florence, a *campanilismo;* it did not include Fiesole.[32] A false philosophy, said Coleridge in *The Friend,* had declared to the eighteenth century that "Cosmopolitism is nobler than Nationality, and the human race a sublimer object of love than a people."[33] As they did to other areas, the English poets brought emotion and attractive cloudiness to patriotic nationalism and subsequently to the justifications of national self-determination. Fortunately they lacked the precision required for the Germanic theories of *das Volk* and *der Staat.* English poetic nationalism is a political version of organic or divine union between people and land rather than an organic submission of land and people to an all-inclusive state.

45

James Gillray, "Presages of the Millenium"

The Climate

The various displacements here traced—of rationality by intuition, of utility by nobility, and of generalization by individuation—may be taken as the chief intellectual elements in the politics of English romantic poetry. Romantic poems are identifiable, not by the ideas of the Revolution, but by such counter-strains as empiricism, moral prophecy, and a sense of history. In the long view, perhaps the major import of the Revolution for the older English romantics came in the shock of disillusionment. The altruism of their concern for the moral position of the enemy encountered the impracticability of believing that Bonaparte only slightly threatened British shores, local affections, and a wide range of liberties. This shock, as much as any, made all the poets, including Byron, discover the basic contradiction between the rational doctrine of equality and faith in the unifying imagination.

V

That the major English romantics were deeply concerned with contemporary politics should not be questioned by students who have read more than the anthology pieces. Like the contemporaries of Milton and Dryden, the romantics were "no less inspir'd by the injur'd Genius of their Country, than by the Muses."[34] The injury began with the official British response to the evidence of expansionist inclinations in France. If, in the long view, the French Revolution acted only as a catalyst for romantic energies, its immediate effect was to make poems by Blake, Coleridge, Wordsworth, and Shelley share with Dissenting sermons an explosion of millenarial and apocalyptic enthusiasm for the new dawn.[35] By 1800 most apocalyptic utterances had turned for imagery from rising sun and purging fire to the whore and beast of destruction. This darkening had already occurred among prophets whose visions enveloped Pitt. Some still awaited the dawn, but now looked to the south of overclouded France.

The romantic bards sought to influence legislation, policy, and current events. Of the European poet, as distinguished from the American, W. H. Auden has said that "in his heart of hearts the audience he desires and expects are those who govern the country."[36]

Politics in English Romantic Poetry

Any attack on freedom of the press, such as the restrictions, penalties, and "taxes on knowledge" of 1797, 1798, and 1819, will bring previously unconcerned writers into intensified opposition. Newspapers and poets formed a natural alliance during the surveillance that began in 1793 under Pitt, Grenville, and Dundas, with zealous aid from judges Braxfield and Eyre and the retired judge John Reeves. The practical concerns of this alliance account for much of the obviously political verse of the romantic period. Later chapters in the present study will attempt to show how such concerns are reflected also, not always indirectly, in major poems of the romantic movement in England.

III

VARIETIES OF
ROMANTIC EXPERIENCE

Given the intensity of the poets' concern and their breadth of interest in matters touching politics at various points and in various ways, it is neither practicable nor desirable to limit an examination of the major poetry to a demonstration of the dilemma posed for each poet by discrepancies between the intellectual principles underlying his first political assents and his romantic intuitions of organic wholeness made apparent by the creative, unifying imagination. It does seem practicable to suggest the boundaries and depth of the dilemma, and to give the outline of several configurations that resulted from it, by presenting briefly some representative case histories.

Samuel Taylor Coleridge provides the model line of intellectual development, beginning with approval of the French Revolution, support of domestic reform, detestation of the British ministers who proscribed freedom, acceptance of associational psychology, and avid proclamation of the necessitarian laws of Nature and human conduct—all this in his brief period as an undergraduate at Cambridge—and ending with efforts to construct a universal philosophy of idealism, expressed in organic analogies intended to glorify the imagination and to strengthen the conservative forces of society. Robert Burns, peasant son of the Enlightenment and too early for the aesthetics of organicism, illustrates as well as Edmund Burke the failure of the American Revolution to clarify in England political principles that would be forced into clarity by later events. The Revolution in France, which separated Burke from his former companions the liberal Whigs, caught Burns ready for alienation from conservative patronage. Burns, born in 1759, moved in the opposite direction politically from Wordsworth (born 1770), Coleridge (1772), and Southey (1774). In each case the French Revolution served as catalyst. William Blake, now commonly regarded as the first English romantic, maintained almost from his birth in 1757 a radical defense of the poetic imagination against the oppressive government, established society, "charter'd Thames," and indeed sense impressions from all nature whatsoever, but the severe strains of this position have been too little emphasized in recent attention to Blake's "system." Thomas Love Peacock and Walter Savage Landor illustrate peripheral effects of the romantic dilemma on two poets who were not clearly romantic. Two of the "National Bards," Thomas Moore and Sir Walter Scott, one Whig and the other officially Tory, provide still further patterns at the periphery. Burns and Blake establish a chronological limit, a *terminus a quo;* Peacock, Landor, Moore, and Scott represent the boundaries of commitment to imagination. John Keats, youngest of the major poets, was the latest to feel the strain of loyalties divided between reform and imagination. Because Keats and Charles Lamb are often considered the most apolitical of the prominent English romantics, they provide the best illustrations of the pervasiveness of political interests throughout the romantic period.

I

We can begin with Coleridge as the paradigm. He completed, and justified intellectually, the movement from radical to conservative that we could most obviously expect to result from the common dilemma.[1] Emerging from boyhood in an environment of humanitarian sentiment, he "got great credit" in his first year at Cambridge for a Greek epitaph imagined as for the tomb of John Howard, revered author of *The State of the Prisons in England and Wales,* 1777, and translator of "historical remarks" on the Bastille. Soon

Varieties of Romantic Experience

the undergraduate was extravagant in praise of the Revolution in France,

> When slumbering Freedom roused by high Disdain
> With giant Fury burst her triple chain!   (CPW, 65:17–18)

He loathed and reviled the government of Pitt for warring against freedom, first abroad and then at home. Falling in with Unitarians and freethinkers, he adopted republican arguments against luxury, expanding commerce, and inequalities of property. He accepted the utilitarian principle of Helvétius, reflected in tracts by Priestley, that our only virtue is to secure the greatest public good for the greatest number. He embraced enthusiastically the doctrine of necessity, developed by Priestley less from Jonathan Edwards or other Calvinists than from Holbach, who depicted Nature as an active whole in which all the parts, necessarily concurring, unconsciously conspire to perpetuate Nature's active existence. Helvétius spoke to Coleridge through such libertarians as Godwin, Priestley, John Thelwall, and William Frend; the legislator must persuade men by self-love to do justice to each other.

What Coleridge most admired in the Enlightenment, the ideal of universal benevolence, thus came in the unwelcome guise of self-interest. Pantisocracy, the principle of communal ownership to be applied on the banks of the Susquehanna, had its sources in doctrines that would have required a quantitative balancing of the constituent members, each presumed to judge reasonably his own requirements and pleasures. Universal benevolence, as acclaimed by such rationalists as Godwin, would require the just balance of interests in the macrocosm of society. A truer benevolence, of a kind acceptable to the awakening Coleridge, would have to grow from the personal experience of affection for individuals near at hand. By 1796 he concluded that Godwinian patriots would destroy the state by dissolving family ties; libertarian began to mean libertine.

No study of the changes in Coleridge's *Weltanschauung* can be successfully divorced from his temperament and personal situation. In rejecting abstract analysis for experiential evidence, he had to give the place of first importance to his own experience. An affec-

51

tionate and pious man who predicted lasting comfort for all in
affection and piety, he yearned for kinsmen and friends who would
return his tempestuous love. He needed a divinity of forgiveness
rather than of reason, because he could not bear the burden of his
own guilt. Furthermore, he was married to the wrong woman and
longed to be free of her: if he listened to the tempting voices of men
who placed utility and reason above the fidelity of a husband, sworn
under God, he could slay his moral being. Virtue, if dependent
only on the frail reed of reason, would bend to earth. Coleridge
had to believe in strength of individual will, and he had to exert
that strength. Epistemologically, too, he needed a better account
than Locke, Hartley, Helvétius, or Priestley had given of the creative
force of such a poetic mind as he felt his own to be.

Reason was also inadequate either to rule or to explain public
events. Previously it had been Britain and her despotic allies who
were "mad with rage demoniac"; even when the Revolution in
France wove a "dance more wild than e'er was maniac's dream,"
the poet had looked for a return to reason; but now the French
under the guidance of Bonaparte were "slaves by their own compulsion."[2] Bonaparte, a corrupt genius, turned the Revolution from
its course; an imperialist Nimrod, he hunted mankind. France
proved to Coleridge that it takes more than the untrammeling of
reason to make a lasting reformation. Nature cannot create, at least
natura naturata cannot; and no government, says Coleridge's recanta-
tory "France: an Ode," can by decree bestow freedom on an enslaved soul.

Despite his alertness to philosophic implications—and both despite
and because of his intense self-scrutiny—Coleridge gives us less than
a classic parabola from naturalistic Jacobinism to a reconciliatory
faith in divine imagination and the organic state. Day after day, year
after year, he looped, back-tracked, redoubled, and reneged. A biographer would be wrong, however, to see these uncertainties as altogether temperamental.

After intense study in the first months of 1801, he announced to
his friend Thomas Poole: "If I do not greatly delude myself, I
have not only completely extricated the notions of Time, and Space;
but have overthrown the doctrine of Association, as taught by Hart-

ley, and with it all the irreligious metaphysics of modern Infidels—
especially, the doctrine of Necessity.—This I have *done* . . ."[3]
This Kant had done. Even so, Coleridge's use of Kant, and later
of Jacobi and Schelling, did not result in submission to any Transcendental system. He did not go to Kant for answers. He had
the answers he wanted. He went to contemporary metaphysicians,
as to earlier Christian apologists, in order to discover more subtle
explanations of the possible relationships among his answers. He
took from Kant the assurance that human understanding is an inferior faculty incapable of reaching or testing the answers most to
be treasured. He borrowed and exploited distinctions, concepts, illustrations, and the language of whole passages in his efforts to discover
and express a Christian Idealism that could acknowledge the creative
value of human experience.

Beginning with *Immanuel Kant in England,* 1931, René Wellek
has frequently objected that Coleridge had "little insight into the
incompatibility of different trends of thought." The objection had
to be put by somebody, because the answers that Coleridge sought
to reconcile included several that do not easily converge: All ideas
are *a priori* in the mind of God, but all of man's knowledge comes
from experience. Nevertheless, with a more creative instrument of
thought than Hobbes, Locke, or Hume acknowledged, man exerts
a positive will both in acting and in imagining, which is "a repetition
in the finite mind of the eternal act of creation in the infinite I
AM."[4] Coleridge, as Alice D. Snyder insisted in *Coleridge on Logic
and Learning,* 1929, had a standpoint rather than a system. From
his theistic standpoint he looked toward what in faith was a gospel
and in logic a goal. He needed to prove that a virtuous man can
know with certainty the existence of a single, omniscient, omnibenevolent, omnipotent God, and can apprehend the truths or truth
of God. In short, Coleridge wagered his whole mental and spiritual being in the effort to reconcile philosophic answers that no
metaphysician has yet reconciled. Kant, the culminating mind of
the Enlightenment, had rejected the certainties for which Coleridge
continued to aspire.

We can see in Coleridge how emphasis upon emotion worked
against generalization by demanding attention to particular experi-

ences. He and Wordsworth first examined the principle of benevolence in the light of the psychology of association, with its empirical
attention to particulars. They soon concluded that liberal rationalists
had deduced universal benevolence logically from the axioms of
unrestricted thought and abstract justice for all. But whatever belief
in liberty and democracy Coleridge and Wordsworth were to retain
had to be consonant with the generalizations that their unifying
imagination could draw from experiences they had personally un-
dergone and thus feelingly remembered. The head affects the preaching; the heart directs the practice. Attention to particulars made
Coleridge, and even Shelley, accept expediency without abandoning
a horror of utility.

By a paradox to become in time the hallmark of the intellectual,
Coleridge committed some of his best energies to the problems of
a society from which he was insulated and in part alienated. He
was concerned passionately for the landscape, skies, church, and
future of his country. He liked the idea of loving the free English
people. In contrast, his distaste for the clear, distinct, and brittle
ideas conspicuous in French thought harmonized with his contempt
for a people who would submit to Bonaparte as emperor.

In 1809-10, with Napoleon rampant, Coleridge was able to turn
from the higher reason of Kant, surrender to the expedience of
Burke, and hold that government should protect itself from the chal-
lenges of abstract reason. In essays first published in his periodical
the *Friend*, known in later editions as the series "On the Principles
of Political Knowledge," he rejected the animalistic doctrines of
Hobbes but sought middle ground between Hobbes and Rousseau.
Against Rousseau's appeals to pure reason, he objected that the
natural condition of man and the organic growth of society require
government to act from empirical assumptions, from "human pru-
dence," from expedience "under the particular circumstances." An
individual finds his political obligation by subjecting his conscience
to reason; government, on the other hand, must calculate a balance
among the unequal understandings of individuals in the society.
As usual, Coleridge was conveying into print little of the subtlety
of his notebooks and marginalia.[5] Even in the notebooks, however,

the conflict between the psychological particulars of experience and the universal principles of reason is evident.

Once Waterloo had put to an end the dangers from France, Coleridge's expressions of political thought shifted toward a more comfortable position on the side of reason. More than ever, he subjected concrete situations in the news to immutable principles. Alarmed by the Catholic Emancipation Act of 1829, on the ground that it weakened religious tradition as well as the Church of England, he argued in his essay *On the Constitution of the Church and State* from the general premise that any attempt to apprehend the universal idea of constituted society must begin by studying a particular nation. Applying this premise, he finds that the universal idea of the state is evident in the average Englishman's sense of the British constitution. In 1830, the ideal constitution called for a strengthening of the conservative forces of society against the overbalancing progressive forces of the middle classes. To complement the aristocracy, gentry, and other so-called owners, who held landed property in trust for the nation, he proposed a timely acknowledgment of the spiritual legislators, the sages, professors, and learned in "all the so called liberal arts and sciences, the possession and application of which constitute the civilization of a country."[6] These, the *clerisy*, including librarians and poets as well as the clergy, together preserve for the nation its spiritual resources and cultural heritage.

In the *Church and State,* if anywhere in English, we have the exposition of a "romantic" theory of government. It was not given to Coleridge to dissolve the theory in a romantically symbolic or irrationally organic work of art. He had constructed a bridge back to the Enlightenment, but not forward across the chasm.

II

The earliest limit of the dilemma faced by Coleridge can be marked by noting how Robert Burns was exempt from it. The poetry of Burns illustrates the catalytic effect of the French Revolution but shows also the advantage of premature escape from the precipitation of conflicting elements. In art Burns belonged to the Enlightenment. He tempered the strong Scottish nationalism of his songs with the universalist bias of the Enlightenment in Scotland and the cosmopolitan assurance of his satiric method: "Bred and educated," he declared himself, "in revolution principles"—the principles of 1688—"the principles of reason and common sense."[7] The language of London, as a language of new ideas, of intellect as opposed to feeling and experience, attracted him as French attracted his countryman Hume. And yet, as he confessed in the "Sketch" inscribed to C. J. Fox, "Mankind is a science defies definitions."[8]

From 1783 to 1795 Burns as a poet went from a half-skeptical, half-Tory interest in recent British history to an eloquent concern with political principles, for a time boldly democratic but modulated at the last to libertarian Whiggery. W. P. Ker, in "The Politics of Burns," called attention to the Tory finesse of such satiric verses of 1784–1787 as the "Ballad on the American War," but he made the case for Burns's early loyalty to Pitt and therefore to George III rather too well.[9] The fragmentary "Ballad," to be sure, breaks off at Pitt's victory of 1784, but the victory occurs in a poetic world of satiric irony, beginning with Burns's ridicule of Lord North in the first line: "When *Guilford* good our Pilot stood." Leadership after Chatham reveals itself in subsequent lines to be nothing but cowardice, intrigue, and asininity. As for George III's family, in the birthday ode of 1786, beginning "Guid-mornin to your Majesty," they are desired to remember that "German-Gentles are but *sma'*." Scottish nationalism made Burns a Jacobite before he was a Jacobin.

As an "independent Briton," he favored Scotch drink, and plenty of it, for the tenant and the plowman; he distrusted, as much in 1786 as later, the gentry, landlord, and steward, or "factor":

> Poor *tenant-bodies*, scant o' cash,
> How they maun thole a *factor's* snash . . .[10]

In an autobiographical letter of August 1787 to John Moore, he traced the ugly development of class distinctions among adolescents after the contrasting democracy of childhood, where a lad's a lad for a' that: "It takes a few dashes into the world to give the young

56

Varieties of Romantic Experience

Great man that proper, decent, unnoticing disregard for the poor, insignificant, stupid devils, the mechanics and peasantry around him. . . ." He wanted the established order to remember the status and value of the independent, educated farmer as a middle link in the chain. Adversity helped him value those he had liked to think of as lower than he. Adversity would later elicit or encourage from him the lines, "Here's a health to them that's awa," his toast to all Reforming Whigs, including the Erskines "of the North" and Fox, "the chief o' the clan."

In Burns's life as a farmer the dignity of independence suffered the indignities of poverty very much as the free Briton of Ayrshire suffered overrule in the Scottish union with England.[11] In moments of pride as a free Briton, Burns opposed the enemies of his country; as a Scotsman of genius, kept down like Fergusson before him by "titled knaves and idiot-Greatness," he nourished strong resentments, not only against the Crown but against his own public moderation. In this self-irritation, if in nothing else, he resembled his longer-lived contemporary, Blake.

It was not only in adversity and resentment that personal experience collaborated with the cosmopolitan ideals of the Enlightenment. The idea of universal brotherhood warmed itself in the pleasures of local fraternity, first in quaffing and later in Freemasonry. Personal feeling as well as received idea brought about his sympathetic treatments of louse and mouse.

In total contrast, liberal principles went for nothing in his sentimental attachment to the house of "beauteous Stuart." Stirred by Jacobite song, he created, in "By yon castle wa'," his own version of "There'll never be peace till Jamie comes hame." If we allow a little for exaggeration in a letter to James Steuart, he kept the Young Pretender's birthday as "a day of the year with me as hallowed as the ceremonies of Religion and sacred to the memory of the sufferings of my King and my Forefathers." Here he faced a contradiction as troublesome as that of the poets who would soon try to fuse rational justice with faith in the imagination. Burns recognized the contradiction. His public protestations of loyalty, influenced by desire to hold his place in the Excise, argue explicitly that the present king is to be preferred because the Stuarts belonged

57

to an age and climate of absolute rule and George III survives in a happier age shaped by the English Convention of 1688 and the enlightened American Congress of 1776.

A man for whom the old answers are contradictory will welcome new answers, even when he finds the new less than satisfactory. Burns's "Ode to the Departed Regency Bill" of 1789, although it takes the Foxite line against the "Premier's sullen pride," unfurls a vision of chaos come again:

> Deafening din and warring rage
> Factions wild with factions wage. . . .
>
> (PSB, I, 462:6–7)

He supports the Whigs as the stumbling supporters of a plowman's liberty in the absence of other support. The democratic idea has bitten deep enough for the Revolution in France to do its work. Next comes Tom Paine. Liberty becomes the freedom to act as an equal.

To explain away the evidence of his complicity when he stood at the theater in the midst of a mob singing the most provocative of revolutionary songs, *Ça ira,* in December 1792, Burns spoke soberly against the "alarming System of Corruption" between the King and Parliament. He spoke drunkenly against some of the upper rungs of what he called—this time soberly, whether or not single-mindedly—"the most glorious Constitution on earth." Like Wordsworth and Coleridge, he recorded his shock at the British declaration of war against the forces of freedom in France. In irritation over an episode unfavorable to France, he wrote an "Impromptu on General Dumourier's Desertion from the French Republican Army."[12] The desertion galled Burns the more because he had celebrated Dumouriez's victory over the Austrians at Jemappes in a contraband ballad, "When princes & prelates & het-headed zealots," set to the air of "The Campbells are Comin'."[13] Meanwhile, Scottish courts acted quickly to enforce Pitt's will, described by Burns in an ironic quatrain "On Politics" as the will to "let great folks know and see," above all to let persons of mean fortune be silent.[14] For stronger protest, Muir, Palmer, Gerrald, and Margarot were transported to Botany Bay. Burns was quieted to a Whig.

58

Varieties of Romantic Experience

Yet the quieted poet sang more universally than an unmuzzled rebel, determined to be raucous, ever can. Against the house of Hanover, Burns had nursed social, humanitarian, partisan, and patriotic grievances. In 1795, for the Dumfries Volunteers, he composed patriotic stanzas against Bonaparte, "Does haughty Gaul invasion threat?" At the close, attempting a final loyalty to all that he had stood for, he brought into synthesis his principles as a Briton, a liberal, a Whig, and a right good fellow:

> Who will not sing, God save the King,
> Shall hang as high's the steeple;
> But while we sing, God save the King,
> We'll ne'er forget The People!   (PSB, II, 766)

This, when a discount is made for intimidation, is not many steps backward from Burns's earlier union of balladry with Tom Paine:

> It's coming yet for a' that,
> That Man to Man, the warld o'er
> Shall brothers be for a' that.   (PSB, II, 763)

His way of universality was not the way of Blake or Shelley. To the end, he saved love for the bed or the rushes. For Dumfries or for Paris, his standards of brotherhood remained what they had been since 1783: worth, independent mind, and sense.

III

It was not because he outlived Burns by thirty-one years that William Blake struggled on the edge of a deeper chasm. For several years before Burns's death in 1796, Blake had espoused the Revolution but worshiped the poetic imagination—a far more jealous god than the Jehovah he renounced. Imaginative energy, or Poetic Genius, could not really approve the commonsense liberalism of Joseph Johnson, the radical publisher who printed *The French Revolution* for Blake in 1791.

An earlier volume prepared for the public, the *Poetical Sketches* of 1783, came from a young man whose closest friends were determined and destined to rise in the world of art. Blake, if equally determined, was tentative. His unbound sheets of verse seemed unexceptionable, but only seemed so, in the age of sentiment, taste, asymmetrical gardening, and vistas of the sublime. The longest fragment allows Edward III to proclaim "Liberty, the charter'd right of Englishmen," as the power impelling him toward the battle of Crécy, a suspicious irony among supporters of the American colonists. At a greater remove of time, place, and fiction, "Gwin, King of Norway" releases the republican cry to be heard later in *America, 1793,* and *Europe, 1794:* "O what have Kings to answer for . . . !"[15] Such combinations of the assertive and the oblique characterize most of Blake's lifework to come.

After several years of promise as an engraver and of almost secret development as a prophetic poet, he revealed in 1789, in *Songs of Innocence,* to those few whose minds and imaginations were attuned and whose purses could afford his method of illuminated printing, a pastoral world open to the innocent Christian in the midst of soiling matter and mortal sorrow. The vision endures. Yet it must be only a segment of the poet's truth, or Blake's admirers must themselves provide irony, when "The Chimney Sweeper" ends with an adage going beyond the Wesleys and Isaac Watts: "So if all do their duty, they need not fear harm." A world of faith in which a child sold by his father must perform his *duty* to the rich is not a world of any innocence worth having. "Holy Thursday," similarly, turns from the assembled charity-children to honor their elders:

> Beneath them sit the aged men wise guardians of the poor
> Then cherish pity, lest you drive an angel from your door.

When a version of "Holy Thursday" was recited by Obtuse Angle, the Mathematician, in Blake's satire "An Island in the Moon," the "wise guardians" were "revrend men." By either epithet, they lead the mind toward Blake's later comment in the margin of Sir Joshua Reynolds' Discourses: England asks whether a man of talent is "Passive & Polite & a Virtuous Ass: & obedient to Noblemens Opinions in Art & Science." The Governors of Christ's Hospital sit uncomfortably in a world of innocence.

Caustic satire, nearly as deep in Blake's being as his secretive self-awareness, certainly plays its part in the contraries of *The Mar-*

Varieties of Romantic Experience

riage of Heaven and Hell, c. 1793, and *Songs of Innocence and of Experience,* 1794. What Swedenborg accepted as Jehovah's Angels, in agreement with the orthodox, Blake took to be accusing imps of evil proclaimed by the hypocritical Elect. Utilizing the limitations of reason, tyranny had contrived to be worshiped under the majestic name of Jehovah. In this religious guise tyranny made war on America, France, and Poetic Genius. For the younger poets, Blake set a pattern: tyranny is one aspect of the evil of mere understanding. What Keats was to call "consequitive reasoning" Blake named Urizen, the tyrannical, limiting horizon of your-reason. Near the beginning of *The Marriage of Heaven and Hell* we are told how to escape from tyranny through the wedding of good and evil: "Without Contraries is no progression." Therefore, "the passive that obeys Reason," which the religious call good, must be countered by the contrary that they call evil, "the active springing from Energy." To Christian meekness must be opposed the energy of revolution as the one way of attaining liberty. Just as tyranny is to be associated with the processes of measuring and weighing, so the highest imagining of eternal man has its political aspect: "Jerusalem is named Liberty among the sons of Albion."[16]

For himself as well as for society, Blake recognized the constant threat of the rationalistic voice, speaking simultaneously through radical acquaintances in London and through the oppressed, angry journeyman that his occupation as engraver had made him and tried to keep him. As one result of this seduction, *The French Revolution* contains the grit of actuality in pedestrian detail: "And the vote was, that Fayette should order the army to remove ten miles from Paris." In *America, a Prophecy,* the giant figures of a universal myth evolved by Blake appear in a "Preludium" to the historical narrative concerning the American Revolution. The following year, in *Europe, a Prophecy,* myth and history coalesce in both "Preludium" and the narrative that follows.

A lesson for the present is implied in the history of *The French Revolution.* In the larger frame of archetypal myth, with periphrastic allusions to reality, *America* and *Europe* both fulfill Blake's requirement for prophetic warning: "if you go on So, the result is So." If George III, with his ministers and allies, continues the present warfare against France, against all opposition to slavery and enslavement, and against the well-being of the sons of Albion, then he and his ministers will witness such plagues as were brought on by the wars of Edward III, will suffer such an end as George Washington effected, will learn what "noble" Louis XVI learned, will face the revolutionary Orc rising in his endless cycle, will in short encounter eternal truth.[17]

The Songs of Experience, surprisingly when contrasted with the pastoral world in the "songs of pleasant glee," but fully in keeping with Blake's movement toward "organized innocence," show a further advance into the Utopian and millenarian. These pieces, from 1791–1794, condemn the interlocking institutions of political, ecclesiastical, and social tyranny as the removable cause of such evils as repressed sex, murder on the scale of war, impressment, the chimney-sweeper's cry, oppression of the laborer, and "the Marriage hearse." The piper of innocence had shown a way of living with evil. The bard of experience, although he begins to discover evil in himself, foresees a way of removing evil. One trouble with innocent charity is that the accusers, who wish you to believe in it, profit when you practice it. In the new Jerusalem the contraries of wrath and pity will reunite in the divine energy. Meanwhile, the trouble with accusatory rebellion is that retaliation makes you one of *them,* the mentally chained, the negated Satanic accusers. You accuse the state (the "Zoa" or condition), and try to forgive the man, but you hit the man in accusing the condition.

The most famous of Blake's poems, "The Tyger," had been a creation of one contrary within the poet himself. He who had created "The Lamb" is here the revolutionary, opposing the "Yea Nay Creeping Jesus," choosing the tigers of wrath over the horses of instruction. He had shown throughout *The Marriage of Heaven and Hell* and *Songs of Experience* that the expression of antagonism is better than repression, which forces the poison of resentful hypocrisy to course through a man's being. Nevertheless, wrath is only a contrary, and its result may be degeneration rather than progression. In the place of moral law, Jesus did not teach mere pity, he did not teach humility, but he did teach forgiveness of sins. Blake backed away from his vision of a political millennium partly because

Varieties of Romantic Experience

Napoleon, the English reformers, and even the American Congress fell short of the dream, but there was also the severer personal problem of self-exclusion from visionary wholeness through hatred, whether of George III, Locke, Reynolds, or Wiliam Hayley. As a well-meaning patron, Hayley had posed a rationalistic threat to poetic vision. By suggesting compromise with the fallen world, he had split Blake's response into pity and wrath. In 1804, when the soldier Scolfield and a comrade accused Blake in court of seditious libel, a suspicion that Hayley had hired the soldier to do it drove the poetic imagination toward the spectrous negation of selfish hatred.[18] Satanic negation is not a contrary.

Nor did the contraries offer a practical way of fourfold vision and integration, now that Blake was writing, not about the supposed Satan of the accusers, but about the ultimate Satan of anti-Christian nothingness. Blake seems to have come solidly against the problem of achieving wholeness through opposition, as well as against the ultimate pettiness of opposition politics, in the manuscript work first entitled *Vala,* much modified through stages of organized innocence to the Christian forgiveness of its final form as *The Four Zoas.* In the palimpsests of this work Urizen still embodies monarchic tyranny and the grinding wheels of dark Satanic mills as well as compass-closing Newtonian measurement. Denunciation of particular wars and measures becomes increasingly difficult, however, not only because the limiting, experiential, naturalistic understanding of Locke affords the sole arguments available in the natural world of particular wars, but also because denunciation is itself a hindrance to the reintegration of Albion, the spiritual wholeness of divine humanity.

Everything that lives is holy. The creation of Adam was the fall of man from divine unity into fragments, male and jealous female, the Urizenic illusion of separable love, imagination, body, and thought. Creative energy involves all of man's parts in fourfold vision. A Last Judgment is available at all times to every man. The poetic imagination must reforge Albion, the whole spiritual humanity; must in London rebuild first the city of art and then man's highest imagining, Jerusalem. To release Los, or poetic genius, is to have social and political liberty. That the condition presently shared by England and Europe is diabolical needs no repetition from the earlier prophecies.

For all the cyclic universality of his system, Blake's prophetic works continued to show how creative energy offered the only solution to immediate public questions. David Erdman, the chief proponent of the historical approach to Blake, has more difficulty in finding and explicating the topical allusions in *The Four Zoas, Milton,* and *Jerusalem* than in earlier works. Part of the difficulty arises within the philosophical import of Blake's vision. In part, also, he had already made the case against his times and needed to explain the bases rather than make the case again. And in part the state trials intimidated him. The prudentially periphrastic becomes in his late works the cautiously obscure. The conventional surface beauty of the early lyrics makes rare appearances in *Milton,* rarer still in *Jerusalem.* Obfuscation came painfully to an artist whose oldest aesthetic principle was clarity and firmness in the bounding line.

Proud of saying, "I also spoke my mind," he introduced as a theme in his prophecies his own lapses into wrath or pity, the one divided from the other. The difficulty of dealing imaginatively with current politics without the disjunction of wrath and pity accounts in part for the poignancy, for us and probably for Blake, of four lines etched at the end of the Preludium of *America* but erased or masked from all of the earliest known copies:

> The stern Bard ceas'd, asham'd of his own song; enrag'd he swung
> His harp aloft sounding, then dash'd its shining frame against
> A ruin'd pillar in glittring fragments; silent he turn'd away,
> And wander'd down the vales of Kent in sick & drear lamentings.[19]

The myth of *Milton,* dated 1804, contains palpable autobiography. It tells how Blake, self-subjected by his own feminine mildness to the insipid William Hayley, then sang with bardic inspiration of his break with Hayley, only to encounter the condemnation of others,

> Saying Pity and Love are too venerable for the imputation
> Of Guilt   (Plate 13:48–49)

The inspired song told how, in the crisis with Hayley, Catherine Blake's courage had exceeded her husband's, and how she was impli-

cated with him in misapplied work as he pushed the etching needle
in anger:

The Harrow cast thick flames & orb'd us round in concave fires
A Hell of our own making. see, its flames still gird me round.

(Plate 12:22–23)

What matters is not the factual detail, but the subjective fervor.
By aligning the mistakes of Luther, Calvin, Cromwell, Milton, and
Blake, the Poetic Genius, "the eternal all-protecting Divine Humanity," teaches itself that the wrath of *America* and *Europe* must
be dissolved: "O go not forth in Martyrdoms & Wars."[20]

Angry with monarchic government for suppressing speech and
constricting life, angry with liberal friends for accepting a contracted
empirical vision, and angry with strangers for ridiculing or ignoring
the everlasting gospel of his art, Blake was angry with himself for
remaining angry, for his fear, timidity, and hesitation, and for the
frustrations inherent in his desire to communicate only by imaginative means. Dr. Erdman has traced through *Jerusalem* the argument
that Britain should pursue peace without recrimination. The turmoil
within the poet is also apparent. As a corollary to *Milton, Jerusalem*
tells how Los struggled against the selfhood that would act in hatred
to split the true manhood that self must become. Erin mourns for
the poet as well as for the society that oppresses him when she
laments that the Visions of Eternity are constricted "Till deep dissumulation is the only defence an honest man has left" (*Jerusalem*
49:23).

Blake appeals to us by the terrors of his conflict as well as by
the awesome array of his archetypes. He appeals also because his
accounts of spiritual warfare for reconciliation and unity convey
in the prophecies a fearful sense of discontinuity, both in history
and in the moral life of the individual.

IV

Northrop Frye could take Blake's radicalism as evidence of man's
discontent with the human condition: "Revolution is the sign of
apocalyptic yearnings, of an impulse to burst loose from this world

altogether and get into a better one, a convulsive lunge forward of the imagination."[21] When we swing from Blake toward what he would emphatically regard as the contrary of classical emphasis represented in Thomas Love Peacock, we find there also a nostalgia for primitive wholeness. Although hardly apocalyptic, Peacock the classicist also yearns for a way out of the absurd paradox of modern life.

Peacock has a great deal of what historians of ideas have distinguished as cultural primitivism. In *The Misfortunes of Elphin*, 1829, he writes ironically of the age of Taliesin, the sixth-century Welsh bard: "They had no steam-engines, with fires as eternal as those of the nether world, wherein the squalid many, from infancy to age, might be turned into component portions of machinery for the benefit of the purple-faced few. They could neither poison the air with gas, nor the waters with its dregs: in short, they made their money of metal, and breathed pure air, and drank pure water, like unscientific barbarians."[22] The gibe against paper money is as characteristic as the rest. Peacock plumped for reform, not for progress. No more than other Englishmen of his day did he have access to a philosophic system that could reconcile his suggestions for political renovation and his disbelief in social progress. Hazlitt and others in the age of progress declared the arts not progressive. In *The Four Ages of Poetry* Peacock declared them degenerative. He saw increase of invention as hand in hand with increase of folly. Yet Mr. Escot of Peacock's *Headlong Hall*, who finds all improvements "only so many links in the great chain of corruption," and Mr. Toobad, the Manichaean Millenarian in *Nightmare Abbey*, 1818, hold their foolish ideas in ways as comic as the theorists who oppose them.

Sir Oran Haut-ton, in *Melincourt*, 1817, illustrates typically Peacock's ambivalence. When this amiable orang-utan is nominated by purchase to represent in Parliament "the ancient and honourable borough of Onevote," he asserts his instinctive wisdom, as well as "the freedom of the natural man," to the extent of refusing altogether the asinine process of chairing the Member. Although Sir Oran's supporters first think that his repugnance to being carried through the streets arises entirely from diffidence, the vigor of his

resistance to human folly leaves the hustings, booths, stalls, and bar-
rows in disarray—until the inevitably aroused rabble converts the
entire borough of Onevote to ashes. Here in a single episode Peacock
not only ridicules Lord Monboddo's primitivistic view of the orang-
utan as an infantine example of our species, from whom we could
properly learn nudity and other primitive virtues, and not only rejects, in the course of ridiculing Monboddo, the soberer theories
of evolution advanced in antiquity by Empedocles and in Peacock's
day by Erasmus Darwin, but also, simultaneously, ridicules man's
claim to superiority in practical reason.

It was during the violent debates over Parliamentary Reform that
Peacock had the perpetually tipsy Seithenyn ap Seithyn, in *The
Misfortunes of Elphin,* speak in defense of the seawall entrusted
to his lax care:

If it were all sound, it would break by its own obstinate stiffness:
the soundness is checked by the rottenness, and the stiffness is balanced
by the elasticity. There is nothing so dangerous as innovation. . . .
Here this immortal old work, which God forbid the finger of modern
mason should bring into jeopardy, this immortal work has stood for
centuries, and will stand for centuries more, if we let it alone.[23]

Seithenyn parallels the arguments of Burke and Canning that privilege and prejudice serve a venerable function in the fabric of the
British Constitution. A sentence I have omitted parodies "The Cata-
ract of Lodore" by the King's Laureate, Southey. Elsewhere, confronted with the proposition that London Bridge should give place
to a new structure, Peacock opposed the renovation. He would retain
the visible signs that "connect the present generation with the ages
that are gone." In the same year, 1830, in the same Utilitarian
Westminister Review, he declared Thomas Jefferson "the greatest
public benefactor that has yet appeared in the nineteenth century"—
with a concession that in the previous century Jefferson may have
been second to Washington.[24]

Meanwhile, with his usual vigorous scholarship he had turned
back to explore the old Welsh materials, to translate and adapt
the ancient songs, to amalgamate the legends of Taliesin and Arthur,
and to bring all these to bear upon the life of his own time. Most

of the lyrics scattered through his novels, drawing their metaphors as often from the amaranth or the sapling as from wine, are sly in tone but nostalgic in effect. His longest completed poem, *Rhododaphne, or the Thessalian Spell*, 1818, is compounded of classical learning, the sweetness of love, and incantation. "Mystic moralisings" and "half-prophetic sense,"[25] though tempting, were less congenial to Peacock than his parodies of Southey, Coleridge, and Wordsworth in *Paper Money Lyrics*, where he was happy to include apostate poets in satire directed chiefly against the Scottish economists. A novelist, poet, scholar, and gourmet holding a position of responsibility in the East India Company, he was rare in accepting not only the politics but also the psychology of the Benthamites while resenting the scars they inflicted equally on culture and landscape.

He was too narrowly utilitarian, even if his arguments are analyzed more tolerantly than Shelley analyzed them in *A Defence of Poetry*, but he was not a faithful Benthamite.

Almost immobilized between classical learning and romantic sentiment, Peacock could not debate public issues with full seriousness. Even in debate, he drew back toward his own ironic center. He took much of his attitude toward dilemmas, along with much of his style, from Hume and Gibbon. Neither his chief dilemma nor its solution changed greatly with the years. In ideology Peacock changed less than Coleridge or Wordsworth and no more than Shelley. But an ironic center is no center at all: like a dilemma, irony points two ways at once.

Peacock and Walter Savage Landor differ from "Jacobin" poets like Erasmus Darwin and Robert Merry, with whom they share liberal politics, in that their classicism constitutes a conscious, nostalgic break with the poetics of the previous century. Yet when Landor puzzled his aging head over "the Classick and the Romantic," in an epistle to the author of *Festus*, the most notorious poem from the Spasmodic School, he could only be sure that "Classic in every feature was my friend." The Spasmodist he addressed was young P. J. Bailey, but the friend was Robert Southey. Landor must have had an odd sense of the classical to associate it so firmly with Southey. Despite political divergence, Southey and Landor had each continued to admire the exuberance of the other's earliest

Varieties of Romantic Experience

poems. They shared almost no important opinions except mutual admiration and a contempt for Byron. Landor's extravagance in private conduct, like his liberal politics, typifies the gulf between them. Yet Landor, a literary critic of notable taste, failed to find Southey inadequate. In somewhat the same way, he left unexamined the grounds of his own antiroyalist, revolutionary opinions.

Landor is more Wordsworthian, in reacting spontaneously to the object before him, than he and some of his admirers have thought. Often, when he read the public news, he was overcome by powerful emotion. Where politics were concerned, he often "seized the pen" when due decorum, according to his poem "So Then, I Feel Not Deeply," would have him wait "near Memory's more quiet shade." Although most of the hundred pages classified as "History and Politics" in the Oxford edition of his poems were history when he published them, they were current, libelous politics when he wrote them. Certainly his works, even those in verse, are more laden with current politics than one would guess from the dozen or so pieces usually anthologized.[26] The guests few and select at his well-lighted table have savored his viands from Hellenic Greece and his wines from the Florence of Boccaccio; they have ignored poniards like "Walcheren 1809" and "Tyrannicide," which have been lost among vast quantities of forgotten verse. In the first he declared the commander of the troops at Walcheren, Lord Chatham, a traitor; in the second he urged "No law for him who stands above the law."[27] His hatred of tyrants, eventually including Napoleon III as well as Napoleon I and Byron (proudest of "Hectorers in proud bad verse"), at all times included the Georges, all "knee-deep in sludge and ordure" and "some in blood." One can understand Shelley better after observing Landor's rash republicanism, his contempt for the mob, and his violent boast, "I strove with none, for none was worth my strife." Shelley and Landor thought of themselves as stern, insistent reformers and restorers.

Landor's "Hellenics" do not espouse the romantic hellenism of beauty as truth; his ideals, like his tastes, were Roman. Here he and Shelley part. Like Peacock, he never increased the difficulties of composition by an imaginative faith in myth or symbol. His hamadryads are endearingly human, but merely human. Unlike

Lydia Languish, Landor had no Captain Absolute to make the dream of romantic hardship come true. He shared her dream, as her creator Sheridan did not, but he sought to achieve it by the unromantic means of compression and revision.

V

Two Whigs, Thomas Moore of Ireland and Thomas Campbell of Scotland, serve the history of politics in poetry as anapestic National Bards. Since he had the misfortune of following Burns, and therefore had no clear claim as the national bard of Scotland, Campbell included among his subjects as Bard of Britain "Ye Mariners of England" and "Hohenlinden." Both Campbell and Moore were widely read until after the First World War.

Even more than the busy Campbell, Moore was active over a broad front. If his amusing satires were what they have been called, "the verbal equivalents of the cartoons of Gillray and his contemporaries,"[28] Moore would have been justified in withholding his name from the title pages, as security against trial for sedition, and such works as *The Fudge Family in Paris* and *Intercepted Letters; or, The Twopenny Post-Bag* would have numerous readers today. But they totally lack Gillray's ferocity. Instead, they almost deserve what William Hazlitt said in *The Spirit of the Age* of Moore's *Irish Melodies,* that a country represented by "these vapid, varnished sentiments, lip-deep," should continue to be "governed as it has been," or what Ian Jack has said more temperately: "Too sentimental to be mischievous, they are rather songs of the sort that a sophisticated imperialism might connive at as a harmless safety-valve for national aspirations."[29] In the words of a sympathetic biographer, Moore "sang at one and the same time the rights of the people and the glories of ancient kings."[30] Yet the importance of Moore's songs for Irish patriotism has not been lessened by their association with hours of conviviality in the public bar. Moore armed the Irish with song.

Perhaps it is representative of Moore the patriot that Fable I of his *Fables for the Holy Alliance* offers no better plan for dissolving the "Holy Brotherhood" than reporting a dream in which the Alliance appeared as the ice-palace of Anne of Russia, an emblem of illusory strength (as it is in several other poems of the time, including, I think, "Kubla Khan"). If the ice-palace was vain, so is the dream. It has been noticed by critics less hostile than Hazlitt that Moore obeyed the opening injunction of his famous song on the most famous of his college friends, the rebel Robert Emmet: "Oh! Breathe not his name! / Let it sleep in the shade." He did not take the risk of naming Emmet in his verses. Nonetheless, despite his typical emphasis on the execution of the unnamed patriot, on failure rather than rebellion, and despite the ease with which Moore combined wit, sentiment, and song in a career acceptable to English lords, he broke decisively with the Prince Regent and derided him openly. One must acknowledge the strength of Moore's subversion when he repeatedly urged his large audience to remember—for example at the end of Fable II—

> That Kings have neither rights nor noses
> A whit diviner than their own.

Divine right is of course not at issue; it is the insistent *whit* that subverts the Hanoverian claim. Long before he corrupted the taste of the young with *Lalla Rookh,* Moore was a popular force. Although lacking many of Byron's interests, particularly in history, he exerted influences of subject and literary device on every stage of Byron's career as a poet. He once challenged Francis Jeffrey to a duel. Unfortunately both his problems and his solutions, on that occasion as on others, were too simple to challenge readers in a later age.

Campbell and Moore avoided the romantic analogies of organicism. Walter Scott, a National Bard on the Tory side, adds a new configuration. He believed in an organically growing state, but avoided the organic analogy for poetry. Except for an occasional partisan poem like the "Health to Lord Melville" of 1806, and verses in praise of Czar Alexander ten years later, Scott exercised his immense influence at first through verse tales, and later through novels, in which political bias is easier to discern than partisan purpose. Although his once-popular poems are no longer much read,

71

Politics in English Romantic Poetry

familiarity with the novels prepares us to expect neutrality on the surface of the poems. Even the dedicatory introduction to the first canto of *Marmion* carefully extends its praise to Fox almost equally with Pitt: the talents and genius of Pitt's great rival did not save him from Francophile error—this qualification Scott must make—but Fox died a Briton; and a noble, loyal death is all-important. Always too generous to deny honorable motives to the opposition, Scott left the leaders of his own day in no doubt about his allegiance to the King and the Tories. Without any of Burns's hesitations, he wrote a "War Song of the Royal Edinburgh Light Dragoons." He voted with those who abhorred rapid change.

For readers alien to Scott's time and place, his novels are politically ambiguous. Mark Twain, in *Life on the Mississippi,* deplored their seductive tendency to turn minds and hearts in the Southern states toward antique manners and codes. Opposite to this view of Scott's "sham grandeurs and sham gauds," the view is older than Twain that all Scott's beggars are kings in disguise. Georg Lukács has best put the case for the significance of popular culture in Scott's novels. He has noted the importance and depth of the fringe characters, the Macwheebles and the Mucklebackits, for the representation of historical change. To Lukács, Scott affirms the progress that results from the antagonisms of classes and nations.[31] Scott assumes a neat role in Lukács's Marxist dialectic. Romanticism, for Lukács, consists of reactionary admiration of the past, escape from social realism, inordinate egoism, and hero worship. For him Scott stands opposite to these vices. Both views, Lukács's and Twain's, can be taken of Scott's great novels, *Quentin Durward* as well as *Waverley, Rob Roy,* and *The Heart of Midlothian.* The novels do show crises in the lives of the people at times of great change, especially—for one more sympathetic than Lukács to Scott's intentions—when shifts in political power impinge on the settled habits of religion. Rejecting what Wordsworth rejected, Scott avoided the romantic dilemma by accepting the conservative implications of his tastes and his ethics.

The probably unintended ambiguities of the prose romances are avoided in the narrative poems (which overlap the novels by about four years), even though the poems allow a juxtaposition of eras,

72

Varieties of Romantic Experience

as in *The Bridal of Triermain,* and employ other devices of historical perspective not practiced in the novels. Even in the novels of eighteenth-century Scotland, conservative elements abound. Lukács underestimates Scott's faith in the durable virtues of courage and loyalty, as well as his belief that moral problems and crises are always and everywhere the same, his antiquarian addiction to the color of the past, his affection for lost causes, his depiction of social process rather than progress, his opposition to the Richard Waverleys as exponents of progress and specimens of moral decay. Such inclinations are even clearer in the poetry. From the beginning of his career, Scott set himself against the ethics of utility and self-interest. The close confinement of the narrative poems gave him little chance to reveal his kindly sympathies in carrying out his desire to revivify and entertain.

These tales of battle, rite, and sorcery show how national loyalty requires and absorbs personal loyalty. To a liberal Protestant or agnostic like Mark Twain, the Scott of these poems would be the seemingly candid white knight of the conservative and royal cause to which Joseph de Maistre was the turbid black dwarf. These poems are an extended gloss on one line, "This is my own, my native land." In tales of the "ancient land where Wallace fought," we cannot disallow the nationalistic implications even of the unfailing charm, for any manly breast, of a fair Caledonian lass. Such implications are present when the fierce Highland chief Roderick Dhu, in *The Lady of the Lake,* loves almost interchangeably, as equally near the essence of Scotland, a conventional "modern" heroine, Ellen Douglas, and timeless Loch Katrine. It was the patriotism of locale, of particular place, that ensnared Scott the Tory. Never attracted toward Jacobin principles and disinclined to struggle against his instinctive loyalties, Scott found that romantic nostalgia, countering his commonsense fidelity to the government on the Thames, had taken him, via a different route from Burns's, toward the lost, misty causes of the Highlanders and the Stuarts. He became a commonsense romantic, loved as a man, disparaged as a poet, oscillating as a novelist between observation and romance. A minstrel, but never, by either vision or illusion, a bard.

73

Politics in English Romantic Poetry

VI

For those writers who believed in either revolution or reform as well as in the creative power of imagination, the persistent temptation was to abandon political concern. Literary historians wishing to exaggerate the degree of abandonment turn to Charles Lamb. Although he openly certified the unifying power of imagination only in his review of *The Excursion,* Lamb was indeed the first of many to exaggerate his distaste for politics. Exactly what he thought has eluded historians. Over and above his disrelish for metaphysics and intellectual abstraction, which he shares with Swift no less than with Wordsworth, Lamb practiced in all his essays, and even in his letters, the devices of understatement, covert allusion self-refuting, exaggeration, and the inversion of fact that he called "matter-of-lie." Aided by these devices, he gradually reduced first the appearance and then the reality of his political anxieties.

Beyond question, he was sorry that the French Revolution had brought its aftermath of Napoleonic expansion; almost as clearly, he resented the social and economic situation that made politics an important concern. Nevertheless, they had become to him as well as to his closest friends a daily and sometimes dominant concern. He maintained at all times the principles of a free press and other civil liberties, increased rights for Dissenters and all other depressed minorities who themselves held to an aceptable standard of tolerance, and—the most persistent of his political positions—a weak Crown. Many of his opinions were those of a liberal Whig, but he shook off in discomfort all feelings of attachment to party. Like Byron he distrusted both religious and political cant.

Of his innumerable paragraphs and epigrams submitted to newspapers, for the combined purposes of political opposition, income, and mischief, those that have both survived and been identified as his fall notably into clusters, particularly of 1802, 1812, and 1820. These clusters do not necessarily represent sudden heightenings of his personal interest in politics, but they represent increases in political tension of a kind to call upon Lamb's special skills for political raillery. By their baldness and vigor these paragraphs and epigrams stand equally apart from his earliest sentimental effusions (which

74

were frequently humanitarian at second hand) and his later playfully ironic explorations into foibles of the human mind. With detachment always from violent opinion, he perpetrated violence of language. He played the game with something of the coarseness and cruelty legitimized by Charles Churchill, William Gifford, Richard Porson, and John Wolcot ("Peter Pindar"). Fallen to the party journalism of John Fenwick's *Albion,* in 1801, he provided epigrams "consonant in no very under-tone to the right earnest fanaticism" of "this infatuated Democrat," Fenwick. So Elia in the essay "Newspapers Thirty-five Years Ago," which tells also of Lamb's epigram against Mackintosh as "Judas, an apostate black," six lines that killed the *Albion* by driving off its single patron, Lord Stanhope.[32] Lamb's best-known political squib, "The Triumph of the Whale," a parodistic paean to the "Prince of Whales," of 1812, anticipated the cluster of 1820, when Lamb supported Caroline's cause without the reservations expressed in faraway Pisa by Byron and Shelley.

Lamb disliked the singlemindedness of political attack. His usual avoidance of public issues came in part from the high value he placed on tolerance and his pride in sustaining difficult friendships. He spoke out, in the "Letter of Elia to Robert Southey, Esquire," partly to strike a blow for religious tolerance, but also because he prized his wish, as well as his ability, to retain on open grounds the friendship of Southey, Wordsworth, and Coleridge, on one hand, and on the other William Hone, Hazlitt, Hunt, and in retrospect Thomas Holcroft: "I own I could never think so considerably of myself as to decline the society of an agreeable or worthy man upon difference of opinion only." What he objects to in the Scotsman, in "Imperfect Sympathies," is not the premises from the Enlightenment or the typically unimaginative conclusions, but the Scot's way to certainty: "Surmises, guesses, misgivings, half-intuitions, semi-consciousnesses, partial illuminations, dim instincts, embryo conceptions, have no place in his brain, or vocabulary." Thus far, and somewhat farther, Elia approached the symbolic mode in literature devised by the "whole man."

In making his case against Lamb as a bourgeois in Biedermeier retreat from heroism, Mario Praz claimed an absence of politics from Lamb's letters during 1814–1830.[33] That the letters seldom mention politicians or parties derives mostly from the pointlessness of arguing politics in those years with Wordsworth, Southey, and Coleridge, to whom the longest extant letters are addressed. Praz's assumption has a second cause: Lamb's allusions are more obscure and seemingly more devious to scholars than they were to the original recipients. When he complained to Wordsworth in August 1814 that the Serpentine "has got foolish ships upon it," he referred to the mock sea battle in patriotic celebration of Bonaparte's surrender. Of this "naumachia" we can learn with difficulty from Keats's sonnet "Nebuchadnezzar's Dream" and scholarly notes to it, but Wordsworth could learn easily from the *Champion* and the daily newspapers. Barron Field in Australia would understand well enough when Lamb asked in 1820: "Pray are you King's or Queen's men in Sidney? Or have thieves no politics?" At one level, this is a simple joke about transportation for felony, but consider the case of the dancing-master unaware in March 1809 that Mary Anne Clarke had used her influence with the Duke of York for the sale of commissions in the Army. "I proposed locking him up," wrote Lamb to Thomas Manning, "barring him the use of his fiddle and red pumps, until he had minutely perused and committed to memory the whole body of the examinations, which employed the House of Commons a fortnight, to teach him to be more attentive to what concerns the public."[34] Lamb set no higher standards of awareness for dancing-masters than for himself. It would take a thief to have no politics. Southey certainly got the point when Lamb explained publicly that, whereas one man will shrink from pronouncing the case of Judas to be desperate, "Others (with stronger optics), as plainly as with the eye of the flesh, shall behold a *given king* in bliss, and a *given chamberlain* in torment . . ."[35] Southey's optics, as all Lamb's readers knew, had been strong enough in *A Vision of Judgment* to see George III welcomed into Heaven by God.

For all his fidelity to political principles, Lamb did retreat. As he himself said in the sonnet of 1795 beginning "We were two pretty babes," he sought through life the Innocence that had fled when he first discovered "love for man's society." This Innocence once resided, but no more, in the "sordid city" he loved. In literature he sought the innocence that had gamboled, before Locke intruded,

Varieties of Romantic Experience

in Spenser, Sir Thomas Browne, Jeremy Taylor, and—by Lamb's lights—Tudor and Jacobean drama. Innocence he retained, too, in the sense of dependence on God's grace for the rescue of frail man from the sin of pride in reason, in artifice, and (see his "Living without God in the World") in the "chymic practices" by which men of the Enlightenment expected to cheat death. Simple innocence was a dream. Elia's was an organized innocence, free of religious, scientific, or epistemological bigotry, but convoluted with amused irony. In political allusion, self-irony is the near equivalent of neutrality. Masked as Elia, Lamb could indulge in self-ironic flights of political unconcern.

John Keats is cited even more often than Lamb as evidence that romantic faith—for example, in the faery power of imagination—was incompatible with all politics whatsover. Of the major poets, Keats is thought to have evaded most successfully the impurities of political reference. Although, he told J. H. Reynolds in 1818, he "would jump down Ætna for any great Public good," he soon discovered and thereafter believed, to the enduring joy of literary people, that he could best serve public good by writing the richest poetry he was capable of; he could best serve England by adding another name to her proud, astounding list of death-shouldering poets. Nor would I deny that in Keats's Hellenism there is a degree of reaction against the Latinate moral statesmanship promoted in the rhetoric of the Augustans, in the public school tradition, in the sonnets of Wordsworth, and in the poems and plays of Byron. Yet Keats's personal adherence to the Opposition side is not in doubt. His letters—the achievement, Lionel Trilling has said, of a hero— show that Hunt and Hazlitt taught him which political views were proper for his confined station in society and his bursting genius. Hazlitt's lectures and essays, which gave him lessons in associational psychology, afforded also a model of gusto, of the rich, patriotic pleasures of hating. In person, Hazlitt provided Keats with the living myth of the constant, fearless, heroic fighter for the democratic idea.

It is easy to wish that Keats had avoided politics in his poems. H. W. Garrod, pleased with the sensuous entanglement of the poetry, seems to have been sorry that Keats had a mind at all.[36] In several

77

Politics in English Romantic Poetry

of the longer poems, pasages of utilitarian, progressive politics and of angry humanitarianism erupt like measles. As Keats raced against disease, on sandals "more interwoven and complete," it is tenable to conclude with Garrod that he never touched the succulence of his poetry with social purpose without corrupting it. He brings off well, or at least endurably, tributes to Leigh Hunt, personal friend and hero of "The social smile, the chain for Freedom's sake," and he musters conventional acclaim for Koscuisko as a thunderer in harmony with Alfred the Great. But here, in couplets and sonnets on patriot heroes, Keats was sowing in ground prepared by older poets. Although still consciously producing imitative exercises as an apprentice, he is full of purpose in the sonnet "On Peace," welcoming the end of war but urging Europe, wherever royal lines are restored, to curb the old "sceptred tyrants" under limited monarchy. Drawing on Wordsworth's praise of Switzerland, he pleads: "Let the sweet mountain nymph thy favourite be." Aileen Ward has broken the code of the sonnet "Nebuchadnezzar's Dream," in which the ministers seem to be ridiculed as "loggerheads and Chapmen" about to topple from power.[37] The less opaque but intricately riddled satire of "The Cap and Bells" has not yet found the scholar to say precisely where its lampooning of the Prince Regent becomes a burlesque of Byron in mockery of Keats's own friends. Professor Garrod is not the only critic who has found Keats's satires and political sonnets tiresome.

Yet politics has an integral place in Keats's canon. The verse epistle to George Keats, of August 1816, passes coherently enough from "knightly Spenser to Libertas" (Leigh Hunt). It moves persuasively from the pleasures and restraints of the bard to the bard's "stern alarum" for the patriot. It rushes playfully but almost convincingly from oats to poppies to Redcoats:

> On one side, is a field of drooping Oats;
> Through which the Poppies show their scarlet Coats;
> So pert, and useless, that they bring to Mind
> The scarlet Coats, that pester human kind.[38]

At a higher level, Oceanus' quietistic affirmation of inevitable progress—"So on our heels a fresh perfection treads"—does not

78

Varieties of Romantic Experience

stop the flow of debate in Book II of *Hyperion*. Oceanus' assertion, as eternal law, that "first in beauty should be the first in might" is no less appropriate to the speaker, just as it is no less quotable, because Keats may have believed it.

It is possible, while admitting that political and humanitarian impulses did not elicit the full strength of Keats's genius, to avoid the error of believing that the political passages interrupt his larger intentions. The first forty lines of Book III of *Endymion*, it is said, jar the reader out of the world of myth:

> There are who lord it o'er their fellow-men
> With most prevailing tinsel . . .
> . . . they still are dight
> By the blear-eyed nations in empurpled vests,
> And crowns, and turbans.   (III.1–2, 10–12)

L'état, c'est moi is a successful but false adage; the many have been deceived into believing that the crowned and turbaned constitute nations. This "stern alarum" may be what Douglas Bush calls it, "the badly written blast of a young liberal against the Establishment and spurious public values,"[39] but it belongs to the poem Keats set out to write. *Endymion*, a self-testing work to assay its poet's power of invention and explore the reaches of his imagination, asks how far Shelley and Hunt are right in assigning humanitarian tasks to literature. Two years earlier Shelley's *Alastor* had depicted a high-minded poet lost to mankind in the solitude of narcissistic pursuit of a vision that arose in the poet's own dream. Can a poet find reality by pursuing dreams? Endymion, sworn to the adoring pursuit of chaste Diana, the Moon, ideality, is guiltily drawn to a living Indian maiden. He finds at last that the human maid and the ideal Diana are one. Book III serves to show that love of the maid connotes not merely sensuous delight in earthly love but attention to one's fellow men. Dreaming and humanitarian service can be reconciled in poetry. Kings deceive; poets illumine.

Book III illustrates the theme by mirroring it. Endymion encounters a thousand-year-old man, Glaucus, treading the cycle in the opposite direction. By secret philanthropy, Glaucus once supplied poor folk with "daily boon of fish most delicate"; restless for freedom

79

from the sea and humane service, he consummated a marriage with the innocent Scylla; in a moment of frustration and sensual greed, the opposite of Endymion's attenuated idealism, he gave himself to Circe; by this excess cursed to explore all forms and substances "homeward to their symbol-essences," and to ensure the piety of his learning by the continuous deposit of shipwrecked lovers in a niche of the sea, he awaits the coming of a certain youth, who is of course Endymion. By ordained ritual, accompanied by the sound of divine harmony, Endymion and Glaucus deliver all the lovers from death. In such a union of music, knowledge, symbol, and sacrifice, true poetry serves mankind. Kings entrap; poets deliver.

In another passage frequently deplored, stanzas 14–18 of *Isabella; or, The Pot of Basil,* Keats attacks the two murderous "ledger-men," Isabella's brothers, for their ignorant rule over an empire of mines and factories, an empire extending its power of misery from Ceylonese divers to dart-filled seals lying "on the cold ice with piteous bark." The poet's protest has seemed extraneous to later critics, for his two Florentine "money-bags" have a larger empire than the plot requires. That "many a weary hand did swelt" for this emblematic pair in "torched mines and noisy factories" is an anachronism at a seemingly different level of conscious artistry from the long carpets on the medieval floor in *The Eve of St. Agnes.* Keats's Ceylonese divers oppressed by two capitalists represent a still larger public issue, in that Ceylon, seized from the Dutch by British forces in 1795, was annexed and retained by the treaties of 1802 and 1815. In sum, Boccaccio's tale of Florentine intrigue is updated by Keats, specifically in the stanzas on the Ceylonese and those on the brothers' "red-lin'd accounts," to one of the subjects of protest in "The Cap and Bells": the growth of British empire in India and the Indian Ocean.

Perhaps the anachronism is in itself a protest against the post-Hobbesian, post-Newtonian skepticism toward such a tale as this. The tale of Isabella becomes in Keats's hands a myth of the natural force of love: her tears combine with her lover's buried head to make a basil plant flourish. Fitted to a later age than the lovers they destroyed, the unnatural brothers stand as a manifestation of

Varieties of Romantic Experience

"hungry pride and gainful cowardice" in empirical selfhood as well as industrial commerce. When they perceive that Lorenzo strays from toil to love of Isabella, the poet curses their unnatural talent along with their spying: "Hot Egypt's pest / Into their vision covetous and sly!"[40] Like the sage Apollonius in *Lamia,* they epitomize contemporary forces antipathetic to poetry. Their way of seeing and knowing destroys love, destroys the beauty of the rainbow or the equivalent basil, destroys the imagination.

Within the four creative years allowed him, Keats regarded his life's goal in a gradually changing light. "Sleep and Poetry," "I stood tip-toe upon a little hill," the epistle to his brother George, and other pieces in *Poems,* 1817, project the development of a poet from the rich entanglements of sense, possibly through an intermediate stage of reflection, upward to the "nobler life" of involvement in human agonies and a distillation of poesy to "sooth the cares, and lift the thoughts of man." He envisions a hard climb to a poetry of humanitarian service. Beyond the entanglements and the distillation lies the possibility that the poet as visionary may "burst our mortal bars." Keats at twenty-one projects this development fully aware of his ignorance; he has not yet achieved the wealth of "spanning wisdom." He must labor toward a full harvest of thought and feeling.[41] As late as the winter of 1818-19 he has Apollo, in *Hyperion,* proclaim as he dies into life:

> Knowledge enormous makes a God of me.
> Names, deeds, gray legends, dire events, rebellions . . .
> (III.113–114)

Meanwhile, however, in December 1817, he unfolded for his brothers the doctrine of *"Negative Capability,* that is when man is capable of being in uncertainties, Mysteries, doubts, without any irritable reaching after fact & reason" (*Letters,* I, 193). Rejecting, like Wordsworth, the consecutive reasoning of a "Godwin-methodist" like Charles Dilke, Keats went on to reject also the "wordsworthian or egotistical sublime." The ideal is now the perfect dramatist, Shakespeare, who reveals no character or personality of his own but enters without prejudice into every variety of mankind. When drama thus superseded epic, political and humanitarian concern

81

had no proper place, at least not as poultices applied to current ills.

Old Glaucus gave way to old Apollonius, whose cold reason, in the process of dissolving sweet illusion, destroyed, along with Lamia, the poet Lycius who had been happy in her embrace. The replacement of Glaucus by Apollonius embodies the dilemma of a poet reluctant to relinquish the liberal principles adorned by Hazlitt but "certain of nothing but of the holiness of the Heart's affections and the truth of Imagination." In the doctrine of negative capability Keats discovered a theory that could, on occasion, stretch across the chasm from liberal politics to imagination. But occasional speculation, however fervent, could not assure poetic practice.

In Keats's last major effort, *The Fall of Hyperion: A Dream,* the stress of dilemma continues. According to the lines preliminary to the dream, only a poet can tell and thus preserve his dreams; but Moneta, or memory, guardian of the innermost shrine, denies (within our narrator's dream) that the narrator is a poet:

> The poet and the dreamer are distinct,
> Diverse, sheer opposite, antipodes.
> The one pours out a balm upon the world,
> The other vexes it. (I.199–202)

Already the narrator has acknowledged the distinction in defining a poet: "sure a poet is a sage; / A humanist, Physician to all men." Probably the implication of learning in the term *sage* does not exclude the ideal of objective drama, as in Keats's description of *King Lear* as "making all disagreeables evaporate, from their being in close relationship with Beauty & Truth." Granting this probability, and granting the apparent contradictions among the several explicit distinctions of Canto I, the highest ideal would nevertheless seem to be a combination of poet and humanitarian. Active humanists, "Who love their fellows even to the death; / Who feel the giant agony of the world," need no pilgrimage to the shrine guarded by Moneta; they live entirely in the present. But the best of the pilgrims, the highest visionaries, are "those to whom the miseries of the world / Are misery, and will not let them rest." Such poets are restless to pour out balm. Compared with other writers of his time,

Varieties of Romantic Experience

the narrator feels entitled to defense; but as to the sterner question of pouring balm or dreaming, he has only imagined, within the dream, a higher goal of service not yet achieved or fully comprehended. Lacking the revisions Keats apparently intended to make, we are left with an inconsistent series of poignant distinctions.[42]

This last great fragment of major effort depicts a physical desolation that represents poetic and human deprivation. The garden, once paradisial, is littered with empty shells and scraps. The temple molders into ruin. At the shrine within, misery must be known as misery. In the first *Hyperion* Keats had created anew the life of Titans and the birth of gods. In *The Fall of Hyperion,* the giants and gods have receded; only memory is "left supreme" (I.226). "Foughten long since by Giant Hierarchy," Moneta explains of that distant, desolating war. Only her "temple sad and lone" remains. Where in the first poem stood those "green-rob'd senators of mighty woods," the poet now enters subjectively, like "a stunt bramble by a solemn Pine."

In the following months, summarized in Walter Jackson Bate's biography as "Illness," before the chapter entitled "Adrift," Keats demonstrated the holiness of the imagination in the stanzas "To Autumn," accepting the progression of the seasons with their anticlimax of twittering swallows and wailful choir of small gnats; he attempted in *King Stephen,* and abandoned, a Shakespearean tragedy—"Scene II.—*Another part of the Field*"; and in a totally isolated part of the forest he began his longest contemporary satire, "The Cap and Bells." With a sense of mission that topical satire could not appease, Keats had a suddenly enveloping sense of the triviality of political concern and the possible triviality of all that he had written. Like the older generation of poets, he found it impossible to carry out what Coleridge in youth had called "the bloodless fight" of "Science, Freedom, and the Truth in Christ." Like the other poets, he gave back to Burke almost all conviction of the holiness of political combat.

By the chronology of birthdates, the story ends with Keats. Thomas Hood, born four years later, began his poetic career as a disciple of Keats, but after such derivative works as "Ode: Autumn,"

83

"Ruth," and "The Plea of the Midsummer Fairies" he turned to his own vein of punning satire—best represented by "Miss Kilmansegg and Her Precious Leg: A Golden Legend," wherein an heiress killed with her own golden leg is judged to have committed suicide—and a typically Victorian denunciation of specific social abuses in such poems as "The Song of the Shirt" and "Agricultural Distress: A Pastoral Report." True "Hagricultural Distress," Hood concludes with an unromantic pun, lies with "the *Farming of the Poor!*"[43] The movement from the travails of basic political thought to proclamations on specific issues can be seen equally in the verses of Ebenezer Elliott, born in 1781 but occupied in the iron trade before and after his popular *Corn-Law Rhymes* of 1831 ushered in what he was willing to regard as an age of prose. The Reform Bill of 1832 forms a watershed for English poetry.

IV

WORDSWORTH

During his sixty years of contemplating the nature of the poetic office, William Wordsworth spent very few moments questioning the degree of a poet's responsibility to society. To the contrary, he increased from time to time his sense of that responsibility, sometimes by intensifying it, sometimes by enlarging its objectives.

Among other metrical projects, he began a sentimental excursion in heroic couplets, *An Evening Walk*, in the year after his matriculation at Cambridge. He began a second, *Descriptive Sketches*, and began to tighten the first, in the year of his B.A. degree. Two years later, in 1793, both poems were published. The second startled Coleridge by its "harshness and acerbity connected and combined with words and images all a-glow."[1] Yet both poems apparently seemed to most of their few original readers, as they have seemed to most literary historians, largely conventional in both matter and devices.[2] The poems came from a young man born to prefer hard-won originality to either flaccid convention or brash novelty; to prefer fresh reports on the enduring forms of the countryside to sophisticated updatings of urban drama. They came from one who had grown up on resentment against cold family guardians and in bitterness against the earl who withheld even yet the boy's modest patrimony. Despite his love of the outdoors, the poet was a reader saturated in recent humanitarian verse. By both temperament and

85

situation sympathetic with the undernourished and the solitary, he praised solitude but practiced fellowship with success and friendship with ardor. He had revealed slight awareness of the Foxite liberalism rampant at Cambridge, probably less than the average student and certainly less than S. T. Coleridge revealed in 1793-94.[3] He and his friend Robert Jones had no contribution to make to international politics, although they did drink in the "joy of tens of millions" in France, when they walked to the Grande Chartreuse, Chamonix, and the Simplon Pass, during the long vacation of 1790, in order to interpret the hieroglyphics of nature in their fullest grandeur. For twelve months beginning in November 1791, however, Wordsworth returned to watch human nature at work in the Revolution, at the time of the first, worst massacres and the proclamation of the Republic. He had passed rapidly from love of nature to trepidation for man.

From such general facts as the letters from the novelist Charlotte Smith introducing him to Helen Maria Williams and other friends of the Revolution in 1791, when Mrs. Smith had not yet been repelled by events in France; from the radical orientation of Wordsworth's publisher, Joseph Johnson; from impressive details recorded, for example, in Godwin's diary; and from Wordsworth's own accounts and references, we know that his associates during 1791–1793 included Girondins in and near Paris and "English Jacobins" in London. At the time of publication, *Descriptive Sketches* would have seemed more partisan, not less, for assigning a French background to its brief vignettes of "social suffering." To the extent that the sketches have unity, the unity comes from clear commitments to French soil and the French Revolution. What England's officials described as the fall of Savoy to France, a footnote to *Descriptive Sketches* called "the emancipation of Savoy."[4]

Vignettes of suffering women, which have been to some critics a signal of Wordsworth's guilt because he begot a child in France without marrying the mother, Annette Vallon, were a different sort of signal in the years of debate over Burke's *Reflections*. Experience with other poems from the partisan Opposition would have led a reader of *An Evening Walk* to count Wordsworth's vignette of the burdened mother, struggling toward an inconvenient cottage, as

86

ill-will toward the King. Just as other poems had prepared the reader to expect, the soldier who left the woman with child soon fell "on Bunker's charnel hill." This *Gestalt* contains three elements typical of its day: a sentimental morality that asked the reader to weep himself into goodness, subversive intimations against the war-waging King and Pittites, and a humanitarian form of the romantic metaphor of the journey. Southey, as already noted, included in nearly every poem the journey of a wretch.

Of course this dark vision is related to a fashionable mode of lamentation that was not quite protest. If some of the melancholy reflects discouragement from analysis of society, some of it comes from as far away as Goethe's *Werther*. As the wits of the *Anti-Jacobin* knew, however, such way-wandering humanitarianism as Southey's and Wordsworth's, if not increasing, was increasingly partisan and ought to be damned. England's war against the Revolution changed an age of sentiment to an age of politics, as one sees in Southey's movement from the elegiac cluster of *Poems*, 1795, around frail Emma, a flower plucked and destroyed by an ungrateful seducer, to the clusters in *Poems*, 1797, around slaves worn with toil, soldiers' wives and widows, and deserters transported to Botany Bay, and on to *Poems*, 1799: "The Sailor who had Served in the Slave Trade."[5]

The solitary figure had entered the verse of Wordsworth's notebooks, notably "The Vale of Esthwaite," as early as 1787. More than literary convention is involved. The poet had tried to keep his eye on the object. From the beginning of the war with the Colonies, such figures had been seen on the roads with increasing frequency. To the prevalence of actual derelicts, letters and journals of the poet and others in his family testify as eloquently as the poetry. Aware both of the actuality and of the literary commonplace with its political implications, Wordsworth wished to record and interpret what he himself had seen. Some single searing experience intensified his continuing disposition to reflect on solitaries observed in the vale of Esthwaite, in Savoy, on Salisbury Plain—wherever he looked for them or wherever they came before him, drear spots in time.

In the Spenserian stanzas eventually reconstructed as "Guilt and

Politics in English Romantic Poetry

Sorrow," Wordsworth gave his image of the vagrant woman shuffling toward an isolated cottage the dual context of social frame and political explanation. Altered over a period of many years, the stanzas have special value as indicators of Wordsworth's intellectual, spiritual, and artistic development. In the evolution of the poem between 1793 and 1798 we learn that an improving and enclosing landlord by "wilful wrong" deprived the vagrant's father of fishing waters and seized all but the bed he lay on. The daughter married an artisan, apparently a weaver, who was forced by the new industrial conditions to ply his trade in a distant town. She was thus uprooted a second time soon after the first. Next the threat of war ruined the artificer's trade and drove him into an army bound for America. Minor afflictions and then further major crises ensued for the soldier and the wife and children who accompanied him. Sometimes the unfolding poem blames society, sometimes it blames the government; never the victims. After losing her husband by the sword and her children by war-induced plague (as in Blake's *America*), the widow returned to England, underwent the "careless cruelty" (reduced in 1842 to "cold formality") of a hospital, and found true succor only among wild gypsies, where "all belonged to all, and each was chief." Although Wordsworthian scholars in the first quarter of the twentieth century may have exaggerated the few signs of republicanism in the poem, its militant opposition to war can hardly be overstressed. Byron was to write nothing more unpatriotic than this poem by Wordsworth. In the 1798 and 1800 readings of "The Female Vagrant," when Britain had lost battles and allies on the Continent and Bonaparte was strengthening his "Army of England," Wordsworth allowed his victim of enclosure and war to cry publicly:

> Oh! dreadful price of being to resign
> All that is dear *in* being! better far
> In Want's most lonely cave till death to pine,
> Unseen, unheard, unwatched by any star;
> Or in the streets and walks where proud men are,
> Better our dying bodies to obtrude,
> Than dog-like, wading at the heels of war,
> Protract a curst existence, with the brood
> That lap (their very nourishment!) their brother's blood.[6]

Wordsworth

As the brother specified is the colonist in America, it might be argued that fraternity is not here extended to the common soldier of France, but this passage is positive evidence that the shock of England's declaration of war on France in February 1793 lasted longer than most students of Wordsworth have thought. And yet it is not longer than *The Prelude* says the shock lasted.

We know from the manuscripts of the sorrow-on-the-plain poem, from Wordsworth's letters, from the unpublished and unsent Letter to the Bishop of Llandaff, and from manuscript and newspaper versions of minor poems like "The Convict" that Wordsworth regarded himself as a republican, that he was working for the removal of political injustice, that he anticipated no good from king or aristocracy, and that he expected general happiness to flow from change in the forms of government and society. By joining the powers arrayed against the Revolution in 1793, says Wordsworth in *The Prelude,* a beloved country "threw me first out of the pale of love."[7] This shock led directly in 1794 to the anger, which he was never entirely to relinquish, against the ministry of Pitt. Besides goading France into war, the ministers subverted civil liberties, like "vermin working out of reach." Wordsworth himself keeps wandering out of sight in 1794-95, but Government spies and Government writers knew him as a man to watch.

In June 1794, in a letter to his friend William Mathews, he declared his position in terms very close to those of Godwin:

I disapprove of monarchical and aristocratical governments, however modified. Hereditary distinctions and privileged orders of every species I think must necessarily counteract the progress of human improvement: hence it follows that I am not amongst the admirers of the British constitution. Now, there are two causes which appear to me to be accomplishing the subversion of this constitution; first, the infatuation profligacy and extravagance of men in power, and secondly, the changes of opinion respecting matters of Government which within these few years have rapidly taken place in the minds of speculative men. . . . To the latter I would give every additional energy in my power. . . . I recoil from the bare idea of a revolution; yet, if our conduct with reference both to foreign and domestic policy continues such as it has been for the last two years how is that dreadful event to be averted? . . . After this need I add that I am a determined enemy to every species of violence?

Politics in English Romantic Poetry

Proposing to Mathews that the title of their projected periodical be *The Philanthropist, a Monthly Miscellany,* Wordsworth made still clearer his position toward the Terror:

. . . While we expressed our detestation of the execrable measures pursued in France we should belie our title if we did not hold up to the approbation of the world such of their regulations and decrees as are dictated by the spirit of Philosophy. We should give also an accurate account of the Polish revolution, and purify it from those infamous representations which ministerial hirelings have thrown over it.[8]

In 1795 a small annuity from the death of an admiring acquaintance, Raisley Calvert, left Wordsworth free to avoid a regular profession without curing his grievances as a dislodged orphan. By the summer of 1797, however, his views had softened, along with his life, under the ministrations of his sister Dorothy, his new friend Coleridge, and residence in the country. For the man attached to his rural boyhood, it was especially hard to maintain a city-sharpened radicalism among loving friends in a rural cottage.

The Borderers, the Sturm-und-Drang play that Wordsworth wrote in 1796-97 and published in 1842, has been taken as a retraction of the allegiance to Godwinian and republican principles variously evident in the letter to Mathews, in the formal if unpublished letter to the Bishop of Llandaff, in the jejune imitation of Juvenal perpetrated with Francis Wrangham from 1795 to 1797, in "The Convict," in "The Ruined Cottage," and in peripheral works. Many of these, unfortunately for the theory of retraction, overlap *The Borderers* in time of composition and even in theme. In truth *The Borderers,* like the "Lines Left upon a Seat in a Yew-tree," which has been thought equally anti-Godwinian, represents a revulsion against unimaginative rationalism; yet what is opposed is not a political position, even by analogy, or the direct results of a political position, but the moral and psychological ground held in common by Paley and Malthus as well as by such varied reformers as Condorcet, Volney, Priestley, Godwin, and Bentham. The events of the play show that the associations of benevolence can be sidetracked by deliberately perverted reason.[9] Neither the subtle Oswald of the

90

play nor the contemptuous "lost Man" who built the yew-tree seat
could possibly be regarded as an adherent of Godwin's doctrine
of general benevolence. Both have declined into arrogant misanthropy. With homage to abstract reason and a daring experimen-
tation in morals, Oswald adheres to an idiosyncratic superstition
(similar to the superstition of Shelley's Cenci) and combines with
this a self-justification through appeals to fatalism, which he miscalls
Necessity.

The Borderers is designed neither to promote Godwinism, as a
doctrine of political reform, nor to attack it. This is not to say that
the play has nothing to do with the doctrines or methods of *An Enquiry concerning Political Justice.* Oswald, when he has seduced
Marmaduke into repeating his own crimes, offers congratulations:

> To-day you have thrown off a tyranny
> That lives but in the torpid acquiescence
> Of our emasculated souls, the tyranny
> Of the world's masters, with the musty rules
> By which they uphold their craft from age to age:
> You have obeyed the only law that sense
> Submits to recognize; the immediate law,
> From the clear light of circumstances, flashed
> Upon an independent Intellect.   (WPW I, 187:1488–96)

Making freedom of the individual depend on untrammeled judgments of the reason, Oswald tries to tie emotional prejudices to
social and political tyranny, but in rejecting conscience he confirms
the traditional view that conscience requires the slowly developed
associations of habit and prejudice. Wordsworth later borrowed key
phrases from Oswald's speech for ironic mockery of the erring faith
in reason that overtook him during the crisis of his disillusionment
with the Revolution (*Prelude* X.820–830). *The Borderers* came from
a man who had awakened to the urgency of defending our affections
both in theory and in practice against aggressive rationality.
Reason must not be abstracted from its anchorage in sense and
emotion. Oswald, like the friend of "The Tables Turned," who sat
without one impulse from a vernal wood, had become "somewhat
unreasonably attached to modern books of moral philosophy."[10]

Politics in English Romantic Poetry

The Borderers, then, is no attack upon reform or upon attempts to promote reform. Yet it gives half-conscious evidence, somewhat as Malthus was soon to give consciously on statistical grounds, that current narrowness in argument for reform and progress would have to be abandoned. For Wordsworth, the reasons were its inadequate psychology, its consequently inadequate ethics, and the frustrations of his own conduct under cataclysmic circumstances. In France he had observed failures of conduct among the morally dislocated. He had already acknowledged, in the passage on the (supposed) desecration of the Chartreuse in the pro-French *Descriptive Sketches* that ruthless action upon general principles of right had on occasion abruptly stripped what was beautiful and dear, and even what had been of utility to the individual stranger, from old institutions and old ways. More and more he was learning that the individual and particular case, in which he put his deepest trust, seldom supported the abstract ideal. Personal affection, but not abstract benevolence, could assure decency and kindness in the individual act. Whatever the changes in Wordsworth's views of French and British leaders, however, *The Borderers* examines the effects of social disruption rather than its cause.

No mere homily, however limp as drama, *The Borderers* imparts also the experience of personal crisis and collapse. The Border of the thirteenth century in the play is Wordsworth's Paris, Blois, and Orleans of 1791–1792 (and perhaps, as I shall suggest shortly, his England in 1793–1795). Among the empirics who had strayed amid the moral dislocations of a lawless time and place, the playwright had to count the Wordsworth of four years earlier, who had contemplated the possibilities of leadership in an alien revolution and had experimented in an irregular union with a daughter of France—one, as it turned out, who had expected him to marry her and had joined the Royal cause. He examined aspects of himself in both the susceptible Marmaduke and the overweening Oswald. In one of the keenest interpretations of the play so far offered, Roger Sharrock points to the implications for Wordsworth's career to be found in Marmaduke's final withdrawal from action.[11] The Marmaduke who proclaims that he will wander on in search of nothing but expiation reaches in 1793 and 1794, as William Wordsworth, the Isle of Wight, Salisbury Plain, the Wye, Plas-yn-Llan, the Lakes, and Halifax and frequently moves out of our view. Impasse in social action engenders the quietistic mode in poetry. In 1795 he turns to Godwin, Holcroft, Joseph Fawcett, William Frend, and other political philosophers, mostly pacifists, in London. When philosophy fails, he begins *The Borderers*. In the first shock of disillusionment with more than himself, when the new French thirsted even more than the old for empire, Wordsworth despaired of all action and all political answers. He recovered his shaping spirit of imagination, but he did so at the expense of confidence in action.

The Borderers represents in no sense whatever a revulsion against acting in concert. Later Wordsworth will give an antidote against abandonment of self to concerted action. *The Borderers* seems rather to depict a nightmare of individual betrayal. Probably the dislocations of chronology in Book X of *The Prelude* are pertinent here. Beginning with the poet's departure from France, after his decision not to sacrifice himself rashly in the French cause, the sequence seems to be (1) anger at England for declaring war on the Liberty-seeking people of France; (2) nightmares wherein he envisioned innocent victims in separate cells and himself pleading before "unjust tribunals," with a sense, "Death-like, of treacherous desertion," in "the last place of refuge—my own soul"; (3) a prophetic afflatus whereby he rose above his fellows to understand the cause of violence in France as a reservoir of guilt and ignorance, and (4) a period when, "all things tending fast / To depravation," speculative schemes and despair over France drew him into erroneous reasoning, "Misguided, and misguiding" (1850, X.414, XI.223, 293). If, as clearly implied, the shame, nightmares, and rationalistic speculation among fellow liberals all occurred after his return to England, then *The Borderers* may analyze the lawlessness of Jacobin London rather than France, and may point toward some sense of his own betrayal of a comrade in London, with Marmaduke's search for expiation— "a wanderer *must I* go"—telling us something about the poet himself, of his journey over Salisbury Plain in August 1793, or perhaps of the puzzling lost months in London that ended in August 1795.

II

In the sequence from "The Vale of Esthwaite" to "Guilt and Sorrow" and the similar sequence from "Incipient Madness" through "The Ruined Cottage" to the first book of *The Excursion,* Wordsworth attempted to keep his eye on the object—or to move his eye away from poetic conventions and toward the object, for fidelity did not come automatically in the idealizing century of his birth. In *The Borderers,* he had been artistically rebellious to the extent of emulating models of passion, such as early plays by Schiller, rather than models of restraint and grace. He made in *The Borderers* no revolutions in language. At about that time, however, as the Adertisement to the *Lyrical Ballads* of 1798 and the Preface of 1800 make explicit, he experimented prosodically with his eye on the humble object and his ear to "the language of conversation in the middle and lower classes of society." In representative poems of *Lyrical Ballads,* Wordsworth's figures, settings, and attitudes were each commonplaces of the day.[12] But he injected into the fashionable sentiments and configurations a novel aspect of the democratic idea. The language spoken by simple people living close to the elemental forms of nature, he argued, comes nearer to a universal language than any other available to a poet who would speak as a man to all mankind. In the union of severely simple method with socially humble subject, Wordsworth resembles the painters Millet and Daumier rather than his own contemporary, George Crabbe, in whose tales a Tacitean syntax clicks with the neoclassic regularity of a metronome:

> There were wives, maids, and mothers on the beach,
> And some sad story appertain'd to each.[13]

Without Crabbe's narrative vigor, but with equal observation and an infinitely greater imaginative penetration, Wordsworth practiced a simplification that far more chastely concealed its art.

More than Crabbe—indeed, as much as the newspaper Jacobins—Wordsworth concentrates in *Lyrical Ballads* on sad victims of social wrong. He gives us Goody Blake, ill-fed, ill-housed, thinly clad, begrudged by Harry Gill the few sticks she pulled from his hedge; he gives us Simon Lee, ancient, one-eyed, weak-ankled, impoverished huntsman emeritus, reduced to tears of gratitude for the single muscular stroke that freed him from vain hacking at a tangled root; he gives us the shepherd of "The Last of the Flock," fallen on lean years with ten children to feed, refused relief from the parish as long as any of his fifty sheep remained unsold. Within the general experiment of applying severely simple method to socially humble subject, we have the child of "We Are Seven," miserable Martha Ray of "The Thorn," the idiot boy and his distraught mother. To paraphrase his Girondin friend Beaupuy, it is for these that the poet fights with his pen. He does not anticipate social security payments for the Simon Lees, but he laments the necessity, even the possibility, of such immense gratitude for small favors as old Simon was reduced to. "The Last of the Flock" contains an implicit argument to be made somewhat clearer in "Michael" and much clearer in Wordsworth's comments on "Michael": statesmen in Parliament should not by inertia force "statesmen" of the hills— small estatesmen—to choose between their children and their real property or livestock. By the conservation of a modest patrimony, "statesmen" serve their children. Concrete attachment to place is thus an ally of family affection.

After 1798, Wordsworth gradually softened the social protest and injected new interests into vignettes of pity such as "Alice Fell, or Poverty," which combines the poet's interest in the psychology of children with the theme of "Simon Lee," that there is a threshold of pitiableness across which no human being should be pushed. "The Old Cumberland Beggar," an argumentative poem reflecting folk balladry less than economic tracts and Parliamentary debates, asserts the utilitarian value of a conspicuous, peripatetic pitiableness that arouses the community to charitable acts and feelings. By bestowing on this beggar her mite of meal, the poet's neighbor "builds her hope in heaven." Beyond the appeal to utility, the poem proposes a humanitarian supplement to the code of laissez faire: leave the Cumberland beggar "free of mountain solitudes"; let him sit "*where* and *when* he will." It is not clear that the beggar feels his organic union with nature.

In the peroration of this oddly flat and inconsistent poem, the malediction on the "House, misnamed of Industry" refers to a venerable institution and not to any innovation of the recent Speenhamland Act, which supplemented wages out of parish rates, in amounts to accord with the current price of bread. Such recent changes in the Poor Laws were concerned not with the poorhouse but with "outdoor relief." Although the utilitarian reforms in progress were in part attempts to reduce vagrancy, the poem opposes acts of state, not for their specific provisions, but in the name of individual freedom from regulation. Yet "The Old Cumberland Beggar" provides as apt an example as any in Wordsworth of transition resulting from ideological frustration. The poet condescends, but he asks his readers to value even this beggar as an independent piece of humanity. His stance is democratic, but no longer so fiercely, so absolutely, or so politically democratic as in 1794. He cannot support, he must protest against, the proposals of every known reformer. His past is England's past. "Art thou a Statesman in the van / Of public business trained and bred?" he asked in the opening lines of "A Poet's Epitaph"; if you are, go home and "learn to love one living man" (WPW, IV, 65 app. crit.).

Writing to C. J. Fox about "Michael" and "The Brothers," included in the new volume of 1800, he asked the liberal statesman to intervene for the purpose of conserving old ways and an old class of modest yeomen. For these humble landowners, Wordsworth makes a claim he does not make for the Cumberland beggar. Through them he shows that "men who do not wear fine cloaths can feel deeply."[14] These poems criticize classical heroism and "pastoral" artificiality in the light of the democratic idea and of spirit-infused realism. Michael stands in his own dignity. Like the poet, he finds one strength within and without, alone "Amid the heart of many thousand mists, / That came to him, and left him, on the heights."

God had not cut these shepherds to fit the accepted political patterns. The Statist (as Wordsworth later calls him) comes first among the villains in "A Poet's Epitaph" because he is trained to abstraction and public conflict rather than to the care of individuals. The Statist is an enemy to the statesman Michael as well as to the Cumberland beggar. Michel Beaupuy could win Wordsworth's assent

Wordsworth

in France by pointing to one hungry girl as a sufficient cause for civil war; but now it is for the shepherd's peaceful possession of small property also that the poet is fighting, and the theorists of the Revolution in France give no answer to his problem. Even Wordsworth's readings in Turgot gave only the negative advice of the physiocrats: leave alone. To preserve freedom, to preserve affection, the Statist must act to preserve small property. Michael's family has been able to live "in the open sunshine of God's love" because Michael's industry has freed his patrimonial fields from all encumbrance, "free as is the wind / That passes over it." In the letter to Fox, Wordsworth condemned the "vanity and pride" of all who had promoted recent utilitarian legislation, but the Statist who is asked to leave the beggar to his roads is asked not to leave the shepherds and landsmen to their present decay. The poet is impelled one more step from French equality toward English "liberty and order." Michael's property is not to be equated with privilege, Wordsworth insists, but with life. At his level, the land simultaneously owns the man and sets him free.

The democratic individualism that underlies these poems enables the poet to hear the "still, sad music of humanity" in the beauteous forms of nature. I take it that this famous but cryptic phrase, line 91 of "Tintern Abbey," grows more organically from the opening section of the poem than is generally recognized. The opening description of the landscape along the Wye implies throughout a contrast with rural life in the middle counties, where neatly trimmed hedges divided the landscape into rectangles, with a square clearing for the house of visible brick or stone, capped by ornamented chimney pots, from which smoke curled away as evidence of warmth and festive meals within. Over this image of commonly evident rural life, the poet superimposes the greener, wilder scene along the Wye:

> These plots of cottage-ground, these orchard-tufts,
> Which at this season, with their unripe fruits,
> Are clad in one green hue, and lose themselves
> 'Mid groves and copses.   Once again I see
> These hedge-rows, hardly hedge-rows, little lines
> Of sportive wood run wild: these pastoral farms,
> Green to the very door; and wreaths of smoke

97

Sent up, in silence, from among the trees!
With some uncertain notice, as might seem
Of vagrant dwellers in the houseless woods,
Or of some Hermit's cave, where by his fire
The Hermit sits alone.   (WPW, II, 259–260)

By mediating between wild nature and trim civilization, the lines reveal that people do live active, social lives beneath the undisturbed blanket of green. The lines make their point by negatives and abatements: "hardly hedge-rows," absence of a clearing "to the very door," smoke sent up "in silence" (a sublime deprivation, according to Edmund Burke in *A Philosophical Inquiry into the Origin of Our Ideas of the Sublime and Beautiful*), "vagrant," "houseless," and "alone"—not houseless, only apparently so. Looking from Westminster Bridge toward the quiet splendor of unawakened London, in 1802, the poet will admire the sleeping power of "all that mighty heart." In neither weakness nor raging power, but in hidden and subdued potentiality, he finds best revealed the "one life" of nature and man. In "Tintern Abbey" the power of ordinary human life, concealed within the blended verdure along the Wye, teaches the poet to hear in nature the "still, sad music of humanity." Although no longer a believer in the unleashed forces of revolution, Wordsworth continued to revere the latent power of the ordinary cottager.

The democratic individualism implied in "Tintern Abbey" and apparent in "The Last of the Flock," "The Brothers," and "Michael" continued less obviously in a series of famous but cryptic poems commenced in 1802. Encouraged toward ambiguity by the increasing discrepancy between reformist ideas and his patriotic feelings, the poet found that what he had to say about fellowship with the poor could not be said adequately in bald statements of fact or in statements merely bewigged with rhetorical ornament. Wordsworth's butterflies, celandines, creeping worms, and frail snowdrops—what Sir Herbert Read has called "but lowly features in his poetic landscape"—are primarily, most of the time, symbols for human features, human figures in the poetic landscape.[15] Perhaps he came to love of man from love of nature; he was next moved to write of celandines from love and study of man.

He did not, of course, merely seek and find objective correlatives for his feelings toward the lonely poor; his cuckoos and daisies glow with a sacramental vision of the one life breathed by Infinitude into man and worm. Religious implications did not await the Dedication of *The White Doe of Rylstone,* with its concern for the small creatures of the forest "to whom Heaven / A calm and sinless life, with love, hath given." Similar implications are present in the reflections on a "tiny glow-worm, lowliest child of earth," assigned by Wordsworth to one of his earliest figures crossing a lonely heath to a lowly hut (WPW, I, 293:30).

From his earliest poems to those of his old age he makes it important to be watched by a star and by one's fellow men. In kinship with Blake's insistence on multiple vision, Wordsworth cares what kind of eye the poet and the politician keep on the object.[16] A utilitarian eye will turn the "meanest flower" or Simon Lee into a thing. Because a dead eye deprives life of divinity, it is important to remain open to the speaking star, the healing heavens, the sensitive breeze, the sympathetic passerby. But theological distinctions come from an intellectual teasing of Wordsworth's early poems rather than from the poems themselves. A reader must stress the word *unassuming* if he is to learn what Nature teaches:

> To look with feelings of fraternal love
> Upon those unassuming things, that hold
> A silent station in this beauteous world.
> *(Prelude* XII.50 52)

Not always fancifully as in the first of four lyrics entitled "To the Daisy," all of Wordsworth's poems and lines in praise of humble creatures carry an ethical, social, and political burden. He does not expect to be read by peony, hawk, or showily beautiful "worldlings" like the brazen buttercup.

Beyond all particulars, Wordsworth sees a unifying Nature, but the vision does not turn him away from the vital particulars. He accepts David Hartley's psychological laws of association as an affective element in the responses and growth of the mind, although he dislikes the prison wherein association would constrict man's use of language to rational communication. Man's moral life is a combination of affective habit and freedom to choose and to conclude.

Politics in English Romantic Poetry

Both the actual and the poetic butterfly and daisy are symbols in this moral life. The creatures Wordsworth sees in life represent a compromise between individual particles of a world given value by the perceiver, which is the poet's subjective version of the physical world of deistic natural religion, and Berkeley's system of arbitrary symbols established and shared by the mind of God—Wordsworth's "Characters of the great Apocalypse, / The types and symbols of Eternity" (Prelude VI.570–571). Man's moral life among daisies requires reflection on the symbolic power of each modest creature. Near as Wordsworth sometimes is to Rousseau, he clearly does not believe that "L'homme qui médite est un animal dépravé." Poetry, according to his Preface of 1800, is "the spontaneous overflow of powerful feelings" in one who has "also thought long and deeply." The poet is one "who rejoices more than other men in the spirit of life that is in him; delighting to contemplate similar volitions and passions as manifested in the goings-on of the Universe, and habitually impelled to create them where he does not find them." Ernst Cassirer's world of myth, a "world of actions, of forces, of conflicting powers," is precisely Wordsworth's world of escarpment, oak, and celandine.

Whether divinely ordered or dependent upon a limited perceiver, the living symbols had to be divested of wrong meanings by hard experience. Dorothy, according to "The Sparrow's Nest" and the first "To a Butterfly," taught her brother that there was a way of looking at butterflies unknown to silly, cruel little boys. "He told me," Dorothy recorded in turn, "how they used to kill all the white ones when he went to school because they were Frenchmen."[17]

The early lyrics and passages in praise of modest creatures do not often make explicit their connection with the human ideals of freedom, simplicity, and humility, but the connection can frequently be deduced even from the titles: "The Redbreast Chasing a Butterfly," "The Kitten and the Falling Leaves," "The Pilgrim's Dream, or The Star and the Glow-Worm," "The Oak and the Broom: A Pastoral." The last poem, written in 1800 in a style one might expect from a shepherd trying to imitate *The Shepheardes Calender*, makes all the connections explicit enough for the meanest skeptic, and was consequently placed by Wordsworth among poems of the fancy. When he placed poems on daisies and green linnets among poems of the lesser fancy, he did so because of simplicity in overt metaphor, not because the subject or the addressee was insignificant.

III

Wordsworth's development to this point is made explicit—deceptively explicit—in the masterwork drafted between 1798 and May 1805, published after his death in 1850 under the half-deceptive, half-instructive title *The Prelude*. As R. D. Havens and Abbie Potts have shown, the work outgrew several schemes for arranging its extensive parcels into a whole. Taken in the spirit of its growth, the work may be described as a letter of inquiry addressed to Coleridge, somewhat as if to another self. Asking how far he is competent to produce the great philosophic poem by which Coleridge expects him to restore the hopes of men, the poet goes more ontogenetically than St. Augustine and Rousseau into the development of his mind, its inner growth and the ecology of it. Taken in the amplitude of its accomplishment, the poem may be described as an empirical epic of spiritual trial and personal victory. Most of the political interest of the poem has usually been found in an area, seemingly discursive, between the extreme poles of epistle and epic. More remains to be said about the politics of the whole. An approach to *The Prelude* through its ideas must be undertaken with some reluctance, not because the work cannot be so read, but because there is a greater need to show just how Wordsworth imbedded the ideas in what we currently take to be his greatest poem. Every idea we extract to examine must be torn from a root-system of literary tradition, sensuous allusion, deep feeling, grandly varied sound. To analyze carefully the political content of the poem, even without consideration of the changes introduced between 1806 and 1850, would produce a heavy book. I should like to try instead to say how far, and in what ways, the work as a whole is political.

Coleridge had in mind an immortal poem that would have at least better ideas than those of Lucretius and Dante. The two friends agreed that the kind of philosophical poem Wordsworth could write was especially needed in their perilous times to rescue contemporaries from disillusion and error. The resultant poem points out for a despondent generation, spell-stopped by the Napoleonic wars, how one mind recovered its health. The universality of this personal theme enabled Wordsworth to select, discard, and modify; in the poem he not only attributes to himself as archetype what actually happened to others, but also, for contrast and a semblance of action, attributes to others what he himself has felt or done.

For the encouragement of others, the poem tells how one mind survived the encounter of its instinctive romanticism with the seductive ideas of the Enlightenment. In the three movements of turn, counterturn, and turn again, the work shows how one poet's imagination was formed in childhood; how this imagination was progressively impaired in Cambridge, France, and London; and how it was restored by Nature through the threefold mediation of Dorothy, Coleridge, and the visible universe. As if by the way, it tells how the imagination grew from a convenience into a supreme power.

The sharpest break in the poem comes at midpoint, before the nadir of the protagonist's descent. In the retrospective summary of Book VIII, the poet examines the stages of his growth from a perspective different from any utilized in the survey to that point. Books I through VII had stressed the worth of solitude in natural settings and the unwholesomeness of most human congregation, whether for dancing, gambling, worshiping, or competing intellectually at college. The first half of the poem had shown the making of a poet by Nature, freedom, and indolence, largely in divorce from art and society. Book VIII tells how, throughout these formative years, the forces of Nature, freedom, and opportunity for indolence had led the poet into an ever-developing love for his fellow men. Perhaps Wordsworth surprised most in 1850 by his frequent references to unconscious forces, to the "under-presence" impelling the active mind. Today he surprises more by his explicit declarations that he first discovered the dignity of man when the human form of solitary shepherds blended with the contour of some distant promontory, in Cumberland and more consciously in Switzerland and France. Although somewhat sentimentalized in his early fancy through the influence of literary pastorals, actual shepherds firmly associated humanity for him with the great, fair, and permanent forms of external nature.

Despite the infectious meanness of men huddled in cities, his earlier perception of dignity in humble individuals seen at a distance helped him discover in London embodiments of such permanent and admirable passions as paternal love. Of such embodiments he gives only one example, but the earlier perception of human dignity helped him also to revere the "weight of Ages" palpable in the streets and buildings of London. No, he will be honest; only momentarily in 1791 or 1793 did he perceive more than the vulgar externals of London.[18] Not before 1802 did imagination enable him to grasp the unity of "the vast metropolis,"

> Fount of my country's destiny and the world's;
> That great emporium, chronicle at once
> And burial-place of passions, and their home
> Imperial, their chief living residence.
> (1850, VIII.593–596)

Here we have a characteristic distinction between his years of error and his years of matured competence to advise the whole people of England.

Interplay between changes for poetic contrast and changes of political viewpoint can be seen in Wordsworth's treatments of his visit to the monastery of the Grande Chartreuse in 1790. That the monastery impressed him deeply, every account shows. But every account is more notable for interpretative color than for fact. In the originally published version of *Descriptive Sketches* we see his readiness, shortly after Revolutionary soldiers had turned the holy place into a garrison (May 1792), to denounce as blasphemous the approach of soldiers in 1790. As late as 1806 he saw no reason to include in *The Prelude* any record of such misconduct by "new-born Liberty" during the gaiety of his visit. And in 1790 no such misconduct had in fact occurred. Apparently it took conversations with Coleridge and Sir George and Lady Beaumont to bring about, in the versions from 1808 on, a passionate arraignment of Revolutionary desecration. In these versions, by dramatic fancy or unconscious fusion of memory, he represents the confiscation, which actually occurred while he was composing *Descriptive Sketches,* as on the brink of occurrence even as he and his fellow-traveler Jones slept the night at the Chartreuse.

The satiric rejections of Cambridge and London in Books III and VII, then, might be taken as conscientious reconstructions, about 1804, of his consciously cultivated reactions to Cambridge and London in the period from 1787 to 1795. The rejections are scarcely qualified by admissions of his initial wonder. In contrast, the mellowness of Book VIII represents reflections in tranquillity on what he had discovered by 1804 about his unconscious as well as conscious development up to 1792. Yet his radical acquaintances in London took politics so seriously, and he himself took them so seriously for two or three years after 1793, that the charge of unreality against London must belong to his later view that Londoners were shallow even when earnest. In any event, the contrast is notable for readers who pass from the petulancy of III and VII to the retrospective Book VIII.

Broadly in the suddenly satiric tone and pointedly in metaphors of play-acting, Wordsworth's Cambridge prepares for Wordsworth's London. Cambridge plays at evil; London is the reality. The poet remembers the interplay of grotesque faculty and frivolous students as

> that inferior exhibition, play'd
> By wooden images, a theatre
> For Wake or Fair.   (III.606–608)

When Book VII turns from frank entertainments like Bartholomew Fair to "others titled higher," to brawling lawyers, droning senators, and mincing clergymen, the chief evil of London is seen to be its disjunction from reality. Thus Cambridge, the shadow of a shadow, was playing at play-acting.

The poet uses satire in defense of principle. His chief exhibit on the stage of Parliament is Pitt, unnamed but identified by epithets ("tongue-favor'd"), by half-puns ("one among the prime of these," his name "a household term"), and by satiric description of his oratory ("What memory and what logic!"). Probably this passage

Wordsworth

was written during Pitt's return to power in 1804. Even after 1820 Wordsworth could not apologize to Pitt, the very emblem of ministerial deceit. Temporarily he inserted an apology to Burke and Fox for omitting from his first account the true eloquence that moved "the ingenuous and the sensitive" in the years of crisis. As the new crisis of the Reform Bill approached, the tribute to Fox had to go. In its place the version of 1850 epitomizes Burke's political and social thought. Whether or not Wordsworth was capable of honoring Burke in 1793 or 1795, both the tribute and the summary came aptly in *The Prelude,* for the poem's defense of experience against the straightjacket of theory is very nearly Burke's:

> While he forewarns, denounces, launches forth,
> Against all systems built on abstract rights,
> Keen ridicule; the majesty proclaims
> Of Institutes and Laws, hallowed by time;
> Declares the vital power of social ties
> Endeared by Custom; and with high disdain,
> Exploding upstart Theory, insists
> Upon the allegiance to which men are born—
>
> (1850, VII.523–530)

A hero of doctrine had come to the poet late but fittingly.

The poet himself had emulated Burke's high disdain for upstart theory in Books III and VII and in V, where he derided the recent utilitarian books for children and their monstrous product, the juvenile "prodigy," a "dwarf Man." When he had to specify, Wordsworth blamed politicians more readily than philosophers for social disaster, but the vigor of his attack on analytic and utilitarian modes of education shows how he realized, independently of Burke, the danger to all he loved in any attempt to defeat the "froward chaos of futurity" by the erection of plans and systems. In Book V, under the slight cover of oblique reference, he likens the mighty artificers of child prodigies to Milton's Sin and Death, who made one world of hell and earth by erecting a bridge and highway between them. Wary of engineering, the poet of *The Prelude* saw no better way out of hell than Satan's original struggle through chaos by the trial and error of experience.

In the course of apologizing for the restriction of his survey in

Book V to books he read as a child, Wordsworth made his charge against the Enlightenment explicit although folded within one of his softening double negatives. In a manuscript of the poem possibly prepared for Coleridge to read in Malta, he made explicit the importance of his reading for his larger theme of impairment and recovery:

> I mean
> To speak of an abasement in my mind
> Not altogether wrought without the help
> Of Books ill-chosen.   (1959 ed., p. 172)

Such poets as Thomson, Akenside, Beattie, and Cowper, with critics like Young and Hurd and such writers on the picturesque as William Gilpin and Sir Uvedale Price, despite their rationalistic tendency to classify and systematize, provided an extensive basis for objection to Augustan modes. Their cultural significance, along with misinterpretations of Rousseau and overestimation of "Ossian," is evident. But it is also worth remembering what opportunities the speaker of *The Prelude* had for help from books ill-chosen. Adam Smith, Bentham, and Malthus published as he grew. Not only Locke, but probably Hartley and certainly Paley in studies at Cambridge, followed by Godwin, Priestley, Thelwall, Fawcett, and the French in later reading, made appeals to self-interest, materialism, mechanism, and rational abstraction as if John Howard and the Wesleys had never lived. Erasmus Darwin and the satirists continued rationalistic modes in verse. Wordsworth was determined to save the Arabian Nights against the siege of utilitarian tales as the proper reading for children.

The satiric passages of Books III, V, and VII, then, mark the increasingly severe reversals in college, in reading, and in London, of the deepening of a poetic mind otherwise joyfully traced from Book I through Book VIII.

The explanation provided in Book VIII, how love of man evolved from prior love of Nature, had to be inserted before Book IX, "Residence in France," which traces the poet's involvement as a "patriot" of the Revolution. Like the retrospective summary, Book IX completely changes the emphasis of the earlier books, if it does not contradict them. From Books III–VII one would gather that the poet who went to France at the age of twenty-one, to learn the language, was prepared for the experience chiefly by the intellectual decay of Cambridge and the sophisticated emptiness of London. Yet Book IX, continuing the dialectical antithesis of Book VIII, asserts that the poet's upbringing had been unusually democratic, free in his home district from scenes of excessive attention to "claims of wealth or blood" and open at Cambridge to "something of a republic. It was not the least of his debts to Cambridge, he said,

> That something there was holden up to view
> Of a Republic, where all stood thus far
> Upon equal ground, that they were brothers all
> In honour, as in one community,
> Scholars and Gentlemen . . .   (IX.228–232)

In truth, as others have remarked, the "something" of a republic held before him must have been an ideal intensified by the notable absence of republican virtues from the actual Cambridge of his day.[19] But Wordsworth is not only taking a case; he is making a case. From the only intimate knowledge conceivable, the knowledge of his own mind, he is showing how to rescue a typical young man of the time from representative bewilderment.

The dialectic accomplished, he turns to the tremendous events of his life in France, which may here be reported briefly. Merely curious in Paris, he drifted from privacy at Blois into a "noisier world" where he soon became a fervid supporter of the Revolution. He gave his heart "to the People." Among a band of Royalist officers, he met a Girondin who memorably said, at sight of a hunger-bitten girl, " 'Tis against *that* . . . we are fighting." This officer, Michel Beaupuy, knew all the current doctrines concerning the purpose and forms of government. Wordsworth, whose judgment was not yet flooded with hope, argued for "the experience of past ages"—which suggests that his education at Hawkshead and Cambridge had not been a total loss. Although he shared Beaupuy's eagerness to see arbitrary government obliterated, the poet would

107

have us know that he paused in his republicanism for visions of the chivalry that had veiled the royal vices of the past in beauty and romance.

To illustrate the evil of *lettres de cachet*—"Captivity by mandate without law"—he ends Book IX with the tale of high-born Vaudracour and plebeian Julia, whose parents thwarted their love. Twice, in the phrase of *The Prelude* of 1850, Vaudracour resorted to "Nature's rebellion against monstrous law," first by getting Julia with child and secondly by killing a functionary who tried to arrest him by "mandate without law." To cut a woefully bad tale short, Julia was shut in a convent and her lover ended childless and insane. The story borrows from both literature and life.[20] In "Vaudracour and Julia" Wordsworth did not, I think, despite its similarity to violations of law in *The Borderers,* simply distort for the public his own unhappy affair with Annette. He brought to a standard republican exemplum, but surely no less for literary force than for expiation, the intimate knowledge that we assume he had of "secret grief" and fugitive rapture. Although brightened with two or three moments of passion, "Vaudracour and Julia" is essentially a melodramatic, second-hand tale. Specifically, it is a tale of young love oblivious of class until destroyed by authoritarian rule and the pigheadedness of parents, both the aristocratic pair and the plebeian. If the poem is to be taken autobiographically, what ought to be a confession of guilt is instead—even though original indignation had long since cooled—an accusation against arbitrary power that would enforce artificial inequality.

Like Book IX (whatever we make of Vaudracour), Book X contains biography. But it is at once more philosophical than the previous book and more narrowly political, more topical and more partisan. Biographically, it tells us how the poet, despite the September Massacres, returned to Paris "enflam'd with hope"; it admits that further atrocities kept him guiltily sleepless; it says that the lack of funds forced him again to his homeland; it tells how he rejoiced with enlarged hope at the fall of Robespierre. More philosophically, although a little obliquely, the poet indicates the importance of his being in France when he discovered the allure of social progress. To be an English youth in France was to stand on a higher cloud in heaven. Doubly free, he could feel one hope for all men; unlike most patriots, he was not then goaded to bitterness either by the Bourbon past or by discovery that "universal benevolence" and "the government of England" could be other than synonymous. Britain's declaration of open war ended his euphoria: "This threw me first out of the pale of love."

An extended passage tells how he reflected in Paris on the urgency, for all mankind, that Parisian disorder end in the ascendancy of men of honor, how he saw that "the virtue of one paramount mind" could have converted outrages into just government; and how he contemplated the possibilities of leadership open to an insignificant stranger, one little graced with eloquence and "all unfit for tumult or intrigue." He would have accepted any assignment to an act of honor, however dangerous. An allusion to the proof by Harmodius and Aristogiton that "tyrannic Power is weak," a proof known to Brutus and to schoolboys, suggests that he had in mind assassination.[21] He is describing the situation of *The Borderers,* where moral anarchy leaves every man adrift, either to sink or to discover his full strength. With the intent of understatement and the effect of anticlimax, Wordsworth says next that the poet who went to France merely to learn the language left it only from an absolute want of funds. In recovery from this anticlimax, he says that the tempting self-sacrifice would have been a "poor mistaken and bewilder'd offering." With fumbling caution, he apologizes because a mad dream ended in sobriety. At the close, he is saying with Keats that he would have jumped down Mount Etna for any human good, but that he can best serve mankind by composing this poem. As a representative figure, he depicts the magnitude of the crisis in 1793; as an exceptional poet, he reports a descent toward annihilation more nearly disastrous than his transit through the superficialities of London, in turn a greater danger than the shallowness of Cambridge had been. Enlightenment and Revolution had wrung his imagination dry.

The poet's intellectual and spiritual history in the rest of Book X (disjoined to form Book XI in the 1850 version) is best skimped, not because its story is unimportant, but because, as the exegetic impasse over it has shown, it is too ambiguous for precise interpretation.[22] Here, rather than earlier with the episodes of his year in France, Wordsworth places the ecstatic lines published separately as "The French Revolution," declaring "Bliss was it in that dawn to be alive." After his return to England, he was soured by and toward the British ministers, not yet by or toward France. The displacement chronologically of this key passage gives us three possible meanings: bliss was confined to his year in France; the declarations of war did not immediately sour his bliss; or the dawn of bliss lasted only during the one month of January 1793. One meaning is certain: in 1793 the hopes of man still lodged with France. When Frenchmen became "Oppressors in their turn" (pinpointed by de Selincourt and Darbishire as September 1794), the poet found his hopes in republican doctrine, which could be planted afresh in some other soil. Already, if the order of passages means anything, he had begun to "think with fervour upon management / Of Nations." What next captivated him can be identified almost certainly as Godwinian belief in individual reason. How tempting, this realm where zeal could realize itself in abstract utopias; where, as he put it with unwonted and uncharitable wit, "passions had the privilege to work, / And never hear the sound of their own names"! The attempt to prove in logic all his propositions and convictions concerning society and government could only end in despair. "This was the crisis of that strong disease," this the soul's "last and lowest ebb" (1850, XI.306–307).

Throughout Book X, Wordsworth echoes the arguments of Opposition newspapers and Foxite speeches. When the Terror was called by English ministers the inevitable harvest of popular government and equality, the poet saw that its cause was something quite different. The cause, he continued to believe even as he wrote,

was a reservoir of guilt
And ignorance, fill'd up from age to age,
That could no longer hold its loathsome charge,
But burst and spread in deluge through the Land.
(X.437–440)

Of the armed attack from Britain, although Wordsworth emphasizes more than Coleridge the resultant madness in France, he employs

110

the metaphor of Coleridge's "Recantation: Illustrated in the Story of the Mad Ox," a metaphor much favored by the Opposition. In Wordsworth's version, "The goaded Land wax'd mad." Unlike Coleridge, he writes with time for reflection. Yet ten years of rebuttal by Pitt and his followers had not shaken him from the Opposition view that only on some later date did Frenchmen change "a war of self-defense" into one of conquest. According to *The Prelude* it was only after "Britain opposed the Liberties of France" that the French became oppressors "in their turn." With this premise he had agreement from Coleridge, but the Tory press still vehemently denied it.

The Government was wrong in actions at home as well as abroad. Upon the poet's return from France, he was too concerned over the war even to worry about the slave trade. In terms of his theme, the growth of the imagination, he was beside himself. Nor was he alone in dislodgment from the normal self. Even yet he blames the Ministers of 1793 for the wild growth of radical theory:

> Oh, much have they to account for, who could tear
> By violence at one decisive rent
> From the best Youth in England, their dear pride,
> Their joy, in England . . .   (X.276–279)

Further, in Shelleyan vituperation that he later mitigated but never retracted, Wordsworth denounced Pitt and his former ministers for such atrocities against civil liberty as the baiting of the disaffected with domestic spies:

> Our Shepherds (this say merely) at that time
> Thirsted to make the guardian Crook of Law
> A tool of Murder; they who ruled the State,
> Though with such awful proof before their eyes
> That he who would sow death, reaps death, or worse,
> And can reap nothing better, child-like long'd
> To imitate, not wise enough to avoid,
> Giants in their impiety alone,
> But, in their weapons and their warfare base
> As vermin working out of reach, they leagu'd
> Their strength perfidiously, to undermine
> Justice, and make an end of Liberty.   (X.646–657)

111

Politics in English Romantic Poetry

That Wordsworth retained this passage, changed in language but not in gist,[23] illustrates the tenacity of human prejudices, for he did not cry out against the Six Acts of 1819 and tended to support later ministries than Pitt's "working out of reach" to undermine civil liberties.

Upon giving up social and moral questions in despair, for lack of certainty, the mind he traces turned desperately to mathematics (*Prelude* X.904). In this desperate turning lies the deepest crisis of self in relation to other. Here all the evils of the city derided in Book VII come to war within the protagonist of *The Prelude*. But because the poet employs against the urban light of reason its own weapon of satiric irony, critics seeking to affirm Wordsworth's existential pessimism have looked elsewhere for evidences of guilt and despair. They have looked, not to the rationalistic flounderings of the prodigal son in the sties of London, but to the probings into the obscure places of the creative mind, to the episodes of childhood and youth wherein Nature shaped the soul through beauty and fear, and to the final emblem of the mind in the roar of waters rising through usurping mists on the heights of Snowden.[24] Yet it was not in the darkest of the spots of time, but in London, that the mind caressed the devil. Only in the rationalistic, fragmented city did the mind fail to transcend its difficulties.

The final books of *The Prelude* tell of the protagonist's rescue from both geometry and the city and of his recovery of native taste and imagination. Both as illustration and as partial explanation of the recovery, Book XII (XIII in the 1850 version) contains important ruminations on society. The vital union of man and Nature celebrated in this poem is not merely individual. Nor is the poet concerned only with the national built on the personal, the "mighty hopes of Nations" rising from the "truths of individual sympathy." He has embarked

> To seek in Man, and in the frame of life,
> Social and individual, what there is
> Desireable, affecting, good or fair
> Of kindred permanence, the gifts divine
> And universal, the pervading grace
> That hath been, is, and shall be. (XII.39–44)

Wordsworth

Kindred permanence is not to be found in the external, hollow "wealth of Nations" currently idolized. In escape from turmoil, the poet had rediscovered the superiority of receptiveness over shows of power. Action is less to be honored than alert passiveness.

Although we could not expect Wordsworth to express it, the negative side of his return to Nature is evident enough in Book XII. He had grown weary of the reformer's constant awareness of social wrong, of the unsleeping search for further evils to reform. He had escaped from endless expectancy, from the excitements of dissatisfaction, from obligatory anger and resistance, from the reformer's inability to rest in a world capable of infinite improvement. Movements of reform will always find it hard to retain their Wordsworths.

The poet had, nevertheless, found a radical truth for contemporaries and posterity. Disillusionment with political leaders, with "power and action" (the version of 1850, more cautious, says disillusionment with "power and energy detached / From moral purpose"), enabled him to see that the grace pervading the frame of life catches up all "unassuming things." Asking "in spirit more subdued" what 9,999 men lacked that the one in 10,000 had, he discovered a new search and a poetical subject never before made sufficiently concrete:

> "Inspect the basis of the social pile:
> Inquire," said I, "how much of mental power
> And genuine virtue they possess who live
> By bodily toil, labour exceeding far
> Their due proportion, under all the weight
> Of that injustice which upon ourselves
> Ourselves entail." (1850, XIII.94–100)

So inspecting, he found in vagrants on the road a depth of soul that not only made ridiculous all claims that society had identified and coroneted its natural aristocracy but also made ridiculous all praise of formal education for its paltry accomplishments. We are given here in Book XII the deepest reason why the books of the adult had to be slighted in Book V. He hails the unassuming man who enhances the land in labor for his kind.

Admittedly the victim oppressed into excessive labor and extreme poverty can achieve love even less readily than the victim of urban vacuity, but the poet now knows it false to say that love requires for its growth leisure and sophisticated language. Part of this argument had been written out about 1800, but Wordsworth stitched it with relative smoothness of seams into the reverent tribute of Book XII to Nature and to "men as they are men within themselves." Postulating injustice in the order of society, he had uncovered the chief source of continued injustice under representative government: a false belief in the innate inferiority of the poor. He does not say, of course, that all men are born equal. He says that we all suffer needlessly both when we allow the wrong men to be pressed toward the bottom and when we allow any man to be pressed beyond all possibility of love. The political voice in the poem has applied balm to its own anger.

We can hardly avoid saying "the poet" and "he" for the autobiographic voice in *The Prelude*. But the liberating doctrine of the persona is applicable to the extent that an inner logic of the poem discovers not only arguments and positions but also the unfolding self that gropes toward communication. Even those later changes in idea that look like expressions of increasing conservatism are adjustments in the dialectic of the poem that the author needs rather than dictates.

Yet the poem never totally abandons its character as an exploratory letter to Coleridge. Its concluding lines, the inventory of an introspective psyche, combine biographical with speculative optimism.

After resigning in despair his attempt to prove the equality and natural goodness of men by such logic as Condorcet's or Godwin's, the poet has reached very nearly the same point through imaginative observation. He accepts the effective meaning of the declaration that men are born equal; namely, that the inequality manifest in society distorts the different, lesser, natural inequality of individuals. I think his conclusion that "the inner frame is good" (XII.280) is to be equated with his conclusion that however low of station a man may be, "high service is perform'd within" (XII.226). If so, then *The Prelude* replaces the theory of natural goodness with the observation that any man may be, for all you know, potentially as good as the next. Among Christians, even some Calvinists had admitted as much. Politically, the poet's conclusion is democratic. Clearly the second half of *The Prelude* does not trace the conversion of a republican into a Tory. It helps explain why the later Wordsworth said he remained a democrat when he outgrew the republican enthusiasm of his youth. It traces the growth of a troubled liberal into a Wordsworthian romantic, who held slightly changed beliefs with deeper reason. The long poem ends with implications somewhat like those of Arnold's "Dover Beach," but with a firmer grasp of eternity: though men sink again shamefully, nation by nation, into enslavement, yet Wordsworth and Coleridge, "Prophets of Nature," can unite honorably to communicate in the brief years left to them the truths needed for man's redemption from ignominy.

IV

In 1802 Wordsworth began to find relief from the endless expanses of his great philosophic poem in the narrow ground of the sonnet. The liberating confinement of this form belongs to the poet who had returned the literary shepherd to his native simplicity and stooped to humanize the meanest flowers that blow. Although his sonnets permitted the clear emergence of Wordsworth the patriot, and afford most readers their clearest view of his patriotism, the form itself can be regarded as a sort of pilewort that Wordsworth rescued from the general contempt (except among newspaper editors) that it had suffered for a century. In his hand as in Milton's, from 1802 on, "the Thing became a trumpet" for political comment and sublimation.

Convinced from childhood that his native regions were sanctified, he had learned from bitterly cold weeks in Germany, in 1798-99, how much more he loved the English soil than he had ever realized. His sonnets progress from love of soil to love of nation and on to love of state. His own dating, untrustworthy as it is, places earliest among the sonnets of his maturity the one asking why Pelion and Ossa, or even Parnassus, should be more highly praised than Skiddaw. On 21 May 1802 he wrote the first of his political sonnets known to us, "I grieved for Buonaparté," which demonstrates the soldier's incapacity to govern by contrasting his training in battle with the ideal training of a governor. The implications are clear. William Wordsworth or another equally close to the upper middle class of England, rather than an alien soldier in a disrupted country, has the experience by which "true Sway doth mount":

> Books, leisure, perfect freedom, and the talk
> Man holds with week-day man in the hourly walk
> Of the mind's business . . .   (WPW, III, 111:10–12)

In another sonnet, one of the most famous of the series, it is largely the man among weekday men that France lacks, when Wordsworth finds in the present and past of France "equally a want of books and men" (III, 117:14). He is not saying that France lacks all signs of genius. He is not pitting Shakespeare, Bacon, and Newton against Racine, Montaigne, and Descartes, but Milton, Sydney, Marvell, Harrington, and Vane—because "These moralists could act and comprehend"—against Voltaire, Rousseau, the amoral Helvétius and Holbach, and the men directly involved in France's perverted revolution. Nevertheless, the patriot in daily fear of Bonaparte's "loaded pistol held at the head of England" does not settle for the simple slander that France has had men who could act and men who could comprehend, but no men who could do both; he must say France has had no men who could do either. His assertion is near enough to epigram to have been often quoted out of context as quite sufficient evidence of his stupidity. At least it should be noted that he accomplished his tribute to the English republicans without any Carlylean hero-worship of Cromwell.

Prejudiced patriotism, love of the "cock that crows, the smoke that curls" only in England, finds its place in several of the early sonnets. But the poet's scorn is not limited to Bonaparte's France. Fearing lest his country not deserve victory, he surveys the "stagnant waters" of casual living, and cries shame on Englishmen pressing to cross the Channel, not on upright business like his (to settle honorably with Annette so that he can marry Mary Hutchinson of Cumberland), but to prostrate their minds in admiration of the glittering First Consul. The Government and countrymen that had given him his nastiest shock by warring against freedom in 1793 were not

116

to be altogether trusted yet. In these months of 1802, however, the public was close behind Wordsworth and Coleridge as they hurried toward the conclusion that the Government must be trusted, because the First Consul was insatiable. Even Fox's opposition to the policy of war achieved less and less public expression. It took a crank like Cobbett to turn in this period from right to left. Very rare among the liberals of the newly founded *Edinburgh Review* was Sydney Smith, who did not need to search for his head because he had never lost it. Wordsworth, who had lost his way in the storm, found it hard to remain calm while rowing his way back through stagnant waters.

Given Napoleon's thirst for empire, Wordsworth's patriotic fervor was not out of keeping with his considered nationalism, which comes to the fore in his sonnets. In prose, the doctrine of nationalism elicited his most significant speculations on the principles of government.

The theory of the modern national state first trailed its infant clouds in the cradle of German transcendentalism, where it was nursed by Herder, rocked awake by Fichte, and breeched by Hegel. Hans Kohn, the most thorough student the subject has had, argued in 1944 that nationalities are fluctuating bodies that arise only when a social group is delimited by such objective bonds as language (stressed by Herder and Fichte), territory, political entity, customs (stressed by Rousseau), traditions, religion, and common descent (stressed by Hitler).[25] To the minds of those who form a nationality by act of corporate will, not all of these bonds need to be present at once. Several bonds could be present but undifferentiated or fused, as we find political entity, traditions, and language interfused in Wordsworth's tributes to political heroes who have spoken and acted in England. The preexistence of nationalism has a long history of loose strands, some of them going back at least as far as the Israelite bondage in Egypt; but the accelerated movement toward full-blown nationalism in Wordsworth's youth can be seen by noting, as an example of what went before, the scarcity of strands (as specified by Hans Kohn), and the emphasis on government, in the essay "Of National Characters" that Hume added to the third edition of his *Essays Moral and Political* in 1748. On one major point Hume did anticipate Wordsworth: national character depends on moral differences, not physical. Although the French Revolution first showed the relation of doctrinal nationalism to a people's readiness to explode, Wordsworth had no trouble in regarding Napoleonic expansion as more than a perversion—it was an absolute contradiction—of the nationalism that had acted as yeast in the Revolution.

In tracing the ideas and feelings that Wordsworth contributed to the understanding and adoption of nationalism in Great Britain, one can pass almost imperceptibly from his prose to the sonnets. His fullest articulation appears in the long essay *Concerning the Relations of Great Britain, Spain, and Portugal, to Each Other, and to the Common Enemy, at This Crisis; and Specifically as Affected by the Convention of Cintra: The whole brought to the test of those Principles, by which alone the Independence and Freedom of Nations can be Preserved or Recovered.* The essay was begun serially in the *Courier* at the end of 1808 and published separately as a tract in 1809. Although Coleridge collaborated on two installments and De Quincey lent many editorial hours to the work, the ideas are Wordsworth's. In 1811 he added what is in effect an appendage, in the form of a challenge to the imperialistic arguments of Captain Charles Pasley.[26]

The essence of his doctrine, more cosmopolitan than Burke's had been, is the self-determination of peoples. Although the doctrine could not have borne fruit in Wordsworth's sonnets without such faith in universal benevolence as grew during the Enlightenment, he insists on the particularity and individuality that make nationalism an arrangement to be cherished. Throughout, the tract implies organic growth and organic oneness. It carries forward from his letter to the Bishop of Llandaff an insistence on the dignity proper to the labor of the individual. Except for this emphasis upon the value of doing, Spain and Portugal in the tract are national counterparts to the linnet and pilewort in his lyrics: all four are natural entities to be left alone so that they may obey in the majesty of solitude their own internal laws of growth. The true nationalist leaves other peoples alone except to rescue them from an invading third power. There is no place in Wordsworth's doctrine for an imperial mission, and none, as there had been in the self-centered doctrine of Locke and the militant expansionist fervor of Robespierre, for territorial expansion under the plea of *Lebensraum*.

Successful nationalism depends upon public virtue. If independence is to be preserved, says the tract, national morality must be "fixed and habitual," for "*Principle* is indispensably required." Above all, as the poet writes in a number of the sonnets dedicated to national independence, for example in "The Pillar of Trajan," there must be no imperialistic glint in the national eye. To retain independence a people must be upright in all their dealings as a nation. Liberty consists, he suggests in "Temptations from Roman Refinements," in maintaining vigorously your own endemic culture. Independence, he sometimes insists, is a matter of moral conviction; you have it if you can believe you have it. By the soul only, he proclaims, "the Nations shall be great and free"; an energetic spirit of nationalism is itself nobility. A mean people, be they English or any other, deserve no freedom; it is to the advantage of a free country like England that every other nation be free; the preservation of liberty is a just cause for war; moral principle, indispensable in all international affairs, makes mandatory all practicable aid to peoples under foreign domination.[27]

Until about 1812, the sonnets express as much fear of England's spiritual ailments as of Britain's external enemy. Sonnets of aspiration and uplift enforce their argument negatively, in metaphors of putridity, poison, and impotence: A "fen of stagnant waters," where a commercialized people partakes of "emasculating food," can enjoy no stream of liberty. The maintenance of true independence requires exertion and sacrifice. But the attainment of independence also—and this works comparatively in England's favor—requires time. By accepting the importance of time for a nation's growth into freedom, Wordsworth slid very early toward a Burkean distrust of all liberty not traditional, "healthy, matured, time-honoured"—accumulated, as he admits in the tract on Cintra, through slow years. Consistent with his psychological and aesthetic beliefs, he insisted upon the importance of human affections in a free nation. "It was not for the soil, or for the cities and forts, that Portugal was valued," he says in the tract, "but for the human feeling which was there . . ."

Politics in English Romantic Poetry

A second conservative vein, more personal to Wordsworth than the emphasis on organic growth, ran through his expressions of nationalism from the beginning. He held a solemn belief in real property, in soil to be cultivated and perpetually improved. A natural and therefore healthy passion for private property, such as Michael's, implementing the passion of land to preserve its dignity by avoiding second mortgages, requires national independence. It is a variation on his theme of the paternal estate that Wordsworth has the Tyrolese speak in 1809:

> The Land we from our fathers had in trust,
> And to our children will transmit, or die;
> This is our maxim, this our piety;
> And God and Nature say that it is just.
>
> (WPW, III, 130)

Before examining two or three sonnets in illustration, let's recapitulate. The doctrine of nationalism that Wordsworth shared with Coleridge rests on twin keystones: first, a people have the right to plow unmolested the soil their forefathers plowed; and second, as he thankfully found it in Abraham Cowley's essay on liberty, a people are free when they are "governed by laws which they have made for themselves, under whatever form it be of government." (WPW, IV, 153) The doctrine evolved from the Whig version of British liberty, particularly as it came through Wordsworth's favorite poets; it evolved from his own faith in natural affections and his belief in the need to assert that the soil has indwelling Presences, vital and divine; from the theory of liberty through law, thought of in his youth as liberty through contract; from the moral ideal of honorable action by independent men, united to form a state; and last—not to be slighted—from the need to oppose Napoleon on principle. Increasingly, between 1809 and 1814, bleeding and belligerency became additional requirements of public virtue.

In the best of the sonnets on international politics, Wordsworth lends to topical commentary the joys of personal liberty among the forms of nature. Requiring freedom of mind and body for his own happiness, he rightly associated these personal satisfactions with his interest in civil and national liberties.[28] The sonnet to Toussaint

120

Wordsworth

L'Ouverture represents most obviously the Miltonic mode of address to a patriot hero which Coleridge had essayed with some success in the *Morning Chronicle* toward the end of 1794. Coleridge's sonnets, however, had used metaphor for ornament or baroque involution, whereas the sonnet to Toussaint directly promotes its theme by assuring the imprisoned hero that he has left behind

> Powers that will work for thee; air, earth, and skies;
> There's not a breathing of the common wind
> That will forget thee; thou hast great allies;
> Thy friends are exultations, agonies,
> And love, and man's unconquerable mind.
> (WPW, III, 113)

One being interfuses the adroitly designated trinity of Nature—land, circumambient air, and distant stars—with the love, exultations, and agonies of man. Or putting it humanistically, the spirit of Toussaint's noble sacrifice has roused kindred spirits which will be aided in the work for independence by man's natural affection for place and his reverence for the noble living and the noble dead. To interpret rigidly either way, humanistically or organically, would be to shatter the crystalline exactness of the tribute, achieved through the several means of enthusiasm, moral and political principle, exaggeration, and metaphor. The poem avoids arid statement, on one extreme, and on the other the evanescence that often blurs Shelley's treatments of the same theme. In the sonnet on Toussaint, tenor and vehicle fuse. The "common wind" becomes the everyday breath of man, and the exultations become the purgative storms of nature. This sort of prophetic vision was recognized by Ruskin as the highest kind of pathetic fallacy, which he could have called pathetic validity.

Two of the best-known political sonnets, though marked by an overflow of powerful emotions, came from a mind that had had long to think deeply on the events concerned. "On the Extinction of the Venetian Republic" followed by at least five years Bonaparte's desecration of Venetian dreams, but came inevitably to the mind of a poet surveying in 1802 the First Consul's worst desecrations.[29] So absorbed was the poet of nature in the metamorphosis of city into maiden queen, he reserved only one line for her marriage with "the everlasting Sea." Yet the sestet solved his problem honestly: Venice was worth praising only as a memory surviving in an ideal. Even with this yearning look toward the past, it is an oddity of party alignment that Wordsworth, who at no time partook of the Whiggish love of commerce, should have been driven by scorn of Napoleon into praise of the republic of Venice several years after his republicanism had passed—and a few years before a partly favorable appraisal of Napoleon by Leigh Hunt, radical champion of small tradesmen, separated the actuality from the ideal by observing that "the Venetian Government might have been wiser and stronger by throwing open its honours and offices to every deserving citizen."[30] Hunt found it difficult to lament the subjugation of an oligarchy. Much of the strength of Wordsworth's sonnet comes from the subdued but daring figure that conveys the kind of principle that distinguishes a poet from a political theorist: Liberty as an idea has produced at least once, in Venice, what royal families find it hard to get—a live, guileless princess worthy of fairyland. A soberer doctrine, foreshadowing support for the Holy Alliance, sneaks into the opening lines. At the height of Turkish power, Venice "was the safeguard of the west."

More predictably, the famous Two Voices sonnet laments the progressive elimination of Swiss independence between 1798 and October 1802—"Thou from thy Alpine holds at length art driven"—with a possible reference, in the phrase "hast vainly striven," to harassment of French garrisons as late as 1806. Of the two voices, one is of the sea breaking against the cliffs and shores of England; the other is of the torrents rushing through the Swiss Alps: "They were thy chosen music, Liberty!" Liberty was not playing the music, but listening to it. Although both voices continue, Wordsworth has a device, the folded negative, for making unneeded facts retire. The folded negative is not a double negative, but one folded to conceal or minimize its positive assertion. The poet reminds Liberty that her ear is deprived of the "deep bliss" formerly enjoyed in her Alpine holds, "Where not a torrent murmurs heard by thee." Alpine torrents still roar, but what difference does it make? The sestet of the sonnet utters a prayer, "Then cleave, O cleave to that which still is left," vague, because multiple, in the person or persons addressed. Under guise of imploring Liberty, the poet prays to his God to preserve England from the French (recently papist, now godless), and prays simultaneously to his countrymen first to deserve and then to preserve their liberties. The imperative to *deserve* liberty, though not explicit, is effectively present; and this sonnet draws strength from others in the series in which the imperative is both explicit and emphatic. On the other hand, the word *chosen* in "They were thy chosen music, Liberty," unveils the celebration in this sonnet not only of the national independence to which the series is especially devoted, the independence of a national people from a foreign tyrant, but also of liberty under representative government, as enjoyed by the British and the Helvetians alone among independent peoples.[31]

As he continued the series through the years, the political sonneteer watched for peoples and their heroes to celebrate. By 1809, despite his intense emotional involvement in the morals and events of the Peninsular War, he had to search such books as *A View of Spain*, by Alexandre de Laborde, for images to challenge his powers of invention and compression. Yet few of his sonnets or longer poems on European struggles are as dully topical as their explanatory titles in his collected works: "Indignation of a High-Minded Spaniard, 1810," "The Germans on the Heights of Hochheim," "Siege of Vienna Raised by John Sobieski, February, 1816." It is evident from the frequent appearance of a caption like "Composed at the Same Time and on the Same Occasion" that such captions are intended to provide continuous orientation for the reader as he follows the ship of state through Wordsworth's "Poems Dedicated to National Independence and Liberty." The captions often include a date, either month and year or year alone. It would be needlessly matter-of-fact to take such a date as either the time of the action recorded or the date of composition. In origin the dates are sometimes those of publication and sometimes Wordsworth's later error concerning date of composition, but either fact is incidental. He tried to convey in the date a particularly intense emotional reference. To achieve the full sublimity of each sonnet, you are to imagine yourself present at the date he assigns. So we have "London, 1802," when the fen of stagnant Englishmen had need of Milton, and "To the Men of Kent. October, 1803," one of a series so dated to indicate a time of threatened invasion.

Let "February, 1816," the date assigned to the sonnet on Sobieski, serve as a fuller example. John Sobieski (John III of Poland) raised the Turkish siege of Vienna in 1683, and Wordsworth's sonnet adapts one of Vincinzo da Filicaia's contemporaneous odes on the event. Filicaia's call to thanksgiving for Sobieski's victory both through and for God came nicely to hand in the afterglow of the Second Peace of Paris. Wordsworth wished to advocate thanksgiving to God, but he remembered the Convention of Cintra too resolutely to pay direct tribute to Wellington as divine champion. He escaped this small moral dilemma by citing an analogue. In the *Champion* of 4 February 1816 appeared "Three Sonnets by Mr. Wordsworth." The first was offered as an inscription for a monument to the men of Waterloo; a second suggested that the bard who would hail the triumph worthily would have to be as pure as Spenser himself. Third, without title, came the sonnet on Sobieski:

> O, for a kindling touch of that pure flame
> Which taught the offering of song to rise
> From thy lone bower, beneath Italian skies,
> Great Filicaia!—With celestial aim
> It rose,—thy saintly rapture to proclaim,
> Then, when the imperial city stood released
> From bondage, threatened by the embattled East,
> And Christendom respired; from guilt and shame
> Redeemed,—from miserable fear set free
> By one day's feat—one mighty victory.
> —Chaunt the Deliverer's praise in every tongue!
> The cross shall spread,—the crescent hath wax'd dim,
> He conquering,—as in earth and heav'n was sung,—
> HE CONQUERING THROUGH GOD, AND GOD BY HIM!"

Translating for ten lines, Wordsworth avoided calling Wellington a divine deliverer but applied to Waterloo the spirit of Filicaia's lines. Thanking God in "Ode, 1815," for "Thou hast brought our warfare to an end," he reduced Wellington, and himself as bard, to fallible creatures in the divine plan:

124

Wordsworth

> But Man is Thy most awful instrument,
> In working out a pure intent;
> Thou cloth'st the wicked in their dazzling mail,
> And for Thy righteous purpose they prevail . . .
>
> (WPW, III, 155)

(Originally this passage included the notorious line, "Yea, Carnage is thy daughter!") It may be charged that in early 1816 Wordsworth's humilities, both the poetic and the patriotic, were a sham; that the translation from Filicaia is to be taken solely as a device and the whole set of poems as an invitation to the reader to compare Wordsworth's accomplishment with Spenser's. Whatever the depth of personal feeling, the poetic devices of humility and distancing needed only a clarification of structure and a greater buoyancy of diction to make the sonnet on Sobieski as reverently joyous as any critic seeking reverent joy could ask. The poem in its final form incorporates exactly those improvements in structure and diction.

The devices of this sonnet serve as a useful reminder that particularity, immediacy, and self-study were characteristics and interests not only of the romantic poets but also of the readers they addressed. Egoism and the verisimilitude of immediacy, perhaps at times obsessive, are also calculated literary modes of the era.

Although he published very few of the occasional sonnets immediately, Wordsworth's chief impulse initially had been to goad all persons who were in any way capable of flagging in the contest against Napoleon. The goading sonnets, through a mixture of rhetorical passion, topical immediacy, lucid political and psychological propositions, apostrophes to leaders who had fallen in a just cause and to whole peoples in the pulse-quickening news, with bookish appeals to historic analogues, originally glowed with purpose. This mixture makes some of them now rather dusty. Although the analogues could give the original reader a sense of rising above his feverish patriotic engagement into the sanity of literature and learning, even while the sonnet quickened his patriotic passion, to the later reader they give a soporific sense of double remoteness. In short, the "literary" decoration is deader than the topical event it once decorated.

Politics in English Romantic Poetry

More awkward still, some of the sonnets try by allusion to make everything explicit except the situation that drew forth the sonnet, so that the later reader feels himself confronted with multiple puzzles concerning obscure events of the Napoleonic era and equally obscure events of Greco-Roman eras. In so far as these sonnets are typical of Wordsworth's later output, they reveal a decline not at all through decrease of passion but rather through increased use of immediate passion for something other than his art. Excited by the moment, he failed to imagine the ultimate coldness of the literary result. He tested his poems by his own galvanic response, and was consequently more successful, at least during his middle years, when the stimulus of experience was mild enough to drive him to a greater energy of creation.

The pressure of events led him to grade informally the major peoples resisting Napoleon. High-minded Spaniards come first, and occupy the greatest number of poems, with the Portuguese as an uninteresting appendage. The Tyrolese stand as high as their mountains. The Germans, Greeks, and most Italians have clearly lost their ancient force and resolution. Like young Oswald in *The Excursion* (VII.800), the goading sonnets turn from the Germans, "taught a base submission," to a "nobler race, the Switzers."

The Italians, despite Wordsworth's love of their language and literature, had little place in his poetry until his visits to Milan in 1820 and down to Rome and beyond in 1837. The 1805 version of *The Prelude* addressed Coleridge at Sicily, the birthplace of pastoral poetry, as living "among the basest and the lowest fallen / Of all the race of men." The tract on Cintra declared Florence, Venice, Genoa, and Rome asleep but not dead. When the poet found the Italians in 1837 still as torpid as their Lago Morto, "indignation mastered grief." Nonetheless expressing hope for Italy, in the sonnet "At Rome" he uses an ambiguous device that seems to place him among those who have talked with men of the Risorgimento, among those

> who have heard some learned Patriot treat
> Of freedom, with mind grasping the whole theme
> From ancient Rome, downwards through that bright dream
> Of Commonwealths, each city a starlike seat

126

Wordsworth

Of rival glory; they—fallen Italy—
Nor must, nor will, nor can, despair of Thee![32]

A later group of critics and readers is untroubled by factual allusion, within the poem, to Campanella's *Civitas Solio* and Machiavelli's *Discorsi;* indifferent to the preceptorial "mind grasping the whole theme"; and unconcerned to ask how far the actual Wordsworth had hopes for Italy. Such readers can value the poem the more for its embodiment of an imagined, as-if situation. The romantic beliefs in imagination and particularity have here had an odd victory over the latter-day reader who can more easily esteem the poem by believing that the poet needed, as a counterweight among the sonnets, one that spoke *as if* he had talked with a patriot at Rome, *as if* he had regained hope for a *risorgimento,* and *as if* he cared. Yet the available evidence suggests that among Wordsworth's political sonnets the approval of the later reader correlates closely with the degree of the poet's caring. Of Wordsworth the man, who wanted to feel that the Carbonari were still at work, we may sense in the sonnet "At Rome" a nostalgia for his days of hope in Revolutionary France. If we thus imagine a talk with the "learned Patriot" Sismondi in Rome calling up for the old man conversations with the republican Beaupuy in 1792, we do not disturb the function of the learned patriot "Beaupuis" in *The Prelude,* or "the noble Roman," peasant, and "learned Patriot" of the sonnet, as archetypal figures in arranged literary conformations.

At sixty-seven and beyond, Wordsworth needed a conjunction of old and new enthusiasms to give life to new verse. In three sonnets, and in twenty lines of "Musings near Aquapendente," he wrestled with the current view of history as the knowledge of individual facts, which had recently, through B. G. Niebuhr's method of philological criticism, attacked those heroic legends of ancient Rome that Wordsworth—and Byron after him—had learned to love in school and college. Because his "Allusion to Niebuhr, and Other Modern Historians" included both his friend Julius Hare, one of Niebuhr's translators, and his friend and neighbor Thomas Arnold, Wordsworth composed one sonnet as a "Plea for the Historian," but his heart remained with the defense of legend, for

127

Politics in English Romantic Poetry

> in our hearts we know
> How, for exciting youth's heroic flame,
> Assent is power, belief the soul of fact.
>
> (WPW, III, 213)

In quoting Horace's invocation to Clio to choose a subject, he suppressed Horace's word *heroa,* demigod, as the alternative to mere man, in fairness both to the historians and to his desire to believe in the lost heroic poets of Rome. It is partly in his role as upholder of noble legend and bold eulogy that he affirms the power of conversations with Sismondi to make hope for a united and independent Italy a necessity of his being.

V

"Not used to make a present joy the matter of a song," Wordsworth did at least make present soberness and sorrow the matter of several songs to mark changes in his psyche between 1802 and 1806. These changes, which we have seen hinted in the sonnets on liberty and national independence, are no more than hinted in *The Prelude* of 1806. The Peace of 1802 introduced and accompanied so much personal strain—settlement with Annette in order to have a new wife share his home with Dorothy, the anguish of Coleridge, which brought a different torment to each member of the inner circle—so much private strain that we cannot profitably speculate on the degree of conscious revolt against fuller acceptance in 1802 of the war against the governor of France. He recorded in the opening stanzas of the Intimations Ode a profound sense of spiritual loss. In "Resolution and Independence" he reported a vision of such terror, in anticipation of "Solitude, pain of heart, distress, and poverty," which Chatterton and Burns suffered and Coleridge seemed about to suffer, that it brought an agony of shame over his past complacency. In 1802 he discovered " 'twas pastime to be bound" within the scanty plot of the sonnet. In the midst of the poet's distresses, the Earl of Lonsdale died. William Lowther, who succeeded, paid most of the debt owed to the Wordsworths, but not rapidly enough to make the poet realize at once his gratitude to a nobleman for acting "worthily and justly, I will not say nobly

128

and generously."[33] Subsequent generosities bound Wordsworth to the new Lowthers with hoops of iron. Hoops of steel were reserved for Sir George Beaumont, 7th Baronet, painter and patron, and his Lady, who began with a present of land in 1803 and continued with intimate advice on pictures, religion, politics, and society. How could a Cumberland beggar compete with such bounty? Would not even the estatesman Michael, alone amid the heart of many thousand mists, be left to the bounty of heaven?

Month by month the poet submitted to new controls. In 1804, in the "Ode to Duty," he celebrated stoic submission to the stern regulator of conscience: "thee I now would serve more strictly, if I may." Although this supplication for the power of self-sacrifice is a deliberate renunciation of "that serene and blessed mood" in which "the affections gently lead us on," the version of 1804–1807 retains the desire to act still "according to the voice / Of my own wish." Submissiveness must come by choice. In February 1805 the terrible loss of his brother John by shipwreck first turned him from poetry and then deepened his theme of submission. By 1806, according to the finest and most famous of his several tributes to John, the "Elegiac Stanzas Suggested by a Picture of Peele Castle, in a Storm, Painted by Sir George Beaumont," the deep distress had humanized his soul. Loss had stiffened the armor of his personal requirements, but also had proved that adequate fortitude would presuppose "frequent sights of what is to be borne." Called from his dreaming "at distance from the Kind," he would hereafter live among the sufferings—what Malthus and the Bible agreed were the inevitable sufferings—of his fellow men.

This resolve had the effect of turning his verse outward to a more objective channel and thereby turning it backward to the clearer diction of Augustan modes. For an early example, the sonnet to a family friend as hero of liberty, "To Thomas Clarkson, on the Final Passing of the Bill for the Abolition of the Slave Trade. March, 1807," beginning "Clarkson! it was an obstinate hill to climb," includes personifications of Duty and Time along with apocalyptic affirmation—"The blood-stained Writing is for ever torn"; it implies submission to duty and conscience in the tributes to Clarkson who "heard the constant Voice its charge repeat"; and it reveals the poet's perseverance in the conviction that *severe* suffering is not inevitable. In another example where an unimaginative mode is adapted to the increased sense of responsibility to man, an expository sonnet declaring a pause to the series on national independence and liberty, he claims as merit that the worst reversal of the war, "the worst moment of these evil days," has not made him shrink from hope:

> From hope, the paramount *duty* that Heaven lays,
> For its own honour, on man's suffering heart.
>
> (WPW, III, 140)

The joyous evangel of *The Prelude,* that man can live with his darkest mysteries, has now become the considered warning ornamented with hope.

Although defense of affection against the false psychology of Jacobinism was no more than the root of the ongrowing change, the full fruit of change was not a "Lost Leader." Contraction was accelerated by what Wordsworth could only regard as the perverse folly of the Foxite Whigs in continuing to oppose the war after threats of invasion in 1803. Memory of the United Irishmen and their attempts to aid Bonaparte, perhaps as much as his belief in Anglo-Saxon liberty versus Papal dominion, made him oppose those who would enfranchise Catholics in England and make *theirs* the established church of Ireland. Almost at once he had carried his nightmares from the Terror into fear of revolution in England. When he asked, "Have I not reason to lament / What man has made of man," in 1798, we probably should read *despots* and *sansculottes*—he laments that bloody tyrants have made bloody revolutionaries. He dreaded a similar process in England. He despised demagogues and feared all whom demagogues could influence. In 1815 he scorned in private the "vile Tyrants" into whose hands the Holy Alliance had surrendered the Italians, but he still feared violent revolt.[34]

Some elements of his change in political views were more positive. He had always honored simplicity of being and revered attachments to the soil. He had found relief in accepting certain prescribed limits within the illimitable possibilities of literary creativity. We have seen him erect stoic barriers to reduce the emotional devastations of calamity. Once a wanderer, he now had a growing family to provide for, and no longer a brother John to return laden from India. In John's stead, God sent Beaumont and the Lowthers. If the poor are to get relief, there must be those stable enough to provide it, and who better than baronets and earls? Wordsworth's brother Christopher (a clerical pluralist, cofounder in 1811 of the National Society for the Education of the Poor in Accordance with the Principles of the Established Church, by 1817 chaplain of the House of Commons, from 1820 master of Trinity College, Cambridge), nephews, and eventually the poet's own son John were clergymen, mutually involved in religious stability. With the years, reverence for the soil became respect for property owners. In his final sonnets, "Liberty" means security of property. To Byron and Hunt, humanity died in Wordsworth in 1813 when he solicited Lord Lonsdale's aid in securing a lucrative post and accepted the Distributorship of Stamps for Westmorland and part of Cumberland, with later extensions at his own importunity. The post was not a sinecure, but it helped him sympathize further with pluralists who employed vicars.

Besides his more objective attention to the public good, the hardening of Wordsworth's style had an external shove. His finest collection, the *Poems* of 1807 in two volumes, was met by reviewers with collective abuse. Although thereafter he was defensively insistent on the high value of his work—sometimes obnoxiously so—he nevertheless veered, both to incorporate the suggestions of friends and to avoid many of the objections of foes.

VI

Retreat is evident in the later books of *The Excursion,* which was published in 1814. *The Prelude* can be interpreted as prescribing a cure for others as it traces the cure of a poet, not only from erroneous political theory but also from political action. *The White Doe of Rylstone,* written in 1807 and 1808, would seem to take the argument one step further. Tracing the ill-fortune of a Catholic family that rebelled against Queen Elizabeth, it offers as worthy of pursuit only those aims that transcend the vanities of this world.

The idealism of this symbolic narrative comes no nearer to political preachment than in its clear advocacy of the Church of England. In succession, *The Prelude* and the *White Doe* throw the reader upon himself and upon his God. *The Excursion* is much more overtly concerned with society. Not that Wordsworth commends "the strife of phrase" in Parliament. He claims no yearning and little respect for "the distempered flood of public life" (VI.435).

The poem does, however, employ the diction of political theorists. Only in his apology for the French Revolution in the unsent letter to the Bishop of Llandaff had Wordsworth thrown about the language of the *philosophes,* as when the letter pursued an argument like Condorcet's and Godwin's against Rousseau's definition of the General Will: "If there is a single man in Great Britain who has no suffrage in the election of a representative, the will of the society of which he is a member is not generally expressed; he is a Helot in that society."[35] *The Excursion* turns back to the more conservative language of the Enlightenment in England and Scotland.

The published work begins with a further revision of the tale of Margaret, "The Ruined Cottage," begun about 1795 and ready as "The Pedlar" since 1802. Although other early tales and passages are incorporated further on, eight of the nine books were mostly the work of 1806, 1810, and 1811–1813. The poet addresses the reader in the acceptable neoclassic form of a series of dialogues, weighted toward particularity with exempla and extended narratives. Speaking through the Wanderer (or Sage, elevated from the Pedlar), the Poet, the bitterly disillusioned Solitary, and the humanely institutional Parson, he disclaims the power of "framing models to improve the scheme / Of Man's existence, and recast the world," but offers instead "clear thoughts, lively images, and strong feelings" in the modest cause of correcting despondency (WPW, V, 2, 85). In the framing of adequate models, political philosophy has been little better than poetry; it has been an absolute quack in its attempts to cure the despair for which it is largely responsible. Since the tearful vale of earth is the only paradise we can ever with certainty know, we may as well enjoy every aspect it shares with the poets' and painters' most ethereal dreams of Elysium. Much of the Solitary's stubborn dejection has resulted from the excess of his expectation that Europe would leap from the Bastille to a Utopia of universal justice and equality. Earth is sick, says the Poet, and heaven weary, of the "hollow words" practiced by states and kingdoms in appeals to truth and justice (*Excur.* V.369–381).

In later poems, the "Vernal Ode" of 1817 and "On the Power of Sound," 1828, Wordsworth will envision, as vision, a Golden Age of transcendental harmony, but in 1814 he has no Utopia to offer or promise. Somewhat unconsciously he suggests one, as we shall see, in the vast and heart-lifting possibilities of colonization. His illusions had never included the Noble Savage or the gentle jungle. The young man who betrayed the titular heroine of "Ruth" had traded vices with American Indians. With a mixture of amusement and awe at human credulity, Wordsworth assigns to the Solitary the experience of expecting an exaltation of spirit, as predicted in *The Hurricane* by William Gilbert, upon beholding the vast savannahs of America, an exaltation to be shared with "Primeval Nature's Child." Instead, the Solitary found the natives superstitious, lawless, remorseless, "squalid, vengeful, and impure" (*Excur.* III.953). The Pastor, in his closing prayer, asks God to take away the "sting of human nature" (IX.639). Wordsworth had always felt that sting. His poetry emphasizes it more and more as pain comes, not from crisis, but from inflictions and sorrows in a generally fortunate life.

From Book II to the end, the debate goes forward for the benefit of the Solitary, sometimes called the Recluse, who sulks in that part of the poet's mind unconvinced by the solution of *The Prelude,* which was emotionally exalted but philosophically eclectic and tentative. Wordsworth told Isabella Fenwick that the Solitary was based on a disillusioned Scotsman who came to Grasmere, with reminiscences also of English Jacobins he had known, particularly the dissenting minister Joseph Fawcett, who "had not strength of character to withstand the effects of the French Revolution, and of the wild and lax opinions which had done so much towards producing it, and far more in carrying it forward in its extremes" (WPW, V, 375). Wordsworth referred to Fawcett's later "habits of intemperance" as if drunkenness were an inevitable result of mistaken faith in the Revolution. The Solitary, despite the acidity of his skeptical responses to all hope held out by the Wanderer for this world and the Pastor for the next, has a clear urge to evade hard problems. The Jacobinical John Thelwall, who probably contributed as much as "poor Fawcett" to Wordsworth's portrait of the Solitary, had lapsed after the storms of 1793–1797 into a lecturer on elocution. Wordsworth, too, had evaded political confrontations, first in France, then in his failure to publish the letter to the Bishop of Llandaff, and later in the establishment of his character as the Recluse who would attempt a great objective poem. For the benefit of the solitary skeptic and evader, the Pastor confirms the Wanderer's recommendation of stoic submission to duty. Specifically, the rural spokesman for the Church prescribes patriotism, daily chores, and acceptance of mutability. Love of country is a strand in the cable of love that binds man to his fellows.

Each creature must accept its ordained place in the great chain of being, says the Wanderer, as Pope had said in *An Essay on Man* and as Wordsworth says in his own voice in the "Home at Grasmere" portion of *The Recluse*.[36] "The vast Frame / Of social nature changes evermore," with "an ascent and progress in the main," but the vital universe is linked together neither appreciably by evolution from low to high nor demonstrably in a band of love suspended from God—and ascent within the frame of society is meagerly proportioned to the "expectations of self-flattering minds" (VII.999–1007). Our best means and our best end are the same, love of child for parent, man for wife, neighbor for neighbor, love until all lie side by side in the calm of the parish churchyard. Love in *The Excursion,* whether proclaimed doctrinally by the Pastor or feelingly by the Wanderer, lacks the desperate energy it would achieve a century later, when the disintegration of religious faith and Christian humanism had continued as Wordsworth feared it would. But he wishes urgently to call love to the attention of the successors of Fox in Parliament.

The equivalence of love, freedom, and life brings the necessity of lectures by the Wanderer against utilitarians and cold analysts in Book IV, against unfeeling industrial capitalists in VIII, and against socially blind legislators in IX. It turns out after all that "the strife of phrase" was not occupationally wrong, but wrong because Lords and Commons should engage in strife of idea, not of phrase, and should accomplish positive legislation that would please the poet by easing the twisted frame of society.

It is established in Book VIII that the owners and managers of factories and cultivated land ought not to grind down children, either for personal gain or for the misconceived "economic laws" of nations. An inventive age ought not to be industrious to destroy. To labor is good, but to have men, mothers, maidens, youths, boys, and girls enter "a many-windowed fabric huge," as their forebears entered cathedrals; to feed the never-resting eater of labor—this is to construct an obscene parody of the curse on Adam. In factory, in hovel, or darting onto the roads to beg, and (interjects the pale Solitary) in the field with hoe or scythe, boys throughout the land subsist in a prison of inward chains, some with a dim, some with a ruddy stare, but all "sluggish, blank, and ignorant." Born to the country's "equal rights," tens upon tens of thousands of boys are strangers to the joys of intellect and strangers to love. Never in this warped frame of society can they rise to love.

Often, as in "The Old Cumberland Beggar" and "Resolution and Independence," Wordsworth had difficulty avoiding the appearance of honoring the poor for their utility to him. *The Excursion* should exonerate his character, if not every passage of his poems, from that imputation. Book VIII displays an objective concern for the individual and for the whole society. Sensitive to charges of bias in favor of rural life and the landed orders, Wordsworth made his Sage explain, after the discussion had passed to another subject, why he had left it to the Solitary to mention the plowboy among the oppressed. He had done so, said the Sage, because in all countries plowboys are oppressed and in Britain "none are proud of it," whereas the oppression of children in factories was new, was systematically promoted, and was boasted of even by mothers.

Returning a third time to the theme of the great chain, at the beginning of the final book, the Wanderer emphasizes "An *active* Principle" that circulates as freedom through "every Form of being." As freedom, it has its "most apparent home" in the human mind.

Politics in English Romantic Poetry

Therefore the child who has no hope, who cannot meditate action, who has no springboard of love, is deprived of all moral freedom to choose, to imagine, and to anticipate.

> Our life is turned
> Out of her course, wherever man is made
> An offering, or a sacrifice, a tool
> Or implement, a passive thing employed
> As a brute mean, without acknowledgment
> Of common right or interest in the end;
> Used or abused, as selfishness may prompt.
>
> (IX.113–119)

In sum, a long way from Burke, he equates the condition of the poor in Britain with tyrannic oppression.

The Sage, before advancing to a triumphant solution of the riddle, pauses to remove the Malthusian objection that no solution can outstrip the pressure of numbers in a mounting population. If once the discipline of virtue takes root in Britain, then the swarms of tomorrow can be dispatched across the seas as successive communities of virtuous colonists. Thus virtue and freedom will be implanted throughout the world. But emigration is secondary.

The simple solution to present disgrace and the key to future hope is compulsory education for all. The realm has manifestly before it this opportunity and this obligation. "British Lawgivers"—the Sage kindles as he speaks—"Ah! sleep not there in shame!" No national emergency, such as this long war, can have priority over these "sacred claims." *The Excursion* not only anticipated by nearly fifty years the national education act of 1870, but exceeded its limiting details.

The machine that made the Wanderer's plan credible to Wordsworth was the monitorial system, by which older children were taught simple lessons which they then attempted to teach verbatim to the younger children. If it seems grotesquely paradoxical today that Wordsworth, Coleridge, and Southey, along with most educators of their time and place, should have thought of this steam-intellect system as a way of defeating the mechanization of the human spirit, it is equally painful to acknowledge that the tens on tens of thousands counted by the Wanderer and the Solitary had been so far debased that the monitorial system could seem to make souls blossom within them. The Lake poets were so concerned that the content of education by the state be moral rather than utilitarian that they plumped for the only method that seemed economically feasible. Only a system economically feasible would be politically feasible. In consequence, paradoxically, they supported a utilitarian system.

Excited by hope, Wordsworth presupposed spiritual growth from Christian gospel and moral precept. *Practical Education,* first published in discipleship to Rousseau by Richard Edgeworth and his daughter Maria in 1798, could have provided better doctrine many years before the poet visited Edgeworthstown in 1829. By vision, however, rather than from direct influence, he shared the concern of the chief educational reformer of the day, Pestalozzi, that education be a communal self-development. In this emphasis on social health along with individual growth, he went beyond the methods of attention to individuals, adapted to the more affluent classes, of Rousseau and the Edgeworths.

It took half a century to pass a bill for national education because adherents of the Church wanted instruction to be Anglican and others wanted it to be secular, moral, or vaguely theistic. The monitorial system itself suffered a tug of war between the "Madras" version of Andrew Bell, the friend of Southey and the Church, and the more flexible version of Joseph Lancaster, a Quaker supported by the Dissenters.[37] The National Society of Wordsworth's brother Christopher may be regarded as an anti-Lancastrian enterprise. In this conflict, the poet would have chosen religious education without Anglican specifications only if he could have seen a clear alternative between non-Anglican education and no improvement at all in schooling for the poor. Yet he was at least as dedicated to democratic education as the Revolutionists in France. Universal compulsory state education, although it had belonged to the rhetoric of Jacobin orators and journalists (and had perhaps been commended to Wordsworth by Beaupuy), had been ignored in France as a matter for practical action.

Despite his grasping at the monitorial device, Wordsworth had considered in his plan, or let us call it his aim, the needs of both the social body and the individual, "active," living soul. He did

Politics in English Romantic Poetry

not share the axiom of Robert Owen that transformation of character could be assured by melioration of the environment. His choice
of education as the base of social welfare was indeed a deliberate
alternative to transformation of the environment, as it was to such
cures for physical undernourishment as Dr. Thomas Beddoes, on
the periphery of the Bristol circle of poets, had suggested in 1796
in a public letter to Pitt "on the Means of Relieving the Present
Scarcity and Preventing the Diseases that Arise from Meagre Food."
Pitt, Beddoes declared, should ask the sages of the nation to provide
substitutes for traditional foods, reduce the amount of foodstuff going
into alcoholic beverages, and introduce foods that could be eaten
by animals until the next famine required people to eat both the
animals and the new foods. However practical and clever, attention
to the alimentary tract was not what Wordsworth regarded as the
proper business of a sage.

Against science as expedience, *The Excursion* speaks out in several
places. In a passage from "The Pedlar" moved to Book IV, the
Wanderer derides the possibility that earth, sky, or man exists in
mysterious vitality "Only to be examined, pondered, searched,/
Probed, vexed, and criticised." In a passage written much later,
the Wanderer exults over physical progress, the strengthening of
man by "dominion over nature," but the Poet objects because he
finds in physical progress little solace for the sad decline in manners,
morals, and love. The Wanderer concedes this round:

> Oh, banish far such wisdom as condemns
> A native Briton to these inward chains,
> Fixed in his soul, so early and so deep;
> Without his own consent, or knowledge, fixed!
> (VIII.296–300)

The significance of all this, for Wordsworth's politics generally,
lay in his insistence that the state, responsible for the welfare of
all whose allegiance it claimed, had a moral obligation to make
life humane for the poor and the unfortunate. In 1816 a Select
Committee on education of the poor reported on the inadequacy
of the current system, or lack of system. More generally, *The Excur-*

sion foreshadowed the legislation of the 1820's to diminish disabilities and to improve welfare. Connections between universal education, a cheap press, public opinion, and the will of the people were obvious enough to many politicians and propagandists, both Tory and Radical.

Later on, Wordsworth would restrict the "sacred claims" to those known in the Victorian period as the deserving poor—ruffians and thieves could hang—but he continued to ask for legislation more humane than the Poor Law of 1834. To speak of Tory humanitarianism is inadequate. It is not to a principle of *noblesse oblige* that Wordsworth appeals, but to the natural right of love, granted by the breathing laws of the universe.

The poet opens Book VI of *The Excursion* in his own voice (as distinct from "the Poet" in the colloquies that make up the body of the poem) by hailing the State and Church of England as bastions of freedom and truth. This belief in the sacred ends of the war against Napoleon does not efface the tempered patriotism of a Hebraic prophecy by the Wanderer in Book IV. Partly the greedy bickering of Russia, Prussia, and Austria, with frequent treaties of defeat and concession to Bonaparte; partly Burke's pleas against overweening expectancy of "a fight celestial," but partly also the Convention of Cintra and lesser betrayals by Britain herself (as at Copenhagen) inform the Sage's warning:

> at this day,
> When a Tartarean darkness overspreads
> The groaning nations; when the impious rule,
> By will or by established ordinance,
> Their own dire agents, and constrain the good
> To acts which they abhor; though I bewail
> This triumph, yet the pity of my heart
> Prevents me not from owning, that the law,
> By which mankind now suffers, is most just.
> For by superior energies; more strict
> Affiance in each other; faith more firm
> In their unhallowed principles; the bad
> Have fairly earned a victory o'er the weak,
> The vacillating, inconsistent good.   (IV.296–309)

He ends by quoting from Samuel Daniel an assurance that the wise man rises as an individual above the storms of power, what Wordsworth in a note calls "an admirable picture of the state of a wise Man's mind in a time of public commotion."

VII

Beneath the sweetness and light, the compassion and elegy, in a landscape of sociable vales, Wordsworth must have suppressed grimmer feelings. In two victory odes (later divided into three) of 1816, when "public commotion" swirled around the internal hardships of Britain, he revealed an aggressiveness, with a declaration in prose that freedom required "martial propensities, and an assiduous cultivation of military virtues,"[38] which shocked liberals into permanent distrust of his motives. He proposed a timely tribute to military heroism from—as he puts it in an accompanying sonnet— "The Bard—whose soul is meek as dawning day." The tribute will come from one who can fitly praise, as antithetical to himself, the happy warrior. In the apologetic metaphor that begins "Ode 1815," Imagination, "ne'er before content" except in restless ascension, "stooped to the Victory" at Waterloo, and "with the embrace was satisfied." One only God brings earthquakes, volcanoes, and carnage. God in just anger, with man as his "awful instrument," sinks the navies of those who are evil as the Corsican was evil. France, too, must rejoice.

To the dozens of powerful lines and phrases, and the effort of shaping them, Wordsworth referred when he told Crabb Robinson that the odes were "poured out with much feeling" but had cost excessive health and strength "from mismanagement of myself."[39] But the odes were themselves mismanaged. They parallel, in allegorical trappings and static positioning, the monuments to military glory that crowd the aisles of Westminster Abbey. One of them recommends just such monuments, but in "civic halls," along with "imperishable Columns" of the kind to be caricatured on the covers of Thackeray's *Vanity Fair,* where the honored hero of the wars against Napoleon has his feet where one might expect the head. One ode, presumably the earliest, later titled "Ode 1814" to put it first in the sequence, makes a heavy commodity of dream-vision. If Milton had left to his greatest disciple a model for such odes, perhaps these victory odes would seem to be innovations in the Pindaric tradition rather than what they in fact seem—forced replicas of Abraham Cowley's plaster imitations of Pindar. In stanza X of "Ode: The Morning of the Day Appointed for a General Thanksgiving" the disciple himself describes the appropriate tones of the organ in language equally appropriate and revealing: "While the tubed engine feels the inspiring blast." He attempts, successfully, to be pre-Wordsworthian.

These baroque odes are the conservative counterpart to Shelley's "Ode to Liberty," in its rococo character as a "progress piece." It is of course not the conservative manner of these odes but the matter ("Almighty God! . . . Yea, Carnage is thy daughter!") that led to Shelley's parody in *Peter Bell the Third*. But Wordsworth had enabled Shelley to turn from parody of "language really used by men" to parody of archaic elevation. If he gave these odes their baroque character partly for archaism and Pindaric stateliness, he did so in part also, I think, to give aesthetic distance to matter much more conventional than twentieth-century readers of *Peter Bell the Third* might assume. Jane Cave Winscom, for example, whose poems Wordsworth would have encountered in Bristol, wrote an occasional piece "On the First General Fast, after the Commencement of the American War," wherein the poet hears the voice of Jehovah:

> Be still before your GOD, and know 'tis I!
> 'Tis I make peace, and I create stern war,
> And ride to battle in my flaming car;
> I guide the bullet, point the glitt'ring sword . . .[40]

Wordsworth tried to lift these sentiments to a literary sublime. That the baroque manner resulted also from his decision to act objectively in a public capacity, whatever the degree of personal conviction or emotional release, is demonstrated by such ceremonial elements as the proposal, in "Ode 1815," of a temple of victory that might well "beseem that mighty Town" of London. Well might Wordsworth feel, when he accepted the Laureateship upon Southey's death

141

in 1843, that this poetic service to officialdom was already behind him. He had built public monuments.

Mrs. Moorman trenchantly describes the situation in 1816: "Politically, Wordsworth had now come to a point of no return."[41] Still another "Ode" in the booklet of 1816 begins with a question concerning the dawn of the French Revolution, but evokes also a vision of Napoleon by asking in the present tense, "Who rises on the banks of Seine?" The poet employs the present partly to trace with a more dramatic immediacy than Coleridge's "France: An Ode" the stages of hope and fear. In addition, he revives old questions in the present tense to suggest that the spirit of opposition to monarchy, which at first seemed the fairest of inspiring spirits, has since threatened the principalities of Europe as a creature of wrath armed with "the live scales of a portentous nature," and now once again assumes a posture of promise to a few "Weak Spirits" (WPW, III, 123–125). The ambiguity of the phrase "portentous nature" may be intentional: not merely "a forboding look," but ominous by its very nature, an inner principle now revealed. Henceforth the bard will not hide like an ostrich from (line 48) "The lion's sinews, or the eagle's wing."

In this year or the next, he tried to exorcise the passion of revised commitment by drifting backward in time to a perennial favorite, North's translation of Plutarch, for an exemplar of political dilemma. He had defined the ideal leader, in a sort of ideal stasis, in "Character of the Happy Warrior." His "Dion" now submits just such a leader to the challenge of severe temptation. Dion returns in popular triumph to Syracuse and kills his usurping nephew. He has thereby "stained the robes of civil power with blood, / Unjustly shed, though for the public good." He faces, in consequence, first the eternal Sweeper in the visions of his own conscience, and then, in his own turn, retributive assassination. Wordsworth's Dion is too noble by far to represent Bonaparte.[42] It is conceivable that he is a surrogate for the poet, reviving the pattern of *The Borderers,* but the poem effectively reexamines the combination of Horatio Nelson, Beaupuy, John and William Wordsworth, and the extrapolated persona of the poet-patriot to be found in the Happy Warrior, with perhaps also a concealed reappraisal of Wellington. In any event, "Dion" achieves an open dignity probably sought in the victory odes, a dignity to be achieved again in Tennyson's formal and public "Ode on the Death of the Duke of Wellington."

Despite the cool dignity of "Dion," Wordsworth did not successfully exorcise the passions of commitment. His famous quietism, more influential than the stoicism and then the reliance on grace that followed, came out of crisis. If his final message is quietistic, it was a message for others, not for himself. Temptation followed on the heels of "Dion." Henry Brougham, who had fallen out with the Radicals and their "rabble" after losing a Westminster election, decided in 1818 to contest one of the seats immemorially held by members of the Lowther family. Conceding that their interest entitled the Lowthers to one vote, he thought it unfitting that Lord Lonsdale should simplify control of the Westmorland vote by sending to Parliament only members of a family that happened to be his own. As a civil servant, Wordsworth could not work openly against Brougham, but he did in secret everything that a suddenly tireless energy could enable one man to do. In verse he produced nothing more reckless than thirty-odd lines beginning "The Scottish Broom on Birdnest brae" (Birdnest being the local jocularity for the manor purchased by Brougham for his nefarious purposes), but he was known to most, including Brougham, as the author of *Two Addresses to the Freeholders of Westmorland,* in which Lonsdale is praised as "a tried enemy to dangerous innovations." For the first time outside London a candidate was making a direct and personal canvass.[43] To Wordsworth, and to Dorothy, electioneering that was overheard by men, women, and youths who had no vote was a violation of good order and a short cut to insurrection. For use against such a public pest as Brougham, ordinary methods of political journalism seemed fair enough.

Brougham was defeated at the Appleby poll. Elsewhere, the "long Parliamentary career of Colonel James Lowther terminated, but still the local constituencies sent four of the name to Westminster, and with them went also, as local members, two of their relations by marriage and their professional adviser."[44] In preparation for Brougham's second attempt in 1820, Wordsworth followed up his many previous steps, such as promoting De Quincey to the editorship of the new and committed *Westmorland Gazette,* by engineering the purchase of land for division into freeholds. This was not to purchase votes, but to create votes by purchase. That Brougham laid before an indifferent Parliament a scheme of primary education had no influence on Wordsworth's sense of duty to Lonsdale and to the public in 1820. The poet's conviction that Brougham was of good character in private acted as no brake on his renewed activity when Brougham made a third attempt to gain the seat—or to gain attention—in 1826.[45] Apparently "Dion" was not only more stoic in its teaching than Wordsworth could be in a political situation, but also so elevated and abstract that Wordsworth could allow its final warning to swing unnoticed above his head:

> Him, only him, the shield of Jove defends,
> Whose means are fair and spotless as his ends.

The efforts against Brougham were not so much political activity as the suppression of political activity in others.

In 1820 Wordsworth had published stanzas entitled "Hint from the Mountains, for Certain Political Aspirants" (WPW, II, 151). His editors have assigned the poem to 1817, because that was the date Wordsworth later mentioned to Miss Fenwick; but the stanzas can hardly be earlier than 1818, for they concern a "TUFT OF FERN," a "dull helpless thing," as dry and "withered, light and yellow" as Scottish broom, mistaken by a stranger for a hawk soaring "on undaunted wing." In the *Poetical Works* of 1827, after Brougham's third attempt in the previous year, Wordsworth changed the word "Aspirants" to "Pretenders."

Wordsworth had much good poetry left to write, some of it excellent, but the excellent and the political did not coincide. The earlier, invaluable uncertainties and hesitations disappear. He had many persuasive reasons for opposing the Reform Bill, but he used his verse to argue and he lost persuasiveness by denying honest motive to his opponents. Manufacturers and tradesmen did not take a moral view toward society. Seeing good in "the influence of individual Peers over a certain portion of the House of Commons"—seeing good, that is, in the existence of pocket boroughs, which he discreetly called nomination boroughs—he thought that the bill to eliminate this influence was bringing "unbridled Democracy" and therefore "the worst of all Tyrannies."[46]

The greatest change of outlook reflected in Wordsworth's later poetry is a movement toward order. From an existentialist assertion of selfhood, with antennae searching all the magnetic darkness outside the self, he moved toward an endorsement of order and coherence. "To the Lady Fleming, on Seeing the Foundation Preparing for the Erection of Rydal Chapel, Westmorland," 1823, not only laments the possibility that some Englishman might delight in "trivial pomp and city noise," but also finds in this possibility an excuse for lamenting the decline in comfortable social coherence:

> Alas! that such perverted zeal
> Should spread on Britain's favoured ground!
> That public order, private weal,
> Should e'er have felt or feared a wound
> From champions of the desperate law
> Which from their own blind hearts they draw . . .
> (WPW, IV, 167:71–76)

He speaks, by more than inference, of those who would reduce the social, economic, and legislative power of the Church of England. If the country is to be saved, it must be through the bolstering of religion, morals, and conscience. Between 1831 and 1845 he produced a sequel to his sonnets on liberty and independence; these short blasts against "social havoc" he carefully detached as "Sonnets Dedicated to Liberty and Order." The cloud, once his most glorious emblem of personal freedom, becomes an emblem of fickle changes. In "Tynwald Hill" a cloud over old Snafell becomes an emblem of mortal change in the state, an irritation which the mountain must brush away. A cadence set by rapidly returning rhymes fittingly rocks back and forth in verses of the same year, 1833, on the birth of a grandchild, "Like a shipwreck'd Sailor tost," and a similar cadence introduces and fittingly drives forward in "The Warning: a Sequel to the Foregoing," which castigates the wayward multitude and their leaders for making England such a wretched sea to be tossed on.

These changes from a young man's unrestraint are not heinous; except in their steady progression year after year, they are not surprising. He could continue to give glancing tribute to republicans of the past like Algernon Sydney. As late as 1838 he could make a slight variation in a line borrowed from Spenser, "All change is perilous and all chance unsound," in order to permit some change where Spenser had allowed none: "Perilous is sweeping change, all chance unsound."[47] Nor is he quite ready to declare all change "sweeping change."

Until almost the end, he maintained his vision of the sacred river of "Liberty and Power." Both freedom and power are potential in the source, but accumulate as the river flows through the infinitesimally eroding hills (*The River Duddon*), through the philosophic and institutional deposits of the human past (*The Ecclesiastical Sketches*), and through the days of the individual (bound, as is the individual in *The Prelude,* to the noble living and the noble dead). In all of these, until Wordsworth was past three score, the flow of the river represents freedom of development according to inherent laws that vary with the individual as preciously as with the type, from Mount Pelion to the meanest flower.

More surprising than his movement toward order is his continuance until at least 1835 as a poet of the underdog. One of his very late calls to be up and doing, the sonnet "Highland Hut," exhorts the reader to "love, as Nature loves, the lonely Poor." Not humanitarian in the sense of exercising a social consciousness that wishes to reform the poor out of their condition, this sonnet expresses a brotherly affection for the downtrodden as they are. According to the elderly Wordsworth's view, the philosophical radical is certain that his own enlightened state is superior to the state of the lowly; finding it convenient to conclude that the poor we shall always have with us, the later Wordsworth remains more humble than the reformer. He believes himself, because of the inclusiveness of his respect, more democratic than the reformer who would have people changed along with their condition. Against the Poor Law of 1834, his Postscript asserted the principle that "*all* persons who cannot find employment, or procure wages sufficient to support the body in health and strength, are entitled to a maintenance by law." As

Wordsworth

for those who had found employment in factories, the Postscript recommended a law to encourage joint-stock companies, partly for such prudential reasons as the containment of "unjust combinations" (trade unions), but partly that workers might, as an end in itself, realize capital gains from their work.

What he really wished was that the upper classes had given educational and economic concessions to the lower "orders" gradually, in the past. Under the impression that he was looking ahead to tomorrow, the older Wordsworth took a very mature, reasoned, and humane view of yesterday. Yet those who would judge his powers as a prophet must answer an unsimple question: Are the overwhelming majority of British citizens better off today, under the tyranny of their own ignorance, than under the refined rule of the King and unreformed Parliament? The privileged few certainly suffer discomfort under this tyranny, and we can be sure that Blake, Coleridge, and Wordsworth would regard the spiritual deprivations of the masses today as more than counterbalancing the great reductions in toothache, backache, exhaustion, and cholera. Although the present writer believes that both the masses and the society as a whole are better off for the changes that Wordsworth opposed, even with the impressive military improvements, our hindsight cannot include the road not taken. The aged poet became hysterical when he saw the nation taking a road of expediency that romanticism had made him abandon long ago.

In defense of God's established institutions, he hardened his responses and wrote what David Perkins has generously called "a poetry of wit."[48] "Hourly the democratic torrent swells": he no longer trusted torrents. Benjamin Disraeli joined the paternal feudalism of "Young England": Wordsworth exploded for the honor of "dear Old England" (WPW, IV, 134). Without our permission, the poet grew old.

V

BYRON

If Coleridge illustrates the dilemma in thought and Wordsworth tests it through feeling, Byron confronts it in action.

From adolescence on, Byron read history. He read steadily of republican virtues that were practiced by few of his friends, either those seeking pleasure or those supplying it. By 1807, at Cambridge, he had joined a Whig Club that upheld the two principles of Fox: *liberty,* meaning freedom for yourself and others and therefore toleration at home and abroad, even at the price of occasional discomfort; and *peace,* even at considerable cost to ministers and monarchy. Understanding no commitment to any particular leaders of the party, Byron was subscribing to Locke rather than to Church and King. At every period, he was more nearly a moral historian than a Whig. The negative, ambiguous, and conflicting goals of the Opposition encouraged individualists like Byron much as it encouraged factionists, freebooters, and runaways like Whitbread, Brougham, and Burdett. Inevitably, Byron was to waver politically from personal affronts. In 1808 the *Edinburgh Review* drove him upward from the intellectual middle class of the party when it "cut to atoms" his *Hours of Idleness.* Perhaps he thought that his lines in defense of Fox against an "illiberal impromptu" in the *Morning Post,* shortly after Fox's death in 1806, had clearly proclaimed his loyalties; if so, he forgot that his lines so carefully balanced praise of Fox with

148

praise of Pitt as to appear nonpartisan. In 1812, when his politics and his talents were better known, Lord Holland made him comfortable among the "Moderate Whigs." Among other disconcerting activities of the Utilitarians and independents, Brougham and Sir Samuel Romilly served as legal advisers against Byron in the matter of the separation from his wife in 1816. Byron exulted at Romilly's suicide and would have done as much for Brougham. Yet he suffered fits of depression whenever his own independent course exposed an apparent incapacity for disciplined service with a junta united in a good cause.

The theme of loyalty continues a subterranean existence throughout his poetry. His earliest volume, in its various transmutations, includes an invocation to Jove, adapted from the *Prometheus Bound* of Aeschylus, quite unlike his later uses of Prometheus:

> Ne'er may my soul thy power disown,
> Thy dread behests ne'er disobey.[1]

Despite the erroneous forecast of these lines, the juvenilia anticipate, to a degree almost dismaying, Byron's later themes, moods, and methods. Here at once are freedom, noble exploits, leadership and fame, fate and death, contempt for demagogues and the demos, angry opposition to tyranny, reproof of commercial gain and luxury, disdain for unreason and dullness, discovery of cant, self-deflation, mountains and ocean, melancholy, tears, *Weltschmerz* ("I rest a perfect Timon, not nineteen"),[2] erotic fervor, eternal friendship, sudden passion, flippancy, misogyny, defiance, bile, hauteur ("I blast not the fiends who have hurl'd me from bliss"), bravura, domination (as assertion, episode, and metaphor), wit, Giffordian antithesis, anapests, double rhymes, anticlimax, and shameless commonplace. The themes are largely classical, pre-Ptolemaic; the moods are largely post-Rousseauistic, those of Goethe's Werther or Schiller's Karl Moor. There are several anticipations of Manfred's regard for "superior science." The emphasis on loyalty, in such forms as "submission to my God," may be allowed to stand for conventions Byron soon set aside.

He would never outgrow, he could not even set aside, a dilemma perceptible in his first volume: craving fame, he hedged lest near-success as a poet qualify great success as a statesman. He saw three main roads to glory: war, statesmanship, and poetry. From Plutarch and other school texts he had learned to honor the Grecian "clime that nursed the sons of song and war." As early as 1807 he noted in his verses several ways to celebrity: military action, Parliament, preferment, companionship with princes, popular verse, transcendent poetry. In time, he would make Marino Faliero distinguish (unless they are synonyms) "Glory, and Wealth, and Power, and Fame, and Name." Although Byron could never refuse celebrity, he was ambitious to win by statesmanship or poetry the ultimate fame that augments the strength and thus the fame of the nation. He was calling on himself, as well as on his fellow Whiggish bards Campbell and Rogers, to "Assert thy country's honour and thine own." The poetry required was moral; often but not necessarily by castigating vices, it promoted public virtue and thereby strengthened national freedom. Byron wished to try for this true fame, but he preferred to conceal or deny the trial as long as any could say he had failed. Not only his paraphrase of the Nisus-Euryalus passage from the *Aeneid,* but more overt poems also, show that he dreamed often at Harrow and Cambridge of conquering Time with a fellow senator, fellow general, or fellow poet. Reversals and losses in love soon helped him exploit the isolation imposed by genius.

Byron revealed his feelings more fully in verse, as Leslie Marchand has acutely observed, than in private letters. Certainly he revealed his aspirations less fully in letters than in verse. Against the advice of the Reverend John Becher that he mix more in society, Byron protested in rhyme that it was one thing to emerge for the purpose of emulating "the life of a Fox, of a Chatham the death," but quite another to "mingle in Fashion's full herd":

> Did the Senate or Camp my exertions require,
>   Ambition might prompt me, at once, to go forth;
> When Infancy's years of probation expire,
>   Perchance, I may strive to distinguish my birth.
>
> (BWP, I, 113)

In letters or conversation, he would have expanded into ironic comedy that hedging word "Perchance." He told himself in November

Clime of the unforgotten brave!
Whose land from plain to mountain-cave
Was freedom's home or glory's grave;
Shrine of the mighty! can it be,
That this is all remains of thee?

Byron's Giaour

Byron in a helmet of his own design

Politics in English Romantic Poetry

1813: "To be the first man—not the Dictator—not the Sylla, but the Washington or the Aristides—the leader in talent and truth—is next to the Divinity! Franklin, Penn, and, next to these, either Brutus or Cassius—even Mirabeau—or St. Just." The next day, still faced with proofsheets of *The Giaour,* he hated the inaction of poets— except Cervantes, Tasso, Dante, Ariosto, Kleist, and Aeschylus, Sophocles, and some other ancients. He needed to make literature an act equivalent to the destruction of a despot. He had to live up to his adage that "true *words* are *things.*"[3]

To paraphrase Theodor Mommsen on Caesar, Byron had liberal ideals to propagate and remember, but he was born to be a king. The ideals cramped his role as an opportunist looking for a kingdom to rule.

Thucydides, Cicero, and Plutarch established limits to the means as well as the ends. In one of his several censures of his friend John Cam Hobhouse for speaking and dining with the "low, designing, dirty levellers," Cobbett and Henry Hunt, Byron distinguishes his kind, Mirabeau and Lafayette, from lawless blood-letters like Robespierre and Marat: "Why, our classical education alone should teach us to trample on such unredeemed dirt as the *dis*-honest bluntness, the ignorant brutality, the unblushing baseness of these two miscreants, and all who believe in them."[4] As a writer, he did not seek the notoriety of Tom Paine. What he did seek produced the result observed by Swinburne: ". . . we find little really living or really praiseworthy work of Byron's which has not in it some direct or indirect touch of political emotion." Politics flowed spontaneously from his nerves to his verse in such images as the *"rotten borough* of the human heart," rats and bats roused (in the drama *Werner*) "in general insurrection," or the declaration that he hated a motive like "a lingering bottle" when the landlord pauses in an argument over politics, or like a "Laureate's ode, or servile peer's 'Content.' " In the final simile he referred, of course, to the placeman's acquiescence in corrupt laws.

In 1921 Walter Graham, a thorough and generally cautious student of the politics of the English romantics, concluded: "Of all the greater Romantic poets except Keats, Byron exerted perhaps the least influence in politics."[5] Graham was demanding "effective

152

protest" against specific acts of government. In a larger context Byron affected youth in a way to determine or strongly influence politics. As much a child of the Enlightenment as the Girondins were, he merged classical precepts in poems designed as happenings for readers whose lives or opinions affected the common weal. Although his aberrations from this line intensified the malaise of the day, he belonged essentially to the eagles of the Enlightenment, not to the profound despair of "Le Point noir" of Nerval:

> Uh! c'est que l'aigle seul—malheur à nous! malheur!—
> Contemple impunément le Soleil et la Gloire.

Byron's cure for envying the impunity of the eagle was to scorn the scramble of the gull and crow.

It was the need to conceal his aspiration for greater fame than an average young lord could easily achieve that made Byron say too much on his title page of 1807: *Hours of Idleness,* "A Series of Poems, Original and Translated, By George Gordon, Lord Byron, A Minor," with mottoes from Homer and Horace and a third from Dryden: "He whistled as he went, for want of thought." Reviewers had hardly begun to react in predictable ways to that title page when Byron began the satirical couplets to be published in March 1809 as *English Bards and Scotch Reviewers.* Patriotism, not personal pride, requires him to speak out. His peroration, conventional but lucid and suasive, declares that he has chastised idiotic corrupters of verse out of zeal for the honor of his country, "As first in freedom, dearest to the Muse." Like Charles Churchill in *The Rosciad* and William Gifford in *The Baviad* and *The Maeviad,* and like Pope, their master and his, Byron defends the classical fame of "lawful Genius" from unlawful shrines erected by every book club to some "leaden calf." In upholding the neoclassical mode he appeals, not to its authority, but to its clear superiority. Inspired by "No Eastern vision, no distempered dream," he seeks by satiric wit to persecute tumidity and dullness till "Common Sense assert her rights again." Those were happier days when Pope's "pure strain Sought the rapt soul to charm, nor sought in vain." Byron, in his turn, attempts to rescue souls enraptured by the rattling tinsel of Erasmus Darwin,

Politics in English Romantic Poetry

the soft sympathy of William Lisle Bowles, the soaring exoticism of Robert Southey (Thalaba is "Illustrious conqueror of common sense"), and the erotic lyrics of Thomas Moore. Wordsworth is mild, dull, simple; Coleridge is gentle, turgid, tumid, obscure, innocent. Throughout, Byron distinguishes writing for fame from scribbling for lucre. Innocence, meaning ignorance of man's destiny, is as dangerous as prostitution. Beneath the foot of true heroic poetry he places the moral confusion of sympathy-whimpering Bowles:

> Whether thou sing'st with equal ease, and grief,
> The fall of empires, or a yellow leaf.

He cannot care about the politics of these poetasters, because they lack the sense to care themselves.

English Bards and Scotch Reviewers had two obvious aims: revenge for personal affronts and the inclusion of all poets and poetasters in vogue. Once included, a poet had to be satirized, but the ruling principle was to include those in vogue. Another principle of selection is almost as readily apparent. Byron derided, although not specifically for their politics, nearly all the poets (whether he had read them or not) that Gifford, Canning, and other wits of the *Anti-Jacobin* had derided. He did not need to go out and gather for himself Erasmus Darwin, Richard Payne Knight, M. G. Lewis, Robert Merry and Merry's fellow Della Cruscans, and the Bristol-Lakes fellowship of Southey, Coleridge, Wordsworth, Lamb, and Lloyd. His condescension to artisan-authors, although partly to protect true poetry, is an echo of Gifford's condescension, not the nobleman's hauteur that Leigh Hunt was to feel so keenly. The author of *English Bards* probably did not know that all of the Bristol-Lake group except Lamb could be called renegades from poetic Jacobinism; what he did know was that Gifford, Canning, Frere, and Ellis had made delicious sport of them. Further, Byron seems to take the side of the Pittites who attacked the coalition ministry of "All the Talents," in the most recent battle of poetic pamphlets, rather than the side of those who attacked the attackers.[6] Certainly he gives no quarter to the moderate Whigs, rich and poor, who then frequented Holland House.

154

Byron

In sum, his personal grievances, along with his neoclassical, moral, satirical bias, helped him to produce what could pass as a Pittite poem. When he put on the cloak of Gifford, he tried the trousers too. In *English Bards* an imitative brashness hides indecisiveness and self-conflict. The poem in its original form would not have been unpleasing to Byron's cousin and guardian, the Earl of Carlisle, who he then hoped would stand as his sponsor in the House of Lords. Even though the dedication of the second edition of *Hours of Idleness* to Carlisle in 1808 seems tardy and casual, Byron probably had the conservative views of his guardian in mind when he designed the first version of *English Bards*. It was only when Carlisle declined to sponsor him, or failed to offer to do so, that a couplet in praise of Carlisle's *Tragedies and Poems* deliquesced into an extended lampoon. Unattended, the young lord took his seat as if carelessly: ". . . But I will have nothing to do with any of them, on either side; I have taken my seat, and now I will go abroad."[7]

Born of contesting Scottish and English blood, Byron had been moved about for several years before ruinous Newstead Abbey became more the symbol than the fact of home. As much addicted to Roman values as Wordsworth, he found no life for those values in England's past. The Commonwealth, which offered to Wordsworth the republicanism of Milton and Harrington, meant to Byron an arbitrary, narrow, destructive Cromwell. Byron had in him less of the international *philosophe* than Shelley, but more of the rootless cosmopolitan. Not yet taught by Wordsworth and Scott to revere the landscape of his childhood, he embarked as a peer in some sort of fraternity of the independent noblemen of Europe.

II

As turbulent and discontented as he was, the Childe Byron who sailed in July 1809 had not yet encountered the dilemma defined as characteristic in the present study. At twenty-one as at eighteen, he wished to escape his "cursed country" and himself. For him the principles of the Roman republic, with little or no filtering through the philosophers of the French Revolution, served adequately all the demands he had so far placed on either poetry or polity. Acquainted with caresses and rebuffs from his mother, from trueloves, and from strangers, he treasured solitude and yearned for assimilation in some ennobling be-all. Converting personal desire into a vague political notion, he "believed in" freedom. Unlike the other poets, he found his own rebellion fated and directionless. He could speak, for example, of "our unsullied John Locke," instead of their stultifying Locke. He made *Childe Harold's Pilgrimage* a poem of search.

His famous Spenserian stanzas record a pilgrimage out of a discontented self in search of a larger role. The moods of meditative adventure and morose exile are almost, but not quite, the thematic unifiers of the poem.[8] Throughout, sometimes on the surface, sometimes not, run the analogies of Titan and Empire, hero and republic. The poet laments the ruin of his own years amid the ruins of empire. Explaining Harold's character in an addition to the Preface, Byron pointed out that all the usual stimuli of travel were lost on him, "except ambition, the most powerful of all excitements." Ambition begets ruins. Harold's wanderings follow a thread of historical fact as he seeks memorials of battle and monuments of mind's conflict with convention. Byron always took comfort from a belief that his poems had a basis in fact. He found it particularly hard to imagine differences between himself and the created Harold. By gradually eliminating the fiction of difference, he turned himself into an imagined observer of geographical and historical fact. Despite the self-deceit, it proved a successful way—not Coleridge's way, but later to be Manzoni's—of making the poet's imagination and feelings constitutive of reality. Uttering what he feels about Europe and himself today, he asks the evidences of grandeur gone by, with the reader overhearing, what he can be tomorrow.

The landscape of *Childe Harold* is a palimpsest of political maps. For Wordsworth the spirit of place arises from the sigh that humble persons have breathed over the grass and stones. In contrast, the topographical imagination that informs Byron's four cantos draws upon historical evidence of public lives and public event, whether encountered on the way or remembered from books. As late as 1822, in *The Deformed Transformed,* we find the idea that Rome as an imperial place gave strength to and through her leaders. Extraor-

Byron

dinary place and leaders mean more to Byron's nationalism than Wordsworthian place and ordinary people. History as the essence of innumerable biographies, rather than as dramatic moments in the lives of the ambitious, is not for Byron. A life merely private, however riotous, is equally inadequate. History records the reversal by the few of the fate of thousands or millions. Harold seeks the scene and breath of such reversals.

Troubled critics have complained of occasional debris on the surface of the poem rather than of the strong undertow. Some have stopped with Newman's persuasive account of the poem as "an extended funeral sermon."[9] True, the work is elegiac. Its title could almost have been *The Pleasures of Ruins*. It coddles the poet's past and honors the past of empires and nations. From Portugal and Spain, embroiled in the war against Napoleon, the first two cantos move thematically as well as geographically to long-fallen Greece. The last two cantos move similarly from Waterloo, through the Switzerland of Rousseau, Gibbon, and Voltaire, to far-fallen Rome. Besides the *Weltschmerz* hospitable to Ossian and Werther, Cantos I and II extend the despair of a Wordsworth in 1795: the war affords no moral choice for the individual. Cantos III and IV, less contrived and dubitable, assimilate a numbing event in visceral politics: even the villainous hero Napoleon has been beaten down. Even moral dilemma is dead. We may grant the presence of melancholy as wide as a continent—still *Childe Harold's Pilgrimage* is not all elegy.

Cantos I and II pursue the morally simple topics of nationalism and romantic Hellenism, in sympathy with the downtrodden, the betrayed (as at Cintra), and the unjustly fallen. Cantos III and IV, some five years later, carry the same topics into the philosophic brambles of power and empire, as Harold travels from the grave of France at Waterloo to the Forum in Rome, "field of Freedom—Faction—Fame—and Blood."

Harold as a pagan palmer on his way to the classical past seeks the heroic ideals of Greece and Rome; or rather, not the surest of palmers, he seeks a renewal of faith in those ideals. It is this search that we can identify as cross-current or undertow. Hope repeatedly interrupts the pleasures of melancholy with question marks.

Politics in English Romantic Poetry

To Harold the hum of men in cities is a torture, but the hum of generals in the field is a challenge. He bears the Byronic mark of melancholy, and yet like Browning's Childe Roland, "quiet as despair," he moves on toward the Tower.

Confronted with ruins where nations have been born, defeated, or divided, meditation becomes expectancy. Looking to the future, the poet retains his Harrovian preference for nations, not empires. His first encounter is hardly propitious, for the Portuguese mix ignorance and pride with bodily filth; nonetheless, "Gaul's locust horde" will have to be driven from "this delicious land." The English generals were simply foolish in signing the agreement at Cintra instead of pressing with military force:

> Behold the hall where chiefs were late convened!
> Oh! dome displeasing unto British eye!
> With diadem hight Foolscap, lo! a Fiend . . .
> . . . . . .
> Convention is the dwarfish demon styled
> That foiled the knights in Marialva's dome . . .
>   (I.24, 25)

This passage reaches back to the mockery of cuckolds, with the suggestion of horns on the head, in the song that ends *Love's Labour's Lost*—" 'Cuckoo, cuckoo,' O word of fear, / Unpleasing to a married ear"—and reaches forward to the mockery of St. Paul's Cathedral as the cap of London in *Don Juan:* "A huge, dun cupola, like a foolscap crown / On a fool's head" (*D.J.* X.82). In this elaborate joke, Napoleon has cuckolded the military dunces of England. Although Byron condemns the Convention of Cintra for military reasons, not moral, he opposes the "bloated Chief" Napoleon on principle rather than from English pride. In the manuscript he derided equally the generals, the Portuguese, and the London press of "the blatant Beast," the mob, that had roared against the Convention. When his cousin R. C. Dallas asked him to cancel his vituperation of the Portuguese and the generals, he omitted the stanzas divorcing himself from the mob but merely toned down his attack on the generals and the Portuguese. Principle stands in relief in Canto I because the nations defended there give it little support.

158

Byron

As in Portugal so in Spain, where *"all* must shield their *all,* or share Subjection's woes," he upholds the principle of nationalism with difficulty. With Parnassus before him as he writes, a contrast is inevitable between ancient Greece and the land of the Inquisition: "They fight for Freedom who were never free." In context this line has a doubled force, for at Cadiz "all were noble, save Nobility." The rest—the peasants, the guerrillas, the "unsexed" maids—are earning independence for a nation whose rulers have deserved the similar uprisings in Spanish America. Byron heightens romantically this turbulence for freedom. Not even in *Don Juan* could he have reduced his Maid of Saragossa to the virgin in *Los desastres de la guerra* who stands tiptoe on the bodies of the fallen to fire a cannon, above Goya's dry caption: "Que valor!" To Byron unsexed virgins are grander than the grandees, who are unsexed, leaderless unleaders.

Portugal and Spain prepared Harold for the debased condition of the Greeks, once first "in the race that led to Glory's goal." In a long note Byron defends the Greeks against the kind of judgment that he himself had made on the Portuguese. The Greeks, like the Catholics in Ireland and the Jews everywhere, need only the opportunity to throw off a viciousness that has resulted from long subjugation. Greece in 1809 was no more leaderless than the Iberian countries, but respect for classical glories evokes a question significantly absent from the stanzas on Portugal and Spain:

> Who now shall lead thy scattered children forth,
> And long accustomed bondage uncreate?

Knowing the answer a proper Whig should give, Byron later gives it: *"Who* would be free *themselves* must strike the blow." Overtly he is making the same point as in his earlier cry, "Awake, ye Sons of Spain! awake! advance!" A timid insistence in 1809, that the Greeks could be "subjects without being slaves," was strengthened in 1811 to a suggestion that they might sustain "even a free state, with a proper guarantee."[10] As if to show that he is no mere sentimentalist leaning on a sad relic, Byron takes the word of the modern Greeks that Ioannina, for refinement, surpasses Athens. Gloomy

Politics in English Romantic Poetry

Harold elegizes vanished glories; ambitious Harold opts for the future. Here Byron begins for the first time to suggest vertigo at the edge of the chasm. Janus may look both ways, but a poet cannot escape and stand at the same time.

Politically, Canto IV emphasizes the wealth and power of ancient Rome and fallen Venice. The opening stanzas on Venice, although uneven in poetic control, surpass other parts of the poem in the concentration of observed detail and historical synopsis. Byron creates myths of state out of aptly banal references to symbolic objects that have survived from the rich past into the troubled present. He begins with the bridge that "divides, or rather joins," he tells Murray, "the palace of the Doge to the prison of the state." The steeds of St. Mark—"Are they not bridled?" Venice still "looks a sea Cybele" (an afterthought), but her *Bucentaur,* rifled by the French and scored by the Austrian, "lies rotting unrestored." Byron has the pleasure of warning Albion that her own fall is prefigured in her agreement to the resubjugation of Venice under Austrian control. Trying to sharpen a detail noted by Goethe, Isaac D'Israeli, and others, he associates with the subjugation of the city the silence of gondoliers, who formerly sang to passing gondolas answering stanzas from Tasso's *Gerusalemme liberata.* Samuel Rogers' *Italy* was to call this decay of tradition "something like the dying voice of Venice." *Childe Harold* says it flatly: "In Venice Tasso's echoes are no more."

Byron does not include the observation by chance. It is true that the long notes and separately published *Historical Illustrations* to Canto IV came from John Cam Hobhouse. Although Hobhouse concealed from both the public and Byron the aid he received from Ugo Foscolo, we need not doubt his later claim that he provided a list of topics used to fatten the poem itself.[11] Walter Scott, reviewing the poem in the *Quarterly,* found the politics of poet and commentator equally reprobative. Yet the passion of a writer's exile belonged to Byron, not to Hobhouse. Harold relives the aspiration and grief of Tasso.

Traveling on from Venice, the poet skips over Padua, where Tasso began his career with the publication of *Rinaldo,* and instead devotes three stanzas to the "miserable Despot" who confined Tasso unjustly

160

in Ferrara—according to the growing legend that Byron had embellished further in *The Lament of Tasso*. He pauses before Petrarch's tomb at Arquà long enough to approve its simplicity. The personal implications continue. He had followed that nineteenth line of Canto IV, "In Venice Tasso's echoes are no more," with a similar analogy: Venice retains the spell of the drama and fiction set there, English as well as Italian. The spell necessarily remains, for the "Beings of the Mind are not of clay"; in evidence, I myself, says the poet, once envisioned a reality that "Outshines our fairy-land"; although now beside a sea far from the "inviolate Island" of my birth, I have tied my fame and fate to the English language; if I cannot be fittingly buried in English soil, "My Spirit shall resume it"; meanwhile, I accept my exile, my fate, and the judgment of posterity. This subjective commentator returned in stanza 11 to the prospect before him: "The spouseless Adriatic mourns her Lord." Wordsworth's sonnet makes Venice the bride; Byron, with his finger on the doge's pulse and his own, knows who tries to master what. The doge, as male ruler, must tame the sea.

This identification with the noble dead recurs in Florence, where the poet finds Santa Croce sanctified with the dust of Machiavelli, Michelangelo, Galileo, and most recently Alfieri. He calls upon ancient factions as if they were present, and upon the "hyaena bigot" of ungrateful Florence today, to answer for the absence from Santa Croce of Dante, Petrarch, and Boccaccio.

In history the poet finds political lessons for the present. Through analogies of historical figures with a certain English pilgrim, he traces programs for the future. "To fly from, need not be to hate, mankind" (III.69:1).

Canto IV, proceeding, will not lose the contrast between the present calm of Lake Trasimeno and the day when soldiers of Rome and Carthage collided there so ferociously that a yawning earthquake went unnoticed. Harold will follow Pliny from this battleground to the temple of Clitumnus and the cascade at Terni. He surveys the ruins of Roman grandeur. But the road of the pilgrim lies also along the monuments where the rebellious creators of the Renaissance are honored or were once conspicuously rebuffed. In Canto III the road had led from Waterloo by way of Koblenz (which

Politics in English Romantic Poetry

afforded an otherwise gratuitous tribute to the crushing general Marceau, who had captured the city for France in 1794) on to the Switzerland of three iconoclasts, Voltaire, Rousseau, and Gibbon. Anticipating and probably feeding Thomas Hardy's conception of the "lord of irony" as a rebel and martyr, Byron portrays Gibbon, like Voltaire and Rousseau, as one who helped to free the modern mind. Tempted in the direction of the patriots Wordsworth and Coleridge, Byron incorporates the language of rejection in his portraits of "the self-torturing sophist, wild Rousseau," who yet knew how "to make Madness beautiful"; Voltaire all "fire and fickleness," but "Historian, bard, philosopher, combined"; and Gibbon, "Sapping a solemn creed with solemn sneer," but serving thereby as godfather to the Pilgrim of Eternity. These join the "Commonwealth of Kings—the Men of Rome." Even as gloom-adoring Harold, Byron could not despise the Enlightenment.

The Titans of the past—including great moral poets, enemies of cant like Machiavelli and Gibbon, and liberators of the kind Bonaparte once promised to be—these give Byron hope that edifices yet to rise will in their turn make magnificent ruins. Because Byronic individualists exist to strike the fires of rebellion anew in Spanish America, although Byron himself stands amid the ruins of Roman might and within the crumpled shadow of the French Revolution, he can shape an image of defiance:

> Yet, Freedom! yet thy banner, torn, but flying,
> Streams like the thunder-storm *against* the wind . . .
> (IV.98:1–2)

In the vigor of his call for the birth and rebirth of independent nations, Harold blends also the siren's call of glory in Empire. A romantic lust for energy was carrying the poet away from reason, which he had hoped to serve under the banner of Alexander Pope and in the company of Voltaire and Gibbon.

The countercurrent of hope itself includes a question. Byron knows about fire in the soul:

> This makes the madmen who have made men mad
> By their contagion; Conquerors and Kings . . .
> (III.43:1–2)

162

Byron

But what of the creators driven mad, like Tasso, what were their minds made of? It is problem enough to comprehend and judge the mountainlike leaders of men; it is much harder to know if the imagination can encompass a reality beyond physical experience.[12] He decides with Coleridge, Lamb, and Hazlitt that true genius is sane, but he wonders in Florence if the Venus de Medici is greater than a live girl; that is, if nature speaks to the senses while a reality beyond nature speaks to the artist. Not surprisingly, he concludes that he should never abandon reason whether for pure fancy, his past excesses of passion, or mere faith; but this conclusion does not put down the possibility that the mind's immortality lies in the difference between ideal vision and realized existence. Byron seems sorry that the question has been raised for him in Wordsworth's poetry and Shelley's conversation, but *Childe Harold* reflects his sense that the question is annoyingly important.

Greece, despite Plutarch, may have been a dream, but Rome was pure fact. With only those modifications required by the medium, a Roman bust imitated the appearance of an individual emperor. Byron had left Cambridge equating this imitative realism with classical strength. The generalizing ideal of the Elgin marbles, or of Roman copies from a Phidianesque Aphrodite, Byron thought of as unreal, imaginary, bathed in sentiment, and therefore romantic. Some of the appeal of Hellas he recognized as an expansion of the ego, a sentiment, the amoral seductiveness of beauty, and truancy from subjection to Phoebus, who commands poets to follow the light of reason. Yet Wordsworth, Coleridge, and Shelley were suggesting that the poet's control over men differs in kind from the statesman's control. If so, then the study of the greatest power available to man may require concentration on the artistic act rather than on legislative and military acts. The man who confronts this question of power had created little stir by three daring speeches in the upper chamber of the most venerable legislature in the world but had overturned London with Cantos I and II.

Part of the much greater stir created by *Childe Harold* came from its confirmation, to a tantalizing degree, of magniloquent rumors concerning the noble bard's own personality and adventures. The verse and the versifier became forever inseparable. Critics who

163

take poems as autonomous objects must either reject Byron's attempts as inadequate—a needless repression—or accept him as an archetypal figure in the myths of his own poetry, a legendary Prometheus-Orpheus who survives in his own singing. The strength of the myth overcomes the carelessness of the verse.

Standing outside the poem, Byron complained that some critics spoke as if he were more concerned with nature than with civilization. Within the poem (IV.61) he protested that a man accustomed to entwine his thoughts with nature in the fields could not be expected to loiter about describing art in galleries. He has a chance of being right in both places, for it is very nearly self-evident that the strong winds and waves are analogues for the poet's Titanic spirit. Even the moments of calm between Trasimeno and Rome throw into relief the cataclysmic power of the human soul for good and evil. Nature is indomitable; the mind, which thinks it may be so, takes encouragement from nature. If there is no identity and little transfusion, there is vital analogy. On this as on the sense of personal mission that speaks through *Childe Harold,* Shelley is reassuring in his generally despairing "Lines Written among the Euganean Hills" of October 1818: From the rekindled Venetian arc, "loud flames" ascend around the Austrian anarch; the deep and dark blue Ocean did welcome Byron, with such emotion that "its joy grew his"; and the remembrance of the tempest-cleaving swan of Albion (even if Tasso is forgotten) will remain in Venice a "quenchless lamp." Through interchange with nature, the hero leads civilization. The pilgrim among political ruins, throughout four cantos, has contemplated reconstruction.

III

In *Childe Harold,* emulating Beattie and Thomson rather than Gifford, Byron felt his way toward subjective satire. Rumors from the Duchess of Richmond's ball, attended by Wellington the night before the battle of Quatrebras, elicited a tender smile, slightly wry, in the stanzas beginning "There was a sound of revelry by night." Between the two periods of composing *Childe Harold,* he had begun to align satiric couplets, as in the *Hints from Horace, The Curse of Minerva,* and *The Waltz,* with the duty of conserving the best in a given heritage. Initially, Horace and notable imitations of Horace provided conservative guides. Soon the satiric couplet became a tool to be picked up whenever Byron had an impulse to preserve old furniture. The form served as if to hold in place every partition of an armoire from Louis XIV.

The vigor of phrase did nothing to reduce the conservation. Gifford as well as Peter Pindar had played the game of couplets with a spiked club and a sharp ax. One of Byron's opponents, in the *Scourge* for March 1811, described him with typical buoyancy as the son of a profligate father and drunken mother and "the illegitimate descendant of a murderer." Byron, like this opponent, knew that effective satire in a good cause required a grain of credibility.

In the dialogue of *The Curse of Minerva,* nearer to frame-breaking than the other neoclassical pieces of 1811–1812, the poet reminds Pallas that Lord Elgin, the barbaric plunderer of her temple, was a native not of England but of Scotland, land of meanness and sophistry; unappeased, Pallas utilizes the last third of the poem to pronounce doom on Britain for her recent perfidy in Copenhagen, her tormenting of Ireland, her guilty confusion in the Iberian peninsula, and her imperialistic tyranny in India. Pallas knows also—perhaps as a subscriber to Hunt's *Examiner* or Cobbett's *Register*—that the "starved mechanic breaks his rusting loom" and that paper-credit is ruining the poet's homeland. The English who have slaughtered, ravished, plundered, and charred "from Tagus to the Rhine" receive their wages in Pallas' prophecy—muddy after the fashion of prophecies—that "Gaul shall weep ere Albion wear her chains." This poetically dull satire lacks the conserving passion of patriotism. Otherwise, by the negative method normal to satire, it urges Englishmen to conserve the ideals handed down from republican Rome through Harrow and Eton. Nevertheless, through stanzas added for topical thrust, it attacks the foreign and domestic policies of ministerial pillagers as worthy of barbaric Elgin. In consequence, as Byron was flirting just then with Lord Holland's moderate Whigs, he had a few copies of the poem privately printed but withheld it from publication.

The vogue of Juvenalian or Giffordian satire, in 1811 fading rapidly, presupposed an interest in current affairs. The vogue of Turkish tales, which Byron exploited for a year beginning in May 1813 and occasionally during the rest of the decade, presupposed commitment to almost nothing. Their prosody could be described as anti-heroic couplets, in some poems a loose tetrameter, in others pentameter, with more expansive rhyming substituted at will. Torn by the dilemma of the age, the poet had split into two inferior parts. Now he acted as the angry man conserving the treasured armoire; soon after, in oscillation, he expressed the emotional libertinage of the Turkish tales. He had not divided cleanly into halves. Enough of him dangled from the edges to make the parts both incongruous with each other and inconsistent with themselves. The tales, going beyond *Childe Harold* as excrescences of personal passion, frustration, and dolor, are calculated sins against Apollo.

Guilt awakens aspiration. In the continuum of Byron's lifelong study of ambition, the tales stress daring and the psychology of domination. The protagonists, variously outlawed or alienated, represent the temptation to force and violence. They charge toward us "fitted for the desperate game." Suffering slightly from the Robin Hood syndrome, their author dissolves a mite of generosity in gallons of sin and gloom. When we first see Conrad in *The Corsair,* he has assumed a stance of musing guilt that keeps his followers in awe. In the sequel, Byron asks of Lara:

> And cared he for the freedom of the crowd?
> He raised the humble but to bend the proud.
> (BWP, III, 357:897–898)

Alp, also, in *The Siege of Corinth,* "had skill" to "warp and wield the vulgar will." The tales are to this extent antidemocratic. But they are unmistakably antiroyalist, and their effect was to make every young reader feel superior to kings. Without having to preach it, they stimulate rebellion against staid arrangements of society. All order under the Turks shows in these tales as the essence of tyranny. And the bitter aloofness of their leaders shows Byron's uneasy awareness that the man who leads others, needs others. Although the tales do not presuppose commitment, they do not void it.

166

These tales have incited generation after generation. Mark Rutherford, in *The Revolution in Tanner's Lane* (1887), has a radical Major Maitland stir the hero's latent individualism by putting into his hands, in 1814, a copy of *The Corsair*. This timely gift elates the hero, Zachariah, by the evident "scorn of what is mean and base, the courage—root of all virtue—that dares and evermore dares in the very last extremity, the love of the illimitable, of freedom"—as well as by the passion, which Rutherford calls love. Since Rutherford was a social observer, like Orwell, without an ounce of fancy, I think it no embarrassment to the argument that T. S. Eliot also admired *The Corsair* and the other tales. Admiring the tales for the driving force of their narratives, Eliot could ignore everything that the tales have said to rebels. The tales speak rebellion only to those fuming against convention and oppression—sentimental girls like those chaffed in the novels of Jane Austen, Frenchmen in 1830, Germans in 1848, Japanese in 1948. In times and places of political unrest and social change, the tales have been much translated and widely circulated.

As characters, the noble outlaws of the Turkish tales reflect specifically the temperament of Byron's friend Ali Pasha, cruel tyrant of Albania and Epirus. In a specifically national aspect, they symbolize Greek insurgency. A century later as in the year of the siege of Corinth, 1715, "Freedom still at moments rallies," and "pays in blood Oppression's ills." Byron did not wait a moment to assert this theme. He began his career as the popular author of Turkish tales with the tribute to Themistocles that opens *The Giaour:* "When shall such Hero live again?" To the Fifth Edition (twelve weeks after the first) he added the present lines 103–141, which denounce the self-abasement of those who live in the clime of Salamis and Thermopylae. Count Pietro Gamba, in *A Narrative of Lord Byron's Last Journey to Greece* (1825, pp. 4, 149), reports the doubled irony of Byron's memory in 1824 of oriental visions from his earliest readings in Turkish history and his "greater personal esteem for the character of the Turks than for that of their slaves." After 1812, however, it is only individual Turks, like his friend the Pasha, who rise to the stature of noble villain.

In the panoramic view, these dark heroes share with Schiller's

Karl Moor and Goethe's Götz, and with the Titanic brood of outlaws after them, the strength of natural leadership. As forces without
sophistication, they could be admired by Europeans who revered
a national culture but disliked or detested its established regime
and the idea of legitimacy that underpropped the establishment.[13]
This exaltation of revolt, although oblique because of the protagonists' guilty gloom, drew energy from, and in turn gave fresh energy
to, the contemporaneous claims of a people's right to cashier their
governors. Among other pleasures for the original reader, the tales
made less surreptitious the widespread sense of superiority over
pharisees, magistrates, legalitarians, and dynasties. A natural, organic
society could and should thrust its own natural leaders through the
artificial crust of arbitrary rule, whether only dynastic or both dynastic and foreign.

Byron accompanied the tales with political gestures. In 1812 he
had urged the Lords to follow the leadership of liberal Whigs and
vote for Catholic emancipation; he had supported the rebellious
weavers of Nottinghamshire in a speech on the radical or "Demo-
cratical Whig" topic of frame-breaking, with an accent on economic
injustice; and still more recklessly, he had supported Major Cartwright's petition for redress of grievances—meaning the right to
present petitions for Reform. The whole spectrum of the Opposition,
from land-minded Lord Grenville to suffrage-minded Sir Francis
Burdett, praised his first speech, that on the frame-breakers. In short,
they courted him. Lord and Lady Holland invited him and sent
him to balls. He joined the Hampden Club, which was founded
by Cartwright, led by Burdett, and aristocratically liberal. If the
Turkish tales as such smack of the libertinage of his stormy affair
with Lady Caroline Lamb, his habit of accompanying each tale
with more explicitly subversive poems suggests the political ardor
of Lady Oxford, whose embraces, more than Burdett's counsel, seem
to have seduced him into the camp of Princess Caroline.[14] Not
notably successful as an orator, and too hungry for action and creativity to be satisfied with Parliamentary maneuver, he appended
to the tales various satires—some hidden, some open—against the
Prince Regent. Despite the fears of Murray, his Tory-oriented publisher, Byron forced into the second edition of *The Corsair* his "Lines

Byron

to a Lady Weeping," which had appeared anonymously in the *Morning Chronicle* two years earlier (7 March 1812). In "the Fracas at Carlton House" to which the lines refer, the Whig leaders rejected the Regent's offer of a coalition government instead of the Whig ministry that they expected. When the Regent flushed, his daughter Princess Charlotte wept; whereupon the Regent sent her from the room. Byron's quatrains had been lost among other attacks when they first appeared:

> Weep, daughter of a royal line,
> A Sire's disgrace, a realm's decay;
> Ah! happy if each tear of thine
> Could wash a Father's fault away!
>
> Weep—for thy tears are Virtue's tears—
> Auspicious to these suffering Isles;
> And be each drop in future years
> Repaid thee by thy People's smiles!
>
> (BWP, III, 45–46)

Byron was prescient: when republished under his own name, the verses caused a furor. They helped draw Princess Charlotte closer to the Whig leaders; they struck a blow for Ireland in that plural, "these suffering Isles"; and they helped drive Lord Byron's latest tale toward a Ninth Edition. In turn, the sale of 29,000 copies by early 1815 made a serious contribution both to Byron's disrepute and to the Prince's unpopularity. Swayed by attacks from the *Courier* and *Morning Post,* Murray omitted the additional poems from the Third Edition, to avoid further offense, but the poet demanded their return to the Fourth through the Tenth (1818). Meanwhile Byron as man and poet "quite captivated" the weeping lady, Princess Charlotte, as he did most of her faction and a large part of her mother's.[15] The Regent, too, had made a soothing bid for cordial relations, but the game had to be played on different terms. Opposing the Regent on the principle of civil liberty and likewise the principle of loyalty to one's friends, Byron disliked those terms of the game that meant attendance in salons, parlors, and buzzing lobbies—places, he said, where he was most alone.

In the long view, he had chosen a side, felt the satisfaction of

169

loyalty to it, and could now look down as outlaw on a pinnacle. He wrote a few squibs and impromptu quatrains as partisan actions to be praised in the salons. These pieces contain inevitable evidences of native skill, but they have survived as actions rather than as art. In the same period Byron tried also to turn into action both moral, Giffordian satire and romantic melancholy.

Chastisement of the Regent for abandoning the Whigs combines heavily with the Giffordian complex in *The Waltz,* which thanks Germany for graciously begetting England's royal family, her sodden alliances, and the new lascivious dance. Continuing the same political campaign in a total contrast of prosody and mood in six stanzas near the end of *Childe Harold,* Byron makes Charlotte's name synonymous with the hopes of freedom. Her early death enters as a new reversal in the hope that has already paused at Waterloo over "an Empire's dust."

Byron's canon of purely political verse is slightly longer than Lamb's. In his varied squibs and *jeux d'esprit,* the public and personal merged sufficiently to mark him as the man of action he wished to be. Shortly after his maiden speech on the subject, he asked James Perry of the *Morning Chronicle* to publish anonymously "An Ode to the Framers of the Frame Bill." Eldon, Liverpool, and the Home Secretary—considering that "Men are more easily made than machinery"—"when asked for a *remedy,* sent down a *rope*" (BWP, VII, 14). The wordplays of his pieces on politics, and some of those on poetry, seize wit in this way from the content; nearly all the rest involve puns and ingenuities that are their own excuse for being. Politics and poetic rivalry were real.

After an important speech, journalistic verse had to follow, even if the speaker must write it himself. In 1813 and 1814, the energies Byron saved from Parliament went into squibs. Sometimes he published; sometimes he started a circulation from hand to hand that usually resulted in publication. "Damn their impudence," he wrote when the *Champion* and the *Morning Chronicle* made public his lines, impudent enough in themselves, on the Prince Regent's banishment of Lady Jersey's portrait from the royal gallery of miniatures. Lady Jersey, to whom Byron had sent the verses, was trying to get him to speak and write more in the good cause. The *Champion* included all of his attack on "that VAIN OLD MAN" except for a few asterisks in the line, "Heir of his father's crown, and of his wits" (VII, 37).

For Byron or any lord concerned with poetry, satire, and politics, we may take as the ideal to be emulated the last two lines of Rochester's quatrain on Charles II: "He never said a foolish thing, / Nor ever did a wise one." Byron's best chance had come in April 1813 when the Regent entered the vaults at Windsor to see the body of Charles I removed from the tomb of Henry VIII. Although he fills ten lines, the argument advances rapidly:

> By headless Charles see heartless Henry lies;
> Between them stands another sceptred thing—
> It moves, it reigns—in all but name, a king:
> Charles to his people, Henry to his wife,
> —In him the double tyrant starts to life: (VII, 35)

The political point is fully made in these five lines, but it took two additional couplets to reveal the full venom of the phrase "starts to life." What good did it do, these couplets ask, to bury royal vampires, since these tombs disgorge "The blood and dust of both— to mould a George." The word *dust*, which generally meant garbage, here had the third meaning of a vampire's vomit. A royal vampire. Obviously Byron was shooting partly for fun, but such shots were undoubtedly of immense service in keeping up the spirits of those who supported the Opposition. He was willing to be used for the purpose of keeping up the spirits wherever he was acknowledged to be able, ready, and dangerous. Usually he wrote first for a private circle. He could—and therefore did—introduce into a series of private squibs on Lord Thurlow's poems raillery at Liverpool's ineptness and a personal jibe at Castlereagh (VII, 20). Although this Edward Thurlow had succeeded in 1806 to the title of his famous and powerful uncle, the lord chancellor, he was a poetaster who could be made to seem more worthy of Byron's powers as a satirist by associating him with the chief ministers. And yet Byron would make clear in "The Vision of Judgment" and *Don Juan* what is implied in his squibs against Thurlow: any writer not in earnest is a serious menace to literature and to society.

Politics in English Romantic Poetry

If the force of the shorter pieces, by Byron's own criterion, proves his earnestness, then "The Devil's Drive" (1813), of twenty-seven known stanzas, puts his earnestness in doubt. Dull in execution, it indexes the topics and attitudes of the Opposition in 1813. It condenses six or seven weeks of the *Morning Chronicle*. The stanzas sweat along from "that standing jest," Tyrwhitt, the Regent's private secretary, to a jest too tired to sit down, the duplicity of George Rose, long a financial adviser to Pitt and currently Treasurer of the Navy. The hobbling meter lames even the best of the triple rhymes: "pervert her," "deserter"; "gloss over," "Philosopher."

The longest sequence in the poem is of little poetic value, but it has an importance. From his earliest juvenilia, Byron had treated war increasingly as slaughter. He had condemned mere generals. The element of glamor, originally strong and always present, had diminished when he passed through Spain and Portugal in 1809. At Leipzig in 1813, Russian, Prussian, Austrian, Swedish, and miscellaneous German monarchs, princes, and generals, with a few British soldiers, had driven Napoleon into blunders. In "The Devil's Drive" Byron's distaste for mere generals finds expression only in conventional formulas: Desolation hurts maidens; Carnage makes widows; Famine makes orphans; Fever hurts villagers and youth; vultures and "allies" are exact equivalents. Nevertheless, the drawing up of these formulas gave Byron training for the later ferocity against war in *Don Juan*. Part of the strength of his later inhospitality to war came from his learning how to be, not merely sentimental or merely "cutting," but blithely savage.

Politics can enter more surprising kinds of poetry than squibs and occasional satire, and can enter in more surprising ways. Of such surprises, Byron's "Hebrew Melodies" afford a remarkably complex example.

A Selection of Hebrew Melodies Ancient and Modern, Part I, of April 1815, "with appropriate Symphonies and accompaniments" by John Braham and Isaac Nathan, bore a dedication to Princess Charlotte, presumably with Byron's approval. The political scope of the lyrics was much larger, although the political implications are not instantly apparent. Byron's solemn bride, Annabella Milbanke, was led to believe that the poems were a wedding present

172

signifying the reform of a sinner. To others, also, these lyrics seemed a turn toward virtue, if not a climb into piety. Some of the pieces he included, notably "She Walks in Beauty," ill fit the Hebrew mold; yet the term and title "Hebrew Melodies" initially designated, not the poems, but "the favourite Airs which are still sung in the religious Ceremonies of the Jews," adapted to Byron's lyrics by his collaborators. The volume aided tolerance, which was badly needed. Although Jews were emerging from oblivion in 1815, British law still excluded them from Parliament, official honors, and even naturalization. The civil disabilities were to outlive the poet by forty-two years. And Byron himself, sensitive to jibes that he had competed in pious gravity with Sternhold and Hopkins, was equally uneasy over his alliance with Jews—who remained in his life, and returned after the "Hebrew Melodies" to his poetry, as moneylenders.

In the first of his "papers" attached to Canto II of *Childe Harold*, Byron had defended the Jews along with "such other cudgelled and heterodox people" as the Greeks and Irish Catholics. Privately he came to like Isaac Nathan. Yet in *Hebrew Melodies* he was supporting the principle and spirit of nationalism more than Zion specifically. National melodies had become a fad. The Braham–Nathan title page echoed a preceding series of selections, by competing publishers, from Irish, Welsh, Scottish, and Indian melodies.[16] Scott, and before him Burns, had contributed to the vogue, in a lost cause. Byron was tuned closest of all to *A Selection of Irish Melodies,* of 1806 and after, with lyrics by Thomas Moore and symphonies and accompaniments by Sir John Stevenson. At least seven of the Hebrew Melodies, even more directly than the Irish Melodies, advance the doctrine and cause of nationalism. The Hebraic distancing lends power to a general application of the doctrine and emotions, rather like Byron's own philhellenism or the medievalism that turned Victorian historiographers from written documents to social ideals. What the anapestic nationalism borrows from Moore—and Campbell—it repaid in 1815 to the cause of Irish Catholicism. By emphasizing Israel's cries for freedom from tyrants, Byron reinforced the use of the Old Testament for political prophecy, already common in verses and caricatures on affairs of state. In a stamping beat too regular for sobs or tears, he asks readers to feel for Irish, Greeks,

Politics in English Romantic Poetry

Italians, Poles, natives of South America, and all "Whose shrines are desolate, whose land a dream." The singer of "On Jordan's Banks" asks all who have known Mussulman or Bourbon, "How long by tyrants shall thy land be trod?" The titular heroine of "Jephtha's Daughter," like the Maid of Saragossa in *Childe Harold,* becomes the bare-bosomed spirit of the people that Delacroix would depict in *Greece Expiring on the Ruins of Missolonghi* and *Liberty Leading the People.* In "The Wild Gazelle" the curse on Ahasuerus is the curse of national deracination. Byron's appeal is to feelings of action. Moore conceals his own stirring of the strings by accepting with a tear the ruin of the harp now "mute on Tara's walls"; in contrast with this sentimental passivity, the "Harp the Monarch Minstrel swept," the harp of David, which "grew mightier than his Throne," belongs now to the noble bard who has called you to hear martial strains. Even of the harp in "We sate down and wept by the waters," which is nearer to Moore in sentiment, Byron cannot resist a nationalistic aphorism: "its sound should be free." He goes on to a second, fiercer version, "In the valley of waters we wept on the day":

> Our hands may be fettered—our tears still are free
> For our God—and our Glory—and Sion, Oh *Thee!*
>
> (BWP, III, 404)

Dealing in commonplaces, as a librettist should, he does not need to point out that the monarch in "Vision of Belshazzar" is on the opposite side from David, who represents our side. Here, and in a second poem on Belshazzar's "sensual fulness" that Murray withheld until 1831, the doomed monarch is clearly the Prince Regent (III, 421). Indeed, we may with no great difficulty find the Regent in the entire series of speaking tyrants faced with visions of retribution.

A fatalistic acceptance of man's evil and man's doom, which is extended and deepened in "Darkness" (Byron's unusually serious contribution to the "Last Man" fad), imbues several of the Hebrew Melodies, but the prophesied doom of Balshazzar is the good child's victory (Byron's Daniel is "a youth") in behalf of all that is free,

174

good, true, and beautiful. Balshazzar is unfit "to govern, live, or die."

Distress over the enslavement of Greece breathes fog into the Turkish tales. The sunny rhythm of the Hebrew Melodies supports their assurance that enemies of natural right have always "melted like snow in the glance of the Lord." In 1817 and 1819 *The Lament of Tasso* and *The Prophecy of Dante,* midway between sun and fog, address more explicitly the public condition of Europe, although the first is the monologue of a victim maddened by love and unjust imprisonment (with a suspicious similarity to Byron himself), and the second is cast in a form traditionally vague in its foreboding of trouble already known to the reader. Since Byron's Dante urges a foreordained generation to rise against the barbarians, "German, Frank, and Hun," and throw off all external and internal restraints to *"one* deed—Unite," it is not surprising that this poem is to be found on the list of works banned by Metternich's agents.[17]

The threats that Byron assigned to Tasso were less transparent. Like the prisoner Bonivard, Tasso becomes on Byron's page a model victim cleansed of historical impurities. Byron wooed historical accuracy, but he would always accept the latest congenial theory and he sometimes accepted attractive legends from such panderers as today point out to tourists, from Chillon to Sounion, where the letters B-Y-R-O-N and B-y-r-o-n are cut in the hallowed stone. No more than these graffiti repeat the same lettering styles did Byron merely do again in *The Lament of Tasso* what he had done better in *The Prisoner of Chillon.* Chandler Beall, Mario Praz, C. P. Brand, and Tasso scholars since 1895 in Italy have shown that Tasso the oppressed was overcoming Tasso the poet in Italy and France as well as England, but Byron goes a little further. His Tasso, as victim, patriot, and poet, is a passion-driven maniac inspiring the limitless human mind in a way to make men divinely mad.

Byron had taken on an especially hard task in the monologues of Tasso and Dante. The less the reader knew about a figure, the easier it was to make a political hero of him. Kosciusko, whom Byron called the "sound that crashes in the tyrant's ear," is a revered name in England only because of the English poets. Byron lifted Bonivard from obscurity into international light as a semihistorical hero of liberty. But he was able to write of Bonivard with an English audience in mind. That audience knew nothing of Bonivard. He aimed the monologues of Tasso and especially Dante toward a European audience for whom he was interpreting poetic prophecy already revered. Of all his works, these must have brought the greatest temptation to write in Italian.

For Byron, the great Italians are avatars of the Titan he depicts in the three stanzas of "Prometheus." Man is a "troubled stream from a pure source." Attempting to reduce the "sum of human wretchedness," the avatars of Prometheus "strengthen Man with his own mind." Although the very act of defying convention is good for society, an actively patriotic poet lifts defiance to the level of challenging man's enemy, Death. Goethe twice surpassed the living English poet he most admired in conveying the creativity of Prometheus. But Byron's Titan is more a figure of suffering, pity, and kindness than the finest interpretation of the pertinent poems, Douglas Bush's *Mythology and the Romantic Tradition in English Poetry*, could admit within its thesis. To Bush, Byron's Titan represented explosive rebellion. G. Wilson Knight's *Lord Byron: Christian Virtues* and *Lord Byron's Marriage* are scarcely models of scholarship or logic in their presentation of Byron as the ideal Christian in his love of dogs, lesser animals, and little boys, yet readers skeptical of Knight's extremes should grant that Byron's ideal of right conduct always reserved a place for unselfish loyalty, operative pity, and daily acts of charity.

Byron esteemed the ideal of patriot-poet the more highly because he had often thought of himself as Napoleon *manqué,* and Napoleon had failed him. No one of his many references to Napoleon can be properly interpreted in isolation from the rest. Many accounts of his troubled regard for Napoleon's ascendancy imply that at some period he completely approved. He never did. But the ideal of "the Scourger of the world," even in the context of disapproval in *Childe Harold* (I.52), was Napoleon's to fill if he would, in a world crying out for the rout of despots. Napoleon had achieved by his own merit an opportunity to bring down the old system of a balance of despots in Europe. The eagle, a frequent symbol in nineteenth-century verse for the strength of freedom, is accepted by Byron as an emblem that Napoleon justly inherited from imperial Rome. In their sunward movement, Byron's eagles dare to gaze into a light that blinds all lesser creatures. In contrast with the mere nuisances committed by the two-headed eagle of Austria, the eagles that were Napoleon's troops became in the carnage of battle positive symbols of evil, sometimes identical with the vultures that Napoleon was born to oppose. Looking from Spanish soil in 1809, as Childe Harold, Byron saw only "Gaul's Vulture," cousin to his earliest anti-hero, Cromwell, in the lust to "swell one bloated Chief's unwholesome reign." In Venice he was to look upon remnants worse than carnage, not merely in the shattered barge, *Bucentaur,* but in a people basely consigned to Austria. Hazlitt was in error when he accused Byron of abusing Napoleon only after the fall, although the accusation made abuse harder for Byron after 1821. Meanwhile, in one of those anachronisms irresistible to dramatists, Byron has Marino Faliero curse the "Sea-Sodom," Venice, in 1355, with the prophecy of ruin by a "bastard Attila," Napoleon (V.iii.49, 99). Yet Napoleon's crimes did not altogether kill Byron's awe of the conqueror who announced a code and constantly renewed his strategy.

Highest of all in Byron's poems stand Sulla, Washington, and Bolivar, those who conquer and retire. Against these Napoleon is judged. That the Venezuelan would retire was unproved during Byron's lifetime, but Byron christened his yacht *The Bolivar* in anticipation. Next after those who retire after victory come Aristides and Dandolo, who conquer but refrain from empire. Napoleon has not been one of these, but he might yet redeem himself by serving freedom more than conquest. Sulla, who had first provided a pattern of cruel devastation, went on to provide a finer model: he reformed the state and retired. When Napoleon seemed destined to repeat only Sulla's devastation, Byron had raised even Cromwell (in *Childe Harold* IV.85) to the level of "sagest of usurpers" and "immortal rebel." For the moment even Cromwell seemed a better model than Napoleon. Yet Napoleon, like Sulla and Cromwell, had reformed the institutions of a state, and he was above all a king-scatterer. When Napoleon made his bold march to Paris in March 1815, after the escape from Elba, Byron took pleasure in casting his vote in the Lords to recognize Napoleon instead of Louis XVIII. Napoleon had redeemed his cowardice, and might redeem his cruelty. He might become less of a "Byronic hero," and more of a hero deserving Byron's admiration. Although passages in the poems and journals sometimes drop Sulla below Washington and Cincinnatus, the ferocity of Sulla and Napoleon had a special attraction for Byron. Ferocity in a just cause could be admired.

Napoleon attracted partly by his personality and career, partly by his opposition to those who maintain the accumulated evils of the past, and partly by the envy his accomplishments stirred among the "great" who attended waltzes in London. Circumstances made Byron vacillate in his contempt for "shrivelled Wellesley," but even in 1813 he had warned the Spanish against applying the title *Salvador del mundo* to a vaunting general capable of accepting homage as the Virgin Mary.[18] The victory at Waterloo, won by Wellington, Blücher, and "God knows who besides in 'au' and 'ou' "—for the Regent, Castlereagh, Metternich, and the devil knew what Bourbons—stung Byron less because of Napoleon's conduct in 1814 and 1815. Having stooped to empire, the least he could have done as a Titan was to fall on his sword or blow his splendid brains out. The portraits in *Childe Harold* of Rousseau, Voltaire, Gibbon, Petrarch, Ariosto, and Tasso show typically that Byron admired Promethean figures no less when they brought ashes down on their own heads. But 1814 made him cry out, in "Ode to Napoleon Buonaparte," because God's world had been the footstool of a thing so mean. The ode appeared anonymously, mostly because he had just declared to the public that *The Corsair* would be his last work "for some years," but the times were as numbing as his debts and his decision to marry. Stanzas set up to praise Washington were withheld by Murray, perhaps because British soldiers freed by Napoleon's fall could now sail and march to burn the White House and the Congressional Library. Byron, whose prophecies often seemed inflammatory invitations to the enemy, was in no mood for public apology. He was much more ashamed of Napoleon's abdication than he was of the ode.

The second meek surrender, in 1815, made him doubt his own

aims and his own daring. So cruel had events been to his sense of fitness and his scheme of fatalism that he attributed Wellington's final victory to the earlier, crucial Russian snows as well as to the "Hero sunk into the King." He repeats this counterattack on fate in *Beppo*: "Crushed was Napoleon by the northern Thor . . ." In "Ode from the French," published in the *Morning Chronicle* in March 1816, he threatens that "Crimson tears will follow yet," not from an end to the captivity at St. Helena, but because the system of deceit that had engulfed Bonaparte must succumb to "equal rights and laws."[19] The storm of emotions almost took him out of himself. The monologues ascribed to Dante and Tasso are nearer in mode to Browning's "Rabbi Ben Ezra" than to anything more convincing dramatically, but two of the newspaper poems purportedly translated from the French, although they attempt no dramatic immediacy, show Byron's power to blend with his own feelings those of a Frenchman loyal to Napoleon. His own loyalty was to illimitable energy.

He sighed to the end, as he admitted in lines added to *The Age of Bronze* in 1823, "to behold the Eagle's lofty rage / Reduced to nibble at his narrow cage." A slight consolation came in chiding the jailers for vying with their captive in meanness. A greater consolation—and one I cannot reconcile with views of Byron as spoiler—came with the threat that Napoleon's aura would inspire next a "Washington of worlds betrayed" who would not take the Corsican's "single step into the wrong." These lines, startling in their ingenuous susceptibility to ridicule from an ironic reader, epitomize all that Byron meant by the morality of satire. Napoleon had come tormentingly near to all that Byron hoped from a Titan, without having the necessary moral fiber.

The hero of *Mazeppa* (1819) belongs to the Napoleonic configuration of action rather than with the bardic fury of Tasso and Dante. Specifically, Mazeppa brings to an end, at least in Byron's own work, the line of the hard-souled, existentialist adventurer begun with *The Giaour*. Byron seems to have intended nothing in particular by publishing with *Mazeppa* his most dithyrambic celebration of commonwealths, the "Ode on Venice," but the extravagant homage to the United States that closes the ode points toward a myth of commonweal in the hazy union of distance, novelty, vigor, and freedom.

The new narrative, based on an episode of the Ukraine in Voltaire's *Histoire de Charles XII,* handles political perspectives more adroitly than any of the earlier tales. In the nine central sections of the poem, Mazeppa tells how, long ago, bound to the back of a wild steed for seducing the fiancée of a rich palatine, he endured "Cold—hunger—sorrow—shame—distress." His topic is endurance. He has for audience the wounded Charles XII, pausing for breath with a small remnant of his troops after their defeat at Poltava. Early in the aged Mazeppa's narrative the reader is reminded of the present occasion, Charles XII at bay, not yet presented as a parallel to any other event:

> I watched her as a sentinel,
> (May ours this dark night watch as well!)

In closing, Mazeppa points the moral of his rescue by a Cossack maiden: "Let none despond, let none despair!" For a fillip in the last line, and because it has been a long tale for a short moral, Byron tries for a laugh: "The King had been an hour asleep!" But all is not jest. Section I had at once pointed to the similarity between Charles's retreat from Poltava in 1709 and Napoleon's retreat from Moscow in 1812. The daring, enduring, lustful Mazeppa overlaps in character with Bonaparte-Byron. Frequently after Waterloo, as here, Byron could look upon Napoleon's fall as merely a notable episode in the struggle for freedom. Liberty here crouches under a tree with Charles XII, Mazeppa, and Bonaparte. The king has failed to hear out a parable apt for his ear. The reader, too, may be a royalist asleep to the political warning that Byron's tale provides. Many an English reader has been more than "an hour asleep," but the melancholy, ironic poet hopes to awaken England and Europe.

IV

In 1818, the year he sought and found a new kind of hero in Don Juan, Byron renounced his exploitation of the personal and the exotic, but did so in the protective irony of doggerel. He admitted that some disliked his romantic style, which they called frantic, while others were equally sick of "repetitions nicknamed Classic." He declared the contest ended:

> For my part all men must allow
> Whatever I was, I'm classic now. (BWP, VII, 55)

Agreeing with Blake, Coleridge, and Shelley that poetry and love "both come from above," he landed at some distance from them. Once landed, he drew back from the whirlpool of the imagination. He meant to adopt reason, sense, and wit. No more unadulterated passion. He had just completed *Childe Harold*. *Manfred* was out of his system. *Beppo*, he professed to believe, renewed his alliance with Moore and Rogers.

His repugnance against the spirit of the age would not down. His three historical tragedies, written between April 1820 and July 1821, were artistic penance—or, it may be, designed to look like penance—for the tales of brigandage and the loosened modes of *Childe Harold* and *Manfred*. Within the fifteen months of atonement, he chose three princes and translated the fall of each from history into five-act tragedy. His first hero, Marino Falicro, although his initial aim is to effect severe punishment for slander against his wife, leads a rebellion against what the dramatist allows him to interpret as usurpation of his office. Francis Foscari tragically opposes a kindred usurpation. Sardanapalus rises from a life of sensual languor to face wicked rebels. Each adheres to a princely code of honor.

Byron imprisoned each hero within the unities of action, place, and time. Like the Greeks, he said, he was dramatizing history. He studied the chroniclers of Venice intensively and ostentatiously, particularly for *Marino Faliero*. Whenever art so bade him, he evaded and transcended his sources. Congratulating himself on accuracy rather than art, however, he would have sensed no oddity in the practice of E. H. Coleridge, editor of the standard edition, who introduced each tragedy with facts from the latest scholarship of his own day rather than with the assumptions of earlier historians taken by Byron as factual. The poet escaped slavery to fact by surreptitious art and by his Harrovian belief that history gives instruction in political economy and morals. Transferring this function to tragedy, the playwright turns from study of the past to its utilization for prophecy in the present. Faliero reminds his nephew that victory, which they missed by a moment, "would have changed the face of ages"; defeat "gives us to Eternity." Example such as theirs "will find heirs, though distant" (IV.ii.275, 314). In April 1820 certain heirs of Faliero's rebellion of 1355 awakened the interest of Lord Byron in Ravenna, whither he had followed Teresa Guiccioli as *cavaliere servente*. Awakened, he began to write *Marino Faliero*. The quasi-classicism of his three tragedies had its origin and license in the works of Count Vittorio Alfieri. Of Alfieri's many similarities to Byron, the most significant in 1820 can be seen in the dedication of one of his "tragedies of liberty," *Bruto secondo* (1789), "al popolo italiano futuro." In 1820 an Italian people—as distinct from a populace—seemed nearer. If Byron worked with the Carbonari only or largely to rehabilitate his reputation in England, as Iris Origo argues in *The Last Attachment,* then the historical tragedies were the advertisements for his conspiratorial activity. He could best emulate the Hellenes in tragedy and in life if he followed "the outline of their conduct" (LJ, V, 217).

Without straining the code of princes, each of Byron's three heroes has compassion for the populace. The Venetian plays, *Marino Faliero* and *The Two Foscari,* dramatize two attempts to retard the encroachment of aristocratic power over the Doge and the people. Faliero joins the "stung plebeians" against the "Patrician pestilence" (III.i.12, 102). With an immoderate sense of personal honor, he dreams of winning and resigning sovereignty. Election as a figurehead is much too little. Even so, if he is a ceremonial figurehead, then slander against his wife demeans the honor of the state. The less power the honor carries with it, the more he must insist that personal and official dignities interweave. The doctrine of the two distinct bodies of the king, private and public, which was exercised constantly in the trials of Leigh Hunt and his brother for seditious libel, has no place in Byron's thought. *The Vision of Judgment* shows his emphatic dissent even more clearly than this tragedy. Without mitigating Faliero's personal pride in greatness, Byron distinguishes such pride from the vanity of lesser men. It is by personal quality that Faliero merits identification with public dignity. In his fall he exploits men of weaker state, whose grievances against the patricians he nonetheless holds to be as just as his own.

The lesser conspirators justify tyrannicide with conventional rhetoric and the inevitable references to Brutus. Byron shows no concern to prejudice the reader either for or against them, despite the Doge's allusion to Calendaro, a sort of bloody-minded Leigh Hunt, as "the plebeian Brutus" (V.i.178). Faliero condemns the plebs only when they forget that he is for them but not of them. Byron sees to it that Faliero, a prince by nature as well as election, laments the use of foul means to a good end. A man of feeling, Faliero confesses to himself the stain of treason in his act (III.i.66, 105). What matters is not the *law,* but unease in his fine conscience. Yet the audience was clearly to find the lessons of limited monarchy and the problems of 1820 in the pellucid theme: opposition of prince and people to strangulation by an oligarchy.

Until this hour, one conspirator asks, "What Prince has plotted for his people's freedom?" (III.ii.438). When the question is asked again, at the imposition of sentence in the hall of the Council of Ten, the Doge himself answers: "Agis," meaning Agis IV, an agrarian reformer who was sentenced to death by the Spartan ephors; he alone, before Faliero, plotted for his people's freedom. In Plutarch's *Parallel Lives* and Alfieri's *Agide,* two versions Byron would know, Agis' fellow king Leonidas acts the same role of implacable nemesis that the patrician Loredano acts in *The Two Foscari.* The struggle against oligarchy as a headless monster is therefore much clearer in *Marino Faliero* than in any of the likely sources. Plutarch, Alfieri, and Byron all exalt the hero who fights patricians for the benefit of the people, but uneasiness over the hero's utilization of popular revolt also begins in Plutarch. Although he describes and portrays Agis as temperate and noble, Plutarch offers Agis and Cleomenes, like the Gracchi, as examples of the ruin that comes from exalting the people out of desire for personal glory. The good man needs no glory. Byron evades the problem by making his hero's pride seek stability, not aggrandizement. He could see as well as

Politics in English Romantic Poetry

we can the parallel in his personal debacle and the rumors of revolt brewing in England.

The personal parallel influences Faliero's language at many points:

> Haply had I been what the Senate sought,
> A thing of robes and trinkets, dizened out
> To sit in state as for a Sovereign's picture;
> A popular scourge, a ready sentence-signer,
> A stickler for the Senate and "the Forty,"
> A sceptic of all measures which had not
> The sanction of "the Ten," a council-fawner,
> A tool—a fool—a puppet,—they had ne'er
> Fostered the wretch who stung me.   (III.ii.187–195)

This description, not so much of a weak monarch as of a ministerial puppet or a Holland House tool—such a tool as Byron could have become in 1812 to ensure his rise in Parliament—parallels his outbursts against current British politics—"how I despise and abhor all these men, and all these things (LJ, IV, 398). The play is emotionally heightened throughout by personal reflections on English politicians. Even Faliero's "wretch who stung me," fostered by the Senate, had equivalents in Romilly, who forgot that he was Byron's lawyer when he advised Lady Byron to bar her lord from her bed and indeed from their house, and in Brougham, whose gossip about the separation outdid the wretch Steno's remark about Faliero's wife. To act now for the vulgar Caroline would mean to collaborate with Brougham, her chief counsel, and that dog Cobbett, one of her most strident supporters. It was one thing to visit the festooned cell of Leigh Hunt, propagandist for tradesmen; it would be another when cooperation with Shelley brought Hunt and family into Byron's palace at Pisa. The first was *noblesse oblige;* the second, an offensive leveling. And now Faliero's stooping to plebeians had its annoying counterpart in the descent of Byron's alter ego, Hobhouse, to join "a pack of blackguards," including Cobbett and the ragamuffin Henry Hunt, in the current Westminster election. To Byron's chagrin, Hobhouse had attacked the Whig jurist Erskine while "Orator"

184

Hunt attacked Burdett. For one sentence in a pamphlet deriding the old-line Whigs, the House of Commons had sent Hobhouse to Newgate. Byron's laughter, in the ballad "My Boy Hobbie O" and elsewhere, was not good-humored: Hobhouse's break with the Whigs cut too near his own dilemma. He was supporting revolution abroad and doubting reform at home. Now that the trading and laboring classes had taken over reform, how could one be sure of leading rather than following? In Italy he could lead. In Ravenna he had been encouraged by Teresa's brother Pietro into the heart of rebel lion. By midsummer of 1820 he had joined the Carboneria and was called the "chief" of "the *popular* part, the *troops*," known as *la turba*—the crowd, the ragamuffins (LJ, V, 358). Their object, Byron said, was "the very *poetry* of politics" (V, 205). So was Faliero's object, for "poetry" here means national self-determination. Byron searched the news for similar poetry in English.

He had told his journal in 1814: "I shall adhere to my party, because it would not be honourable to act otherwise . . . If you begin with a party, go on with them" (LJ, II, 381). Hobhouse, who had irritated him for a year by protesting the "indelicacy" of *Don Juan*, had now violated the clear principle of loyalty to the Whigs. Worse, he had made Byron wonder what loyalty he should require of himself. If Hobhouse had done wrong to bolt the Whigs, was it wrong to make Faliero heroic in conspiring with commoners? The defense seems to be that one chooses one's party but not one's birthplace or class. Faliero protests that he did not wish to be doge. Byron was free to acknowledge British citizenship or to renounce it.

Somewhere, though, in Italy or Greece or America or England, without letting friends see how important it was to him, he had to cleanse a state. Complaining of "Orator" Hunt to John Murray, Byron had to insist on his own approval of "a Constitutional amelioration of long abuses," but he felt more at ease assuring Augusta that he could take part in the miserable contests only if the Funds sank and he had to fight to save "what remains of the fortunes of our house." With his usual need for an appearance of nonchalance, he offered a personal, petty reason for contemplating a major action. He could threaten to lead a revolution, but he could

Politics in English Romantic Poetry

not comfortably confess in his own person the ideal of reform that he assigned to Faliero:

> We will renew the times of Truth and Justice,
> Condensing in a fair free commonwealth
> Not rash equality but equal rights,
> Proportioned like the columns to the temple,
> Giving and taking strength reciprocal,
> And making firm the whole with grace and beauty,
> So that no part could be removed without
> Infringement of the general symmetry. (III.ii.168–175)

The English, too, should be restored to equal rights without rash equality, but there should be no damned cant about it.

Marino Faliero exalts the single noble leader. It deplores the corporate power of rich patricians. In keeping with the sentiments of its author, it has no good word for mixed government, that balance of forces praised by Plato, Aristotle, Polybius, Locke, Montesquieu, and many between. The proper sequence for the truly Byronic hero, such as Washington, is win, *rule,* retire. The struggle of a doge for the just renewal of power to rule provided a more congenial subject than Byron would have found in Spartan kingship, with its tandem yoke over two kings. Ignoring stronger rebels historically more important, Byron selected the doge Faliero to dramatize a generous prince's plot for his people's freedom.

His other Venetian tragedy, *The Two Foscari,* likewise argues the lost cause of the dogate against "the stern Oligarchs" (II.i.407). The title points to a contrast of father and son, worked out in the Latinate theme of a father who reveres law above the life of his own son. Although in the end the doge sacrifices his son and his own office for the stability of the state, he appeals tacitly, like Faliero, to natural law. When the Council of Ten, augmented by a Giunta of twenty-five, command his abdication, he offers his own life for his country:

> But for my dignity—I hold it of
> The *whole* Republic: when the *general* will
> Is manifest, then you shall all be answered.
>
> (V.i.55–57)

186

Byron

Within the historical frame, this assertion is both anachronistic and illogical. Historically the Doge had the right to convene the Grand Council, but that body had been closed since 1297 to all but the aristocrats against whom Foscari is aiming his defiance. The historical Foscari had been elected doge by a complicated system of lottery and veto devised to assure the aristocracy full and permanent control of government. It is possible theoretically for the House of Lords to embody the general will of the English people, but that is exactly the theory that Byron's Venetian plays deny. Most English readers in 1821 probably would have translated the doge's plea into the hoary complaint of the Whigs that the power of the monarchy, working through ministers, placement, and the law of seditious libel, had increased, was increasing, and ought to be diminished. As early as 1813 "the freeholders of Middlesex" had denounced the "detestable Oligarchy" aligned against Caroline;[20] the Venetian plays invite their sympathy. As downtrodden rulers, Byron's doges are his outlawed corsairs on stilts. Only fitfully in *The Two Foscari* does the Council of Ten become the Austrian anarch that has gone so far in "exorbitance of power" that "the most contemned and abject" will rise to check it.[21]

In the second Venetian play Byron greatly relaxed his scrupulosity over the details of ancient sources. Probably he noticed also the inherent contradictions in *The Two Foscari*, but he had expended all the patience he had available for historical tragedy. At least he had the fun of depicting in the son, Jacopo Foscari, a young man whose love of country is so intense that he had rather rot alone in a Venetian prison than live in exile with his wife and children.

Meanwhile, he had turned backward to Diodorus Siculus for the story of Sardanapalus. Byron's version sets forth the situation at once: strength buried under sloth. Sardanapalus epitomizes indulgence. He indulges equally his people, himself, and suspected conspirators. Warned that luxury is a tyranny that multiplies tyrants, he answers that the vice of luxury is better than the glory of leading hordes to death. "I hated," he says when disaster is upon him, "All that looked like a chain for me or others" (IV.i.339–340). An earlier Byronic hero, Manfred, confessed that his noble aspiration in youth, to be the "enlightener of nations," had faded because he could not

187

Politics in English Romantic Poetry

tame his nature down to soothe and sue the masses—the only way to become a "mighty thing amongst the mean" (III.i.114–123). In situation Sardanapalus resembles Manfred, but in him aspiration has never risen above the wish to live and let live. Unlike Byron's doges, his Assyrian acts from purely personal motive, even when he rises with a courage and understanding not at all apparent in Diodorus' account. Yet he lacks the urge to drive men mad that makes a Dante, Galileo, or Napoleon. He is Byron in Venice.

Upon the first sign of conspiracy, however, Sardanapalus explains himself ominously:

> Ne'er
> Was man who more desired to rule in peace
> The peaceful only . . .   (I.ii.370–372)

Descendant of Nimrod and Semiramis, he will be a tiger when roused. Others find his effeminate life degrading. He feels degraded only when those below him can interrupt his princely pleasure. He scorns (like Coriolanus and Childe Harold) the "popular breath," the "rank tongues," of the "vile herd" (I.ii.339–341). The ignorant masses blame their rulers for the natural, inevitable dirtiness and misery of life. (The text has no ironic ripple to suggest that Sardanapalus speaks as a conscious Malthusian.) It is the baseness of mankind that forces their master to abandon rule by sloth for active tyranny:

> Oh, men! ye must be ruled with scythes, not sceptres,
> And mowed down like the grass . . .   (I.ii.414–415)

His paramour, the Greek slave Myrrha, has a racial memory of freedom. Educated to hate monarchs as well as chains, she also disdains the "vulgar mass." Partly we have here the essence of a historical situation—a potentate and his concubine in a trap set by antiquity—as we have when Memmo, the Chief of the Forty in *The Two Foscari*, expresses his choice of belonging to "an united and Imperial 'Ten' " rather than rising to the gilded loneliness of a doge (I.i.193–195). These passages give us also the troubled

188

judgments of Lord Byron. Sardanapalus, called by Sfero a slave of circumstance, calls himself "the very slave of Circumstance," but he adds, "And Impulse" (III.i.320, IV.i.330).

In protesting to his publisher that *Sardanapalus* is "nothing but Asiatic history," not by any intent "a *political* play," Byron meant that the play did not allude to George IV. He had to say, whether or not he could say honestly, that he did not write the play with any King George in mind. Murray could hardly have proceeded without some such disavowal on file. The opening line, "He hath wronged his queen, but still he is her lord," calls rhetorically for the third, "He hath wronged his people—still he is their sovereign." As the second scene opens, Sardanapalus orders his pavilion to be garlanded. No milkmaid in Lincolnshire could have missed the allusion to the royal extravagance at Brighton. And were the royal brothers, with George at the top, not bywords for the "despotism of vice" resplendent in Sardanapalus?

Byron could be certain that Murray and other readers would look for disclosures about himself. His letters had exposed his sense that languishment in the Sea-Sodom came to an end only because Teresa now led him by the nose, just as Myrrha, his kind of ironist, feels debased by loving, but loves. His letters included Teresa's relatives among the Italian patriots who had helped him decide to "take rebellion when it lies in the way" (LJ,V,153). He was hinting to friends in England that the passivity he had claimed in earlier affairs had intensified to a Sardanapalus-like languor with Teresa. Sardanapalus calls for a mirror to admire himself in armor; Byron asks Murray to look up a similar character in Juvenal, as if his own habits and portraits, both known to Murray, did not authenticate such vanity. The meeting that Byron imagines for hero and wife in *Sardanapalus* fits the possibilities of his own situation, not George IV's, although it has the dramatic purpose of preserving the royal line. Sardanapalus more than once expresses a suspiciously Voltairian disbelief in omens and deities. Sardanapalus' final generosity, in encouraging his servants to escape with treasure that legend assigns to his pyre, is no act that Byron would attribute to England's new king. In short, the neoclassical unities of this tragedy of liberty were too scant to hide the old impulses of self-examination and self-disclosure.[22] He planned another work of the kind on Tiberius, to explain how a mild governor could decline into cruel misanthropy.

Possibly Byron had a sense of considerable success in distinguishing his protagonists from himself. Closer study of the historical records, he said, changed his view of Faliero's motives. However that may be, the three plays reveal less interest in theme than in character. In prefaces to *The Borderers* and *Ruy Blas,* Wordsworth and Hugo claim to have shown how disordered times affect individuals; Byron's analogous dramas show how, when the structure of power changes, the leader most affected reacts in and on society.

He felt little strain in building the historical tragedies. Their substance and form seem Harrovian and Cantabrigian. Without any challenging contradictions between form and subject, they served for rebellion against the unbuttoned modes of Shakespearean drama currently in fashion. They illustrate the paradox that all neoclassicism in England since about 1780 has been in revolt. But Byron's satisfaction was both incomplete and brief, for the tragedies represented his feelings and experience only in repression. Except for the expression of their themes through the mouths of partially imagined characters, the momentary pleasure of unleashing their rhetoric, and a passing hope of success on the stage, the plays did not warm him.

The burden of their classicism appears in the tedious purity of their four principal women. The three faithful wives are less Senecan than bourgeois. Jacopo Foscari's wife Marina serves in that play as the voice of reason and virtue. The old doge argues for obedience to the laws of Venice; Marina prefers the laws of nature. When she descends from aristocratic wit, which distinguishes her spirit of rebellion in Acts I and II, to visit her husband's prison in Act III in the domestic spirit of *Fidelio,* Byron has brought her into the bourgeois world of Beaumarchais.

Marina's husband Jacopo loves home and family. He represents the hearth-living ingenuousness that Byron tried to like in Leigh Hunt. Faliero had soared like a Napoleonic eagle against the sun; Jacopo is characterized as a dove.[23] Of course Jacopo is neither a hero nor the protagonist; we are to remember eagles like Faliero

Byron

when Jacopo declines a challenge to soar: "The Mind is much," he says, "but is not all" (III.i.87). The contrast with Faliero nevertheless leaves us on Jacopo's side, sympathizing with a patriotism more appropriate to innkeepers and apothecaries. No such feelings of preserving house and shop from authoritarian search motivated, as far as one can tell, Byron's revolutionary activities in Tuscany.

V

In February 1821 Austrian troops crossed the Po. The Neapolitans who had seemed so brave in 1820 were easily routed. Patriots in Ravenna returned their firearms fearfully to Byron's house. The authorities exiled Teresa's brother, Pietro Gamba, as a conspirator, and his father as well; next they got rid of Teresa by threatening to shut her in a convent for violating the agreement of separation from her husband, Count Guiccioli; and finally they accomplished their aim: Byron applied for a passport to Tuscany and agreed to settle in Pisa. Upon the collapse of excited hopes in Italy he turned in hot fury to the affairs of England. The fury shows in the Moore-remembering anapests of "The Irish Avatar," on the theme that "Each brute hath its nature; a King's is to *reign*" (BWP, IV, 558, st. 16). He had written, but not published, a sonnet in praise of the Regent for restoring the rights of property to the heirs of Lord Edward Fitzgerald, an Irish rebel who had fought against George III on both sides of the Atlantic. From the magnanimity of the sonnet he now claimed the right to vilify the newly crowned King, who came as "the Messiah of Royalty" to Ireland's shores, but the stanzas against George IV lack the wit of those against the Irish who received him in state with "a legion of cooks, and an army of slaves" (BWP, IV, 556, st. 5). Again a Roman adage—the slave makes the tyrant—combines with versification of matter from the *Examiner* or possibly the *Morning Chronicle*. "The definition of a true patriot," Hazlitt wrote in the *Examiner,* "is *a good hater.*" The King was accompanied in actuality and in Byron's verses by Castlereagh, an Irishman who had earlier supervised a bloody suppression of the Irish. To the people so supinely hospitable to a reptile red with Erin's blood and so quickly forgetful

191

Sing we Now Apollo's praise

DOCTOR SOUTHEY'S NEW VISION.

George Cruikshank, "Doctor Southey's New Vision"

of Grattan, who had combined in their behalf the skill of Orpheus with the fire of Prometheus, the poet addresses an Irish question, "Is it madness or meanness which clings to thee now?"[24]

Tiger-springs like "The Irish Avatar" die with their events, but Byron had meanwhile given enough thought to a series of related personal and public events to finish a masterwork he had begun four months earlier, *The Vision of Judgment*. A King died, a King succeeded, but Robert Southey remained Poet Laureate to tell in the hexameters of *A Vision of Judgment* how the absolvers, including George Washington, put down Wilkes, Junius, and the few other accusers when George III sought the gates of Heaven. Although racked by these few, the good King had remained faithful to God and country. Byron ridiculed the title, content, and meter of Southey's poem. Even Hartley Coleridge felt that his uncle had put "the wind-gall'd, glander'd, stagger'd, bott-begrown, spavin'd" monarch into a long trot of extreme cruelty both to the departed monarch and to the reader. One sample from Southey's eulogy will show how the satirist in Byron was provoked. The King ends his plea:

Bending forward, he spake with earnest humility. "Well done,
Good and faithful servant!" then said a Voice from the Brightness . . .

—let this sample suffice.

Only in *The Vision of Judgment* did Byron achieve such simplicity on the surface with so much complexity beneath. Few poems of equal compactness can boast so many levels of parody, satire, comedy, church-window symbolism, factual history dissolved in comic myth, and moral argument.

The Vision parodies not only *A Vision* but much else that the language and structure of that work suggested: George III's own stammer; the courtesies of lethal Parliamentary debate; the stationing of supernatural personalities in *Paradise Lost;* comic discrepancies between the Bible as Byron considered it now and the rigid interpretations of his childhood under a Presbyterian nurse; the idea of an ultimate power that blesses or condemns monarchs—and barons—for all eternity; the complacency of Southey, and of Anglicans still punier, in the face of such power; and the idea of parody itself. Parody had become an issue of political freedom. To climax their spatting, Southey had challenged Byron into this area by ending his attack on the "Satanic school," in his introduction to *A Vision,* with an earnest request that the government look to it. In *The Vision,* as in short passages of *Don Juan,* Byron combined "seditious libel" and "blasphemy," elements in the parodies for which William

Politics in English Romantic Poetry

Hone was tried before Lord Ellenborough in 1817. Acquitted, Hone had published similar parodies, with drawings by George Cruikshank, during the trial of Queen Caroline. He now carried on with such pieces as his own parody of Southey's hexameters. Byron's method is even closer to the political caricatures of James Gillray— for example "Sin, Death, and the Devil," which borrows from Hogarth but burlesques simultaneously the sublime in Fuseli's paintings, Milton, Milton's publishers and illustrators (including Fuseli), and "sublime" reverence for royal actions. For Gillray, Hone, Blake, and Byron, parody is politics.

Fresh from his state funeral, Byron's George III continues his noisy progress to the gates guarded by Peter, much to the surprise of that splenetic but recently inactive saint. In the hearing that follows, Satan has Wilkes, Junius, Horne Tooke, Franklin, and Washington on his side, with many English, Irish, Scottish, French, Spanish, Dutch, Danish, and other witnesses ready to testify. Just when he is about to overwhelm the court with these hordes, in proof that this king has the same qualifications as the recent headless one from France, the last third of the poem suddenly begins: Asmodeus, one of Satan's plainclothesmen, has arrested Southey, a hack, for the blasphemy of anticipating divine judgment. Southey—who has turned his coat and would have turned his skin; who knows which side his bread is buttered on because he buttered both sides; who violently denounces the republication of his own *Wat Tyler* and forgets his slightly more recent pacifist poem on Blenheim in the chauvinism of *The Poet's Pilgrimage to Waterloo*—now offers to add to his biographies of Nelson and Wesley a new one of Satan. When he begins to read from *A Vision*, panic ensues, St. Peter's keys cudgel him into the Lakes, and George slips into Heaven unobserved.

Comedy and satire coalesce in the Parliamentary debate. Early stanzas had been libelous in the poet's own voice. Satan is not chargeable with libelous intent, since he pleads positively for due possession of this soul. He would willingly address George in Southey's own words: "Thou who hast lain so long in mental and visual darkness." Though no tyrant, George shielded tyrants. Even personal madness and physical blindness are a considerable disadvantage to a country so ruled, but spiritual blindness begot political madness. Satan liked that. Besides his shielding of tyrants on the Continent, the King's one body (with its "rottenness of eighty years") begot tyranny in Eldon, Ellenborough, Castlereagh, and their predecessors. He became their tool more than they were his. As for the Continent, this shielder of tyrants died in "the first year of Freedom's second dawn," a dawn predicted in Byron's "Ode on Venice" and celebrated in the present poem. The *Annual Register* for 1821, surveying events across the Atlantic and in Spain, Portugal, Naples, the Romagna, and France, from the point of view of British ministers, concluded: "A new era of political conflict seems about to open upon Europe." Before reminding Saints Michael and Peter that George as the rabid foe of Catholic emancipation lessened their stature, Satan sketches this larger political scene and slips into a Byronic threat:

> The New World shook him off; the Old yet groans
>   Beneath what he and his prepared, if not
> Completed: he leaves heirs on many thrones
>   To all his vices, without what begot
> Compassion for him—his tame virtues; drones
>   Who sleep, or despots who have now forgot
> A lesson which shall be re-taught them, wake
> Upon the thrones of earth; but let them quake!   (st. 47)

Whether or not Lucifer speaks for Byron in *Cain*, as the reviewers charged, here it is certainly the poet, not Satan, who is concerned to threaten despots with education.

Similarly, but without breaking the comedy, Byron looks to the audience when Satan grants George III's domestic virtues. Did his constancy to one ugly woman help the men and nations who cried for freedom while oppressed by "this old, blind, mad, helpless, weak, poor worm"?[25] Perceiving, like Bentham, that George's constancy as husband and farmer, along with his madness, had made him finally popular, Byron exploits the reputation for total inconstancy, bruited by the radical press, that all the royal dukes and their crowned brother shared alike. The sole claim of royal virtue was buried.

Politics in English Romantic Poetry

Byron is using, without having to mention, the wails of the Hunts' *Examiner* and Cobbett's *Register* that royal mistresses account for an increase in taxes. Direct allusions to taxes could be accommodated in *Don Juan,* but less easily in *The Vision,* which kept its sedition pure and narrow. When Murray avoided publication of the manuscript, the poem went into the *Liberal,* edited by Leigh Hunt, published by his brother John, and taken by readers as a literary overflow from authors currently puffed in the *Examiner:* Shelley, Hunt, Hazlitt, and Byron. Periodicals and pamphleteers supporting the government attacked the *Liberal,* and particularly Byron's satire, more vociferously than any other publication of the Hunts. Specifically for publishing *The Vision,* John Hunt was fined £100 and ordered to give sureties for five years against any similar act of sedition.[26] Although Byron squirmed because his connection with the Hunts sickened Moore and other friends in England, he could enjoy the fatefulness of linking the poem to a pair who had for fourteen years sickened the royal family.

The old King had in Southey a fitting Laureate. Aside from a deepening personal quarrel, Byron exercises against the Laureate Pope's moral fervor against dullness. Southey's very existence is a threat to poetry. He smuggles lead into the saddles of Pegasus because he has no aim beyond wages. He shares the drabness of all prostitutes. A few months later, Byron was to call the historian Mitford's wrath and partiality virtues in a writer, "because they make him write in earnest" (*Don Juan* XII.19n). It is suspicion of shallow purpose, as much as aristocratic scorn for an apothecary-poet and anger at Keats's description of the school of Pope as "dolts to smooth, inlay, and clip," that made him reprimand Murray for sending him "*p-ss a bed* poetry" by Johnny Keats, that "tadpole of the Lakes." Southey's dullness, like his King's, came from indifference to things that matter. The turncoat's own poem, with its libel on Washington, gave all the hints Byron needed for Michael's diplomatic retreat—"I ne'er mistake you for a *personal* foe; Our difference is *political*"—when Satan's host of witnesses darkens all surrounding space.

In the blistering Dedication to *Don Juan,* which Byron wrote and suppressed in 1818, Southey's accomplice is not George but

196

Byron

Castlereagh, the "intellectual eunuch" who learned to pant for wider carnage by dabbling "its sleek young hands in Erin's gore." He is the "vulgarest tool that Tyranny could want." Besides his equivocal role in Ireland, where he opposed relief to Catholics as early as 1793 and made unkept promises in achieving the Union of 1800, Byron held it against Castlereagh that he had been demonstrably inept, for example in planning the Walcheren expedition of 1809; had agreed secretly at Paris and Vienna to return Lombardy and Venice to Austria and to transfer Genoa to Sardinia (he simply and systematically opposed Italian nationalism); had left unchallenged the public association of his name with Metternich's against everything Byron wanted in Poland, Spain, and Greece; and had gone out of his way to speak in the Commons for Sidmouth's suppressive acts of 1817 and 1819. Byron apparently meant the word *eunuch* to be privately invidious, for elsewhere he counts among impossible things the day when "Castlereagh's wife has an heir," but in the Dedication he fuses the personal with a charge of political impotence. Impotent to perform any good he might have in him, Castlereagh like Arbaces in *Sardanapalus* is a kind of "human sword" in another's hand. The King, his Laureate, and his Foreign Secretary—all are tools and tools of tools.

Does part of the explanation of incapacity, even in George III and Castlereagh, lie in the neutral space between the spheres and within the individual? In neutral space, in the central section of "The Vision of Judgment," the Two Eternities of light and dark, brilliantly defined by G. Wilson Knight,[27] hold their debate. Manichaeism, which is perceptible in *Manfred,* blatantly unrefuted in *Cain,* and basic to *Heaven and Earth,* seems to guide the opposition of "his Darkness and his Brightness" when Satan confronts Michael in *The Vision of Judgment.* Original sin and the curse of fatality may coincide in a divided nature where the halves are ruled by equal powers. The speaker of the poem benignly runs the risk, if the Anglican catechism holds the final truth, of committing himself to eternal damnation for the "large economy" of allowing that George may have escaped just damnation. By a universalist heresy or Voltaire's easy deism, he could escape all black alternatives; in a world of alternating moral noon and midnight one risk is as good

197

as the rest. Although the poem avoids a conclusive Armageddon, it does not retreat beyond good and evil. Its satiric thrust bursts through the vision of warring powers as well as through the comedy. Moral choice confronts a king, his historian, and his historian's historian. As for Manichaean or "any-chaean," Byron saw no habitable ground between his own view that he followed Alexander Pope and the view of those who called him Manichaean that he worshiped the devil (LJ,V,563). Leslie Stephen, recognizing that his day saw Pope, at best, through the eyes of Byron, said that dullness was to Pope "the literary Ahriman." Although Byron lacked the neatness of Pope's faith in reason, order, and rule, he put down Ahriman, romantic obscurity and gloom, whenever he took up the Ormazdic pen of satiric light.

His own success had deprived him of the pleasure of smothering nonentities; but Wordsworth, because he was an annoyingly good poet of the wrong party, made worthwhile the occasional jests at a complacent bard who distributed excise stamps and sought praise from "Sir George Beaumont, Baronet." Henry Gally Knight was worth lampooning because he was an M.P., rich, and like Southey a dull and therefore conscienceless contriver of verses. In short, Byron still held before himself the ideal of a Renaissance courtier: statesman, military leader, knower, vital poet.

More tightly ordered than any of his purportedly classic satires in heroic couplets, *The Vision of Judgment* differs from them mainly in its easy demeanor. Although it represents a deliberate attempt to do Southey in once and for all, it is free from both the oppressive preachments of the egotistical sublime and the anxieties that underlie Keats's search for disinterested empathy as well as Byron's earlier tempestuous self-pity. Remembering his half-madness in 1816 and for some time afterward, when he gathered strength in hatred, experienced the grandeur of solitude, and saw in mountains and tempests extensions of his own personality, he no longer lived and wrote in the shadow of his failure to conquer either Parliament or his wife—not to mention his wife's advisers. To read the signs in reverse, to say that he now concealed his cold malice in the pretense of condemning public malefactors, might be tenable were it not for his victory over cant. Following up the discovery that he was at his best in exposing cant and hypocrisy, he had now discovered how to free the expression of his own emotions from cant without selecting any one of the neoclassical cages. His ambition had not died, perhaps was undiminished, but repeated evidence of his own superiority had reduced his desperate reliance on fate. The uprisings in Italy had made it harder to continue the role of blasé sinner. As the last infirmity of a martyr is pride in martyrdom, so Byron began to brag of avarice, to him the dullest of sins, in his final pose of non-poseur.

VI

Byron owed much to "Whistlecraft" (John Hookham Frere) for introducing him to the work of Pulci and other Italians who had used the *ottava rima* stanza for comic effects. After trying the stanza and its deflationary devices in *Beppo,* a narrative comedy of Venetian manners, he embarked on *Don Juan.* His stance was casual. At times he pretended not to notice that he had hit upon the way to write the epic of modern times. To object that it has little of the noble simplicity that Matthew Arnold describes as characteristic of Homer is merely to confirm the point: *Don Juan,* although it has the disadvantage of haphazard construction, supersedes *Paradise Lost* and transcends *Faust* on the way out of antiquity. Not epic, it is the successor to epic grandeur. Shelley perceived this, but Gifford, Hobhouse, and other advisers to Murray perceived only that slashing satire made a shocking mixture with naughty-nice comedy of the *Beppo* kind. Why, then, replied Byron, "Do you suppose that I could have any intention but to giggle and make giggle?" In truth he had found in the medley of comic and satiric effects the one form with which he could meet the new subjective requirement of sincerity in art.

Wordsworth's solution to the conflict of political and aesthetic principles was a reconciliation so complete that it chilled his verse; Byron's solution was to accept, after fierce struggle, the failure of reconciliation. In *Don Juan* he achieves organic unity, in the Coleridgean sense that it "blends and harmonizes" antithetical materials without subordinating nature to art. Wherever you look into the poem, its tissue is both alive and dependent on the living tissue

199

Politics in English Romantic Poetry

around it. E. E. Bostetter has said before me: the poet of *Don Juan* sang as if his song could have no ending.[28] This approximation to the *élan vital* forms a portion of the extent to which Byron fulfilled his aim of making literature a human act. Another portion came with the creation of art out of carelessness; not merely *sprezzatura,* the nobleman's nonchalance; not simply art concealing art; but sloppiness that eases communication. Bluffness in manner as in matter was one positive force in making *Don Juan* more honored abroad, in translation, than in London and the counties.

Byron did not apply in the poem a solution, either philosophical or literary, reached beforehand. He discovered the solution in the poem itself. He did not owe everything to the stanza, or even to the devices of incongruity, surprise, deflation, anticlimax, and abrupt reversal fitted to the stanza's structure of alternating rhymes, *ababab,* prolonged thus from the usual fourth to the sixth line, then suddenly an unanticipated *cc.* Although he had scattered most of the devices through his earliest volume, and had learned from Francesco Berni, Luigi Pulci, and G. B. Casti how to concentrate the effects in *ottava rima,* he soon saw that the stanza and its devices yielded minor effects except as they served the larger discovery of digression. Byron interlarded the comic stanzas of narrative in the past tense with satiric commentary in the present. He had found in the commentary, as Elizabeth Boyd observed in 1945, how to show the domination of his immortal mind, "that fiery particle," over a congeries of material facts. He continued his ostentatious homage to fact, in part to underline the satirist's allegiance to truth, even more to show the power of skill and personality to subdue and assimilate, and most to refute charges of romantic irresponsibility. Mistakenly, like many after him, he had taken the romantic impulse as illusion, avoidance of reality, what he now called Platonism, very nearly the opposite of romantic adherence to particulars. Often when the narrative flowed most freely he interpolated additional commentary to impede it. Canto III is mostly commentary, with splendid narrative digressions. The poet mocks the narrative, itself basically mock-heroic, and he mocks his mockery of it.

To mock so is not to abandon. Byronic irony, gazing into the chasm between its visions of man as despicable monster and man as glorious power, commands no stoic withdrawal from experience merely because glorious, strenuous, awesome, terrible, idyllic love falls down the stairs of time and lies exposed in all its silliness. The Byron of *Don Juan* is no Prufrock in ironic suspension. The bardic warrior had reached Canto V when he devised an epitaph to be used if he fell in the anticipated battles for Italian independence:

> When a man hath no freedom to fight for at home,
> Let him combat for that of his neighbors;
> Let him think of the glories of Greece and of Rome,
> And get knocked on the head for his labours.
>
> (BWP, VII, 70–71)

Deflation leads him straight to the final word of the two stanzas, *knighted:* "Then battle for Freedom wherever you can, / And, if not shot or hanged, you'll get knighted." But the power of deflation does not take from him the sense of grandeur in commanding guerrillas to gain a nation's independence.

"I want a hero," he begins—an odd pursuit when gazettes have brought the price of heroes down to tuppence a peck and exposure to battle has so reduced their value that he can pack them six to a line—"Joubert, Hoche, Marceau, Lannes, Dessaix, Moreau"—and then return to his problem. In later cantos, particularly VII and VIII on Suvorov's butchery at the siege of Ismail and the stanzas on Wellington's pension that open IX, military glory is equaled with successful practice at spattering brains and slitting windpipes. To the satirist obligated to strip away illusion, all fame is *vanitas vanitatum,* and the seeker of fame is a pig chasing the wind.

> Not so Leonidas and Washington,
> Whose every battle-field is holy ground,
> Which breathes of nations saved, not worlds undone.
>
> (VIII.5:2–4)

Other stanzas on the "all-cloudless Glory" of Washington evade with equal aplomb the irony that keeps the poem spinning. The satirist leaves much for the historian to praise. Nor do the satirist's quips against epic structure and epic devices reduce the implied heroism of the moralist emulating Pope. Nevertheless, probably in life and certainly in literature, the democratic idea has put an end to the heroic hero. By default, the old commentator takes as non-hero a young Byron, more pursued than pursuing.

Juan is a natural man, a Rousseauistic innocent. Perhaps Byron meant him to disrupt society more by his beauty than by his innocence, but his guilelessness, evident in the first episode when he returned the love that Julia mistakenly believed to be Platonic, continues until he stumbles backward into a medal for heroism. Although less surely than his forerunner, Tom Jones, he learns from encounters with the hard-souled and self-centered, like the Sultana Gulbeyaz, the professional soldier Johnson, the curiously dull Catherine of Russia, and ultimately—just as the poem breaks off—from England's forthright highwaymen and icily hypocritical ladies. Through Juan's natural passivity, the positive satirist exposes Wellington's claims to distinction. The victor by force, particularly through Wellington's avatar Suvorov, becomes the anti-hero, the classic hero at last seen through. Napoleon ducks in and out as a "sucking hero" who grew to fit the sorry pattern. Juan drifts as the non-hero. The author looks into the narrative, into prophets like Cervantes, and into the daily news, to ask what true heroism consists of. At last in this poem what is drawn from dreams does not exceed what is drawn from observation and experience, but the stuff of dreams is present, so that political principles emerge in *Don Juan* from the context of daily life. The callow Juan is forever learning what the commentator has long known from experience.

It is inaccurate to say, as several critics have said, that the commentator is a harlequin who believes in nothing. He believes in continuing the poem, in continuing the search for liberty and love, and in continuing to question even what he prizes most. A skeptic, he goes completely through the bottom of skepticism: he doubts that "doubt itself be doubting" (IX.17:8). The voice in the commentary admires both reason and the mystery of creative imagination, doubts the efficacy of either, and comes to terms with the doubt. In choosing targets for satire, this voice maintains a high level of discrimination.

Byron

Recent emphasis on the contrast of unfolding narrative and spurting commentary requires a counteremphasis on the binding element of satire. The poem darkens as it goes, but Canto I, a bedroom farce, satirically rejects a large number of follies: the unreason of marriages of convenience and similar arrangements by social convention; Platonic idealism that tries to ignore the flesh; unintelligent systems of education (particularly those that rely on untried virtue); chivalric mounting of horses that have to be dismounted; the hypocrisy of condemning such cantos as this but reading on; and pride in industrial and charitable progress—this "patent age of new inventions" for "killing bodies, and for saving souls" (I.132). Seven rejected stanzas on Brougham, although more splenetic than the narrative they were to interrupt, are less effective as satire than the pedagogical misadventures of Donna Inez, who sought solace from failure with her son by teaching children in a Sunday school "to suppress their vice and urine."[29] Satire, which saturates the commentary, varies in intensity throughout the narrative, but persists.

Again, it is not enough to note the similarity of *Don Juan* to picaresque novels unless one notes also Juan's performance of the picaro's satiric function: his geographic and occupational mobility permits the exposure of a wide array of conduct. Continuing the picaro's rise from street crime through the trades to the professions, Juan moves mostly among Byron's own set, the hereditary leaders. Despite this heroic environment, Juan sees the underside of heroism, like Candide, from a combination of bumbling and enslavement. *Don Juan* is close cousin to *Joseph Andrews, Tristram Shandy,* and *Vanity Fair.* As a prose epic in verse, it inherits from Henry Fielding the problems and opportunities of a literary form addressed to persons of middle income and regular but limited leisure.[30] If any example is valid in Mario Praz's survey, *The Hero in Eclipse in Victorian Fiction,* then Juan signifies the decline of the English hero under bourgeois ministration.

As one might predict from his insistence on fact, Byron sometimes moves from the exploration of political principles, as Coleridge, Wordsworth, and Shelley explore them, toward the humanitarianism of Dickens and Mrs. Gaskell, for example, in XVI.61–67, devoted to the pregnant country girl brought as a "poacher upon Nature's manor," along with two actual poachers caught in a steel trap and ready for "jail, their place of convalescence." Brought before Lord Henry, the magistrate sitting in his own multiple interests, the girl is soon forgotten in the press of legal suits, mortgages, and dinner. Along with a sly confession of his own affair with a servant girl some fourteen years earlier and a hint that the lord of the manor may be the father in the present case, Byron seems to satirize the political shilly-shallying of Lord Holland while confessing in shifts of tone his own awkwardness of 1812, when he declared the frame-breakers guilty of "the capital crime of poverty" and of "lawfully begetting several children"—this in his maiden speech before the Lords—within a month of accomplishing a partial solution to his own debts in the raising of rents at Newstead. (Admittedly the situation was as involuted then as the tone is in Canto XVI.) In any event, if some of the lines seem too flippant for self-awareness, others mount a heavy attack against two double standards: the woman pays and the most deprived pays most.

Domestic politics and manners are thoroughly blended in the "versified Aurora Borealis" of the commentary, asides, and sudden retractions. English ladies who read the poem to see who was pilloried or tattled on complained that the manners were out of date, but the narrative was supposed to be of past events and the commentary was almost abreast of political contention and intrigue in London, "from Carlton palace to Soho." Hobhouse, like other old friends, agreed increasingly with Evangelical and mercantile acquaintances that flippancy and frankness should be guarded or suppressed, but many stanzas of the commentary parallel Hobhouse's newly donned Westminster radicalism, except in the notable absence of democratic sentiments.

The political and economic inferences of *Don Juan* become sharper if we have three sets of facts in mind. First, Cantos VIII through XVI, where the commentary turns toward economics, were written between July 1822 and April 1823. Secondly, the dominant concerns of Parliament and the English press had in recent years fluctuated: famine and crisis in 1816, precipitating mob violence and retaliatory Coercion Acts in 1817; better harvests but fear of revolution in 1818, signalized by the defection of independent Whigs from the masses and their demogogues and resulting in Parliamentary concessions to landowners; in 1819, mass meetings and sporadic violence in the industrial countries of the north, countered by the Six Acts but not disrupting the new cooperation of Benthamite industrialists and the artisans; expectation in early 1820 of revolution in the name of the Queen; then, after the bursting of this political bubble, a renewal of the economic debates; and finally, in 1822, movements toward liberal reform on numerous fronts.

We want to know, thirdly, what choices of information were open to the poet in exile. Until the autumn of 1821 Murray sent him the *Quarterly, Edinburgh,* and occasionally the *Monthly* reviews, with items of special interest from *Blackwood's* and other magazines. Although *Galignani's Messenger* came from Paris with extracts from the English papers, Byron had followed no London newspaper since his departure in 1816. Snippets were reprinted in Italy; others were quoted to him in letters. Weary of spatting with Southey, Bowles, and others, he ordered Murray, on 24 September 1821, to send thereafter "*no periodical works* whatsoever—*no Edinburgh, Quarterly, Monthly,* nor any Review, Magazine, Newspaper, English or foreign, of any description."

He needed a mixture of passion and aloofness, with the appearance of slapdash topicality, more than certifiably late news. A moment's comparison with *The Dunciad,* with Gifford's satires, with *All the Talents,* or with his own earlier pieces shows one of Byron's great satirical advances in *Don Juan* to be the reduction of footnotes. Other satires carried outside wallets of fact and forced wit; *Don Juan* swallows topicality whole.

The interdiction of 1821 left available the *Messenger,* the *Annual Register* (slow news indeed, but a kaleidoscopic reminder), and whatever he accepted from his colleague in the Pisan school of Satanic poetry. Shelley had written to Thomas Love Peacock in May 1820:

We know little of England here. I take in Galignani's paper, which is filled with extracts from the *Courier,* and from those accounts it appears probable that there is but little unanimity in the mass of the

205

people; and that a civil war impends from the success of ministers and the exasperation of the poor. I wait anxiously for your Cobbetts . . .[31]

Peacock regularly sent batches of Cobbett's *Register* and the *Examiner,* which usually reached Shelley two months or so after publication. Of course news could travel faster. "My Boy Hobby O" appeared in the *Morning Post* thirty days after it left Byron's hand. *Galignani's Messenger,* published in Paris daily except Sunday, reported Parliamentary debates, with editorial opinion from the London papers, within two to five days. When the arms of the telegraph signaled across the Channel such dramatic news as the death of Queen Caroline, the *Messenger* stopped the press to insert a "Second Edition." Besides the *Courier,* it quoted the *Times, Post, Morning Chronicle, Bell's Weekly Messenger, Statesman,* and other British papers, and it quoted them on the subjects mentioned in *Don Juan.*[32]

When Shelley drowned in July 1822, Leigh Hunt had just arrived in Pisa. The supply of *Examiners* from Peacock probably overlapped a supply from John Hunt, and Byron may have succumbed. Although Byron liked to appear in the *Examiner* because of its large circulation, he did not cite it, as he had previously cited the quarterlies, in letters to Murray and Moore. Nevertheless, it is to be observed both that the last cantos coincide with the period of Hunt's uncomfortable proximity in Pisa and Genoa and that the commentary takes up the same topics as the weekly editorials headed "Political Examiner." More to the point, it reflects similar attitudes, except when the *Examiner* condemns the House of Lords outright as a legislative institution. Byron had come to share many of the Hunts' aversions.

Like the *Examiner* of 1816-17, but more than the *Examiner* of 1822-23, *Don Juan* emphasizes the financial and economic aspects of government. *The Curse of Minerva* and *The Waltz,* like most other satires from the Opposition, had blamed various kinds of corruption on paper money. In 1820, when paper money poured from county banks as well as Lombard Street and the Bank of England, the landowners defended it with the full support, according to Halévy, of the great Whigs. Landowners and fundholders were put in conflict. Byron suffered a period of freedom from rents. He had long since, but only after previous years of effort, dissolved Newstead into investments at interest. His Rochdale estate, up for sale, provided an income from mining until its sale was realized shortly before his death. Always alert to income, debt, and instant philanthropy, the baron had first declined his royalties as a poet, then asked that certain royalties go to friends in need, soon had others assigned to his creditors, and finally accepted the income for his many purposes. He regarded as a danger to his stake all ministerial tampering with either the British Funds or the Sinking Fund, which Pitt had designed for repayment of the national debt. Pitt had not reckoned on endless borrowing. Shelley had written to Peacock in 1820: "Cobbett persuaded you, you persuaded me, and I have persuaded the Gisbornes that the British funds are very insecure." But suddenly, at the beginning of 1822, the death of Lady Noel gave Byron an income of £6,000 a year in addition to some £2,000 in royalties, restored him to the class of landowners with an eye on rents, and simultaneously enabled him to deny kinship with landowners by such generosity as the payment of Suliote troops and a loan of £4,000 to the Greek cause while the London Greek Committee dallied. *Don Juan,* much more ruminative than the earlier satires, speaks both for these personal concerns and for the avarice of what Tom Moore called "the d—d sturdy Saints of the middle class."[33]

Nor could the accumulation of economic allusions be altogether unconscious. The commentary of Cantos VIII–XVI observes the "House of Commons turned to a tax-trap," the "Sinking Fund's unfathomable sea," the "foul corruption" in "the dear offices of peace or war," the probable cost to taxpayers of royal mistresses, the certain cost of Wellington's awards and pensions, the loot taken in the righteous cause of replacing Napoleon with restored Bourbons and the Holy Alliance. The poet asks Cockneys to recall "the taxes, Castlereagh, and debt" when ministers propose another bout of the "pious pastime war." In a metaphor directed against such evangelists as Elizabeth Fry, the Quaker who preached to prisoners, he sideswipes the Corn Laws, which were strengthened in 1822 by a sliding scale against imports. Packing still more into the metaphor, he contrasts his own deep satiric trenches with the shallow plough of Mrs. Fry, which skims the vice-manured surface only "to keep its corn at the old price." Elsewhere in Cantos IX and XII he laughs at country gentlemen because their rents fell with the emperor they hated.

A passage of 1817 in *Beppo,* anticipating the devices of *Don Juan,* had proclaimed love of England for its freedom of speech, press, and quill; "the Habeas Corpus (when we've got it)"—in 1817 they hadn't; "the taxes, when they're not too many"; and, to prove his loving-kindness, "Poor's rate, Reform, my own, the nation's debt"—"so God save the Regent, Church, and King." The list, which included also beefsteak, beer, and the weather, went downhill all the way to the King. The intention, as in the later poem, was to expose English character, just as in his references to litigation as the way a nation of shopkeepers settled affairs of honor. The Rochdale estate, which provided income from mining rather than rents, was subject to parish rates and tithes; but Byron's first angry readers would accept the topics of taxes and tithes as national. The poet who puts these topics into stanzas is not complaining; he has simply grasped the English idea of the constitution of the church and state. In a sense, this is exactly the protest against commercialism that Coleridge was making.

Although the commentator in *Don Juan* ignores the parish rates, he never mentions the Church of England without a reference to its takers of tithes. In lampooning magistrates (XVI.60), he jibes at the choler of Dissenters over tithes, but three stanzas later, and once again in the same canto, he joins his protest to theirs: the clergy are "takers of tithes, and makers of good matches." At Ismail the Russians fought as if a preacher, spurning all earthly goods "save tithes," had urged them on (VII.64:6). To summarize, a country that takes idealistic language home from services in church, instead of listening to a skeptical satirist, will live in hypocrisy, money-madness, and carnage.

Suspicion of Byron's way with his own motives is justifiable. When he defends his attention to money at the beginning of Canto XII as the stripping of illusion, because in life "Cash rules the grove, and fells it too besides" and because Napoleon's daring has been replaced by "Jew Rothschild, and his fellow Christian Baring," it takes sixteen stanzas to move toward another subject. The cash nexus does not alienate him from, as much as it binds the satirist in him to, the land of "white cliffs, white necks, blue eyes, bluer stockings, / Tithes, taxes, duns, and doors with double knockings." Byron is English enough to concentrate on these topics.

When Canto XII refers to the miser's ingots and diamonds from a distant mine, the poet does not, as Keats does in *Isabella*, turn aside to pity the thousands of miners "in troubles wide and dark." Yet Byron's Idenstein does just this, at *Werner* III.i.338, in alluding to the millions of hearts that bleed to lend luster to a monarch's crown. Even in *Werner*, the point is explicitly political. I have mentioned a humanitarian tint in the narrative. The commentary darts among the political subjects common to the *Examiner*, Cobbett's *Register*, Wooler's *Black Dwarf*, Carlile's *Republican*, and the conservative journals set up to put them down. The radicals try to leave pity to the Methodists and Evangelicals they despise; their own theme is injustice. Similarly, *Don Juan* leaps to the Queen's trial; "the people ridden o'er like sand" (at Peterloo) by "slaves on horseback"; "carotid-artery-cutting Castlereagh," whose suicide is thus made a symbol of power diplomacy, self-defeating oppression as in the Six Acts of 1819, and of Anglican hypocrisy, which imprisons a Carlile for blasphemy but honors a murderer of Ireland and self by burial near Grattan ("if a poor radical, such as Waddington or Watson, had cut his throat," Byron's Preface complains, "he would have been buried in a cross-road"). Support for Irish Catholics, with much more, is implied in every mention of Castlereagh's name. He recurs in synecdoche, a part for the whole. His name reverberates with Sidmouth's sins as well as his own. Something of the same antiministerial effect is gained by jests at the eccentric judgments of Lord Chancellor Eldon (Byron's objections are personal); at Wellington as the symbol of imperialistic Britain, a carnage-cobbler in India and jailer to the world (X.67–68); and at their philosopher Malthus, as the symbol of dry reason, heartless orthodoxy, and obstacles to Reform. As an emblem of subserviency, the *Morning Post* will do. To some extent, these things enter Byron's satirical revue as automatic jokes. *Don Juan* includes references to all persons, institutions, and practices against which the Opposition was united.

Politics in English Romantic Poetry

The leaps in context belong to Byron. Stanzas on the slaughter at Ismail-Waterloo assimilate the famine in Ireland: "Though Ireland starve, Great George weighs twenty stone." The paradoxical character of the pirate Lambro as a professional man, a "sea-solicitor," violent only in vengeance for the degradation of Greece, is reversed in the sad trimmer of a Greek Laureate, who "sung, or would, or could, or should have sung" the lines Byron must provide for him. It is because Mrs. Fry restricts her preaching to Newgate ("Newgatory teaching," said Hood) that *Don Juan* must assume the responsibility of preaching to nobles and royalty. The poem leaps from praise of Wilberforce's cause, anti-slavery, to laughter at the man, a Tory.

Outside the mesh of quips, Byron gives less attention to the internal state of his country than to its corrupt influence on international conditions. Before 1793, when the Prince of Wales looked "full of promise"—especially to the Whigs—Juan visited Westminster and saw constitutional monarchy in action: "That noble sight, when *really* free the nation." Now Britain's alliances have entrapped her to perpetuate the "yokes of iron" in Poland, the Austrian anarch in Venetia and Lombardy, and the tarantulas that were just beginning to be stung by "the Spanish Fly and Attic Bee." Perhaps nothing else in the poem shows so well how flippancy serves its specific and thematic protests as this union of insectival and aphrodisiacal imagery for peoples "strongly stinging to be free." You cannot make a subject sacred simply by risking your freedom or your life for it.

In Spanish America the commercial interests of London are investing in revolution, but private vices have supported only public vices where "I have seen a Congress doing all that's mean." Byron inserted this reference to "a Congress," with a context of three stanzas, after the Congress of Verona in October 1822. This latest in the series was called to deal with the Greek revolt against Turkey but was concerned more immediately with the uprising of the *descamisados,* "the shirtless patriots of Spain," against their local Bourbon. The assembled sovereigns and delegates (except Wellington) condemned the Greeks as "rash and culpable" and the revolution in Spain as mere "disorders and convulsions." Although *The Age of Bronze*

210

shows that Byron did not excuse England from the results of the congress of 1822, here in *Don Juan* "a Congress" goes behind Verona to evoke the Metternich-Castlereagh chain of conferences that had made Italy "a geographical expression" and fixed to the principle of legitimacy—at least in the liberal view—Czar Alexander's vision, embodied in the Holy Alliance, of the despotic powers as "all members of one and the same Christian nation."

The commentator esteems all new revolutions, large or small. Like Canning, he thinks of calling the New World into existence to redress the balance of the Old. But *Don Juan* is no trumpet for democracy, despite its prediction that the tyranny of kings will end: "I think I hear a little bird, who sings / The people by and bye will be the stronger" (VIII.50). Toward the end of Canto VIII, in three prosodically crude stanzas, the poet exults in this prophecy. He urges "our children's children," if they should hear of vanished thrones as of painted savages, mammoth's bones, or impenetrable hieroglyphics, to disdain even a dim memory of those who painted the limbs of others—as the savage Picts did not—with gore. This is a direct echo of the kingless world of *Prometheus Unbound*.

In general, though, and perhaps even here, the author of *Don Juan* merely opposes the conduct of all kings presently enthroned. He prophesies to warn. Thirty stanzas later, at IX.25, he affirms his disinterest by refusing to adulate either king or people, tyrant or mob. Although free from the Czar's fear of democracies and republics, he hates demagogues and will not flatter. As a poet, he knowingly combines wrath, augury, and hyperbole.

As the theme to hammer, he chooses freedom from tyranny, in a sense large enough to keep the argument gaily unconfined. Even the narrative, which grasps and releases the theme of freedom as if indifferently, exhibits in sequence the tyranny of convention in marriage, the tyranny of the flesh when challenged by Platonic fantasy or Byronic aspiration; the flatness of mere physical slavery; the contagious, silent tyranny of the harem; the dainty devices of the despots; and last, in its endless wardrobe of disguises, the blind and blinding tyranny of English hypocrisy. George Ridenour, in one of the best studies of *Don Juan*, remarks that tyranny "is seen as essentially sterile," but only the tool is sterile: the needle is sterile, the drug is potent; the trigger is neutral, the mind behind the hand is vicious.

Of course the overthrow of political tyranny is a subtheme only. By precept and example, *Don Juan* opposes the larger, amorphous tyrannies over the human mind. The *Liberal,* announced Leigh Hunt, for himself, Byron, and Shelley, would worship wherever "we see the mind of man exhibiting powers of its own, and at the same time helping to carry on the best interests of human nature." Byron's backing of the *Liberal* was brief, impatient, and harassed by friends like Moore, but *Don Juan* endorses everything in Hunt's statement except the longwindedness; it fights whatever impedes the mind's powers. Its persona becomes a kind of metaphor for volatility. Intimidation and cant, whether on a throne or among the noble nincompoops gathered in Canto XII at Norman Abbey, bring Byron's thirst for freedom into union with the hunger of the downtrodden and deceived. His Preface to the later cantos shows pride in the popular association of his *Cain* with the blasphemies of Richard Carlile. When the poet withdraws from prophecy into the assertion of independence, at the beginning of Canto IX, he withdraws momentarily from irony:

> And I will war, at least in words (and—should
> My chance so happen—deeds) with all who war
> With Thought; —and of Thought's foes by far most rude,
> Tyrants and Sycophants have been and are.
> I know not who may conquer: if I could
> Have such a prescience, it should be no bar
> To this my plain, sworn, downright detestation
> Of every despotism in every nation.   (IX.24)

Lord Byron had learned, and in the japery of *Don Juan* teaches, that superior political views cannot precede the observer's cleansing of himself, not merely of vileness, as the Presbyterians taught in Scotland, but of timidity. If *Don Juan* is a poem of acquiescence, what it accepts is the explosive potentiality of the human being for good and evil in this world.

Man should be at once natural and awake. The contrasts of volatile flippancy versus cant, truth versus feigning, reality versus appearance, fact versus the "Platonism" of Alfonso's Julia or the innocent champagne of Lady Adeline Amundeville—these terminate in nature versus civilization. The poet steps back from civilization not only in Juan's ingenuousness, the idyll of Juan and Haidée, and the casually ranged daughters of nature—from the libidinous Dudù to the helpless orphan Leila—but most notably, because least expectedly, in the seven stanzas on Daniel Boone, "the Man of Ross run wild," backwoodsman ever pressing beyond each new frontier.[34] "Simple, serene, the antipodes of shame," Boone is surrounded by a "sylvan tribe of children of the chace," whose "young, unawakened world was ever new." The opposite of this unawakened dawn is civilization, with its carnage at Ismail, its bullying of wild animals, its tedium indoors, and its quintessential meanness: "Thy cliffs, *dear* Dover! harbour, and hotel." The commonplaces are blasted into truth by the language of experience.

With the biblical account of our first parents' fall from paradise, Byron combined a Hobbesian view of man's uncivilized state, as represented in the cannibalism of all but Juan after the shipwreck and equally in the uncivilized ferocity of teeth and hands at Ismail. In the lifeboat Juan remained above the bestiality of his mates. At Ismail bestiality resulted from exactly those conditions that Europe has come to call civilization. Boone's life gives factual proof that human life comes in two sizes: the colossal, like Boone's, which has almost escaped the fall of Adam by rising clear of savagery but evading the coils of civilization, and the smaller size within backbiting society. Man's nature is such that the artfulness of civilization reduces it to meanness. In Europe every mean or self-serving action is ascribed to human nature, in the absence of any natural humanity to set the standard.

From the shifting antitheses of *Don Juan* we can see more clearly than from Byron's earlier works the chief importance of fact. We discover one important reason, if we have not before, why he venerated the *Iliad* "as the truth of *history* (in the material *facts*) and of *place*": "Otherwise, it would have given me no delight." It is not fidelity to fact that matters, but the existence of fact behind the poem. Belief in reality of any sort comes hard. The poet can reveal the politics of the future only if he sees the "poetry of politics"

Politics in English Romantic Poetry

in the present or past. Since Boone and Washington are not beings of the mind only, a mad Byron may be able to throw off the guilty torpor of a Sardanapalus and rise anew as a liberator somewhere in the Americas or in the visionary isles of Greece, where "all, except their sun, is set." Vision become fact is the very politics of poetry. Juan is on his never-ending way to hell or marriage, but the commentator was on his way to Missolonghi, heart high, morals in confusion of high and low, self-distrust gaining steadily. Byron had always said, *aut Caesar, aut nullus,* and now *aut Caesar, aut nihil,* either Caesar or dead; but unlike Caesar he waited to be asked. Was he accepting the call of the Greek Committee because he had tired of Teresa? Then he would tire of the sniveling Greeks and return.

VII

When Murray began to censor and defer, John Hunt took over *Don Juan* at Canto VI and gained *The Vision of Judgment* for the *Liberal.* Hunt published also the last poems completed by Byron, *The Age of Bronze; or, Carmen Seculare et Annus Haud Mirabilis* and *The Island; or, Christian and His Comrades.* The first ends the lineage of heroic satire. The second is a codicil distributing among three sons the legacy of the Byronic hero. Those who grow restless when Byron is earnest should rush on to *The Island;* students of his politics must linger over his last satire.

The Age of Bronze tells how Europe fared in 1822, the year by no means marvelous when games epitomizing the age were held at Verona. Byron's subtitle, "Carmen Seculare et Annus Haud Mirabilis," thus indicts jointly the Congress of Verona and the decay of human metal that brought it about. This poem, crowded with politics, seems dull today because Byron was entirely serious. He weights the couplets with the Midas touch of detail and allusion that had always made *The Dunciad* a dangerous model for his satire. A casual reader could take the poem as still another versification of the *Examiner* or at best a concentration of the topical satire scattered through the last several cantos of *Don Juan.* But the three-part title points to a tight, complex structure. The first five sections concern the good old days of the giants—at least in

214

memory and by comparison—Pitt, Fox, and Napoleon in his prime. Sections VI and VII look toward the world's struggle to begin a new cycle. The last eleven sections depict the nadir of life under Wellington, Metternich, and the Rothschilds. In the golden age before Pitt, the name, idea, and reality of *Congress* "freed the Atlantic," but the name hallowed in America has become polluted by the congresses of despots. This change in the meaning of *Congress* adequately explains the present suspension of liberal hopes.

Although mockery touches the characterization of the age of Pitt as silver on the verge of bronze, the cohesive metaphors greatly strengthen the earnestness. Cosmic and cataclysmic imagery magnifies the satiric rage. The poetry stirs restlessly, violently, amid the stultifying brass that burdens it. Section I opens with Byronic melancholy and *memento mori*, but when lines in the next section convert the emblems of Cleopatra's (supposed) mummy and Alexander's (supposed) urn into laughter at the "madman's wish" for more worlds to conquer, the true tone and scale of the poem emerge. The Napoleon of section III, greatest of eagles, changed his style of play by throwing human bones as dice across the table of earth. Physically reduced at St. Helena to "daily squabbling o'er disputed rations," he remained the spirit of Aeschylus' Prometheus, appealing from his rock to "Earth,—Air,—Ocean,—all that felt or feel / His power and glory." In Horace's *Carmen saeculare* pure girls and boys pray to the presiding deities for a glorious Roman future. More stridently, Byron's section V calls on all forces where Napoleon was himself a power, on Heaven, Earth, Isle that saw the eaglet's birth, Alps, Rome beyond the Rubicon, Egypt with its tombs of Pharaohs, the cities he conquered and lost, the Fire of Moscow—sublimer than Etna, Vesuvius, or Hecla (Byron was correcting his previous errors about this Icelandic volcano)—and the other element, Ice, that broke the conqueror. Napoleon thus becomes a cosmic force like Shelley's west wind, with his career a mountain range of those peaks of civilization that could be associated with him. All these forces and entities testify that Napoleon's fall resulted by natural law when he crossed the Rubicon "of Man's awakened rights" merely to "herd with vulgar kings and parasites," but they should witness, too, the reawakening of his Promethean spirit in Spain,

215

Greece, South America, and (the poet hopes) Poland, which Napoleon himself had betrayed. Though his dust be denied rest in the Pantheon, yet his name shall be the talisman against legitimacy, like Guesclin's (when the keys of a city were surrendered to his bier) or like "Ziska's drum," which legend and Voltaire say the dying man ordered made from his own skin, to lead Hussites into battle against the Catholic Imperialists. In the Napoleonic cause Byron both adapts and answers a question that Edmund Burke addressed to the Whigs in *A Letter to a Noble Lord:* "Must I be annihilated, lest, like old *John Zisca's,* my skin might be made into a drum, to animate Europe to eternal battle, against a tyranny that threatens to overwhelm all Europe, and all the human race?"

Besides Alexander, Cleopatra, Guesclin, and Ziska, the Titanic sections (through vii) allude to the insatiable Caesar, Anthony, Pompey's pillar, Hannibal, Cambyses, Sesostris who yoked kings and princes to his chariot, Roland, the Cid, Gustavus Adolphus, Charles XII, Frederick the Great, and—as counter to Kosciusko—Catherine of Russia. Later monarchs appear mostly in the guise of vicious animals. After Leipzig the Saxon jackal led against Napoleon the bear, wolf, and fox of Russia, Prussia, and Austria. Pizarro and Cortes enter as reminders of Spanish lust for gold and gore. Against all these the poem invokes tyrant-tamers and heroes of liberty: Harmodius, Pelayo, Washington, Kosciusko, the Maid of Saragossa, Bolivar, and José de San Martin, who had just acted the Cincinnatus by liberating Peru and retiring. Just as important as these, to point out what a true congress would be like, statesmen, sages, and orators gather in the contracted space of the middle sections: Cicero, Franklin, and Patrick Henry, "the forest-born Demosthenes" whose "thunder shook the Philip of the seas." These belong to the tides of freedom rolling across the Atlantic. Two of the lines paraphrase Turgot's hexameter on Franklin's seizure of the lightning from heaven and the scepter from tyrants: *Eripuit coelo fulmen sceptrumque tyrannis.* Henry as Demosthenes to George's Philip: this barter in great names, despite its banality, conveys the sense that other Agamemnons and Ciceros may be, today and tomorrow.

After assembling the noble literary associations of Verona, from the Scaligers through Romeo to Pindemonte (died 1828), the poem descends to Chateaubriand and Constant, who debased their talents at the Congress, and Canning, who demeans his wit in Liverpool's service. The poet himself plays the role of Diogenes searching faces of bronze for an honest monarch.

The cosmic and cataclysmic imagery for the golden sunrise of freedom collapses into tokens of mediocrity in the second half of the poem. Section ix deplores the tameness and paltriness of the Veronese in gaping at monarchs whose greatest accomplishment was the formation of a blessed, earthly Trinity to "melt three fools to a Napoleon." Lacking the ferocity and variety of wolves, bears, and foxes, the monarchs of the Holy Alliance merge in a dull sameness. Czar Alexander, half-promiser of aid to the Greeks and similarly halfway in all endeavors, is "just as fit for flirting as the helm." Despite the grossness of his gut, the mild gourmand Louis XVIII fits neatly into an antithetical balance of couplets:

> A scholar always, now and then a wit,
> And gentle when Digestion may permit . . .
>
> (524 525)

Don Juan points to the murderous instincts of despots: *The Age of Bronze* pulls their teeth. The French Parlement, noisier than the kings, is equally impotent. A few cataclysmic metaphors return in xiv. The method of exaggeration in this section inflates the agrarian "patriot bill" of April 1022, which erected a sliding scale of import duty on grain, into the most awesome event of the decade. Its ninety lines berate English landlords who fattened when they farmed out the war against Napoleon—"farmers of the war, dictators of the farm"— but now grumble when asked to share the cost: "gorged with blood," these "high-market patriots" would not have their earthquake engulf the *price* of land. The poet meets their outlandish claims to patriotism with ironic exaggeration of metaphor.

A plateau of flattened metaphor, beginning in section xiii, surrounds these mock-heroics. Albion stirs only over trade and taxes; Wellington is an eagle only in the hook of his nose; Castlereagh, by slitting his goosequill, gave way to the better promise of Canning. The threat of revolution in England is reduced to an image of Canning as a strong huntsman riding an "unwieldly old white horse," the "royal stallion," who may stumble, kick, or stick fast, with "his great Self and Rider in the mud." After the Titanic Napoleon, the poet gives an adroitly compressed portrait of his Imperial bride and widow, France's widow, Marie Louise, an Andromache of the Age of Bronze, who willingly leans on the arm of the foe, Wellington. Into this vignette Byron injected a second prediction that Napoleon's "embers soon will burst the mould," and ended it with justification of poems like *The Waltz, The Vision of Judgment,* and this one:

> So much for human ties in royal breasts!
> Why spare men's feelings, when their own are jests?
>
> (763–764)

From the age of tyrant-taming we have fallen to the mimic court of Marie Louise, who rules Parma's "pastoral realm of cheese." In this daintily slashing vignette Byron's homage to Pope serves him well.

The foe, Wellington, is handled mildly throughout the poem, and yet unjustly, for Canning had now made obsolete England's part in such congresses. Following Canning's instructions, Wellington had dissented from the agreement to allow French intervention in Spain. The epigraph on the title page, punning on half a line from the *Aeneid,* "Impar *Congressus* Achilli," would seem to imply "a congress unequal to Achilles." Richard Garnett (BWP, V, 535) suggested a reference to a monument, still standing, whose purpose, misnaming, and inscription received much attention in London periodicals after midsummer 1822: TO ARTHUR, DUKE OF WELLINGTON, AND HIS BRAVE COMPANIONS IN ARMS, THIS STATUE OF ACHILLES, CAST FROM CANNON TAKEN IN THE VICTORIES OF SALAMANCA, VITTORIA, TOULOUSE, AND WATERLOO, IS INSCRIBED BY THEIR COUNTRYWOMEN. PLACED ON THIS SPOT ON THE XVIII DAY OF JUNE MDCCCXXII. BY COMMAND OF HIS MAJESTY GEORGE IIII.[35] The temptation to accept this allusion is strong, for the printshops reveled in this "first public nude statue in England," called in a caricature by Cruikshank "the *Ladies Fancy-man.*" Whether Byron knew of this joke or not, its existence gave a dangerous second edge to his knife. Identification of Achilles with Wellington would make the

218

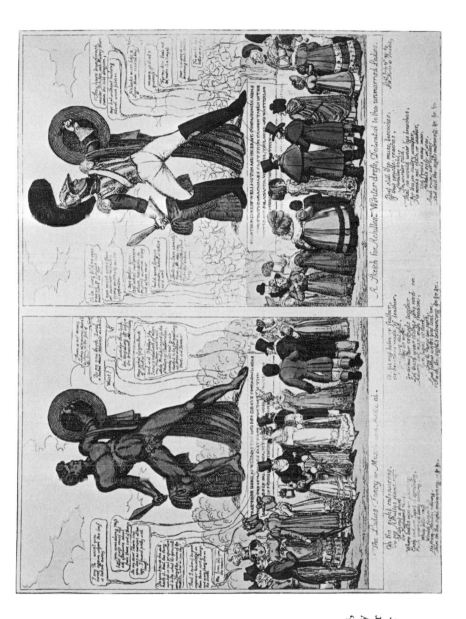

Charles Williams, "The Ladies Fancy . . . A Sketch for Achilles's Winter Dress"

epigraph to *The Age of Bronze* admit that Wellington emerged from the congress undefeated. Again, if Byron's enemies had applied the whole line to Napoleon as Troilus, "infelix puer atque impar congressus Achilli," then Wellington would have remained victor over the "unhappy boy" and emerged victor over the poem. Byron must have wanted the epigraph to declare what the poem describes: a whole congress unequal to one Napoleon.

From volcanoes to Parmesan cheese in seventeen fyttes. Napoleon ended meanly (v), but his liberating spirit was stirring when the Congress intervened for a last accumulation of bronze and brass (viii). The sameness of the despots (ix-xii) tempts a glance at their functionaries. In constitutional England (xiii) the functionaries represent their masters, the "land self-interest," who have shorn the prelates of "proud pluralities" and the fund-holders of dividends (xiv). The impoverished country is rich only in Jews (xv), a scandal that takes us, fiercely prejudiced, by way of the Rothschilds back to the Congress (xvi) and on to exhaustion in Marie Louise (xvii). The final brief section seeks and finds an absurdly petty image in Sir William Curtis, alderman and former Lord Mayor and M.P., who affected a kilt when he accompanied the King to Scotland. This throwaway in closing suggests hope for fresh woods and pastures new: "you'll have, perhaps, a second 'Carmen.' "

Byron's mastery of the commonplace had endured. From his reading after college he could include the "magic palace of Alcina," from Ariosto, in two sentences on the Rothschilds involving also Midas, his golden river Pactolus, and the Symplegades, crushers of all who venture. But most of the allusions, packed into the poem from the Bible, classical myth, history, and popular lore, would have been familiar to the original reader. At worst, they are today more readily accessible than the political tenor of the poem.

Because he valued the intersections of legend and history, Byron has suffered a loss of impact from the shift of knowledge away from his collages of history. Allusions in *The Age of Bronze,* although less oblique than those in his earliest satires, are more intricate and concentrated. In xiv, the landlords as Sabine Cincinnati ("Farmers of War") evoke Napoleon as Triptolemus scattering wheat for English farmers; the "grand agrarian alchymy, high *rent*"; the loaves and fishes of the parable; Esau's birthright sold "for a mess"; sympathy with the sluggards of Proverbs 6:6 against the "agrarian ants"; the proposition—almost self-parody—that death comes to all, so why not to high rent; "Fortune's equal urn," a Cornucopia that farmers turn off for "fear that plenty should attain the poor"; the Mother Church weeping like Niobe over "her offspring—Tithes"; and a dozen other mixtures of commonplace and surprise. Today Byron's sense of history as palimpsest escapes us, largely because we are far more reductive than he in turning the historic detail of his day to dead footnotes, except for the still-visible loot of Wellington and anecdotal legends of Nelson and Napoleon.

Earlier in the satire than the crowded collage of myth and history we have just looked at, Byron notes that the Czar stands between Greece and freedom as (an earlier) Alexander stood between Diogenes and the sun. He makes the Turkish port of Sinope, birthplace of Diogenes, epitomize the "Russ and Hun" he threatens with Greek independence: "His tub hath tougher walls than Sinopè." A poet could hardly achieve greater viscosity by emulating Dante. Annotators take a long way round the reference to royal logs who crush nations so stupidly they leave little work to "the revolutionary stork."[36] Even the Irish bull of line 271, "Where Greece *was*—No! she still is Greece once more," seems reflective: she has been Greece all along, but just now, for the first time in centuries, she lets you know that she is, and the letting-know is what makes her Greece. More simply, the preceding lines tell how the Spaniard revives— "and where?"—in the New World, where old Spain was synonymous with the crime of putting down life.

The rocking-horse balance Byron learned from Gifford gives way in *The Age of Bronze* to quilting on a large scale and to centrality through play on words. The country gentlemen are most "*un*country" in unpatriotic actions which ruin the country and "make a malady of peace." Byron complains, in the interest of his daughter Ada, that they will found on the Exchange "a *Fundling* Hospital." Afterthought, foresight, and patience all appear in a virtuoso passage added after the manuscript had gone off to John Hunt. Lines 608–609, with the rhymes *spent, content,* prepare for the series of fourteen rhymes: *sent, rent; cent., rent; meant, rent; malcontent,* *rent; mis-spent, rent; lent, rent; discontent,* and line 631, "Being, end, aim, religion—*rent—rent—rent!*"[37] Then on to Esau. Though I find only two sets of triplets (*wave, grave, slave; martyrs, Tartars, charters*), well below Dryden's average, the couplets rock in antithesis only when fitted to indifferent virtues in the subject. The poet's own values are graded: he laughs at abuses by the Established Church, while showing it as a victim of the landlords, who are worse. Without achieving the unique cadence of *Don Juan, The Age of Bronze* solves better than any of Byron's earlier satires the problem of uttering jacobinical opinions from an aristocratic elevation in a true voice.

The Island, blunted pinnacle of the exotic tales, is a flawed poem of great interest. It introduces three heroes in turn: in the opening sections, Lieutenant Bligh, the "gallant Chief" of H.M.S. *Bounty,* set upon by villainous Fletcher Christian; in Canto II, Torquil, a Scottish mutineer, drawn from the historical George Stewart; in Canto III, Fletcher Christian, leader of the mutiny, noble outlaw, unlike Conrad because misanthropic only during rages. For the mutineers' island, Byron admitted to only one source. For the precipitating events, he relied solely on the account of "bold Bligh."[38] Although this reliance may explain genetically the apostrophes to Bligh and his loyal few to beware Christian's lawless rage, the poem's own thematic structure requires stern judgment: "Roused Discipline aloud proclaims their cause." Byron had long been a patriot in the sense of one who lashes the conscience of his mother country as Hamlet lashed Gertrude's; in *The Island* he sounds more like the patriotic Dickens described by Chesterton, "the man who feels at ease about his own country." Whether or not Byron turned sentimental when he heard "God save the King" sung in Genoa, as Lady Blessington reports, the change of tone resulted only partly because absence from England kept him ignorant of Bligh's record of tyranny; *The Island* pays tribute repeatedly, as none of his poems since *Hours of Idleness* had paid, to loyalty, discipline, authority, and "whatever Duty bade."

The poem incorporates even Bligh's report that Christian, charged with ingratitude and the frustration of his own hopes to "blazon

Byron

Britain's thousand glories higher," at once (instead of countercharging, "I was in hell," as other records show) confessed: " 'Tis that! 'tis that! I am in hell! in hell!" In Canto III Christian has not only remorse of conscience but other characteristics of the dark heroes of the Turkish tales. Like them and like Manfred, he chose to be, "In life or death, the fearless and the free." Ending as "an extinct volcano," he has been an eagle (IV.312) or, on second thought, a falcon (IV.327). He emerges suddenly as a Byronic hero in Sections IV and VI of Canto III. The two passages describing him, which are set off by a facetious drop to his trivial companions, Bunting and Skyscrape, have the Miltonic cadence and stationing of *Hyperion*, wherein Keats contrived "to talk about the Gods" (says *Don Juan* XI.60) much "as they might have been supposed to speak":

> Stern, and aloof a little from the rest,
>
> . . . . . .
>
> Still as a statue, with his lips comprest
> To stifle even the breath within his breast,
> Fast by the rock, all menacing, but mute,
> He stood. . . .   (III.85–94)

Like the earlier outlaws, Christian has a tender regard for women and weaklings. A lion with cubs, he repents most for the imminent ruin he has brought to Torquil and other followers. The generosity of his remorse either indicates a maturer Byron or demands that we grant a degree of altruism in the mixture of guilt and defiance in Manfred and the sternest Byronic outlaws. Yet Christian, dying, performed a last act of ingenious ferocity. Emulating an anecdote known to his author—still an unsurpassed borrower from anecdotal history—Christian loaded his musket with a button from his vest and felled a dutiful Briton. Concluding this "last rage 'gainst the earth which he forsook," he plunged like a Roman to his death. Waves of the unsympathetic ocean washed over him, but the universalist poet who declined to send George III to a black eternity hesitates also to consign to heaven or hell an instigator of mutiny who bears the felicitous name Christian.

Even without the mediating portrait of Torquil, the conflict that had torn Byron for ten years, between the poet of outlawry and

223

the satiric conservator, seems to have been healed by taking Lieutenant Bligh on his own terms as one of the glories of British discipline and then dropping Bligh except to see through his eyes a lawless passion-maddened culprit. Yet Bligh is merely repeating a theme of the Turkish tales, that such a culprit could seek atonement only in his own conscience.

With Torquil, our questions increase in number and import, but they begin to find answers. A follower, he is yet of heroic mold. Typologically, he is Byron to Christian's Napoleon. A child of the Hebrides, he loves the island of Toobonai, but sees within its fairness the features of his birthplace; so for the poet, "Loch-na-gar with Ida looked o'er Troy." Luxuriating in the "promiscuous Plenty" of an "equal land without a lord," Torquil is Sardanapalus in a Rousseauistic state of nature. "Tempest-born in body and in mind," he might have been a proud rebel in Greece, Chile, or any other land eulogized in *The Age of Bronze*. Pleasure and ease took him in an opposite direction from his eaglelike beginnings:

> His heart was tamed to that voluptuous state,
> At once Elysian and effeminate,
> Which leaves no laurels o'er the Hero's urn . . .
>
> (II.312–314)

The wilds undermined him much as they corrupted the "lovely youth" of Wordsworth's "Ruth." Toobonai is a simpler, slightly staider Venice.

For the entire band, until avengers crossed two oceans in pursuit, "their guilt-won Paradise" had shielded them from every system of justice. Torquil wins exemption even from the poem's own declared system of discipline by his domestic bliss with Neuha, "Nature's child in Nature's ecstasy" but "all a wife." Christian dies vicariously for Torquil, that the values of discipline may be maintained. Torquil, whom Bligh thought justly dead, lives happily ever after. The idyll of Juan and Haidée returns as an endless dream, free from European politics, British justice, steel utensils, and Byronic irony. More than once affairs of the heart had provided escape from the bickerings and delays of politics. The primitive island would provide escape from the risks of failure that even Byron's

224

yearnings for adventure in Spanish America could not provide. Yet it is Armida's bower. Political embroilment achieved through an affair with Lady Oxford or a liaison with the Gamba family mutilates a hero's initiative and makes him dream.

Byron knew nothing of the mutineers' settlement on Pitcairn. The declaration of his "Advertisement," that the "foundation of the following story will be found partly" in Bligh's narrative "and partly in 'Mariner's Account of the Tonga Islands' " has been taken to mean that he found in the latter Torquil's island paradise. Now, most disinterested readers would find in *An Account of the Natives of the Tonga Islands,* as told by Mariner to John Martin, M.D., a people declaredly superior to their neighbors in the Fiji and Sandwich Islands but living under a king and priests in rigid social stratification, strict taboos, murderous suspicion of strangers, frequent child-sacrifice, and well-motivated cannibalism. Apologizing for these few excesses, Mariner and Martin chiefly wanted to show how similar these people were to Europeans. Byron ignored both the cannibalism and the feudal rigor.

He did find in Mariner the means of escape, a cavern hidden deep behind a shelf over the ocean. Neuha leads Torquil (in a reversal of sexes from the legend in Mariner) by diving through the ocean toward what pursuing strangers take to be certain death. Far more secret and awesome than the cave where Haidée nursed Juan, this cathedral of nature, womb of all beginnings, is a microcosm for Toobonai itself, where natives escape Adam's curse by feasting on coconuts and breadfruit. Although "even the mildest woods will have their thorn," no greater harm is done than to shred Bunting's European trousers.

The poem reaches much sooner than we have its explicitly political implications. The uncivilized can be civilizing. Toobonai is a "yet infant world" (last line of the poem), in contrast both with the hypocritical Old World, where you see the "prayers of Abel linked to deeds of Cain," and with the world called New but no longer so except where freedom is newborn in Colombia. The island, uncontaminated by the guilt of those who won it, in truth "Did more than Europe's discipline had done, / And civilised Civilisation's son!" (II.270–271). Real discipline belongs to the shibboleths of modern European culture, but not to its practice. What power a disciplined Napoleon could have exercised and kept!

Torquil, who could have been a "patriot hero or despotic chief," lacked the self-control of a gallant Bligh. He might have been Nero the shame of Rome, but not the consul Nero, a disciplined patriot who defeated Hasdrubal and thereby (according to Byron) saved his country from Hannibal. Weakened in Elysium, Torquil can be no Caesar. But what of that? The "gory sanction" of Caesar's glory has spread throughout Europe the tyranny of "ignoble fowls," "bugbears," and "mousing owls," "mere mock-birds of the Despot's song" whom the roused millions should sweep from their perch as Brutus swept Caesar. Nature, Reason, Freedom, and patriot Glory call upon natural leaders to do this sweeping. Europe has work to be done. The important discipline, we see, is said not to be of civilization because it is discipline not of the sailors and masses but of the chiefs. The important discipline belongs not to the sheep but to the sheep-dog and the shepherd. Even the highest of us, says Ulric in *Werner,* must bear the arrogance of Satan. There is no rebellion, echoes the demon Caesar in *The Deformed Transformed,* against "fixed Necessity." Except insofar as deformity of its own nature compensates by daring, deformity must transform itself. The Byronic legend encouraged individuals to irritate governments throughout Europe, but the Byronic "cult of egoist despair," from which the historian John Bowle tries to evolve a good part of Schopenhauer and Nietzsche, is systematically starved in *The Island.*

Although tamed on Toobonai by union with the highborn Neuha, Torquil on his own island was of no imposed rank, a natural leader undisciplined and *manqué.* He became a mutineer, as Hobhouse did in 1819, through failure to subordinate self to the communal need for a loyal leader. Hobhouse, as the poet's alter ego in England, ought to seek victory only in a respectable cause.

In *The Island,* as in *Don Juan,* Byron accepts the littleness as well as wickedness of some of his favorite acts: he abandons his earlier claims to God-shaking evil. In letters to Leigh Hunt and others he affected to avoid eulogizing mutiny only to increase sales to the "enlightened public." But the interest in leaving "something to my relations more than a mere name" denies neither his interest

Byron

in leaving a name nor his desire to "sprinkle some *un*common-place
here and there." To leave a name a man would have to stir from
his Neuha. The poet himself felt the same call as his Arnold, in
The Deformed Transformed, to go where the world's workings were
thickest; specifically, at that pregnant moment,

> Spain—Italy—the new Atlantic world—
> Afric with all its Moors.   (I.i.498–499)

At worst, he would not endure chains.

Most of the mutineers, abandoning both freedom and a name,
surrendered at last to their captors:

> But though the choice seems native to die free,
> Even Greece can boast but one Thermopylae
> Till *now,* when she . . .
> > dies and lives again!   (III.55 58)

Not allegorically, but symbolically, Torquil is Greece, diving as if
to death but rising cleansed in the security of the cave.

Childe Harold (II.73) had made a callow plea for rebirth of
the "gallant spirit" of Thermopylae. The song of the laureate in
Don Juan prayed for "but three" of the original three hundred
Spartans to "make a new Thermopylae." He who would lead Greeks
to make another must first look to himself. He must forget the crown
and seek new glory for Greece. He who would avoid another Thermopylae but achieve a second Marathon must master Greeks and
logistics before he can master the Turks. Fallen Greece holds out,
most persistently and most enticingly of all, the temptations of the
primitive, the challenging prayers of the debased, and the hope of
the worthy for fame.

Meeting the challenge, Byron died at Missolonghi. Much of what
he had hoped for came to pass. It is of course impossible to guess
what face Byron would have shown toward the Reform Bill had
he lived until 1832. If the bill that actually passed had been presented in 1816, Wordsworth would have opposed it in the name of
the working classes as well as of the landowners. In *On the Constitution of the Church and State,* 1830, Coleridge opposed the increas-

227

Eugène Delacroix, *Greece Expiring on the Ruins of Missolonghi*

ing power of just those commercial classes that won political dominance two years later. To judge from the asides on economics in *Don Juan,* Byron had much more sympathy with the commercial classes than had Coleridge or Wordsworth, and certainly he had less sympathy with the agricultural landowners. All three, and Shelley as well, feared political control by the uneducated. In England, Byron wished to act as an aristocrat to liberate the powerless, not to make them his masters. He would give his life for them, but not endure a life under them. In Greece, without any question of a social revolution that might unseat him, he contributed his intelligence to promote political liberty as the collective base for individual freedom.

He had perhaps betrayed many times his boyhood aspirations for success as senator, general, and poet. Acquaintances had reason to regard him as a mad, bad man. Yet the man and poet who was generous enough to recognize the contributions of Gibbon, Rousseau, and Napoleon to ultimate liberation of the human spirit, despite their inferiority to Aristides and Washington, deserves at least the generosity of an acknowledgment that death found him still in service to the actuality behind his watchword, Liberty.

VI

SHELLEY

The discrepancy between the philosophic bases of the Revolution and a faith in the unifying imagination is aggravated in the study of Shelley by our current preconceptions as students. Expecting to confer value upon his major poems by interpreting them as unified, metaphoric wholes, we resist and resent the presence of practical politics. We do not easily accept the topical as a part of the metaphor in major poems that we are determined to serve with holistic interpretations. We readily perceive the universals caught by Shelley in the topicality of "The Mask of Anarchy," but we do not like to meet Castlereagh in *Prometheus Unbound*. The more obscure the symbolic structure, the greater our resistance to the grit of politics. Although Shelley produced topical satires, his major works are lyric, symbolic, and—in both image and syntax—evanescent. He observed event and detail, but lacked Byron's respect for fact as the point of origin in any search for truth. His intense interest in theories of man, society, politics, and history preceded his interest in the practical, daily workings of legislation and power. Selective observation seemed to confirm what selective reading had told him of social and political wrong.

The difficulty of writing persuasively about the kind and degree of Shelley's political concern appears notably in the irreconcilable explanations of how his politics relate to his religious views. He

Shelley

has been regarded as a metaphysician who left political interests behind as he grew to Platonic idealism. In an unusually moderate form, this interpretation is reflected in Carlos Baker's admirably balanced survey, *Shelley's Major Poetry: The Fabric of a Vision*, 1948. In its immoderate form, Shelley is made a Christian Platonist. On the opposite hand, he has been regarded as a rebel who had no religious interests except in political opposition; as E. L. Woodward puts it in *The Age of Reform*, "Shelley's 'atheism' was a figure of speech, a form of attack upon the abuses and vested interests of church establishments." Still again, he has been eulogized as a saint with the disinterested desire to make love rule in the world. And he has been condemned as a narcissist who fought church and state as substitutes for his father and the pack of hateful classmates at Eton. The evanescent surface of Shelley's poetry encourages these contradictions.

The obscurity of his major poems is deepened not only by evanescence—as well as by true profundity—but also by flashes of excessive clarity. He sometimes shapes his statements in extreme form even when they represent halves of a paradox held in suspension. To urge fraternal peace, he will say, "Rise like Lions after slumber . . ." We have no great difficulty in reconciling Byron's stanzas against the glories of slaughter in *Don Juan* with his praise of military heroism in the cause of national independence. But Shelley's extremist manner makes him seem baldly self-contradictory when, within a few pages or a few lines of denouncing war as an unmitigated evil, he praises noble assassination in the cause of violent revolution. Aware of the paradox, Shelley studied with increasing care the relation of power to force.

In *Shelley and the Thought of His Time*, Joseph Barrell made a distinction between young Shelley the active reformer and the subsequent unacting radical. This distinction allows for a radical poet, but not for a reforming poet. Among other ways of interpreting the language of the poetry, I think that Shelley became a reforming poet by age twenty and remained such until his death at thirty. At all stages of his career, he believed in the power of mind to allay wickedness and evil. Although obviously more inward than Byron, he too regarded the creation of poetry as a social act.

Politics in English Romantic Poetry

I

At eighteen Shelley gaily read and wrote Gothic romances, but
he also read ancient and modern philosophy, and gladly taught.
In August 1810 he ordered "the cheapest edition of Locke on the
Human Understanding" for his cousin Harriet Grove, the first of
his several Héloïses; these, with passions simultaneously competing
and merging, he loved and taught. He particularly wanted young
ladies to learn from Locke that we can have no innate idea of God.
He found that God's failure to make His existence known to any
except the superstitious, a point made with supercilious force by
his coauthor and fellow prankster at Oxford, T. J. Hogg, had been
known at least to Lucretius and Livy among the ancients and to
Hume and certain Frenchmen more recently. Eagerness to teach
dons as well as their students "that there is no proof of the existence
of a Deity" ended the Oxford careers of Shelley and Hogg abruptly
in March 1811. Although Shelley's earliest verse reveals a capacity
for personal spite, it is not easy to disentangle the personal from
the impersonal in his wrath and contumacy against the established
religion. By his own account, he sought revenge against Christianity
for alienating the affections of Harriet Grove, but such disinterest
as mankind is capable of played its part in his initial and continuing
insistence on the logic that offended his superiors. Even his rejection
of most that his father accepted—the calm of their Field Place estate,
the comfort of a baronetcy and a Whig seat, the repose of the
Church of England—includes in its seeming insolence the excitement
of discovering the idea of freedom as well as the psychic rewards
of rebellion.

Available details, though remarkably full, do not tell us how far
Shelley read the *philosophes* one after another because he was predis-
posed toward their conclusions and how far he waited to imbibe
from them what Peter Gay has summarized as "a program of secu-
larism, humanity, cosmopolitanism, and freedom, above all, freedom
in its many forms—freedom from arbitrary power, freedom of
speech, freedom of trade, freedom to realize one's talents, freedom
of aesthetic response, freedom, in a word, of moral man to make

232

his own way in the world."[1] Shelley sought everything in this program, including free trade, which he welcomed as the eradicator and successor of war and monopoly. He first regarded Adam Smith with Tom Paine's eyes, not Wordsworth's.

From early youth he found it obnoxious to exempt a personal action from a general rule. Although he borrowed rhythms as well as ideas from Tom Paine's blunt prose, he embraced the abstractions of the Enlightenment too fanatically to find much use for either Dr. Johnson's or Paine's common sense. To rescue Harriet Westbrook from the tyranny and persecution of family and schoolmates, he eloped with her to Scotland. Although human enough to resent an attempt by Hogg to seduce his bride, Shelley explained his opposition objectively: ". . . I cannot consent to the destruction of Harriet's peace."[2] He expected reason from Godwin when he chose to elope with the daughter of that rational opponent of marriage.

In morals he accepted the utilitarian argument that whatever gives the greatest pleasure and widest happiness is the best. Godwin had spoken for him in the declaration of *The Enquirer* that "the cause of political reform, and the cause of intellectual and literary refinement, are inseparably connected." To seek reform was to serve the truth. As an intellectual worker and active philanthropist, Shelley followed in principle Godwin's insistence that the rich man must take upon himself part of the labor of the poor. The sharing of labor serves truth, because only through the enlightenment made possible by leisure can the manual laborer rise above hereditary poverty.[3] From avid belief in the Godwinian doctrine of Necessity, he ingested very quickly the materialism of *l'homme machine,* as applied to moral and social questions in Holbach's *Système de la nature.* A physical dimension of certainty thus joined temporarily his desire to believe in the improvement of society through increased knowledge. Wherever in his wide reading he found opposition to the irrational bonds of marriage, there he found support for an element in his thought that is usually called Platonic. The good citizen will love enlightened virtue, or "intellectual beauty." The love of such beauty in a soul mate (whether or not a body mate) leads the lover toward benevolence. His earliest verses assert the utility of sexual attraction for social sympathy as insistently as the later poems. And he would not totally drop the appeal to utility even when both sex and sympathy became manifestations of a cosmic force, or what men perceive as a cosmic force, that needs no utilitarian justification.

Shelley's political verse begins somewhat incidentally in *Original Poetry by Victor and Cazire,* an unoriginal collection of imitative pieces and outright plagiarisms issued in the autumn of 1810 for Shelley and his sister Elizabeth. "The Irishman's Song," purportedly of October 1809, differs from its models in Moore's *Irish Melodies* by inept versification. More happily, it differs also by a personal twist to Moore's sentiment. The pieces in *Original Poetry,* as the heroine of *Northanger Abbey* would wish them, are "all horrid." In "The Irishman's Song" the "yelling ghosts" of the heroes of Erin ride on the blast "And 'my countrymen! vengeance!' incessantly cry."[4] The resemblance of the Irish ghosts in this early poem to similar specters in the tales of terror represents exactly the degree to which we ought to accept F. W. Bateson's charge that the "political façade" of Shelley's poems "was a form of unconscious hypocrisy—the tribute of the escapist to the social conscience."[5] Shelley both exploited and shared the popular taste for the horrid. There is another difference from Moore less conventional than the ghosts. In the tearful sweetness of Moore's songs, cries to battle echo in the present but cling to the distant past. Shelley's Irishman rises from the melancholy of reminiscence, the harp unstrung from its once-rapturous measure. But here Shelley's passivist violence takes over. His Irishman rises to a tripled melancholy, because his countrymen have been driven to sound again the note of war, heroes have died, and "thy courage O Erin" must lead to further death. Moore feigns fortitude and belligerence; Shelley drives his forces dolorously into combat.

The only piece in the volume with references to daily politics, to "parliament votes" and "Burdett's reformation," was written, according to the available evidence, by Shelley's sister. But this verse epistle treats politics more lightly than poems of Shelley's already written though not published.

As if to support the theory that the imitations and thefts of *Origi-*

Shelley

nal Poetry add up to a playful hoax, Shelley came forth upon his arrival at Oxford with *Posthumous Fragments of Margaret Nicholson; Being Poems Found amongst the Papers of that Noted Female who Attempted the Life of the King in 1786,* "Edited by John FitzVictor." Both the plagiarizing Victor and this editorial son of Victor suggest a strong element of impish mystification in the genesis of Shelley's career as a rebel. Yet the mad Margaret Nicholson, who was not dead in 1810 but confined, already had an important place in Opposition satire. The third of the "Political Eclogues" that joined *The Rolliad* in 1790, entitled "Margaret Nicholson," has as its subject Pitt's exploitation of her approach to the King with an open knife. Line 116, "Thou 'scaped'st a danger that was never near" (*Thou* being the "wise King"), is explicated in a footnote to a line on "the famish'd poor": ". . . the world will be very well pleased to hear that the miserable woman whom the Privy Council have judiciously confined in Bedlam for her life, never even aimed a blow at his August Person."[6] Shelley and his readers could have found this sally in some eighteen editions of *The Rolliad,* with another to come in 1812.

The first of the poems offered by FitzVictor, titled "War" by a later editor, opens on the evils of monarchy: "Ambition, power, and avarice, now have hurled / Death, fate, and ruin, on a bleeding world." It ends with the faith of an "enthusiast" that heaven's voice will increase, through the murmurs of those oppressed by tyrants, until "peace, innocence, and love" return to earth.[7] Not only the diagnosis, but the prognosis as well, stands ready for refinement in *Prometheus Unbound.*

If a chance reading of Godwin's *Enquiry concerning Political Justice* first brought the commonness of unreason and injustice to Shelley's attention, as the poet repeatedly declared, it is clear that he went on rapidly to Godwin's French masters and to English journalists for more indignant language than Godwin's. In the poems of 1809–1812, both those in the *Posthumous Fragments* and those in the Esdaile notebook, which were gathered apparently for publication, melancholy and horror alternate with monarchs of black heart and "unlovely brow" who laugh at the groans of the famished.[8] The poet, not yet out of his novitiate, has found in political im-

235

moderation a way of putting his pleasure in the Gothic and the lurid to a practical use other than earning cash for private expenditure. Hereafter he will want cash for philanthropy. Now he snatches every opportunity to chastise priests and other "tyrant-slaves" of monarchy. He ranges from Foxite rejection of the war to republicanism, at a time when republican phrases were seldom shouted even by the mobs that cheered Sir Francis Burdett's defiance of the House of Commons. Stanzaic forms used by Southey for political verse contain in the Esdaile book the standard arguments of English Jacobinism: kings beget wars; wars beget impressment, cruelty, widowhood, famine. "A Retrospect of Times of Old" reconstructs from archaeology and imagination the "darksome times" when a "Royal Bloodhound" could still feel a tremor of remorse after murder. This philosophic myth of vanished times, explained in Volney's meditation on the ruins of empires before Shelley wrote it down, means in Shelley's book not only that George III feels no tremor of remorse but also that he is doomed to join the upward spiral anticipated in the first line of the poem: "The mansions of the Kings are tenantless."

Since religion upholds the process of government, and English bishops bless the war against France, the poems attack "Prejudice, Priestcraft, Opinion and Gold" jointly with monarchic slaughter (EN, 126:30). Shelley, who seems to have made the aesthetic transition from horror to political radicalism by way of contempt for religion, says in the poems that the established religion has itself created a bridge from superstition to bitterness in politics. One of Shelley's early fragments on the Wandering Jew shows the poet reaching beyond the Church to abjure its everlasting Tyrant, God.[9] The anti-Catholicism of most Gothic fiction in England and Germany would have been an early, if circuitous, influence on Shelley's anticlericalism. Soon, though he continued to seek and find evidence and illustrations of the inhumanity of religion, he reached the point of needing no further "influences" even from bitter personal experience. He loathed the clergy.

The Lake poets, through works of their Bath and Bristol days, formed part of Shelley's background. During his apprenticeship of 1809–1812, except for the simple diction and pacifist humanitarianism of "A Tale of Society as it is" ("from facts"), which is Southey supported by Wordsworth, the sentimental republicanism of the political poems takes us back to volumes of 1794–1796 by Southey and Coleridge, which represent almost exactly where Shelley was. His title echoes such works as Robert Bage's *Man as He Is,* of 1792, and Godwin's *Things as They Are; or, The Adventures of Caleb Williams,* 1794. He attempts an objective mirroring of corrupt society. He has not yet learned to make the poet's mind, as he will in *Alastor,* an image for all it mirrors.

"The Voyage," a fragment written in the unrhymed stanzas of Southey's *Thalaba,* shows the technical advances he had made by August 1812, particularly in its blending of humanitarian melo drama with a persuasive realism. Its attacks on the press gang ("smooth-faced tyrants" chartered by the King); on a "Rapacious, mean, cruel and cowardly" landsman, who married for gold; on commitment to the House of Industry; and on politicians, along with "Some priestly pilferer, or some Snake of Law," convey a sense of recent experience. And yet he fills his account of the voyage with the same political materials that Wordsworth had worked into his sketches of weary wanderers. The doctrine of Necessity injected into "The Voyage" may have come partly from sources shared by Coleridge; it need not have been directly indebted to Coleridge's early poems, but it parallels their expression of the doctrine. The point is that Shelley began very nearly where the older poets began.

In 1812 Shelley could write as an eyewitness about Robert Emmet's grave, although his anapests derive from Moore, who had published three poems on Emmet. Shelley's interest in the Irish rebel had been stimulated also by Southey and even more by Godwin's warning that Shelley resembled Emmet in "pure mind" and impetuosity (SL, I, 278). In other poems he avoided immediate experience and turned to recent history for stimulants to his revolutionary passion. Oddly, for a rebel so young, he drew on events of five to ten years past, as if he were versifying old "public prints."

Presumably about 1811—if we are to believe him the author at all—he illustrated the meanness of "Coward Chiefs" in five stanzas on an event of December 1805, Napoleon's victory at Austerlitz. The stanzas address George III's cowardly allies in a minatory present tense, but the title, or explanatory caption, treats the event as history: "To the Emperors of Russia and Austria who eyed the battle of Austerlitz from the heights whilst Buonaparte was active in the thickest of the fight."[10] Shelley in no sense makes a hero of Napoleon, "the restless fiend" whom "neither shame nor danger daunts." The stanzas carry out the spirit of his footnote to "A Retrospect of Times of Old": "Frederic of Prussia, Buonaparte, Suwarroff, Wellington and Nelson are the most skilful and notorious scourges of their species of the present day." The application of recent history to the moment of writing comes in the final stanza, where the two Emperors, Alexander I of Russia and Francis I of Austria, are described as slaves to a greater tyrant:

> Be sure
> The tyrant needs such slaves as you.
> Think ye the world would bear his sway
> Were dastards such as you away?
> No! they would pluck his plumage gay
> Torn from a nation's woe
> And lay him in the oblivious gloom
> Where Freedom now prepares your tomb.   (EN, 49)

In Shelley's developing political myth, the tyrant who needs imperial slaves is Jehovah, but the reference to "plumage gay" torn "from a nation's woe" points to Jehovah's viceregent, George III's eldest son, who assumed power in England when he was sworn in as Regent on 5 February 1811. Although both Russia and Austria could be thought of as wavering between France and England in 1811, the "tyrant" of England could count Francis I among his slaves at no time between November 1809, when Austria signed a treaty with France after the defeat at Wagram, and March 1813, when Francis rejoined the alliance against Napoleon. Therefore the poet's address to the emperors in the present tense can be carried from the scene at Austerlitz to the time of writing only if the final stanza is taken as concerning a political idea rather than a political situation.

In a longer poem, "Henry and Louisa," the young author seems to conflate Egyptian battles of 1801 and 1807. Although the abortive expedition against Alexandria in 1807 could have encouraged the

Shelley

choice of Egypt as the setting for the narrative of "Henry and Louisa"—"She died for love—and he for glory"—the British defeat in 1807 is apparently not the occasion of Henry's death, however much it throws into relief the vanity of his fall. As one of "Britannia's hired assassins," he would have died in and for the glorious victory over Bonaparte's forces near Alexandria in 1801. Either the initial inspiration came through an intermediary, or Shelley was beginning to give his opposition to war a slight aesthetic distance through historical reconstruction.[11] Despite his lurid invective, and acknowledging his efforts to assert universal truths rather than topical facts, his return to earlier years of the decade, in this poem as in the stanzas on Austerlitz, suggests a groping for the imaginative means of poetic genre rather than blasts of indignation. He shows none of the academic inclination of Byron and Wordsworth to review the contrasts of Roman republic and Roman empire in illustration of immutable law. If the choice of sites of renewed shame, as in "Henry and Louisa," does not represent the cyclic view of history that Shelley was soon to adumbrate in longer poems, it points to a less inclusive theory that he was never to abandon: the pendulum or dialectic of needless struggle.

One poem involving a site of repeated shame seems to concentrate on the more recent of two events. The "Fragment of a Poem the original idea of which was suggested by the cowardly and infamous bombardment of Copenhagen" (which may be Elizabeth Shelley's work) concerns—at least in its descriptive title—the British bombardment of defenseless noncombatants in September 1807 rather than earlier episodes of shame.[12] In the three surviving stanzas, the "ice mountains," frozen streams, and "whirlwinds of sleet" seem extreme either for September or for April, when Nelson in 1801 won a victory over the Danes by ferocity, disobedience of orders, and dubious display of a white flag. The title and the stanzas are associated ritually, rather than topically, through the "bloodreeking bed" of men left slain by the Britannic Lion. Shrill though these notes are, Shelley would have found Southey equally adamant, in their friendly conversations of 1811, against the "everlasting and ineffaceable infamy" of attack on a neutral country.[13] Seeing himself as a youth in the present Shelley, and expecting his own present

Politics in English Romantic Poetry

wisdom in the Shelley of tomorrow, Southey could sympathize with the ritual exaggeration of ice and sleet in a poem of protest; he would also have recognized in the Esdaile poems, as echoes from his own work, the "lone female" who breathes the "carnage-smoke," hears the "death shrieks," and sinks on the form of the man she sought.

Derivative as the juvenilia are, independence and coherence emerge. As related to Shelley's reading, the early pieces could be distributed under the categories of love lyric, the "horrid," melancholy flirtation with death, and burgeoning political thought. But their relation to Shelley's life, prose, and later poetry points to an adolescent integrity. A religion of humanity was erupting. In this religion he was candid (and so, we unfairly add, priggish) in the adoration of virtue. Although Shelley despised glory, he studied immortality. Throughout his dozen years as an author, immortality was the great question. A searching insistence on immortality puts a great burden on practical politics and a considerable burden on political theory. To Shelley the one solution was love—physical, moral, and spiritual.

Sex, like benevolence, must pervade more than mere action. A poem addressed by Shelley to his first wife, beginning "Harriet! thy kiss to my soul is dear," concludes characteristically, and for the marriage ominously, that his heart "beats for its country too." He means, of course, not what Lucasta's lover meant on going to the wars, but that the patriot, spurning honor and wealth, must thrash his country for its own good. Physical, moral, and spiritual love, he came increasingly to see, required not a way of doing, but a way of being. Byron, tincturing logistics with passion, sought for fame as the surest survival. Shelley's brief career was a persistent retreat from the useful. So retreating, he constantly reinterpreted the one solution of love.

Shelley differs from the earlier poets in that he began to mix his own contradictory thought into borrowed extravagances from the very beginning. He did not fret under the preceptors of reason, as Wordsworth and Coleridge did, but he soon put love before Necessity. In prose he approached the problem of immortality logically and skeptically. His earliest verse provides, instead, sensational ver-

240

sions of the rituals that sustain virtue by dignifying love and death. In the society that suppressed his dissent, the reader is to understand, "Gibbets, disease, and wars, and hearts as hard as they" suppressed also the potential nobility of love and death (EN, 154:180). The early poems combat these evils with rites equally sinister.

Second in the *Posthumous Fragments* comes the supposed epithalamium of Francis Ravaillac, the regicide whose "dear knife" tore a "tyrant's heart-strings from his guilty breast."[14] "Congenial minds will seek their kindred soul"; therefore, the regicide's "maddening passion" mingles with that of "Charlotte Cordé," who had assassinated the fierce Jean-Paul Marat in his bath. According to the bizarre cosmic joke of this fragment, presaging Shelley's cyclic theories in more serious poems to come, the heroic murderer of Henry IV of France in 1610 will forever hear "the music of the spheres" with the virtuous Charlotte Corday of 1793 (who had been depicted in a caricature by Isaac Cruikshank as "A Second Jean D'Arc" and in one by James Gillray as "The Heroic Charlotte La Cordé"). With similarly bizarre humor, "The Monarch's Funeral: An Anticipation," in the Esdaile book, moves through Gothic arches to anticipate Byron on the Sacred Majesty reduced to "one frail mass of mouldering clay." In another piece, equally but less openly anticipating George III's demise, "the bloated Wretch on yonder throne" seditiously resembles the Regent-to-be (EN, 46:70). Always implied is the proposition that an honest man's death would be noble, as a monarch's is not.

The ode "To Death" is a spell to dry up the unnatural luxury of kings. Paraphernalia from the fiction of terror, serving in other pieces to deepen the gloom of love, set up the stanzas beginning "Dark Spirit of the desart rude" for a closing conceit: the "desolate Oak" is a king that sucks all the sap from every living thing nearby and yet doth "upon the spoil decay." "Falsehood and Vice: A Dialogue," in which Falsehood is the mother of religion and Vice is the royal companion of "Famine, Murder, Hell, and Power," reaches back to Macbeth's witches by way of Coleridge's "Fire, Famine, and Slaughter." Despite its greater extravagances—Falsehood's "tyrant-slaves" have bound the innocent baby Truth to a dungeon floor—Shelley's poem is less incantatory and more argumentative than Coleridge's. For both, political and poetic revolt coincide, in that the medieval *débat* form, as a return to "our old authors" (illustrated also in a dialogue of Shelley's between Death and a Mortal), represents a revolt against the Augustan satire of sense.

Later, Shelley would transform ephemera into vatic prophecy; in youth he versified his outrage and spite in rituals resembling Gothic tales, expressed in diction that seems to combine "Monk" Lewis, Southey, Erasmus Darwin, and such disciples of Paine's prose as Carlile and Wooler. In the context of Shelley's novitiate, verses that might seem unallied with politics, if found alone, link still more securely the sentimental and the horrific to the imprecations against religion and tyranny. They coincide with the general shift of apocalyptic writing from emblems of the glorious dawn to those of menacing demons.

A major link between the horrific and defiant opposition is formed by Shelley's compulsion to vindicate outcasts. By 1810 he had taken the Wandering Jew for a totem. "To Mary III," in a series on a virtuous suicide, concludes with an argument later central to *Prometheus Unbound:*

> Such, loveliest Mary, was thy fate,
>   And such is Virtue's doom . . . .
> Contempt, neglect and hatred wait
> Where yawns a wide and dreary gate
>   To drag its votaries to the tomb.
> Sweet flower! that blooms amid the weeds
> Where the dank serpent, interest, feeds![15]

The four dots, which are Shelley's, signal a weighty pause: from contemporary society, virtue can expect only death. The tentative universalism of this series, including Shelley's footnotes, treats life after death as hypothetical, but categorically rejects eternal punishment. The Esdaile version of lines "On an Icicle that Clung to the Grass of a Grave," related to the Mary poems at least in the plaint for buried virtue and advocacy of "a spirit so fair" that sought its kindred in heaven, omits two stanzas involving praise of the patriot-warrior as a spirit even fairer. In place, as they are in a letter to Hogg of 6 January 1811, the two stanzas are self-canceling. In the preparatory stanza of the two, the speaker would have the "pure

Shelley

gem" of a frozen tear—the icicle of the title—melted and mixed with the "taintless spirit" of patriotism in "the stern warrior his country defending," even though acknowledging that such patriotism is red with the "guilt-reeking gore" of the felled tyrant. The canceling stanza, identifying this tyrannicide with "the Altar of Glory," gives preference to the lowly:

> Oh! fame all thy glories I'd yield for a tear
> To shed on the grave of an heart so sincere.[16]

Suicide is better than tyrannicide, because the cruelties of organized religion have made the self-destroyer the ultimate outcast and therefore the greatest deserver of sympathy from those who hate tyranny. The boy who "sought for ghosts," memorialized in "Hymn to Intellectual Beauty," turned against all violence of man against man but continued to honor the "low-laid shrine." The lowly could commit pacifist self-murder.

The speaker in "Dares the Lama," dated 1810, likens himself, in flight from "the grasp of Religion," to a fragile llama attacked by a lion or tiger. He, like the llama, has dared to "draw from the purest of fountains." Whatever his motivation, Shelley supports his praise of outcasts with the reasoning that expulsion identifies those who combine courage with virtue. Dares, and less obviously Mary, are virtuous outcasts of great courage.

Biographically, these poems come from one who considered himself persecuted for opinion. As heir to the baronetcy and the estate, he proclaimed his "atheism" with full knowledge that his family regarded church and state as politically indissoluble in a time of war and rebellion: to threaten bishops is to threaten the king and all hereditary property. A close student of Sir Francis Burdett and Lord Cochrane, who were harassed by the government for their radicalism but not deprived of title or estates, Shelley expected to enjoy or reject privilege and comfort on his own terms. His righteous fury against authority and privilege had practical limits. From the oscillations of his unfilial letters, it seems unlikely that he intended to push his father too far for reconciliation. He did at some point, nevertheless, and probably more than once, deliberately renounce a sure seat in Parliament and whatever else the somnolent Whigs could provide for the heir of a second baronet, himself a nominee of the most liberal of Whig boroughmongers, the Duke of Norfolk.[17]

Despite this renunciation, and despite his pursuit of idea and essence, Shelley had more interest than Byron in the drizzle and dry weather of politics in the daily news. Even the ritual magic of tyrannicide in his early poems is less unreal than the fervent prophecies by Blake and the Coleridge of 1794-95 that the breaking of the fifth seal in France would lead directly into the final apocalypse. His wildest execrations were designed to aid specific victims of the law of seditious libel, such as Peter Finnerty and D. I. Eaton. Without knowing anything about the bonhomie of compromise, Shelley scrutinized its Parliamentary results with an increasingly cool eye. On the one hand, he had extraordinary acumen in philosophical analysis; on the other, he shared the absorption in particulars that Leslie Stephen charged against Hazlitt: "He sees every abstract principle by the concrete instance . . . Tyranny with Hazlitt is named Pitt, party spite is Gifford, apostasy is Southey, and fidelity may be called Cobbett or Godwin . . ."[18]

A vegetarian and pacifist, young Shelley startled his elders by extraordinary activity. De Quincey, who started walking toward Wordsworth in 1802, 1805, and again in 1806, reached him in 1807. Shelley, besides issuing *The Necessity of Atheism*, which brought about his expulsion from Oxford in March 1811; besides his publication in Dublin of *An Address to the Irish People* and a second pamphlet, both urging the Irish to work, "think, read, and talk," as individuals and in an open association, for the immediate aims of Catholic Emancipation and repeal of the Act of Union that yoked Ireland unequally to Great Britain; besides writing in Wales *A Letter to Lord Ellenborough* on the sentencing of Eaton to prison and pillory for reprinting a tract of Paine's as "the third part" of the *Age of Reason;* besides attempting to reduce the diseases of violence and criminal madness by practicing and propagating "the vegetable system of diet"—besides these and other general acts, Shelley within little more than a year made his writings known to Sir Francis Burdett; addressed Leigh Hunt as "a common friend of *Liberty*"; spirited Harriet Westbrook from under the tyranny of her father and schoolmates and into a marriage of righteous ex-

Shelley

pedience in Scotland; corresponded, conversed, and debated with Godwin so pertinently that the noted inquirer set out from London to Lynmouth in the hope of further conversation—and, no doubt, financial aid. In keeping with these acts, Shelley persuaded Southey to believe, mistakenly, that he would outgrow his excesses and thus become an honor to his country; he met several Irish patriots, not without disappointment; and he added an hour's oratory to an address by Daniel O'Connell, whose name was synonymous with Irish nationalism then and until his death in 1847. By such activities the eager youth stirred several informers to add Bysshe Shelley to the Home Secretary's list of persons to watch.

Like his missionary voyage to Ireland, Shelley's efforts in Wales to raise money for preserving the model town of Tremadoc, where W. A. Madocks, M.P. for Boston, had salvaged land from the sea, constituted rites of passage, self-imposed, from his Zastrozzistic adolescence into manly, altruistic service for man.[19] His overblown sense of ritual should not blind us to his deepening perceptions. Nor were the symbolic acts of launching his militant Declaration of Rights in a balloon, and in several bottles, the vain gestures they inevitably seem to Laughter holding both his sides and ignoring the arrest and imprisonment of Shelley's servant for complicity. The Home Secretary, Sidmouth, was warned by the Inspecting Commander of Revenue Cutters of the Western District that seditious agitators, by "this novel mode of disseminating their pernicious opinions," might "do incalculable mischief" among seafaring persons.[20] When Shelley solemnized these acts of propulsion by transubstantiating them in two sonnets, one "On launching some bottles filled with Knowledge into the Bristol Channel," beginning, "Vessels of Heavenly medicine!" and the other "To a balloon, laden with Knowledge," as a "beacon in the darkness of the Earth," he was particularizing a belief in progress from increase of knowledge, knowledge first of nature and then of man in society: *knowledge* is the antonym of *religion*. He was also bringing the ceremonial generalizations of his early verse around to the realism of empirical particulars.

The sonnets on the launching of knowledge signify a new awareness of his own individuality in the pursuit of social causes. Recording the emotions of specific physical acts, the two sonnets are more realistic than the imitative matter-of-factness of "A Tale of Society as it is"; they are more empirical than the predetermined ingredients of "The Voyage." Though weak in execution, the sonnets were rich in function. Despite Shelley's delight in ritualization, the acts of sowing in bottles and balloon were practical in intent. The sonnets, celebrating the teaching more than the gestures, were themselves didactic, with a rationalistic clarity that would be increasingly mythologized or overlaid with metaphor in the later poetry.

Other pieces in the Esdaile book show as well as the sonnets his advance in fusing the personal with the public. The stanzas "On Leaving London for Wales" make personal the conventions of dedication to "Mountain Liberty," humanitarian concern for the oppressed, and enmity to all that obstructs the work of reason, whether from "passion's soothing voice" or "interest's cold control." He was creating his own voice as reforming poet.

II

By 1812 Shelley saw that hope for reform would require a congenial theory of history, which in turn would involve a theory of man's place in the universe. Where has man been, and where is he going? If society is corrupt, did it become so by a sequence that can be reversed? Must all revolutions fail as the Revolution in France failed?

The twenty-two thousand lines of *Queen Mab* represent his first attempt to synthesize all his thought in a poetic form. *Queen Mab, a Philosophical Poem* "with Notes," of about 1812 and in about seventy printed but unpublished copies, set forth certain doctrines, of which the first is sovereign Necessity: the universe, sufficiently awesome in its immensity to need no "childish mummeries of the God of the Jews," keeps to "the paths of immutable necessity." The principle of necessity imbues and binds all things:

> Spirit of Nature! all-sufficing Power,
> Necessity! thou mother of the world!
>
> (VI.197–198)

In the words of Holbach, quoted by Shelley in a note to VI.171, "chaque molécule agit précisément comme elle doit agir." Nor is

246

there a single act or thought in any political convulsion not a necessary consequence of the chain of causes. Necessity, then, is "the
great chain of Nature" (II.108). We can know only "a constant
conjunction of similar objects," but we may recognize in "the consequent inference of one from the other" the law of necessity.

This inference is rather more than Hume concedes, but Shelley
has his eye on the loose economy of Christian faith. Coming so
quickly to the end of perceptible causes, man has erroneously given
to the unknown the name of God and attributed to this mythic
being such human motivations as vainglory, anger, and revenge.
Prostrate before this illusion, man failed to understand, he failed
even to study, the natural law with which he ought to be in harmony.
The infringement of natural law inevitably brings evils to disturb
what Holbach has shown to be the retrievable symmetry of nature,
"Soul of those mighty spheres" and likewise "Soul of that smallest
being" (III.227, 230). In 1812 Shelley selected from Holbach the
unitary and the mechanical, not the animistic. He ignored Holbach's
emphasis on the separate vitality of every monad.

The purpose of emphasizing man's departure from natural law
was of course to counter the doctrine of original sin and the Malthusian argument against the possibility of effective reform. To explain the historic fall of redeemable man, Shelley based his case
largely on the argument of vegetarians. Although "every heart contains perfection's germ" (V.147), man has wandered into such error
as the eating of animal food. The consequence, described with economy in tracts by Shelley's friend J. F. Newton, is summarized in
the first sentence of Shelley's footnote on the value of a vegetable
regimen: "I hold that the depravity of the physical and moral nature
of man originated in his unnatural habits of life." The note becomes
as extravagant as Newton himself, but heat is reserved for the text:

> He slays the lamb that looks him in the face,
> And horribly devours his mangled flesh,
> Which, still avenging Nature's broken law,
> Kindled all putrid humours in his frame,
> All evil passions, and all vain belief,
> Hatred, despair, and loathing in his mind,
> The germs of misery, death, disease, and crime.
>
> (VIII.212–218)

Politics in English Romantic Poetry

Inevitably, priests exploited the vain but convenient belief in "Man's evil nature" (IV.76). Mighty hunters rose to be kings. To enforce the dogma of man's evil nature, kings needed not only priests but also judges, lawyers, ministers, and placemen. Pampered by error, selfishness intensifies: self-interest begets commerce; then "venal interchange" begets "the wealth of nations" (V.38, 80). In short and in fact, wealthy kings rule a superstitious mob of prostitutes. Vice, kings, priests, lawyers, statesmen, and a soldiery of "hired assassins" add up to the crime of war. Christianity has accomplished the spread of slavery. The virtuous few who have pointed the way out have been sometimes ignored, more often persecuted, and frequently disposed of by force, like Jesus, so that their teachings could be perverted. When man listens, and therefore ceases to infringe natural law, he may come to enjoy perpetual spring on earth, "Symphonious with the planetary spheres" (VI.41; cf. VIII.18). The "atheism" of *Queen Mab* consists in the assumption that an unproved, highly dubious doctrine, involving certainly a miscomprehension of natural and moral law, has survived because it is essential to the privileges of a powerful, unscrupulous minority. "Necessity" is merely a theoretical description of the way we can perceive matter to behave.[21]

The hyperbole of a return to symphony with the planets means that, despite Laplace's theory of oscillation, there "is no great extravagance in presuming that the progress of the perpendicularity of the poles may be as rapid as the progress of intellect; or that there should be a perfect identity between the moral and physical improvement of the human species."[22] Faith that the precession of the equinoxes would end the severities of winter and summer was both ancient and contemporary; but the original imbalance at some point in time, as a physical cause of man's moral failure, made trouble for Shelley's argument that man is able to will a return to moral health. He duly inserted a sentence on the problem in his note on the vegetable diet. "The date of this event"—when "man forsook the path of nature"—"seems to have also been that of some great change in the climates of the earth, with which it has an obvious correspondence" (SP, 826). This linkage of climatic and moral dislocation shows Shelley's early reliance on the materialism of La Mettrie and Cabanis, filtered through the vitalistic and humanitarian doctrines

248

of Holbach.[23] He was to retain the linkage in the loosened form of analogy.

Queen Mab is more at ease in laying out a program for man's self-reform. When benevolence, called "love" in the verse, replaces the present chaos of passions, Reason can once again embrace her sister, Passion, as a "sportive child" (IX.55). That is, when Reason rules, sexual passion need be neither feared nor restrained. When benevolence thereby conquers time, tyrannic fetters will give way to "sensation's softest tie," the "kindred sympathies of human souls" (77–79). Shelley had already taken fire from *A Vindication of the Rights of Women,* by Mary Wollstonecraft, and James Lawrence's *Love: An Allegory,* but it was not until he read Lawrence's fuller argument, in *The Empire of the Nairs, or The Rights of Women; an Utopian Romance,* that he realized the responsibility of marriage for "prostitution both *legal* and *illegal*" (SL, I, 323). When enslaving marriage gives way to "that sweet bondage which is Freedom's self," then "O happy Earth! reality of Heaven!" (IX.1, 76).

Except for the vegetarianism, a few passages of deliberate blasphemy, and the cry for free love, all segments of Shelley's argument sound like the motifs of the progress-poem in Coleridge's "Religious Musings," transposed occasionally into the meters of Southey's *Thalaba the Destroyer* but kept near the tone and syllogistic method of the *philosophes.* The ruins and "moral deserts" in section II recur in spirit both in the occasional architectural metaphors and in the glaciers, stormy oceans, and deserts of section VIII, which are transformed by love to "fertile valleys, resonant with bliss." Taking off from Volney's *Ruines, ou méditations sur les révolutions des empires,* section IX depicts with gusto the picturesque inutility of decayed palaces, cathedrals, and prisons in the golden age of benevolence and universal equality. Such delight as young Coleridge took in draconic horrors, Shelley now takes in milder images of melancholy winds and ruddy children playing among the ruins of usurpation. He will deepen these images in *Prometheus Unbound.*

Images there are, but the preceptorial Shelley at twenty heightens his argument less often by metaphor than by exclamation points. Between the author and the reader, except in the footnotes, he interposes Queen Mab, who reveals these truths to the stainless Soul of Ianthe. The good fairy, whose rational detachment prevents any heightening of her affirmation that "There is no God," calls in Ahasuerus, whose eighteen hundred years of retribution fit him better than Queen Mab or Ianthe to denounce vengeful Jehovah, sneer at the Son born in "an unnoticed corner of the earth," and proclaim the Satanic motto of rebellion; he prefers "Hell's freedom to the servitude of Heaven" (VII.13, 137, 195). In rhetoric designed for the writer's own voice, in the Preface to *Prometheus Unbound,* this seeming Satanism is reduced to epigram: "For my part I had rather be damned with Plato and Lord Bacon, than go to Heaven with Paley and Malthus." Mab and Ahasuerus, as intermediaries, serve little more than the protective function of confusing the censor, as such intermediaries do in *Gulliver's Travels* and Volney's *Ruines.* Gulliver colors all with his own character; Volney's Génie and Shelley's Mab speak in total obedience to the doctrines currently held by their authors. From disharmony with nature, man has declined; by new comprehension, he can and will recover his collective virtue.

Recasting parts of *Queen Mab* as *The Daemon of the World,* of which he published Part I in the *Alastor* volume of 1816, Shelley stripped much of the diatribe against society from the more positive images, which consequently seem more vivid than when they were sheathed in explanation. He omitted attacks on the name of God but retained a disinclination for the "bloodhound of religion." Most of the changes indicate precaution, as when "the lone cathedral's roofless aisles" became "The fanes of Fear and Falsehood" (SP, 11:500, 798:103). The few additions are significant. Shelley introduced one of his favorite emblems, "the vast snake Eternity," and replaced Ahasuerus' "almighty Tyrant" with "the proud Power of Evil." The introduction of Mediterranean emblems of fate, with their endless duality of good and evil, might at a glance suggest a sense of blame for man's misconduct more remote than the malfunctioning machinery of society that Shelley had previously blamed. To the contrary, it signifies his growing sense of internal responsibility in every individual. He begins to ask if a change of clothing will purify a corrupt conscience.

He begins also to conceive of poetry in a less didactic way. To

A POLITICAL
CHRISTMAS CAROL,
𝔖et to 𝔐usic.

TO BE CHAUNTED OR SUNG

THROUGHOUT THE UNITED KINGDOM AND THE

DOMINIONS BEYOND THE SEAS,

BY ALL PERSONS

THEREUNTO ESPECIALLY MOVED.

" Go draw your quills, and draw *six Bills*,
" Put out yon blaze of light."—

Carol.

D

George Cruikshank, "A Political Christmas Carol"

hear and understand the truth is not automatically, he now sees, to put reform into action. That Shelley became disillusioned with man means in this first stage that he ceased to believe in the power of rational instruction. His prose on political topics became less hortatory and more syllogistic as his poetic structures became less preceptorial and increasingly mythopoeic. He now expected to reach and modify fewer minds by either prose or poetry. He begins to use such phrases as "the capricious multitude" and "the majority of base and vulgar minds." He includes in these phrases not only the uneducated masses but also the unregenerate majority of the governing classes. The "polluting multitude" are all those who put difficulties in the way of the sacred few true reformers.

Before the end of 1814, he began to accomplish verses that smoothed the briars of didactic politics by the union of form and matter in a common purpose. This maturation came with, and no doubt partly from, his elopement with Mary Godwin, in whose earnest face he saw the wisdom and fierce independence of her mother, Mary Wollstonecraft. With Harriet, Shelley had been subject to nervous, abrupt shifts of habitation. All his life he fell rapidly in and out of infatuations of the sort that Byron took Platonic love to be. Supported afterward by hard work, the two tempestuous months of desiring and seeking either Mary or death, with the equivocal and indeed unprincipled jettisoning of Harriet, brought Shelley toward the counterpoise of objectivity and passionate commitment that his poetry needed.

If we pass by "The Devil's Walk" of 1812 as derivative and undistinguished, except perhaps in its figure of the court growing fat on the news of carnage in Spain, "Fat as that Prince's maudlin brain," then Shelley's first short, skilled, explicitly political piece reached the public in the *Alastor* volume of 1816. Of three original sonnets there, one proclaimed Mutability as lord over man's desires, one mourned Wordsworth's fall from grace, and the third assessed Bonaparte's fall from graceless power. The sonnet on Bonaparte, indebted to Wordsworth for its clarity and perhaps to the Coleridge of 1794 for its irregularity of form, is flaccid in its abstractness but strong in its apology for continuing to hate a bloody tyrant. It laments the discovery in 1815 that virtue has a foe worse than

Shelley

Bonaparte's force and fraud: "old Custom, legal Crime, / And bloody Faith the foulest birth of Time." This last line, at once cryptic and pale, compresses opposition to both the Holy Alliance and the Established Church as products of corrupted civilization, void of divine breath. Shelley as evangelist takes up the challenge to single combat against the unitary foe of prescription, systematic injustice, and blood-spilling faith.

The maledictory quatrains "To the Lord Chancellor," not published by Shelley, begin in the spirit of this evangel:

> Thy country's curse is on thee, darkest crest
> Of that foul, knotted, many-headed worm
> Which rends our Mother's bosom Priestly Pest!
> Masked Resurrection of a buried Form!
>
> (SP, 542:1–4)

Mary Shelley identified the resurrected evil as the Star Chamber, but the line of priestly pests, passing here from Shelley's earliest poems on the way to *Swellfoot the Tyrant*, threatened resurrection specifically of the ecclesiastical High Commission of Elizabeth's reign. In fact it is not institutional evils that concern most of the sixteen stanzas, but Lord Eldon's decree depriving Shelley of the custody of Harriet's children on the grounds of his unworthy tenets, writings, and actions. For circulation among friends, this curse emulates "A Sketch," Byron's vituperative lines on Lady Byron's governess, and imitates even more closely and more puckishly the "Incantation" first published with "The Prisoner of Chillon," inserted in *Manfred,* and probably represented to Shelley as an imprecation against Lady Byron.[24] Perhaps, then, the curse strikes as low as Harriet. But Eldon had a knack for making his judgments against poets seem personal, as when he refused Southey's injunction to suppress piracies of *Wat Tyler* on the ground that the work was written to injure the public.[25] Shelley's attack is personal, strident, and radical, but Byron had made their point: a system of justice is reduced to absurdity when its head practices personal or political recrimination.

The chief poem in the volume of 1816, "Alastor; or, The Spirit of Solitude," an excursion through a mental landscape in Words-

253

worthian blank verse with an epigraph and directly imbedded quotations from Wordsworth, concerns the student of politics in Shelley's poetry only in its new element of inwardness. Yet its warning against social isolation, clearer in the Preface than in the elegiac close of the poem itself, is akin to earlier warnings by Coleridge, Wordsworth, and Lamb. Wordsworth, in "Lines Left upon a Seat in a Yew-tree," and Coleridge, in lines "Addressed to a Young Man of Fortune [Charles Lloyd] Who Abandoned Himself to an Indolent and Causeless Melancholy," had each chided an excessively solitary friend. Shelley finds a similar danger in the idealistic poet's own method of inward vision. He makes a great step forward from angry mirroring of society to self-examination.

III

Queen Mab was a poem of argument. In 1817 Shelley made a more sustained attempt at a poem of epic proportions and epic elevation. Its original title, before the publisher asked for revision to remove calculated incest and denunciation of God by name, was *Laon and Cythna; or, The Revolution of the Golden City: A Vision of the Nineteenth Century*. It was published early in 1818 as *The Revolt of Islam: A Poem in Twelve Cantos*. In the Preface, Shelley sets forth at length the credo, form, and method of the poem: it is "narrative, not didactic," it is "a succession of pictures" designed to kindle in his readers "a virtuous enthusiasm for those doctrines of liberty and justice, that faith and hope in something good, which neither violence nor misrepresentation nor prejudice can ever totally extinguish among mankind." He finds the age in an understandable but needless despair. A union of virtuous enthusiasm and reason could not have been expected of men who had groaned, as the French had groaned, under the calamities of injustice. "Can he who the day before was a trampled slave suddenly become liberal-minded, forbearing, and independent? This," he goes on, "is the consequence of the habits of a state of society to be produced by resolute perseverance and indefatigable hope, and long-suffering and long-believing courage, and the systematic efforts of generations of men of intellect and virtue." The renovation of man is obviously no longer for Shelley a matter of weeks or months. Because he perceives "a slow, gradual, silent change" from despair to hope, he provides the time with the narrative of a revolution that failed physically but points the way to moral victory.

In *Romantic Poets and Epic Tradition,* Brian Wilkie has shown how many episodes of the poem, as well as its machinery, suggest parallels from the classical and Renaissance exemplars of epic elevation. The Spenserian stanzas convey also a suggestion of Spenserian allegory. Following up these suggestions, Carlos Baker has proposed that Cythna as Justice and Laon as Truth, joined by their winged child Freedom, oppose Othman as Tyranny or Political Oppression. Coming from the author of *Queen Mab,* the narrative contains the new particularity of Wordsworth and Southey, but it also sets its street battles within a theory of history. Men fell long ago from some golden age to which they have the potential to return. In the interim, good and evil forces battle within both individuals and societies. Canto I depicts the battle of eagle and serpent as emblematic of the eternal warfare of darkness and light. The Morning Star of light descended as "a dire Snake, with man and beast unreconciled" (SP, 46:369). In the *Revolt,* the snake represents wisdom against force. For centuries the rational few, who could have led men to improvement, have been taken for dangerous serpents and so martyred with fire or hemlock.

The Golden City, according to lines 1630ff., is a walled city of Islam, near a bay, in a plain ringed by mountains. Materially it is Constantinople, city of beauty and repeated siege. Other particulars are unhistoric. Islam afforded symbols; it afforded aesthetic distance; it afforded a site for action to one who could imagine into myth a revolution that would free the modern Greeks. A vital universe that cherishes freedom, with values unperceived until man imagines their counterpart in his own being, defies argument. It encourages inquiry and quest. The myth of *The Revolt of Islam* consequently reduces argument to moments in the quest.

Quite obviously the particularized setting is an ideal France. The revolt of Islam, although it fails, is carried out morally as the revolt of the sans-culottes should have been carried out. The revolt in Islam is crushed, as the revolt in France was perverted, by external forces. Unlike the revolutionaries of Paris, those who failed in the Golden City have nothing to repent and no reason for sudden pessimism concerning man's fitness to win freedom another day. Laon and Cythna each acted the heroic role that Shelley imagines as his own if he had been in Wordsworth's place. The ravages of war that Shelley has looked on in France need not occur again.

After Peacock and along with Byron, he now depicts the conflict of two eternal forces, the eagle and the snake, or might and wisdom, each having a strength of its own. The emblem of warring eagle and snake, as suggested above, is not so much metaphysical as moral: the soul of man is a world forever torn. Shelley's alternate depictions of certain warring snakes as good or evil come basically from the emblematic attribute of intellect, sometimes sagacity, at other times guile. He prefers intellect to vegetation, for man finds his value in conscious choice. Necessity means to him what the doctrine of consequences was to mean to George Eliot: since no act can be recovered and every action has numberless consequences, you must in conscience acquire as much knowledge, sympathy, and empathy as you can in order to meliorate the consequences of every act you contemplate. How one applies in action one's interpretation of Eden affects the future of all.

Some of the Gothicism and rage of the Esdaile book—"tyrant-slaves" bound to a stake or a dungeon floor, the pains of famine, and a soldiery of hired assassins—continues in the *Revolt*. But these conventions fade beneath the force of Shelley's own symbols, which scholars are only now beginning to comprehend. He synthesizes the physical and mental in the images of a rain of enlightenment, the ameliorating whirlpool destroying wrecks, and the volcanic, cleansing fire of revolution.[26] He introduces in various images the strong theme of union in love as a narcissistic mirroring of one's highest aspirations. Cythna undergoes metempsychosis as Laone. The yearning for total union of psyche with epipsyche seems to have been the chief reason for what attraction the theme of incest had for Shelley. He introduced incest directly into *Laon and Cythna* partly for this reason and partly as one more episode in his constant campaign for tolerance.

From Canto IV on Shelley concentrates his political ideals in images of love between man and woman. Intense love not only involves what is called body and soul but also generates these, generates all that can be called body or soul. The search for the ideal other half, in which Shelley himself recognizes narcissistic aspects, he employs as Schiller in *Don Carlos* employs the vow of fraternity, "with sweetest intimations of equality."

The force and ubiquity of love in *The Revolt of Islam* indicate a power of myth not adumbrated in *Queen Mab*. If we construct logical steps for the change, then Necessity, synonymous in the earlier poem with "the Spirit of Nature" and "Daemon of the World," produces a procreative cycle of birth and death that assures a continuation of life. When this permanent cycle of generations and seasons, teeming with life, is seen as empowered by a unifying World Soul, love can be regarded as a cosmic process. Necessity is now coincident with the law of love.[27] The actions of Laon and Cythna symbolize, in a blurred way, the workings of Necessity as love.

The episodes of *The Revolt of Islam,* in kinship with "Alastor," "The Witch of Atlas," and Act II of *Prometheus Unbound,* end in a symbolic, psychological voyage through immateriality in a spirit-winged canoe. Most of the poem, however, is urban. The architecture is not hidden in willows, pools, or the mouth of caves, as fanes and vanes tend to be in most of Shelley's poems. More clearly than in *Queen Mab,* and despite strong influences from the Lake poets, the goals affirmed are the goals of civilization, with the city-state and the town meeting as the apparent ideals.

It is noteworthy that *Queen Mab* contains nothing like the general assembly of nations called by the legislator in Volney's *Ruines* (chap. xix) to announce the ideals of justice, equality, and union. Shelley rejected Volney's emphasis on self-interest as the basis for these ideals, but he rejected also Godwin's opposition to association. In the light of Shelley's proposals for an association of philanthropists in 1812, one might have expected the cosmopolitan *Queen Mab* to follow Volney's *Ruines* in recommending a general assembly. *The Revolt of Islam,* although it moves a long step from the cosmopolitanism of *Queen Mab* toward the individual conscience as the ground of reformation, makes much of solidarity. In Canto V, shortly after an assertion of the Christian theme of the exchange

257

of burdens, expressed as fraternal solidarity to contrast with the dissociality of empire, the rites and feast at "the Altar of the Federation" come straight out of the days of hope in France, as Helen Maria Williams had described them and Wordsworth had compressed them in blank verse.

At "Liberty's uprise," forces of the tyrant rush in and begin hacking. Then follows a cry "to arms," the rescue of Laon, and escape on a Tartar horse. The choice of narrative has led to the representation of open conflict, but Shelley does not allow the mode to overthrow his principles. Not only do the good avoid violence; their nonviolence is their strength. Just as the torturer released Cythna, so it was fortunate that Laon was wounded, for the wounding made his foes contrite. Shelley provides this motivation as a "beautiful idealism" to be emulated by the reader. In Canto X an inverted federation, a decidedly unbenevolent meeting of murderous slaves, leads to fresh outbreaks of oppression, stabbing, famine, and related outrages. The sectarian priests fall into dissent: it is easier to proclaim that divinity has been offended than to identify the offended god. Here Shelley seems to echo Volney, but the anticlerical irony is congruent with the rest of the poem. An "Iberian priest" ("Christian priest" in the first version) recommends that Laon and Laone be caught and burned at the stake in expiation. To stop the flow of sacrifice, Laon surrenders, but only after exacting a promise that Laone may go free to the new, rude land of liberty and truth, America. Of course Cythna joins the sacrifice, but heroine and hero survive as winged thought to tell the tale. The spirit of the revolt survives. It would have been pointless to search history for a successful revolution; men of good will had to be assured that the failure in France was not, as they had thought at its beginning, the pattern for the future.[28]

IV

Shelley always had difficulty in objectifying conflict. His unfinished "Marenghi," of late 1818, is the kind of narrative Byron would have finished avidly. To refute the error that "ill for ill should be repaid," the fragment begins to retell from Sismondi's *Histoire des*

républiques italiennes the exploit of a Florentine patriot stripped
of all possessions and exiled, who nevertheless risked his life to destroy
a ship hostile to his maternal city. The fragment contains a notable
acknowledgment that "good and ill like vines entangled are." The
example is Florence, foster-nurse of Athenian glory but ravager of
Pisa. From Tacitus, Shelley began a poem on Otho but abandoned
it long before it reached the proportions of Keats's failure in *Otho
the Great*. Although Shelley believed in resolute defense of idea
and principle, only in *The Cenci* was he to sympathize with a com-
bative character enough to sustain his own interest in the presentation of conflict.

Shelley's kind of poem, "Lines Written among the Euganean
Hills," begun and completed at Este in October 1818, a poem of
substance and configuration but not of action, enfolds its own political context. The lines assume as axiomatic (as the juvenile experi-
ments and imitations could not) what they embellish in metaphor.
Man, voyaging in a sea of agony, sustains life by anticipating the
flowering islands where he occasionally strands, before he washes
finally ashore as "One white skull and seven dry bones." This day
in the Euganean Hills has been such an island to the poet. The
sunlit scene—a composite of the hills, Venice, Padua, and sister
cities of the plain of Lombardy—appears as a flowering island, but
the bulk of the poem reveals the enslavement, wretchedness, and
decay hidden beneath today's transit of the sun. Sin and Death,
after playing at dice for the tyrant Ezzelino, propagated incestuously
(as prophesied in *Paradise Lost*), and now both rule in Padua under
the Austrian tyrant, begetter of anarchy. In Gillray's "Sin, Death,
and the Devil," a savage caricature on Pitt's ouster of Lord Thurlow
in 1792 (a caricature that may have influenced Blake's *Europe*),
the artist had applied Milton's myth to a political situation, without
regard to general implications.[29] Shelley applies the myth to the
facts of history but also makes use of the theological implications
to convey political theory. Without any comment on the doctrine
of original sin, he accepts the durability of moral evil while attributing the sting of evil to false arrangements in the political state. From
1818 on, he distinguishes between cosmic evil and the sting of evil
in daily life.

James Gillray, "Sin, Death,
and the Devil"

Shelley

The poem pursues a contrast of appearance and reality. The cities of Lombardy, dancing like a band of graces in the sun, are in fact chained ingloriously, like the shimmering palaces of Venice that conceal the enslavement and spiritual decay within. But the beauty of the surface is the ultimate reality that must one day again inhabit the appearance.

The theme of the personal tyrant, which Shelley imbues with all his hatred of the anthropomorphic God, is anticipated in the introductory lines: winds howl around the unburied bones of the mariner (who is everyman)

> like a slaughtered town,
> When a king in glory rides
> Through the pomp of fratricides . . .   (SP, 555:57–59)

In the central lines, Shelley pleads with the cities to throw off their debasement under "the Celtic Anarch" and unmake the tyrant: "Lo, the sun floats up the sky / Like thought-wingèd Liberty . . ." The trochaic tetrameters, leaning forward, seem to hasten the thrust against tyranny and misery, in counterpoint to the despair, first over Venice, which Byron may have prodded as vainly as Shelley prodded Dublin, and next over Padua. Though the sparks from the ancient light of learning in Padua have been stamped dead by despotism, the tyrant shall—it must be soon—find the fire spreading again, just as the Norwegian finds the flames of the forest renewing their vigor around him.

Over this simile we need to linger a moment. Often Shelley's similes appeal to analytic reason rather than to the sympathetic imagination, but the identification of the Norwegian woodsman with a tyrant has an emotional as well as intellectual base. A lesser poem, "The Woodman and the Nightingale," equates the woodman with a Nimrod: "And so this man returned with axe and saw" after insensitively "killing the tall treen." Such woodmen stalk everywhere:

> The world is full of Woodmen who expel
> Love's gentle Dryads from the haunts of life,
> And vex the nightingales in every dell.
> (SP, 564:68–70)

Politics in English Romantic Poetry

Identification of the ordinary woodman with a mighty hunter is symptomatic. The poet feels himself surrounded by Nimrods. Association of self with Nature has positively increased the isolation of the humanitarian intellectual. The temple of Nature (erected in lines 54–59 of "The Woodman and the Nightingale") permits the poet to approve one form of religion without decreasing his ferocity against clerical institutions, but this is a religion of solitude, not of benevolence. Wordsworth, even in *Peter Bell,* regarded every man as capable of revering a primrose; Shelley, like most "liberal intellectuals" after him, defied the antagonism of the common man, who vexes the nightingale that "sits in darkness and sings to cheer its own solitude with sweet sounds" and, thus withdrawn, functions as unacknowledged legislator of the world. Despite the parlous state of love and reason in Padua and Venice, "Other flowering isles must be." The poet in the solitude of the Euganean Hills therefore postulates, for him and those he loves, a Paradise so healing that even the "polluting multitude" will be subdued to brotherhood. Where Wordsworth could prophesy flatfootedly of education and emigration in *The Excursion*—as *Don Juan* has it, "Writ in a manner which is my aversion"—Shelley was driven toward metaphor and myth to express his hope for polluted man.

An avid student not only of metaphysical debate but also of accounts of discovery in pamphlets and periodicals, he sometimes found the needed metaphor at hand, as for "Ozymandias."[30] Pleasantly self-conscious in its preachment, this sonnet has an additional charm in its long, lonely perspective on politics. The periphery of the argument, that nature outlasts art, has an analogue in a fragment published by Mrs. Shelley in her second edition of 1839:

> Rome has fallen, ye see it lying
> Heaped in undistinguished ruin:
> Nature is alone undying.   (SP, 588)

But Rome fell because, like Ozymandias, it had a "sneer of cold command." The sculptor must have mocked that sneer, says the sonnet, even as he recorded it. Shelley's warning against lusts of command goes beyond the stanza Byron added earlier that year (1819) to *Don Juan:*

262

Shelley

Let not a monument give you or me hopes,
Since not a pinch of dust remains of Cheops.   (I.219)

In "Ozymandias," it is failure to build the state on love that is
the vanity of vanities. Although less obviously as he inquired more
and more into the techniques and the essence of poetry, Shelley
continued to ask how political change should be related to the short
and long cycles of nature.

V

Given his need to try all the poetic forms, especially those used
with success by others in the propagation of political opinion, and
despite his growing recognition that good and ill are entangled,
Shelley's political verses inevitably included the exaggerations of
satire.

News of Peterloo, which sounded to the exiles in Italy like a
provocation to sudden and violent revolution, excited him to speak
directly to a wider audience than he had recently sought. He is
at his purely political best in the poems for plain men. These are
Shelley's songs of experience. His "Song to the Men of England"
sounded menacing enough for secret distribution by militant
Chartists.[31]

> Sow seed,—but let no tyrant reap;
> Find wealth,—let no imposter heap;
> Weave robes,—let not the idle wear;
> Forge arms,—in your defence to bear.
> (SP, 573:21–24)

Taken with Shelley's other declarations, this has to be interpreted
as an angrily defiant and active form of civil disobedience. It advises
a show of force, rather than the use of force. To end conflict, it
recommends that the people's strong hand be laid on the table.
It calls upon workers, not to seek the occasion of disobedience, as
a challenge to law, but to be fully prepared for disobedience. Although Shelley had argued against Godwin that reformers must band
together to secure change, he abandoned only in brief periods of

passion Article 9 of his Declaration of Rights: "No man has a right to disturb the public peace, by personally resisting the execution of a law however bad. He ought to acquiesce, using at the same time the utmost powers of his reason, to promote its repeal."[32] Sabers seem to rattle through the eight quatrains of the poem largely because of the emphasis on "weapon, chain, and scourge" that workers have been tricked into forging for the benefit of the "stingless drones": "Ye see" the "steel ye tempered glance on ye." The song closes with tight ironic fury. Borrowing the spell woven by Gray's Bard as the "winding-sheet of Edward's race," the singer, with fierce irony, advises the men of England to go on without revealing their power:

> With plough and spade, and hoe and loom,
> Trace your grave, and build your tomb,
> And weave your winding-sheet, till fair
> England be your sepulchre.   (SP, 573:29–32)

The stanza takes the middle ground between exhortation and the satire of despair over England's masters. Radical leaders did in fact follow this perpetually inconclusive method of implying the threat of numbers without preparing to man barricades, probably because they shared Shelley's belief in the rights of Englishmen under law.[33] But the drones controlled the law.

Under an "old, mad, blind, despised, and dying king," begins the sonnet "England in 1819," these are the rulers who "leech-like to their fainting country cling." Where Wordsworth's "London, 1802" acknowledges that "We are selfish men," Shelley leaps from high to low, from the king's ministers to a "people starved and stabbed," without pausing to implicate the complacent reader. Despite this deficiency, if it is one, the sonnet moves to the subtlest of Shelley's denunciations of the monarchic system of rule by gold and blood: "Golden and sanguine laws which tempt and slay." Not only does the system falsely known as justice serve the rulers' thirst for gold and blood, but it *tempts* starving workers and compromised criminals to serve as informers and *agents provocateurs* in order to tempt and thereby slay on the gallows the hapless victims provoked by entrapment.[34] Perhaps it is Shelley's distance from the

264

laborers in the provinces that makes him stress the actions of the cavalry at Peterloo, in his poems to the men of England, rather than the greater horror to workers (as we know from Carlile, Hone, Henry Hunt, and Wooler) of the government's stooping to suborn spies. Domestic spies were supposed to have ended with the Stuarts.

Shelley received word of Peterloo early in September; in November he still wanted to remind readers of the *Examiner* that he was informed how a troop of factory foremen "massacre without distinction of sex or age, & cut off women's breasts & dash the heads of infants against the stones" (SL, II, 117, 136). Verse designed to influence people who were having experiences of that sort would need special pungency.

"Lines Written during the Castlereagh Administration," complex in myth and more complex in stanza than the occasion called for, shows a great technical advance over the Esdaile pieces similarly conceived as at once ceremonial and abusive. Beginning "Corpses are cold in the tomb," the stanzas identify these corpses as abortions killed along with murdered Liberty, whose funeral din is the bacchanal epithalamium of the Tyrant's marriage with Ruin. The obvious comparison is with Blake's succinct "marriage hearse." C. D. Locock judged this "certainly the most powerful" of the six or more pieces that Shelley called "*popular songs* wholly political, & destined to awaken & direct the imagination of the reformers."

"The Mask of Anarchy" is the longest and most imaginative, most visionary, of the poems for the people. It has seemed much too long to those interested in it only as satire.[35] Political it certainly is, but less satiric than prophetic. The allegorical aspects suggest a masque, but the portent of the title is that Murder and Fraud, who recently manipulated Bonaparte, now ride in England as Castlereagh and Eldon. These two, with their placemen, lead in Anarchy, masked as the present condition of England. The allegorical equivalences take this odd turn because of an implication, usually called Shelley's Platonism, to be strengthened in later stanzas. True, England is *masked* as what she now seems. Yet this opening is not allegory in the sense of metaphor extended into narrative, but only in the sense of assigning abstract epithets to define the public effects wrought by specific, actual, living, named office-holders.

Politics in English Romantic Poetry

"The Mask of Anarchy" treats the mode of prophetic dream-vision as apocalypse, a final uncovering and revelation, at first of horror and then of what horror hides. This sequence follows the movement of Revelation from the seven-headed beast empowered by the great red dragon to the victory and marriage of the lamb. At first, Murder, Fraud, Hypocrisy, Anarchy, and a miscellany of Destructions ride a progress through England, adored by the multitude because they are triumphantly disguised (just like "Bishops, lawyers, peers, or spies") as justice, charity, religion, order, and limited monarchy. A bishop is to pastoral care, a lawyer is to justice, as Oliver the spy is to fraternity. The stripping of these hypocrisies begins emblematically with Eldon's notorious habit of weeping. Children looking up, "Thinking every tear a gem, / Had their brains knocked out by them"; that is, going inside the fine solid metaphor, Shelley's children were deprived of enlightenment from their father. In this pageant, false as the vivid dance of graces in Lombardy, even Hope appears as Despair.

Then, when Hope has lain down in the road exhausted, expecting to be trampled by Murder, Fraud, and Anarchy, suddenly a "mist, a light, an image" arises between her and her foes. This Shape, as the antithesis of Anarchy, makes that "ghostly birth" drop dead, drives away the pale horse of the Apocalypse, and addresses the sons of England along the pragmatic lines of *A Philosophical View of Reform*. This Shape is active love. In part benevolence, but not of Godwin's sort, with its reliance on individual acts of reason and justice rather than acceptance of the compromises, rhetoric, and threats of association, she is the solidarity of action through fraternal love. As Freedom has lost the sense of her own identity through the pretenses of liberty in England, the Shape redefines freedom, in address to Freedom herself, as including comely food and shelter, comfortable dress, absence of inequities in wealth, justice, "Wisdom" (religious tolerance), peace, true charity. What she outlines is not the liberal's freedom, but the socialist's. Apparently she believes some of the essential blessings to be founded in fiscal stability, with a decrease in taxes, for she counts paper money among the instruments of slavery. Giving heart to the men of England, she communicates Shelley's advice to the leaders of reform.

Shelley

The last line strikes the note of "Song to the Men of England":
"Ye are many—they are few." Meanwhile, the mode has been expansive enough to allow for a stanza of unmistakable clarity in its prescription of passive defiance:

> Let a vast assembly be,
> And with great solemnity
> Declare with measured words that ye
> Are, as God has made ye, free—

Troops made up of Englishmen probably will not attack. If by miscalculation or mischance they do, stand your ground.

> With folded arms and steady eyes,
> And little fear, and less surprise,
> Look upon them as they slay
> Till their rage has died away.   (SP, 344:344–347)

Once you are strong, the Shape advises, do not as the French did, but bring to an end the exchange of blood for blood.

The Shape, as the spirit of solidarity, has a progressive program, but she represents in herself reform or renovation, a sloughing-off of recent anarchy to reach the enduring reality of English life, just as Hope was always Hope, and despair only what she seemed to those who did not read her aspect aright. It was not really in despair but in clear-eyed prescience that Hope threw herself in the path of the ruling pretenders. Stanzas just before the close make a concession to Burke that poems addressed by Shelley to the more sacred few do not make. Passive resistance will succeed because the spirit of the "old laws of England" will reduce "the bold, true warriors" to shame for any violence against a countryman. The concession passes immediately into implications more typical:

> And that slaughter to the Nation
> Shall steam up like inspiration,
> Eloquent, oracular;
> A volcano heard afar.   (SP, 344:360–363)

Leigh Hunt, whether because he focused on the volcano and missed the comic vigor and elation of the whole, or because he despaired of explaining its complexity to a packed jury, delayed publication of the poem until after the Reform Bill had passed.

"The Mask of Anarchy" breaks down the neoclassic walls of genre. In slighter pieces Shelley sometimes practiced the prevailing modes; in others he made still further transformations.

Fun and sadness mix with satire in *Peter Bell the Third,* which takes much more than the first *Peter Bell* as its target. The satire aims bifocally at Wordsworth's latter-day dullness and the social follies and inequities of London. The impulse to parody arose from poetic aspects of Wordsworth, but the aspects attacked include his unpoetic support of the Lonsdales against Brougham in 1818. Shelley emphasizes the still fouler sins, poetic and unpoetic, in Wordsworth's odes of 1816, particularly the already much-abused lines on divine use of carnage, which Shelley restates interpretively in one of Peter the third's Odes to the Devil:

> May Carnage and Slaughter,
> Thy niece and thy daughter,
> May Rapine and Famine,
> Thy gorge ever cramming
> Glut thee with living and dead!
>
> (SP, 360:636–640)

Shelley's parody must have helped Wordsworth decide to cancel the offending genealogy—Carnage as the daughter of the "Father and Judge of all"—many years later, when the air had cooled enough for the cancellation to seem like temperance rather than retreat.

In 1820 the trial of Queen Caroline brought Shelley still closer to the ways of parody and invective in political journalism. William Gifford's and John Wolcot's excesses in invective had been imitated by countless versifiers in the partisan newspapers. Parody, made respectable by Horace and James Smith's *Rejected Addresses* of 1812, had been returned by William Hone to the venomous methods of the *Anti-Jacobin,* simplified for a wider audience, and converted to what the orthodox called blasphemy and sedition. Shelley's satire, *Oedipus Tyrannus; or, Swellfoot the Tyrant,* applies parody to the royal indiscretions of 1820 in much the same way as "The Political

Shelley

House that Jack Built," "A Political Christmas Carol," and other
pieces by William Hone collected in his *Facetiae and Miscellanies,*
appropriately illustrated by George Cruikshank. These works employ
parody not to ridicule the work parodied but to turn mock-heroic
burlesque against the royal Court, bench, and cabinet.

In 1820-21 the royal follies were so exaggerated as to defy caricature. Caroline of Brunswick's troubles had begun when she married
the Prince of Wales in 1795. Her husband not only had mistresses,
but was already married, as newspapers and pamphlets informed
the public, to Maria Anne Smythe (Mrs. Fitzherbert), a widow,
a commoner, and a Catholic. He deserted the Princess in 1796;
had a commission investigate the possibilities of divorce from her
ten years later; banished her from his Court in 1814; created in
1819 a new Secret Commission of Inquiry to investigate her conduct
abroad; had her tried before the House of Lords for adultery with
her courier, "Count" Bergami; had her name removed from the
liturgy; and barred her from the long-delayed coronation of 19
July 1821. Meanwhile the obstreperous Caroline was seldom quiet.
With Henry Brougham as her Attorney-General and mobs surrounding her carriage, she embarrassed every proceeding—and embarrassed her leading supporters as well—until her death, one month
after she failed in her attempt to enter Westminster Abbey for the
coronation.

Shelley's Advertisement to *Swellfoot* describes the work as a translation from a tragedy in two acts by "some *learned Theban.*" Swellfoot, a vain tyrant, claims infinite superiority to the hungry swine
who surround the magnificent temple where he worships the goddess
Famine. Purganax (Castlereagh), Chief of the Council of Wizards,
reports the words of their oracle:

> Boeotia, choose reform or civil war!
> When through the streets, instead of hare with dogs,
> A Consort Queen shall hunt a King with Hogs,
> Riding on the Ionian Minotaur.   (SP, 393:113–116)

In making Swellfoot king of the "dull Swine of Thebes," Shelley
efficiently combines the otherwise worn topics of George IV's corpu-

Politics in English Romantic Poetry

lence and Edmund Burke's unfortunate reference in *Reflections on the Revolution in France* to "the swinish multitude."

True to the oracle, Iona Taurina (Joan Bull, the Queen) arrives, borne by the old true Minotaur (John Bull) and noisily surrounded by pigs. The arch-priest Mammon—presumably Prime Minister Liverpool, for he has dismissed his son Chrysaor (gold coin) and married his "accomplished daughter" Banknotina to an heir of Tyburn—opposes Iona with the "poison BAG of that Green Spider huge" (the essence of domestic espionage). In the final scene, just when Iona is about to undergo the trial of her virtue by the test of a large dash of hogwash from the green bag, veiled Liberty enters and calls her eternal enemy Famine to a brief alliance for the welfare of the swine:

> I charge thee! when thou wake the multitude,
> Thou lead them not upon the paths of blood.
> (SP, 408:90–91)

Iona snatches the green bag and empties its contents over Swellfoot and his Court, whereupon they turn into small predators and flee. Iona mounts "the old traditional Man-Bull" and rides in full cry, with her loyal pigs, to rout all the foxes, otters, and wolves.

Shelley had no illusion that the great noise over Caroline might bring about permanent revolution. The triviality of her cause made his usual prophetic intensity inappropriate. His letters indicate an ambivalence similar to that expressed in Byron's epigram, "Why should *Queens not* be *whores?* Every *Whore* is a QUEAN," and its added comment: "This is only an epigram to the *ear*. I think she will win: I am sure she ought, poor woman" (LJ, V, 65). *Swellfoot the Tyrant* builds on topical ugliness more than any other of Shelley's works; in method, too, it belongs to its time. It shares with other pasquinades of the period a similar ancestry. Treating Sophocles' matter in the spirit of Aristophanes, *Swellfoot* has all the Scriblerian pedantry customary after Pope and Swift; but contemporaneously, both in its way of laughing and in what it laughs at, it verbalizes caricatures by Gillray and prolific current work by the Cruikshanks, Hone, and one S. Vowles, who was employed by Mary Ann Carlile during her husband's imprisonment. *Swellfoot* extends and amalgamates the skits of Hone. We know that Shelley

Shelley

subscribed to funds and followed Hone's career; the similarities are even more remarkable if Shelley was not seeing Hone's work in 1820.

They may be wrong who find *Swellfoot* one more proof that Shelley lacked humor. The green bag of secret evidence against Caroline had been derided before *Swellfoot,* often and more succinctly. It required no great ingenuity to include in the fable, as "a LEECH," the King's chief emissary in the case, elevated for just such services to Vice-Chancellor, Sir John Leach. Of those involved in the blunder of hiring Italian witnesses against the Queen, perhaps William Cooke, K.C., had not been previously called "the Gadfly," but John Allen Powell, who had earlier acted for Burdett, was in consequence of his defection already known to caricaturists as "the Rat."[36] Yet Shelley's "dull Swine of Thebes" are both funnier and more pertinent than the average when they claim descent from "the free Minotaur" but follow the gross Joan Bull ("Iona Taurina"). He can be credited with a deft touch in his observation that the sows, defying Malthus, have loaded the earth with pigs despite the starvation, typhus-fever, war, prison, prostitution, and "moral restraint" prescribed by their rulers. He works the National Debt and the Rothschilds aptly if coarsely into the theme and action by having Swellfoot, when other checks to the population fail, order the Jews to spay the sows. The arch-priest Mammon, with empty mind and mouth full of outrageous anachronisms, would make a serviceable role for a clown trained on Shakespeare or Shaw. The satire of *Swellfoot* harbors comedy. We expect and we find burlesque of Castlereagh's speeches, but should note also the self-parody when we come upon bulls

> with sweet breath
> Loading the morning winds until they faint
> With living fragrance . . .

or again the warning to pigs who take Iona Taurina for divine love or intellectual beauty:

> Smoke your bits of glass,
> Ye loyal Swine, or her transfiguration
> Will blind your wondering eyes.
>
> (II.i.64–66, 185–187)

Indeed the structure as well as individual passages of *Swellfoot the Tyrant* parodies the "beautiful idealisms" of *Prometheus Unbound* and *Hellas*. Lurking throughout the whole history of the pigs who claim descent from the Minotaur is a joke on the Whiggish, and latterly the Unitarian and Dissenting, claim to a Gothic origin for English liberties.[37] Swellfoot, Goths, and boars ("crowned with thistle, shamrock, and oak" to include Scotland and Ireland) consort well in a "magnificient Temple, built of thigh-bones and death's-heads, and tiled with scalps." *Swellfoot* will never displace *The Rape of the Lock,* but there is fun in it, as there needed to be in any attempt to acquit Caroline.

The play takes religion seriously as a political tool. Liverpool and his fellows serve as priests in the magnificent Temple of Famine. Each little gibbet, born after Mammon married his daughter Banknotina to the gallows (a conceit enlarged from *Cymbeline* V.iv.206),

says its catechism
And reads a select chapter in the Bible
Before it goes to play.   (I.216–218)

The general point is that summarized in a phrase used by Hone throughout his *Reformists' Register and Weekly Commentary* of 1817: "Political Priestcraft."[38]

VI

Peterloo evoked from Shelley odes as well as satires. The most stridently exalted is "An Ode Written October, 1819, before the Spaniards had Recovered Their Liberty." The title, which has been called a "publisher's dodge," was changed by Mrs. Shelley to "An Ode to the Assertors of Liberty." The reiterations, "Arise, arise, arise," "Awaken, awaken, awaken," and "Wave, wave high the banner," recall simultaneously the bombastic conventions accumulated by the political ode as a journalistic form and the devotional tread of a state funeral. Taking for granted the approach of revolution, Shelley's stanzas ask that mourners forget neither the day of conflict nor the deaths inflicted by the prolonged condition of slavery. Those who attend the car of Freedom, however, are urged, as in the satires, to avoid aggressive violence:

272

Shelley

Lift not your hands in the banded war,
But in her defence whose children ye are.
(SP, 575:20–21)

A final stanza, left in manuscript until it was published by W. M. Rossetti, urges foeman and friend to gather in love and peace (SP, 576). As late as 1819 Shelley still wavered between the release of passion in a just cause and rational restraint of violence.

The allusion to the Spaniards in the title, meant partly in scorn for an Englishman's "liberty," was initially excused by its presence in the *Prometheus Unbound* volume near the "Ode to Liberty," a more ambitious work explicitly celebrating the success of the Spanish *Liberales* in 1820. This ode, and the studied but unsuccessful "Ode to Naples," are antiphonal to Wordsworth's sanguinary odes of 1816. However conscious or not the contrast, their uniform stanzas provide a disciplined alternative to Wordsworth's perseverance in Cowleyan freedom. The nineteen stanzas of the monostrophic "Ode to Liberty" rival in intricate repetition Coleridge's "France: An Ode," which Shelley much admired.

The method of the "Ode to Liberty" is one associated with progress in the age of taste and sensibility, further Hellenized by Shelley. The subject is not handled analytically, as in representative odes by Akenside or Collins—or, in fact, as in one of the direct kindlers of Shelley's fire, "The Progress of Poesy" by Gray. Shelley's handling is thoroughly historical. Like the scientific aspirations hymned by Akenside, the stanzas "seek / Eternity to trace." The procedure was obvious enough among Jacobinical patriots for the editors of the *Anti-Jacobin* to parody Richard Payne Knight in "The Progress of Man: A Didactic Poem."[39] Shelley's "progress," beginning with the emergence of the sun and moon out of primal chaos, is spoken by a "voice out of the deep," an art-seeking, poetry-revering Queen Mab. Milton Wilson has told how the ode mixes Jacobin argument and Platonic texture,[40] but there is more of Lucretius than of Plato.

As a romantic Hellenist, Shelley breaks decidedly on one point with such progenitors as Collins. After Athens and Rome, according to Shelley's progress-piece, one looked for liberty in vain among the Christians and Goths. The voice reminds Liberty: "For neither

273

didst thou watch the wizard flocks / Of the Scald's dreams, nor haunt the Druid's sleep." Neither royalist nor pedestrian enough to praise kings like Henry II for legal reforms, Shelley skips from Alfred, as the equivalent in law of Italians in art, to English prophetic poetry, ended in the disillusioned old age of Milton.[41] Left in naked honesty at the close, when the Spirit returns to the abyss, the poet has a double question. Will the return of liberty signalized in Spain sustain poetry, and will the poet's own art sustain or promote liberty? The ode subsides at the close, or rather it plunges, more than traditions of the genre required. The poet's song declaredly drooped "As a brief insect dies with dying day." Like Coleridge's "Ode on the Departing Year," it leaves the reader staring into darkness.

This is the rhetoric of passion, high style lifted toward the sublime, without any free, subtle, Wordsworthian movement of the mind. Although Shelley's three odes on Pindaric stilts are not equally conventional, they illustrate as a group, and their inequality itself illustrates further, the distinction between straight imitation within an accepted genre, where acceptance nearly always paralyzed the romantic poets, and the renovation whereby they careened or upended a genre to make it new.

"Ode to the West Wind," at a deeper level of success, speaks with inspiration from those English prophets honored in the "Ode to Liberty" for taking Liberty as their queen. It represents Shelley's profoundest response to Peterloo. This is not to say that the poem is merely a reaction to the apparent imminence of revolution, but that its force derives in considerable part from reaction to the public situation in England—from a distance of one thousand miles away in subjugated Tuscany.

The first three sections establish the character of the wind as a cosmic power, simultaneously destroyer and preserver, seen only in its effects on earth, sky, and sea. The mode of the poem as prophetic prayer is anticipated in the opening phrase, "O wild West Wind," but the anticipation is almost surreptitious. It comes forward only in the repetition, at the end of each of the first three sections, of the supplicatory words "oh, hear!" We think of this first three-

Shelley

fifths of the poem as subjective because of the exhortative excitement and the haste of metaphor, but these sections on leaf, cloud, and wave report effects universally exciting to human contemplation. They do not involve the poet or speaker as an individual except in his capacity as the particular consciousness that perceives the effects of the wind and comprehends their meaning.

Section iv, where the "I" first appears, concentrates on the history and present situation of the prophet who exhorts. Praying for a controlled impulse from the uncontrollable strength of the wind, he asserts that even such vitality as he possessed in boyhood would increase his readiness to be the lyre, as explained in section v, conveying the "tumult of thy mighty harmonies":

> Oh, lift me as a wave, a leaf, a cloud!
> I fall upon the thorns of life! I bleed!
>
> (SP, 579:53–54)

Shelley cries out here with something of his own voice, autobiographically, but "the thorns of life" are less personal than public, and more the result of corruption in government than of the sin of Adam, as the final section of the ode makes clear.

As the west wind is to the universe of perceived objects, so the poet would be as prophet to the universe of perceiving man, the "unawakened earth" of mankind:

> Drive my dead thoughts over the universe
> Like withered leaves to quicken a new birth!
> And, by the incantation of this verse,
>
> Scatter, as from an unextinguished hearth
> Ashes and sparks, my words among mankind!
> Be through my lips to unawakened earth
>
> The trumpet of a prophecy! O, Wind,
> If Winter comes, can Spring be far behind?
>
> (SP, 579:63–70)

The analogy of "unawakened earth" holds equally for autumn, poet, England, Europe, India, and Latin America.

Politics in English Romantic Poetry

In offering himself, his skill and his being, as a vessel, an Aeolian lyre, to the destroyer-and-preserver seen only in its effects, never in its essence, the poet assembles conventions from fervent Greek, Hebrew, Italian, and English poets. From the repetitions in other poems we know that he thrust himself into the moment of prophetic despair: "I fall upon the thorns of life! I bleed!" But the creative act of perfecting the prayer transforms the union of projected self, felt storm, and observed society into a phenomenon of language without any didactic trace.

In the humility of the prayer, which extends through the two final sections, although the ordered violence of the imagery conveys a cry for action "to quicken a new birth," the pacifist's problem of having his potentiality taken seriously in a world of force, a problem much clearer in Shelley's satires, is here evaded. In the myth, clustered metaphors, and counterpointed ambiguities of this poem, Shelley found an aesthetic solution to the conflict between his enlightened politics and the poetics of the imagination. Beyond Shelley's own needs, the prophetic contrivance permits the reader either to accept the solution without further questions or to ignore the political implications altogether. A critic need not, like F. W. Bateson, declare the political hope present but unearned.

There is no *Weltschmerz*, no *Sehnsucht* of undirected yearning. The speaker confronts a nadir, not a private but an epidemic nadir, when things are so bad that Europe must get better or die. If England is on the verge of an uprising, it will be, if unguided, no awakening, but a nightmare, the bankruptcy of sleep, death-in-life. The poet finds in himself no way out. The only promise comes from the character of the west wind as destroyer and preserver. All is ready for a thorough renovation. The dark dome of the storm will close the sepulcher where the poet's dead thoughts lie prostrate with wintry earth and deadened humanity. Through analogy, the lines equate cycles of infinitely different duration: plague and recovery, death and rebirth, the seasonal cycle of decay and new growth, sleep and wakefulness, despair and prophetic fervor, suppression and evolution. Although death is acknowledged and progress perhaps implied, the analogy of the seasonal cycle defines the limits of both despair and hope.

276

Shelley

In tension with the botanical image of burying seeds in the soil, the second section equates the coming of the wind with the death of the growing season as a variation on Shelley's frequent symbol of the volcanic revolution that prevents earthquake: the dome of stormy night, vaulted with a "congregated might" of vapors, will collapse under the weight of purifying "rain, and fire, and hail."

The relation of seasonal renovation to politics had been demonstrated by Cythna in her assurance to Laon that "violence and wrong are as a dream."[42] In this earlier passage, as in "Ode to the West Wind," the sleep of winter connotes the frost of tyranny, privilege, superstition, and priestcraft.

In the ode, the poet offers to submit his own selfhood to the fierce spirit of renovation. *The Revolt of Islam* cannot tell us how long the renovation predicted at the end of the ode is expected to last. By the seasonal analogy of the poem, spring will be followed eventually by new winter. Meanwhile, the west wind sounds the dirge of the dying year; "this closing night / Will be the dome of a vast sepulchre." In the political and social terms of the final section, the situation of unawakened earth seems so bad that only a better is imaginable. Yet mankind, even in lethargy, is susceptible. Earth is in a condition to be awakened: sparks can come from "an unextinguished hearth." Just as the whole poem is the prayer of a prophet overheard by the reader, so the final question, "O Wind / If Winter comes, can Spring be far behind?" is addressed to the immanence of incomprehensible, unseen, but "evident" power. The question has the force of Abraham's when he thought a few good men might fall with the bad if the Lord obliterated Sodom: "Shall not the Judge of all the earth do right?" Unobtrusively the poem utilizes the primitive sense that lengthening nights threaten the death of the year, until now always prevented by propitiatory rites. Spring has always followed prayer. If mankind hearkens to prophecy, regeneration will come.

Hope intensifies in the detail of the "sapless foliage of the ocean," thought to respond sympathetically to the climatic changes on the surface.[43] For Shelley's purposes, this concurrence is a version of the organic interpenetration, described in "The Sensitive Plant" and other poems, which is discernible throughout a "mutual atmosphere"

277

filled with radiance, fragrance, dew, vapors, and pollinating insects—a scientifically defined atmosphere of universal benevolence. So animated, the civilization of Baiae, Herculaneum, and Pompeii, seen of late only as excavated ruins reflected in the summer dreams of the sleeping Mediterranean, may reawaken through a Neapolitan revolution, now stirring, against the Bourbon King Ferdinand, "a brutal and treacherous tyrant" (according to mild historians) "who was under the thumb of Metternich."[44] This political circumstance, although it presses upon Shelley, is of course not explicit in the third section. It is implicit in the whole prayer, arising out of "sore need" to discover a renovating force for unawakened earth. The poet appeals to a power within sick nature because tyrants and slaves are the earth off its proper axis: the argument of *Queen Mab* now carried on by implicit analogy expressed in myth.[45]

So powerfully does the urgency of hope burst through the seasonal trammels of the poem that most critics have found in the final question something like the certainty of a Godwinian paradise ahead.[46] This advantage has come to Shelley through his avoidance of the language of politics as well as from the fusion of political vision with religious fervor. In "Ode to the West Wind" myth has freed itself completely from the strident certainties that encumbered the attempts at ritualization in the Esdaile poems. Acceptance of myth as the sovereign mode of the unifying imagination had brought Shelley a long way from the rationalistic program of *Queen Mab*.

VII

Of his attempts to avoid poetic forays into politics by creating poems that place politics within the whole frame of life, as Dante and Shakespeare had done, Shelley's greatest work of synthesis by far is *Prometheus Unbound*. So central is it to a study of politics in Shelley's poetry that we can properly devote to it a major portion of our investigation.[47] *Prometheus Unbound: A Lyrical Drama*, a renovation of Aeschylus' stillest but most eruptive tragedy, is a philosophic romance. As such, it is also a tempered, skeptical, scarcely illusioned romance.

In Aeschylus' *Prometheus Bound*, where Shelley began, the proud champion of man, bringer of fire and arts, has refused to relinquish the secret—known only to him but vital to Zeus—that union with Thetis will produce a son more powerful than the father. Power and Force bear Prometheus to a Scythian crag, where Hephaestus binds him. In lines adapted by Shelley to proclaim that "the deep truth is imageless" even to Demogorgon, Aeschylus represents the Titan's opposition to Zeus as fruitless defiance of Fate, Destiny, and Necessity. The commiserative Chorus of Oceanides scatters at the close when Prometheus is hurled into the abyss. According to tradition accompanying a fragment of Aeschylus' presumed sequel, *The Unbinding of Prometheus,* the Titan divulged his secret, after 30,000 years, in return for freedom.

To avoid this compromising preferment of tyranny and rape, Shelley reforms the myth. In the process, he dislocates causation, geography, topography, chronology, genealogy, and gender, not only in relation to classical mythology but internally as well. Dealing with cosmogony as process and with elemental questions, he transfers the scene of the Titan's suffering to the Caucasus Indicus, a move eastward toward the icy dawn of civilization. With setting meant as metaphor, the drama progresses from a moment before dawn to high noon, and simultaneously from early spring to lasting summer. In Act II, to take a further example of derangement, spring and the day rise together as one dawn, yet Apollo, out of wonder at the light from Asia, holds back the sun until noon. As the dramatis personae return from hate to love, the movement is backward from winter to spring, from age to infancy, from ice to warmth, from iron and stone to such melting affinity as the earth and moon begin to feel for each other in Act IV. Few if any of the dislocations can be confidently said to result from inadvertence.

In Act I the Furies that plague Prometheus externally as the fear, mistrust, "clinging crime," and hate exuded by government also exist within—in the words of the Third Fury to Prometheus—as "foul desire round thine astonished heart." As the retributory history of man in Europe, they are both external and internal. They are external beings as in Coleridge's "Fire, Famine, and Slaughter"; they are what is perceived as external history; they are also externalizations of inner lusts, like the witches in *Macbeth.*

Prometheus is tortured by awareness of what the human mind has done throughout Europe to the message of Jesus. A gentle ghost wails for "the faith he kindled"; we recognize Jesus the more certainly when we find the words that outlived him, "like swift poison," matched with the smoke vomited forth by "Many a million-peopled city." An "outcry of despair" comes both from the many and the One "of gentle worth." The nation that has dedicated to Truth and Freedom its leap from desolation, only to wade in blood like new wine in "the vintage time for death and sin," is identifiable as France in 1789–1796, and the subsequent period, when Despair smothers the "struggling world, which slaves and tyrants win," recognizably extends from 1796 to the time of Shelley's writing. Kingly conclaves where "blood with gold is bought and sold" occurred almost annually from 1814, as we have seen, with signs of acceleration when the Fourth Fury described them.[48] There is, then, at least a suggestion of ironic anachronism, as in a comedy by Shaw, Giraudoux, Brecht, or Bridie; but the irony is in the general conception only, not in the details, for Shelley relates the Promethean myth of timeless foreseeing hardly at all to Grecian times or specifically Grecian thought.

Even such events as the French Revolution flash as examples only. The vomiting smoke might come from military assault as readily as from industrial smudge, and the Fury-torn Prometheus is describing every revolution that resorts to force instead of forgiving wrongs darker than death. The revolution in France remains no more than illustration when Prometheus summarizes the vision that crawled like agony through his veins. The nations thronged round to cry "Truth, liberty, and love," but suddenly confusion fell and tyrants divided the spoil. Whereas we can say that the revolt of Islam is really the revolution in France, we need to say that the torturing of Prometheus reveals certain laws that underlay the revolution. Even the redundancy when a Fury holds before Prometheus an emblem of a youth "nailed to a crucifix," instead of "nailed to a cross," seems almost apt, as if it depicted one youth after another, nailed in turn, not to a cross, but to Christ on the cross, to the crucified Word. The Fury advises:

Shelley

Behold an emblem: those who do endure
Deep wrongs for man, and scorn, and chains, but heap
Thousandfold torment on themselves and him.   (I.594–596)

The lines that follow, on the pallid, dabbling Jesus and his hunted followers, are immoderately elaborate, as much in *Prometheus Unbound* is; but the point to be noted just here—and a point to be returned to later—is that the crucifixion of Jesus and the persecution of the truly Christlike, which belong in part to Prometheus' internal torment, have occurred since he cursed Jupiter. It is the curse that gives currency to the emblem of the suffering martyr. Some of the suffering is shame.

The description of the latter-day avatars of Christ shows Shelley's method of generalizing with political particulars:

> I see, I see
> The wise, the mild, the lofty, and the just,
> Whom thy slaves hate for being like to thee,
> Some hunted by foul lies from their heart's home,
> An early-chosen, late-lamented home;
> As hooded ounces cling to the driven hind:
> Some linked to corpses in unwholesome cells:
> Some—Hear I not the multitude laugh aloud?—
> Impaled in lingering fire: and mighty realms
> Float by my feet, like sea-uprooted isles,
> Whose sons are kneaded down in common blood
> By the red light of their own burning homes.
>
> (I.604–615)

The lines evoke scenes in England, Ireland, Italy, and Spain. The opening has been taken as autobiographical, but it includes Byron, "lofty" if not "mild"; of others it includes at least Joseph Priestley, who fled to Pennsylvania after a notorious incident: a Birmingham mob, opposing the Constitutional Society in 1791 with the cry of "Church and King," had burned his house, including his laboratory and library, emblems of knowledge and truth.[49] The quoted passage brings Dante also to mind, although I take the fifth line to mean a country early chosen by divine Liberty and later to be lamented for its apostasy, rather than simply chosen and lamented by the

281

"hunted." Far from autobiographical cryptography, the passage constitutes a set of deliberately conventional allusions to a "chosen people" and their lapse from virtue.

The linked prisoners, kneaded sons, and burning homes evoke as one of their worlds the Ireland of 1797, vivid in the reprintings of Coleridge's "Fire, Famine, and Slaughter" in 1817. Shelley had denounced in 1812, as all of one worldly kind, "such as burnt the House of Priestley, such as murdered Fitzgerald" (in Dublin, in 1798), and "such wretches as dragged Redfern to slavery or (equal in unprincipled cowardice) the slaves who permit such things" (SL, I, 294–295). Disorders were continuing in Ireland, with new Police and Insurrection Acts to quell them. Cobbett and Carlile reported often, especially in 1818, on poor hawkers and printers chained and fettered in cells for blasphemy or sedition. The unwholesome cells belong also to the Lombardy of the Celtic Anarch, as in "Lines written among the Euganean Hills," with perhaps a hint of the fettered criminals that Shelley saw in the great square before St. Peter's in Rome just as he was finishing Acts I–III.[50] The "lingering fires" go backward from Ferdinand VII (whom Shelley execrates in *A Philosophical View of Reform*) through the Spanish and Roman Inquisitions. The pitting of nominal against true disciples of Jesus epitomizes the thousand years of "myriads of hecatombs" to be charged against the nominal disciples in Shelley's last note to *Hellas* (SP, 480).

The external tortures repeat themselves endlessly, as the Fury within next reminds the Titan, because the heart has created disgust and terror of itself, "Vexing the self-content of wisest men." As fully as caves of the mind and boats on the streams of life—although in a different way—these tortures illustrate Shelley's assertion that the imagery "will be found, in many instances, to have been drawn from the operations of the human mind, or from those external actions by which they are expressed." Through the fusion of day and season in the framework of the drama, the reader is led to a syncretic chronology of external and internal torture.

In the evanescence of this work, clusters of subliminal suggestion, working usually through metaphor, provide firmer guidance to the reader than the symbolic interactions of the sometimes allegorical and sometimes mythic characters. Winter, cold, iron, granite, dusk, gloom, rigidity, tyranny, arteriosclerosis, hardness of spleen—all these coalesce for thematic clarity. Crawling glaciers, earthquakes, and the "winged hound," transferring pollution from Jupiter's lips with "poison not his own"—these together eat into Prometheus' heart. Spring, dawn, flowers, warmth, airs, dissolution, expansion, liquidity, tears of pity or of joy, reacceptance of innocence, and freedom (or the opportunity to achieve self-empire) all flow onward in unison. The spectrum of unblemished light, the correspondingly rational order of the diatonic scale, tones and murmurs from an Aeolian harp, the ridges and exhaled music of the conch—prophetic trumpet of Proteus-Triton, natal source and nuptial gift to Asia—all these give assurances to man of the blindingly invisible, perfect light of love.

It is chiefly through the metaphoric clusters that the action, as well as every aspect of the theme, proceeds. Shelley explains in *A Defence of Poetry:* "The grammatical forms which express the moods of time, and the difference of persons, and the distinction of place, are convertible with respect to the highest poetry without injuring it as poetry . . ."[51] Conversions and transmutations control the structure of this "lyrical drama."

The greatest danger to the critic in looking first to the characters, rather than to the vehicles of the myth, has been to seek allegorical equivalencies and thereby to make their connotations more constant than the poetry warrants. Despite the danger, it is a great convenience to delimit, for purposes of discussion, the atmosphere that each character carries through his various interrelationships with others in the dramatis personae.

Prometheus represents something like the spirit or essence of human thought in its highest capacity. He is not too abstractly intellectual to retain at all times his will to resist. He is by moral necessity the "saviour and the strength of suffering man" (I.817). Although the advent of Prometheus came as a burst of joy to Earth, the chronology otherwise suggests a gradual birth (I.152–163; II.iv.33–46). Professor Ross Woodman does not greatly exaggerate the possible functions of reason in Prometheus when he describes him as in one sense "the psychic potential of the dreaming divinity in man."[52]

Politics in English Romantic Poetry

What Prometheus epitomizes has been too long absent from Asia, from love, the Life of Life, the soul of mind's being. A ray of what man can know as the eternal One, Asia is love, beauty, and light. This is one value of myth: Shelley calls her love; if you know of something better than love, Asia will be that something for you. To thought she is warmth. A daughter of Ocean (treated here and often in Shelley as the ground of being), she is also suprarational feeling. As intuition she comes from the continent of Asia, abruptly segregated by the fall of Troy and classically represented as "in deep distress for the sufferings and desolation of her people." (The words are those of *Bell's New Pantheon,* 1790.) Separated from intellect, Asia inspires love, but does not feel it (II.v.47). Separated from each other, Prometheus and Asia are potentialities of wisdom and love. When parted, they achieve, at best, pity and sentiment.

Suffering and enduring that man might be free, the mind in restraint has been comforted by two of Asia's sisters, Panthea and Ione, whom we may regard as lesser modes of love. The name Ione would seem to begin in the Io of Aeschylus' tragedy, a granddaughter of Ocean of whom the Ionian sea is a matronymic. Possibly the character should suggest Hellenic culture. An Ione is named among the Nereides, lesser nymphs whose long hair floats on waves of the sea. As pity, or with such balm as is afforded by pity—a soothing but dull-witted mode of love—Ione has comforted the human mind during its enchainment. Prometheus had not achieved love when he learned in his misery to pity Jupiter (I.53–59). Ione is with him, but not Asia. Even if his words "I would recall" mean that he wills now to withdraw his curse, and not merely that he chooses to remember it for renewed contemplation, his will has not at this point been purified by full reunion with love.

Panthea, a Pan-thea, etymologically a kind of universalist faith, has been a faithful guard against despair. Prometheus called her a shadow (meaning an emanation) of Asia. In the first scene of Act II, Panthea tells her impatient sister two dreams. In the first, Prometheus, bathed in the atmospheric fire of love, dissolved in her blood until "it became his life, and his grew mine." Asia looks into Panthea's eyes to read the dream and find the "shadow of that soul by which I live." What can she see, asks Panthea, but "thine own fairest shadow imaged there?" (II.i.31, 81, 113). Her question refers at one level to the direct reflection of the perceiver, but probably also to the union of Prometheus and Asia: through recent years they have been united only in the eyes of hope. As hope, then, Panthea for us is both a mode of Asia (more alert than Ione) and an aspect of thought. Even when the absolute perfection of love is absent, Panthea has remained as an attribute of Prometheus, an affirmative part of his character. Without her, chained thought would not aspire.

Asia sees also Panthea's second dream, now remembered by Panthea herself, of a quick shape with "rude hair" (like the traditional Demogorgon) passing in early spring, when the buds that have burst prematurely from the "lightning-blasted almond-tree" blow down (as did the premature hopes of France), but the leaves are marked with a message that Asia also remembers as printed on "each herb"—"O, follow, follow." Echoes now repeat the injunction, and the sisters obey it. That is, the dream lives.

The mutually shared dreams are stages in the process of returning love to its full power. Ione and Panthea act as modes of Asia, modes insufficient to make Prometheus really himself in separation from Asia. Absence from Asia is presence with Jupiter.

Jupiter, whom kings of old proudly claimed as father, embodies the idea and institutions of arbitrary rule: Jehovah, empire, superstition, claim of divine right, infallibility, the self-interest of Paley's utilitarianism, custom and prescription, the Inquisition, the Holy Alliance, the eternally evil trinity currently repeated in Eldon, Sidmouth, and Castlereagh. Jupiter's obscene union with Thetis can be taken as a whoring with Babylon, as the perversion of Christianity in the conjunction of church and state. We are given only the tyrant's own version of the way he overpowered her, but Thetis sits beside him and hears his words without protest. Even the union itself Shelley arranges in defiance of classical versions of the myth, wherein Jupiter avoids Thetis when warned (some say by Prometheus) that she would bear a son greater than the father. If we make analogy with such other poems as "Lines written during the Castlereagh Administration," Jupiter has wedded Ruin, to him "bright image of eternity" (III.i.36).

Prometheus, allowing Jupiter control over all spirits but himself and all wills except Prometheus' own, gave him his very existence as ruler over the minds of men (I.1, 381). When Prometheus wills to hear again his curse of defiance against the tyrant, he hears it from the Phantasm of Jupiter; that is, from the shadow left in time of what Prometheus had for ages become. Jupiter is government in business for itself, in neglect of the established principle reaffirmed in Shelley's *Proposals for an Association of . . . Philanthropists:* "Government can have no rights, it is a delegation for the purpose of securing them to others." Jupiter is tyrannous illusion. He is the stumbling of reason into unreason. He is illusion crowned as Reason.

Jupiter exists interchangeably in monarchy, oligarchy, and anarchy. Prometheus' temptation and torture by Furies shows how tyranny begets anarchy. Torture through anarchy is in one aspect the historical reflection of Prometheus' fall into a condition that includes Jupiter. It illustrates the argument in *A Philosophical View of Reform* that it was not the power of the monarch that increased during the reign of George III, but the power of the rich who exploited monarchy. Jupiter is both tyranny and the acceptance of tyranny. He remains within character in the Pecksniffian hypocrisy of his final appeal beyond justice to the charity of "Gentle, and just, and dreadless" Prometheus (III.i.68). The Titan, in his opposition to Jupiter, is both the better self of man as he has been and man as he may through love become. In this opposition, Jupiter remains man's worse self.

Sometimes the opposition is objectified in historical conflict, as it must be in order to have such intermediaries as the timorous Mercury and the vulture that brings "poison not his own" from Jupiter's lips to Prometheus' open side (I.35). This vulture is apparent in the Castlereagh of the Dedication to *Don Juan,* who had "just enough of talent," according to the draft of the Dedication in the British Museum,

> To lengthen out a chain already fixed
> And offer poison by another mixed.
>
> (12:7–8; Steffan and Pratt, II, 17)

Shelley

Sometimes the opposition is presented in metaphors of spiritual, intellectual, and cultural change. Prometheus supervises the "sun-awakened avalanche" of thought that gathers in "heaven-defying minds" (such as Voltaire, Rousseau, and the Encyclopedists)

> till some great truth
> Is loosened, and the nations echo round,
> Shaken to their roots . . . (II.iii.36–42)

This avalanche on the slopes of Demogorgon's volcano is the political equivalent of "that great poem," celebrated in the *Defence*, "which all poets, like the co-operating thoughts of one great mind, have built up since the beginning of the world." Icy hardness must be melted by the warmth of love and thought. In opposition, Jupiter throws down antithetical, freezing curses (III.i.11–17); he throws cold water on thought.

Mind has enslaved itself with a vengeance, for the tyrant is his own worst slave. A Fury describes the effect on man of the separation from Asia and the concomitant rule of Jupiter:

> The good want power, but to weep barren tears.
> The powerful goodness want: worse need for them.
> The wise want love; and those who love want wisdom;
> And all best things are thus confused to ill. (I.625–628)

As Yeats declared—when he borrowed but tightened this passage in "The Second Coming"—"Surely the Second Coming is at hand."

Apparently there had been a first coming, an original golden age, but *Prometheus Unbound* emphasizes the possibilities of renewal rather than the likelihood of past perfection. The period of perfection remains indefinite and contingent. Although the Love that is Light antedates Saturn, it is not clear that Saturn's subjects enjoyed the full presence of Love. He abused his timeless, vegetable reign by denying, to the flowers and other vegetative things of earth,

> The birthright of their being, knowledge, power,
> The skill which yields the elements, the thought
> Which pierces this dim universe like light,
> Self-empire, and the majesty of love . . . (II.iv.39–42)

Politics in English Romantic Poetry

To live under Saturn was to suffer determinism without consciousness. Essentially Shelley is accepting, first, the doctrine that the dignity of man requires freedom to fall (the cornerstone of Milton's justification of God's ways to man) and, second, the argument of plenitude, as defined by Arthur O. Lovejoy in *The Great Chain of Being:* by its own infinite nature, creative divinity must provide consciousness and whatever else can be imagined. It is better to risk the ascendancy of Jupiter than to be without consciousness and therefore without love.

Prometheus is not a divine creator, nor can he be said to carry out the will of a personal God. Assigned the role of protagonist, he simply carries out a program that the poet regards as beneficent for man. By bestowing wisdom, and thus enabling life to achieve full stature in man, Prometheus gave Jupiter the power to reign, but gave it with the conditions of a social contract: "Let man be free" (II.iv.45). As Asia now perceives, but apparently Prometheus then did not, the nature of dominion is to know "nor faith, nor love, nor law" (II.iv.47). Jupiter broke the contract, as all his crowned, robed, and mitered sons have done ever since. Did Shelley leave the reasons for Prometheus' lack of foresight unexamined merely because the myths of the Golden Age and Paradise came automatically equipped with falls from perfection, because he had no omnibenevolent God to exonerate, or because he chose to place all blame squarely on the will of man? In any event, the evident lawlessness of dominion required the shattering theory concerning government that emerges in Acts III and IV.

Although the existence of a primordial paradise is elsewhere implied, as when the Spirit of the Earth remembers long noons of talk with Asia (III.iv.25), Asia's own account in the presence of Demogorgon suggests a condition, perhaps only a potential condition, rather than an era. In short, the earth may have acquired simultaneously a being of superior intelligence, man, and the errant rule of Jupiter, just as Asia's birth and wedding, both symbolized by the "curvèd shell," may be considered as simultaneous. If we may count the "alternating shafts of frost and fire" in winter and summer as among the remediable evils of the earth (as felt by man), then the rule of Jupiter and the curse of Prometheus concurrently and collaborately rocked the earth from its true axis. Put another way, man in his aberration as tyrant and victim has for centuries incapacitated himself. Each looks before and after without allowing himself or others to drink the eternal beauty of spring. For all its temporal metaphors, the poem subordinates questions of sudden or slow change to the moral and psychic present.

However long it took intellect and tyranny to conjoin, was the conjunction inevitable? Demogorgon, master of the terseness that comes with the smoke from Greek oracles, and abetted by the words assigned to Asia, seems to say that an omnipotent, merciful God created the living world perceived by man and all that makes the perception possible: "thought, passion, reason, will, Imagination." Here, in Act II, scene iv, in the cave of Demogorgon, Asia questions that shapeless spirit. Who made all that the living world contains? "Almighty God." Who made "terror, madness, crime, remorse," and every evil thought of man? "He reigns." Understanding this last to mean Jupiter, Asia asks if any masters Jupiter. Equating Asia's question with the problem of "Fate, Time, Occasion, Chance, and Change," Demogorgon answers that "the deep truth is imageless." Discovering that Demogorgon answers as her heart answers, she asks, "When shall the destined hour arrive?" As her heart desires, he points to two cars, each driven by a Spirit of the Hour. Demogorgon ascends in one; Asia (with Panthea) in the other.

Without any evasion or reticence, then, Demogorgon declares Jupiter responsible for all the evils, errors, and illusions of the human mind. In this Jupiter we recognize a self-distorted or self-abandoned Prometheus. The economy of the drama does not require Asia to ask at this early point who made floods, thorns, worms, and the germs of disease. The truth about ultimate origins is imageless. On the relation of ultimate reality to man's perceptions, Shelley is firmly agnostic. Taking the "intellectual philosophy" from Sir William Drummond rather than directly from Berkeley, he leaves questions of cosmology open. "All things exist as they are perceived"; but in *A Defence of Poetry* he continues the sentence, "at least in relation to the percipient." It may be that what we can imagine as the infinite, the eternal, and the one is so cosmologically, but an answer could not change what is for us the ultimate reality; we must be satisfied with

289

the divinity in man revealed in poetry that "reproduces the common Universe of which we are portions and percipients."[53] The law of Necessity enters *Prometheus Unbound*, not to explain cosmic origins, but to release man from needless struggle. Shelley adapts to his own purposes Aeschylus' several passages on ἀνάγκη, necessity.

In the "Ode to Heaven," published with *Prometheus Unbound* and perhaps once a part of that work, three successive Spirits define the abode of Power variously, inconclusively, and with an increasingly nominalistic skepticism. First Spirit: "the eternal Where and When," the "glass Wherein man his nature sees." Second: "Thou art but the mind's first chamber . . ." Third: "a globe of dew." Shelley wished to free man from the illusion of certainty so that beauty, love, and improvement, however illusory, would be felt as real among men. Demogorgon is a power available to Prometheus through the reunion with Asia. It is to be emphasized that Shelley's epistemological skepticism is not a moral skepticism. His doubt that man can know the ultimates of reality does not act to diminish his faith in the power of "beautiful idealisms" to awaken the sympathetic imagination. In unfolding for the sympathetic imagination a model of moral consequences, *Prometheus Unbound* locates the idea of inevitability in Demogorgon.

Necessity is "Demogorgon's mighty law," which draws, attracts, and impels those who believe that their limbs obey the "sweet desires within" (II.ii.56). Some allegorists have defined Demogorgon as Necessity. He is not necessity alone. When he tells Jupiter that one aspect of his being is Eternity we know that he is not eternity alone. He himself calls Eternity "Mother of many acts and hours" (IV.566). Shapeless on his throne, an unpersonified power, Demogorgon in action gives others the sense of something dread, dark, rough, hairy. The Demogorgon of such tradition as Boccaccio transmitted for the mythological dictionaries of Shelley's day, or at least for some of the dictionaries, was head of terrestial deities, a demon dwelling crudely in its deep domain with Eternity and Chaos. From the womb of Chaos, Demogorgon was sometimes said to have ripped Discord, Pan, the Earth, and Erebus. (All this appeared in as popular a source as Bell's *New Pantheon*. That Godwin's *Pantheon* and Lemprière's classical dictionary omit Demogorgon does not mean that Shelley's use of the figure was esoteric.) Linked to this crude Genius of the Earth, Shelley's Demogorgon bears inevitability as well as awfulness into our world.[54] In addition to his attributes of power and necessity, he accompanies revolution, all abrupt change. In connotation, the etymological *daimon* attracts through sound the meaning of *demos:* "Ye are many—they are few." The connotations of *gorgon* are also appropriate. Demogorgon is powerfully anti-Newtonian. Over against the plumes of Ione's angelic wings and the soothing strands of her hair, Demogorgon swells with snaky gloom, shudderingly shapeless to Panthea, terrifyingly dark to Jupiter. For Jupiter, he is Justice or Doom. For Asia, he is the realization of her own power.

G. M. Matthews, in an article cited earlier, has shown the political implications of the seismic metaphor that runs through Act II. Panthea and Asia, two cold winds from Ocean, are drawn by "Demogorgon's mighty law" toward the "meteor-breathing chasm," over the rim of the crater, and "Down, down" to the volcanic cave of Demogorgon. The consequent explosion shoots lava upward, as a volcanist would expect but Jupiter did not. Volcanic eruptions, relieving the pressure from the central fires, prevent earthquakes of the kind threatened by Jupiter at III.i.50, when he still believes that Demogorgon moves in his behalf. Great change afforded by the ruling classes, from either sudden generosity or unwonted foresight, would prevent violent revolution. Violence, the way of the tyrant, the quake of Peterloo, begets further violence, further tyrannic self-enslavement. Darkly shapeless is how sudden change looks to those who have suffered—when they thought they were enjoying—prescriptive privileges.

In the *Prometheus Bound* of Aeschylus the Titan refuses to divulge the secret that would enable Zeus to protect his rule against a more powerful son by Thetis. But of course Aeschylus and his audience knew that Prometheus' foreknowledge was fulfilled, after due warning to Zeus, in Thetis' son Achilles, who was greater than his father Peleus. Prometheus is by etymology the foreknower. In an ironic turn to the myth, Shelley has Jupiter expect a powerful son, a "fatal child, the terror of the earth," with the further delusion that the son will rid him of irritation from Prometheus. In one sense, when

291

Politics in English Romantic Poetry

Demogorgon retorts to Jupiter in Act III, "I am thy child, as thou wert Saturn's child," he means that he is mightier than Jupiter and that Jupiter will get in turn what he gave to his father Saturn. In the metaphor of paternity utilized throughout the drama, tyranny begets its own downfall. Demogorgon acts as Jupiter should expect a child of his to act, according to the precedent when Freedom-denying Saturn gave birth to rampant tyranny. Since Shelley has modified the myth to imply that the ancients were deceived—for Jupiter did cohabit with Thetis after all—we can take it that Demogorgon is Jupiter's filial punishment for the crime of being Jupiter. He, or *it*, is the ugly necessity required by Prometheus' freedom to err.

Greater difficulty arises when we try to give shape to Demogorgon's shapelessness. The essence of inevitability has in itself no power. When Prometheus repented of his curse, both Panthea and Asia dreamed of his release. Demogorgon is an instrument in their dream.

After evading the problem of cosmic evil and other dilemmas of cosmogony in the colloquy of Asia and Demogorgon, in part by following very closely the language of Aeschylus, the poet faced the problem of avoiding retaliative anger in the overthrow of Jupiter. The drama does almost avoid it, for the Conquest that is finally "dragged captive through the deep" is the human heart's own impulse to conquest (IV.556). A positive act of self-renunciation expells from the mind a negative shadow of itself. The fall of Jupiter ends Manichaeistic deceit. Whatever the ultimate permissive source of evil, the reign of Jupiter, in the chasm of each human heart, created in man's perceived world "terror, madness, crime, remorse." The "retributive Justice" of *Prometheus Unbound* is the "retributive memory" of *Queen Mab* I.174, which plants a sting in "the hard bosom of the selfish man." When Jupiter feels Demogorgon's victory darkening his fall, he mistakes for a darkening cloud a regenerative light too bright to see. Overthrowing its own bearded error, the mind grows young with love. To make a contemporary parable of the renunciation, Parliament, or the landowners who elected its members, might gain the foresight to remove Sidmouth from office; the reform of society might make government by Sidmouth impossible; a self-reformed people might be so forgiving that the government would be embarrassed into reform; or Sidmouth might have the illumination to quell the tyrant enslaved within himself. All or any of these would fulfill the terms of "Demogorgon's mighty law" and topple an aspect of Jupiter from his throne.

What Europe commonly regards as the governing laws of necessity, then, is a mere reversal of the truth. The law of self-interest for survival, to take one aspect of the error, is a misunderstanding of the law of survival through benevolence. C. E. Pulos has given a more specific example, based on associations with *The Revolt of Islam* and Shelley's prose.[55] Jupiter feels the confidence to say "henceforth I am omnipotent" because he has "begotten a strange wonder," the "terror of the earth," from the demonstration by Malthus, the "Jeremiah of a fruitful age," that reform for the benefit of the poor is mathematically hopeless.[56] The law of Necessity is inequity, sometimes known as divine right, established by God and policed by Nature. When Jupiter orders Ganymede to pour forth heaven's wine (III.i.25), he wishes to salute the laws of divine right, infallibility, and overpopulation. Tyranny mistakenly expects a continuation of the status quo through the law of Necessity; concerning that same law, which is really the omnipotent law of love, Prometheus has a secret. The motif of paternity seems to be anticipated in *The Revolt of Islam,* where Cythna at the end claims as her own daughter a child previously nestled by the tyrant.

From the time of the Shelley Society's first papers in the 1880's, most critics have agreed that motivated conflict ends when Prometheus echoes the Jehovah of the Old Testament ironically at line 303 of Act I: "It doth repent me . . ." As we shall see, this is by no means the moment of Aristotelian *peripeteia,* reversal, or even of *anagnorisis,* the protagonist's recognition of his plight.[57] In this lyric romance, however, not at all Aristotelian in structure, repentance anticipates resolution. The thaw begins; Panthea and Asia dream of Prometheus transfigured and of the command to follow, which they resistlessly obey.

Delicate music draws Asia, first in the shared dream and then by her expressed wish (II.i.207), to the realm of awful Power and the car of the Hour. By irresistible law, Demogorgon withdraws Jupiter into the abyss and the earth grows young again. Yet the evidence of cause and effect to be drawn from assertions in the

Politics in English Romantic Poetry

drama is minimal. The strongest language of causation appears in the songs addressed to Asia by Echoes and Spirits. The first statement comes in a self-contained stanza:

> In the world unknown
> Sleeps a voice unspoken;
> By thy step alone
> Can its rest be broken;
> Child of Ocean! (II.i.190–194)

Later, when the sisters have reached the pinnacle above Demogorgon's cave, a chorus of Spirits addresses only Asia—"thee alone":

> Resist not the weakness,
> Such strength is in meekness
> That the Eternal, the Immortal,
> Must unloose through life's portal
> The snake-like Doom coiled underneath his throne
> By that alone. (II.iii.93–98)

When the manipulated sequence of events and the dovetailing metaphors of compelled movement are conjoined with such phrases as "By thy step alone" and "Must unloose," we can confidently take these lyrics to say that power rests with love alone because it must. What the Echoes echo is a reverberation of a tone emitted through Earth by Asia. The "Song of Spirits" counsels love to submit to the law of love. The circle of Doom will open to love's submission. Hercules, who unbinds Prometheus in Act III, scene iii, thereby functions as the strength of love.

In Demogorgon's final exposition of the "immortal day" of Act IV, the day that "down the void abysm . . . yawns for Heaven's despotism," Love rises "from its awful throne of patient power" in "the wise heart" (IV.554–561). This power, as the medium of "Heaven's despotism," is the strength of meekness that forces the Eternal to unloose the "snake-like Doom." So long as "Gentleness, Virtue, Wisdom, and Endurance" abide under the healing wings of Love, the serpent Destruction will remain sealed in the pit (IV.562–569). In *The Revolt of Islam*, according to the final sentence of its Preface, "Love is celebrated everywhere as the sole law which should govern the moral world." In *Prometheus Unbound,* Love is the only law that can govern the world. Love is the law of Nature pursued in *Queen Mab* and now found in the lyrical ideal of the sympathetic imagination.

Tyranny destroys itself, but tyranny held its power as an aspect of Prometheus' hatred, so that expulsion had to come from within. Jupiter's fall and Asia's descent are two ways of looking at the same mental act.

Although it makes comprehension of the structure difficult to say that all caves in the poem are the same cave, they are all aspects of the same symbolization of the human mind. In terms of what is symbolized, everything that happens, in and out of the caves, happens within Prometheus as perceiver. Demogorgon rising from his ebon throne in the cave of the volcano to drag Conquest through the deep is equivalent to Love springing from "its awful throne of patient power" in "the wise heart" (IV.554–561). Similarly, the volcano itself is a source of "oracular vapour," or inspiration essentially linguistic, which in the past has driven men to maddened and maddening prophecy, the "voice which is contagion to the world" (II.iii.1 10, iv.12–18, III.iii.10–24, 124–147).

The scene that begins with the unbinding of Prometheus proceeds thereafter to juxtapose the vaporous caves and other sources of prophecy. To Asia, "thou light of life," and her attendant sisters, Prometheus tells of a cave where they could retire and talk "of time and change," which belong to the mutable world of man. The Spirit of the Hour that transported Asia is dispatched to release over "the cities of mankind" the "mighty music" of that mystic shell which was given by Proteus as "Asia's nuptial boon." Indeed there is a cavern, says Earth, where once her own anguished breath maddened inhalers, who then built a temple and lured "erring nations round to mutual war"; but now the exhalation inspires calm and happy thoughts. And, says Earth to Asia, "This cave is thine." She directs her torchbearer, in the likeness of a winged child, to guide the company to the temple beside the destined cave.

Men affected by oracular vapors have raised divisive temples;

now true prophecy returns to man's use the contrasting (even if taken as identical) cave and temple of Prometheus and Asia. It is false prophecy and delusion to believe that man can know any power over Demogorgon except the power of love.

Why Asia has this power, Demogorgon cannot reveal, for "the deep truth is imageless" (II.iv.116). Mind perceives, it does not create; or, in Shelley's more careful words at the end of the brief essay "On Life," it is "infinitely improbable that the cause of mind, that is, of existence, is similar to mind." The God within man's perception has been described by D. L. Clark: "Shelley's God is the soul of goodness pervading life; he is the charity men feel in their hearts; he is the principle of harmony throughout nature; he is the music heard in the heart of man; he is Intellectual Beauty."[58] This God is not, however, a *cause* of goodness or charity. Goodness, charity, and harmony do not result from "the will of God," but from the eternal possibilities of improvement in "the relations which arise from the association of human beings" (SW, V, 287). Man's duty remains the same in similar situations from age to age. To idealize the similarity is to see Intellectual Beauty instead of the moral standards of one's own era, limited by space, time, and custom, as one's own imperfect mind perceives them. To perceive truly what a human mind can perceive is to love. It is to rejoin Asia. To hate is to dream death, to give death a reality in man's mind, to thwart man's desire for freedom and for belief in permanence. It is to give Jupiter dominion. To imagine is to synthesize particulars into a single reality permeated and given life by love. To imagine is to communicate by love (SW, VI, 201). To imagine is to see and even to create, in the sense of changing perceptible reality as argument cannot change it. Argument lacks proof; imagination needs none. All this says to the individual, "We must love one another or die"; to man it says simply, "We must love one another."

Since to exist is to be perceived or felt, everything known to occur occurs in the mind of man. The reunion of thought and love consequently makes the earth grow young in the mind of the only perceiver any one of us knows. The renovation of earth, celebrated in Act IV, makes palpable the adage of Socrates: No harm can occur

Shelley

to a good man. In Milton's Paradise were "Flow'rs of all hue, and without Thorn the Rose"; in Shelley's, thorns remain, but the virtuous man knows no pain from their pricking.

Prometheus Unbound celebrates the power seated as a shadow of divinity on the throne of every human mind, a power that can be released only by and for love. The earth, when perfectly perceived by love, will be "Fit throne for such a Power!" (II.iii.11). Release may come instantaneously, gradually, bit by bit, or imperceptibly. In what has been called the biography of an Hour, Shelley exploits the ambiguities inherent in the Hours of Greco-Roman myth, the *Horae,* or seasons—nurses to Venus, harbingers of Apollo, born with the spring. Accepting the Godwinian principle of man's infinite capacity for improvement, the drama depicts the ideal, which could be realized instantly and totally if all men were capable of instant and total love. The chief difficulty in Earl Wasserman's emphasis on Prometheus as the One Mind is that it removes you as the reader from the conflict, the urgency, and the invitation to celebrate redemption.[59] Prometheus is potential in you. His problem is your problem.

Even in a lyrical romance of beautiful idealisms, dystopia does not give way to utopia without strain. Although several generations of critics have tended to agree that the millennium of bliss was certain from line 303, when Prometheus renounced his curse, or even from line 53, when he withdrew his disdain, Prometheus as an actor in the drama does not share this certainty. Temptation and agony follow his withdrawal of the curse. Earth regards the withdrawal as disaster. At line 634, when Prometheus pities even the loftiest (like Southey, for example) who are not tortured by the realization that "They dare not devise good for man's estate," the Furies depart. Yet the Titan repeats his refrain: "Ah woe! Alas! pain, pain ever, for ever!" Next he hears "something sadder, sweeter far than all," four spirits, each combining love and calamity, and then a fifth and sixth, dissolving into sound Vergil's *lacrimae rerum,* the sweet sadness of things, as they mingle Love with despair of Desolation. "Though Ruin now Love's shadow be," pursuing Love on the steed of Death, the blended Spirits try to convince Prometheus that he can quell "this horseman grim." "How fair . . . ," Prometheus responds, "and yet . . . alas!" Here, at the end of Act I, he utters his last speech of self-revelation in the drama:

> alas! how heavily
> This quiet morning weighs upon my heart;
> Though I should dream I could even sleep with grief
> If slumber were denied not. (I.812–815)

Confident that all will end in reunion with Asia, but not knowing when, he can at best say to Panthea, who still hopes beside him: "I said all hope was vain but love: thou lovest" (I.824). Instant perfectibility may be attainable by the renunciation of his curse, but in the temporal structure of the poetry it is not attained. When Asia suggests that her breath might drive the Car of the Hour faster, the Spirit answers, "Alas! it could not" (II.v.7). The speed of their coursers "makes night kindle," but the "Alas," repeated this late in the drama, hangs heavy. *Prometheus Unbound* encloses more than the metaphysics of love. It pauses to consider the demands of time. Earth has lamented that the one defense of good "Lies fallen and vanquishèd" (I.312). Jupiter, proceeding at the beginning of Act III as if he overheard or sensed the echoes of that lament, now threatens.

All these impediments to the eternal golden summer of Act IV belong to the realm of spirit. Man has yet further weights to carry. When Prometheus depicts the ideal microcosm of imagined perfection as the primitive innocence of a mossy cave, in still another variation on those places of the mind hidden from European civilization, he describes it as a sanctum where changeless spirits may "talk of time and change" (III.iii.23). For, he asks, "What can hide man from mutability?" Although Earth finds it impossible to explain death to immortals, except as "the veil which those who live call life," she can promise for man nothing better than a death no longer fearful. The poetry here, ignoring the needs and capacities of the immortals to whom Earth purportedly speaks, assures the mortal reader that man can move toward a cave of thought where "retributive memory" of the veiled life of the past cannot reach him. He can be purified beyond memory of the fear of death. Death will remain, but not the fear of death.

The imperfection of the improved condition is shown again in the response of the Spirit of the Hour to the magnificent change. Where the Spirit of the Earth, representing man's awareness that earth has a spirit, found in the new age that toads, snakes, and worms "had put their evil nature off" (III.iv.77), the Spirit of the Hour could judge the transformation by an ideal standard,

> And first was disappointed not to see
> Such mighty change as I had felt within
> Expressed in outward things . . .   (III.iv.128–130)

Revolutionized by the overthrow of "Thrones, altars, judgement-seats, and prisons," man nonetheless retains chance, death, mutability, and passion.

What the Spirit of the Hour did find in the transformed actual life of man, as set forth in the long speech concluding Act III, can be best understood with the relationships of the various ideals and spirits freshly in mind.

All the speaking characters, except Demogorgon, are anthropomorphic. They move and speak in the realm of myth as impermanent but millennial generalization. Prometheus, as man's enduring conception of what wisdom can be, finds himself unable to believe, understand, or (by extension) hear the voices of systolic and diastolic charity and ruin. Earth, as the enduringly perceived world in flux, understands the language of both mortality and the immortals, individual death and continual regeneration, although she is slow to understand Prometheus' motives. Echoes and Voices appear to the senses as if from the earth. Furies from within poison the springs of perception. Although drawing on *Faust* and *Manfred,* Shelley diversifies the literary duties of miscellaneous, numbered Spirits. Each of the two Spirits of the Hour combines the means and ends of destiny. One conveys Asia to the inevitable reunion with Prometheus; in coincidence, the other brings about the despairing of Jupiter: "The elements obey me not" (III.i.80). And we know that all things work together for good to them that love Good. Earth is the imagined assemblage of all that man perceives as physical organisms and objects. Beyond the role of foster-mother, which she shares with the "homely Nurse" in Wordsworth's Intimations Ode, Earth is both the object of man's thought and—as limited man must suppose—its source (I.152–158).

Politics in English Romantic Poetry

Earth exists in perception. The Spirit of the Earth, quite unlike the Demogorgon-like *Erdgeist* in Goethe's *Faust,* is a mood responding to changes in man. The volatile shadow of the essence or permanent spirit of the earth, this Spirit is represented dramatically as the perceived state of the earth at a given time. Whereas the Spirit of the Hour sensed a lesser change relative to the potential of perfectibility, by a contrast already noted, the Spirit of the Earth grows young again with Asia. Ephemerality, as much as rejuvenation, brings about Asia's coy remark that the Spirits of the Earth and of the Moon cannot beget children by gazing on each other's eyes. Ingenuity, vagueness, and self-contradiction try at this point to cooperate: "yet not old enough" in the practice of growing young, the Spirit of the Earth belongs to a perpetually variable and unaging present. In one of the many cosmic puns in the drama, Ione says of the Spirit of the Earth, when the great change comes, "Sister, it is not earthly" (III.iv.1). In the changeless warmth of Act IV, when Asia has passed beyond Infancy and "Through Death and Birth, to a diviner day" (predicted at II.v.103), the Spirit of the Earth "is laid asleep" (IV.265) in permanent reunion with Earth, whose speech is joy without mood:

> The joy, the triumph, the delight, the madness!
> The boundless, overflowing, bursting gladness,
> The vaporous exultation not to be confined!
>
> (IV.319–321)

Poetic participation "in the eternal, the infinite, and the one" puts to sleep the Spirit of the Earth. In the imagined state of perfection, there are no moods.

Other realms cling to the eternal. Know, says the Earth, "there are two worlds of life and death." Besides the commonsense world of actuality, there is a second realm of life and death, that of phantasms,

> The shadows of all forms that think and live
> Till death unite them and they part no more;
> Dreams and the light imaginings of men,
> And all that faith creates or love desires . . .
>
> (I.198–201)

Shelley

This realm has been the more difficult to interpret because critics have expected a Platonic dualism of ephemeral actuality and eternal forms or ideas. In truth, the phantasms lie equally far from the Orphic myth of metempsychosis utilized by Socrates in the *Phaedo* and from the infinite, the eternal, and the one. They belong to a second world of life-and-death.[60] The Furies and Spirits of ruin and love that surround the chained Prometheus have a common existence in many minds; the phantasms, like the gnats and flies that throng from lawyers and theorists in "The Triumph of Life," debouch from individuals. Similar, too, are the "quick dreams" and "twilight Phantasms" that were Adonais' flocks. The phantasms are released into being as motive and intention. They belong to a realm of effects and consequences, but not as links in an endless chain of necessity: upon death, as men call it, the dreamer and his dreams, the doer and his deeds, the motive and the motivated, die together into vivid life—the life of Act IV, where the latency that characterizes phantasms is without strength. The Phantasm of Jupiter that echoes the curse came into phantom existence in the hatreds of millions of men as individuals; Jupiter is the collective reality of their hatred.

The drama seems to juxtapose three worlds: appearance (the reader's world), enduring idea and its varying mood or state (Earth and the Spirit of the Earth), and intent (phantasms), where the last is treated also as the consequence of intention. Prometheus must always be the foe of Jupiter, but the Phantasm returns to Prometheus as the evidence of corrupt conscience at the time when mind contemplated evil and thereby activated it in the realm of idea as Jupiter.[61] The curse, if repeated by Earth, would have added to the derangement of earthly life—made emblematic in excessive heat and cold—as felt by man (I.141). Surviving as a consequence of motive, the curse has remained potential, and therefore available for repetition, in the phantasm of each who was turned into the "all-prolific Evil" of Jupiter at the dire moment when the curse brought retaliation into being. Here, as throughout the drama, sequence in time and moral causation are mutually convertible; a moment interchanges with a condition. Despite set speeches like the Earth's, "For know there are two worlds of life and death," all

301

the "realms" of *Prometheus Unbound* merge in the one spiritual life of man-in-society.

After making it glacially clear what the everyday dyspeptic life of man in civilization has been like, the immortal spirits in human thought free their great frame of beautiful idealisms from its recent trammels. Most of the ends sought by Holbach, Helvétius, Condorcet, Volney, Godwin, and Mary Wollstonecraft have been attained. After carrying the shell of prophecy around the world that all may hear, the Spirit of the Hour reports what reunited Asia and Prometheus already feel: no external law or custom now distinguishes one man from another. None tyrannizes, none fears. None prevaricates, in the old way, until his soul is ashes. Wherever the Spirit went, "None fawned, none trampled . . ." Women have gained freedom, wisdom, and equality with men. Such potentates as Ozymandias have left much marble, but the lesson conveyed is more complex than that in Shelley's sonnet. Although physical structures remain as monuments to once-powerful myth, the horror of their message is no longer understood. Not only are there no "Mighty" to look on either the monuments or the ruins of Ozymandias "and despair"; there are none left to understand what is meant by the term "Mighty." Consequently, when the Spirit of the Hour has blown the shell of prophecy and thereby blown utopia into view, he must speak of man's future in the past tense, as conditional on prophecy in the passing world, which is the present of Act II. "Thrones, altars, judgement-seats, and prisons" *were* as the hieroglyphics on obelisks are *now*. These obelisks, emblems of forgotten mysteries and tyrannies, were captured and re-erected in Rome, under subsequent tyrannies, as emblems of the power of later kings and priests. All these once-potent mysteries, which were as strange, "savage, ghastly, dark and execrable" as the forms of Jupiter they enveloped, have left only their astonishing monuments, which will no longer deceive or tempt. All institutions and implements of class have vanished. Thrones lack both sitters and an intelligible setting.

Tomes of "reasoned wrong," presumably from such reasoners as Vicomte Louis de Bonald, Joseph de Maistre, Augustin Barruel, Burke, Malthus, and Blackstone (as interpreted by Ellenborough and Eldon), along with all other emblems and weapons of Jupiter, have ceased to be regarded.[62] Wicked books are not burned or otherwise destroyed or suppressed; they are "not o'erthrown, but unregarded now."

Man "Equal, unclassed, tribeless, nationless"; this is the heavenly city attributable to the *philosophes,* a cosmopolitan, supranational brotherhood of man. The last clause of Shelley's *Declaration of Rights* of 1812 has been fulfilled: "If man were to day sinless, to-morrow he would have a right to demand that government and all its evils should cease." Paine's "principle of universal civilization" is realized with no if's or but's.

Yet man restored to the cave of loving thought is not passionless, as many of the *philosophes* would have made him. Not only has he achieved his happy state through love rather than through a purification of reason; he retains his passion that he may maintain justice, gentleness, and wisdom. This, Shelley confesses in the Preface, is to be damned with Plato and Bacon. Rational benevolence has become passionate benevolence.

In the process, it might seem that all Dantesque and Miltonic degree and order have been overthrown for an indulgent anarchy. To this objection two important qualifications need to be made. Man, in willing an end to his chains, must accept bonds of another sort. The poet, in one of his least persuasive but most persistent suppositions, extrapolates benevolence from erotic love.

> True Love in this differs from gold and clay,
> That to divide is not to take away.
> (*Epipsychidion,* 160–161)

As part of Shelley's fight during "the Victorian prelude" to keep morality from shrinking to the narrow closet of sexual morality, *Prometheus Unbound* makes free and complete love a duty that individuals in pairs owe to society. True love produces a stressless general will. Therefore the Earth, interpenetrated with love, can renounce the isolated individuals of Locke:

> Man, oh, not men! a chain of linkèd thought,
>   Of love and might to be divided not,
> Compelling the elements with adamantine stress;
>   As the sun rules, even with a tyrant's gaze,
>   The unquiet republic of the maze
> Of planets, struggling fierce towards heaven's free wilderness.
> (IV.394–399)

303

Politics in English Romantic Poetry

The law of love, like the law of gravity, converts an "unquiet republic" into "one harmonious soul of many a soul" (IV.400). Not self-interest, as in Adam Smith, but each man's passions, strong though subjected to the power of Asia, now subserve the best ends of society. The adage running from Locke to Emerson, that the least amount of government is best, presupposes coercive government. Act IV proclaims that the greatest amount of self-government is best: self, "struggling fierce" but governed by love. Only then will "Labour, and pain, and grief, in life's green grove / Sport like tame beasts . . ." (IV.404–405). The physical causes of grief remain, but the sting of grief is lost in communal joy.

John Stuart Mill was to record in his *Autobiography* the shock of realizing that when each works for the happiness of all, the happiness of the worker for good remains forever unassured. The total structure of images in *Prometheus Unbound* evades this objection by substituting a cosmic law of love for a utilitarian rule of seeking the greatest amount of pleasure, by immersing the individual in the mental substance of all-pervading love, and ultimately by replacing argument with image and myth. The ends of poetry, as Shelley describes them in *A Defence of Poetry,* are moral, but the means, the synthesis of images that gives delight by revealing the eternal beauty of love and thereby acting as the best instrument of moral good, is distinguishable from didactic teaching. Works of imagination need not assume an unwarranted certainty in what is called truth by utilitarians. Reason cannot undo symbols. The poet attempts to image forth, rather than to argue, the intricacy of love. In Act IV, after penetrating the granite mass of earth, Love penetrates the frozen frame of the moon.

In considering further the usual interpretation of Act IV as a world of indulgent anarchy, we must admit a second qualification by distinguishing the ideal from the pragmatic suggestion of steps to be taken. Man is not changed by wishing him changed. At the close Demogorgon speaks of how to do it: love, forgive, suffer, endure, defy, hope. He is not telling how it has once and forever been done. Nor, in the career of any conceivable politician or statesman, will it be done. The poem prophesies as poems do. Not, says Shelley in *A Defence of Poetry,* "Not that I assert poets to be prophets in the gross sense of the word, or that they can foretell the form as surely as they foreknow the spirit of events: such is the pretence of superstition, which would make poetry an attribute of prophecy, rather than prophecy an attribute of poetry." A poet can show infallibly what spirit of events is possible. He foreknows because he perceives the present truly and fully. Equality of property is not to be effected by political or social means, according to *A Philosophical View of Reform*, but by moral regeneration that begins in the knowledge and feeling that each has equal rights.[63] The poet knows through imagination the means to moral regeneration.

Even within the myth that foretells the spirit of events, banished Jupiter is left the possibility of return. Like the tools and emblems of his reign, Jupiter in the abyss is "not o'erthrown, but unregarded now." Eternity, "Mother of many acts and hours," may free the "serpent that would clasp her with his length." Once more the virtues of Prometheus would have to reassert their strength (IV.562–569).

Although the shagginess of Demogorgon threatens the "government party" with cataclysm, political changes specified in the drama would not require sudden violence. Taking prophecy in "the gross sense," thrones and altars in Europe have become since 1819 fewer and weaker; judgment seats, if not fewer, have become less rigid; and penal servitude has become steadily more humane. These changes evolved from what *Prometheus Unbound* presents as a union of thought and love. But the drama prophesies equally the Crimean War and the advent of the Fascists. And unless it can be shown that these also resulted from a union of thought and love, Prometheus is entitled to his victory and the poet to his prophecy: this will happen *if*.

Progress has two faces in the drama, one ideal, the other historical. The steady line of development from the womb of time, through the Saturnian era of vegetation, on through the present and toward a millennium, has obviously been deflected by man's belief in Jupiter. Speech created thought, which deepened into poetry and music; astronomy learned the intricate harmony of the heavens; through navigation "the Celt knew the Indian" (II.iv.94: this is an expansion of knowledge, not declaredly of trade); cities raised "their snow-like columns" (in Greece); but, all along, Jupiter must have been there, combating truth, for "Science struck the thrones of earth and heaven," which "shook, but fell not." Such irregularities of the past continue in Act IV.

Science, an enemy to superstition, warred and yet wars against the desire of Earth to keep her secrets. The beams of light shooting from the Spirit of the Earth, as Panthea tells us, now lay bare the geological strata beneath the archaeological strata of the past. Although the steadiness of scientific progress suggested by the passage might suggest also the uniformitarianism of James Hutton, as clarified by John Playfair in *Illustrations of the Huttonian Theory*, 1802, the details of the uncovering (IV.270–318)—for example the bony, twisted serpents and the "earth-convulsing behemoth" drowned in the deluge—suggest Georges Cuvier's theory of cataclysmic change rather than Erasmus Darwin's "mighty monuments of past delight."[64] In a related paradox, the beams shooting from the forehead of the Spirit of the Earth, now asleep in its final infancy, resembled spears overtwined with the "tryant-quelling myrtle" of Harmodius and Aristogiton (IV.272). Thus the fraternal love of "heaven and earth united now" is symbolized by the classical emblem of assassination.

These gritty details from the actual life of the planet do not contradict the symbols of an ideal existence, but they help determine the proper reading of those symbols. The seamless, circular argument that love is the essence of all order appeals at its circumference, especially in Act IV, to the Pythagorean harmony of the spheres. Rebirth in harmony appears also in the utopia of sexual interchange, whereby the moon warms with "love, and odour, and deep melody" from the fraternal earth. In a utilization of the doctrine of measured harmony as restated after Newton, the thawing of the moon says also that love can dilate from the cottage or the Chippendale bed through politics to astronomy, and can convert into symphony activities denounced by Wordsworth as murderous dissection. The unfreezing of the moon, like the melting of glaciers on earth, is a stripping away of cloudy veils, as performed by a conjunction of science and love.

Such juxtapositions of cosmic harmony and disruptive conflict dislodge one's presupposition that *Prometheus Unbound* celebrates steady progress toward perfection. Even so, we must still ask how far the heavenly temple and cave of Act IV could be reached through incremental progress. That Shelley himself held several basic tenets of the religion of progress, daily and in his happiest moments, there can be no doubt at all.[65] Earth, in her efforts to conceal her secrets, has much to fear from the poet's pride in scientific progress. One of the easier ways of going to hell with Bacon was to begin with self-knowledge but move on to increased knowledge of "natural philosophy." Promethean man defies physical evil, "the immedicable plague," rained down by the unknowable creator of such evil (II.iv.101). Now, the basis on which all symbolism in *Prometheus Unbound* rests, the separation and reunion of the Titan and Asia, implies a rebuke to the very term *Enlightenment*. In poetic method, Shelley advocates return, reform, regeneration. Yet nothing in his great lyrical drama supports Rousseau's denial that increased knowledge in science and the arts has in itself increased happiness. With reservations, Shelley had expanded his belief in progress from the natural sciences to the social. In "A Discourse on the Manners of the Ancients," he declares that modern Europeans, in changing the spirit of sexual intercourse and in the abolition of slavery, have "made an improvement the most decisive in the regulation of human society."[66] Where miscellaneous improvements have been made, more are possible. One implication of the unfreezing of the arctic zones and the moon is made clearer by a sentence in the fragment on government by juries: "Public opinion would never long stagnate in error, were it not fenced about and frozen over by forms and superstitions." Even Malthus, at the beginning of his essay on population, had admitted "the progress of mankind towards happiness," though impeded, in the past; Malthus' challenge to hope for progress in the future could not be allowed to freeze into superstition.

A Philosophic View of Reform, written concurrently with *Prometheus Unbound* although not published until 1920, advocates progress by incremental steps. Its immediate program is moderate. It deplores such means of demanding universal suffrage and full justice as would bring violent reprisal. Leaders not only should instruct the people in the clear grounds of their rights, but should also impress upon them "the just persuasion that patience and reason and endurance" can secure "a calm yet irresistible progress." After attaining a limited portion of their rights, the people should be exhorted "to pause until by the exercise of those rights" they "become fitted to demand more." The essayist was willing to wait twenty years in order to achieve a better Reform Bill; meanwhile, he proposed generally the acceptance of a limited benefit rather than the delusion that action without great sacrifice could bring an unlimited one, "something more absolutely perfect." These proposals for incremental progress find symbolic expression in *Prometheus Unbound*.[67]

The drama does what the essayist thought the Constitution of the United States had done; it "acknowledges the progress of human improvement" as something to be projected for the future. In addition, in the ideal of perfect love, it does what Shelley thought the United States did not; it sets an ideal standard for "the full development and the most salutary condition" of the will of the people. Yet every practical appeal to the ideal standard of the drama must be tempered by Shelley's definition of right government as "an institution for the purpose of securing such a moderate degree of happiness to men as has been experimentally practicable." It is precisely his faith in ultimate victory that encourages moderation.

The essay gives us hints concerning the coexistence of a paradisial garden and death, of apocalypse and the relics of time, in Acts III and IV of *Prometheus Unbound*. If the essay dampens the ardor of reformers by advancing a moderate program, it instills hope and enthusiasm by arguing that the spirit of the times favors reform and progress. In evidence, it points incidentally to signs that Parliament will provide better legislation in the decade to come. At greater length it cites the evidence of abrupt revolutions: after a dark night of suppression, revolutions are erupting in South and Central America, the West Indies, India, Greece, and elsewhere in the Turkish Empire, and in the spirit of Zionism. These revolutions the essay specifies. The lyrics of the drama also convey the poet's sense of glorious crisis in the destiny of many locales.

Perhaps, if life were simpler, a lyrical drama with Prometheus as antagonist, even if written by a youth of twenty-seven, could avoid a combination of love and revolution and could evolve a per-

Shelley

sonal apocalypse, perhaps a Christian one, without concern for politics. Under the conditions that prevailed, however, Shelley could Christianize the suffering Prometheus and Platonize the redemptive Christ without diminishing his commitment to politics as the manipulation of power. His excited study of the Platonic doctrine of love in the *Symposium* and the *Phaedrus* did not greatly change his interest in political renovation. I do not mean that Plato's role was lessened by Shelley's finding that "his theories respecting the government of the world, and the elementary laws of moral action, are not always correct." Plato, as a poet discovering by intuition "the before unapprehended relations of things," made it easier to show not only that erotic yearning and social empathy are mutually involved, but also that benevolence and total heterosexual love are interchangeable. He made it easier to offer what Douglas Bush calls the typically Shelleyan household in Prometheus' cave—man, wife, and two sisters-in-law—as a subordination of family to social union, in congruence with Matthew 12:50: whosoever shall put social union above the family, "the same is my brother, and sister, and mother." Above all, however, Shelley's study of Plato influenced the conclusion of his later years that poetry not only speaks of love, but functions through love, which superintends all unification. Imagination, which combines and synthesizes as an analogue with the eternal and the infinite, seeks identity with the beauty of love as the poet's way to achieve the true and the good.

It is only by taking *Prometheus Unbound* and *A Philosophic View of Reform* together that we interpret Demogorgon's final speech as a program of civil disobedience, based on the social psychology of unyielding patience. The drama attempts to give delight by showing how it works, and why, in a vision that exists irrefutably in its own language. "If the majority are enlightened, united, impelled by a uniform enthusiasm and animated by a distinct and powerful apprehension of their object,—and full confidence in their undoubted power—the struggle is merely nominal." Shelley proposes by the drama to impel, through delight, a few readers who will impel a few more leaders who will impel the majority. He does not design the poem merely as "an astonishment," like the hieroglyphs on an obelisk whose meaning is lost; he tries to dissolve the

309

manners, morals, and issues of his own day in the moving beauty of myth. The error of the critic would be to ignore the application and value of the myth for Shelley's own day.

In *Prometheus Unbound* Shelley avoided Coleridge's impasse and Keats's torment by carrying into his supreme work of imagination the agnosticism that had freed him from materialism, Cartesian dualism, hunger for certainty, and appeal to the reader's capacity for rational analysis. As the texture of his poetry thickened with symbols of the ideal, the stridency of his search for absolutes subsided. Violence, for example, was still a two-edged weapon to be used late, sparingly, and despondently, but it was not, in a just cause such as a revolution for national independence, an absolute evil. More than the other poets, Shelley could break new ground without giving up the old. He could insert a higher utilitarianism into mythic vision without any irritable reaching after God. Divinity, no more or less than the eternally best in and for man, would be the ultimate subject for choral hymning in a lyrical drama. The history of Shelley's reputation contains a remarkable testimony to his success. Although he has been charged with almost every other weakness man is capable of, he has not been charged with cynicism. His atheism had come to this: the inherited sin is Malthusian despair of reform; love is the effectual fulfillment of the law and the commandments; the duty of love exceeds any conceivable reliance on an external redeemer.

VIII

In most of his important longer works subsequent to *Prometheus Unbound*—namely, in *The Cenci, Hellas, Adonais,* and "The Triumph of Life"—Shelley explored the relationship of political idealism to the empirical validity of hope. He has been described, but falsely described, as oblivious of all experience. He could modify more freely than Coleridge and Wordsworth the epistemology of British empiricism, but he adjusted his hopes for political and social renovation whenever he found them contradicted by experience.

From visions of ideality, Shelley turned to the chillingly negative lessons of real life in *The Cenci*. He began the tragedy in May 1819 partly as a shocker for the stage and partly as a corollary to *Prometheus Unbound*. Where the larger work belonged to his series designed as "visions which impersonate my own apprehensions of the beautiful and the just," *The Cenci* depicts "that which has been," a "sad reality" (SL, II, 96). In the drama intended for the stage, the poet teaches self-knowledge, as his Preface declares, to the human heart. To the "most enormous injuries," the ideal Prometheus fitly returns "kindness and forebearance." In direct contrast, revenge and retaliation were the "pernicious mistakes" of the tragic character Beatrice. In his earliest years Shelley might have handled the theme of this play in glee with destructive spells and contempt. *The Cenci* puts vile bodies on the stage but does not revile them. In the despotic lusts of Count Cenci, who gives a rich banquet to celebrate publicly the economy of murdering his sons, Shelley attempts the Shakespearean sublime. Beatrice, who resembles in several ways the murderous soldiery of his earliest verses, is presented so sympathetically that critics have mistaken the portrait for a projection of self-pity.

It is true that Beatrice begins in an innocence that appears absolute by contrast with the corruption around her. It is true that she, like Harriet Westbrook, is engulfed by the lawlessness of a legitimized tryanny that leaves no outlet to honest action; true that her monstrous father is part and emblem of a monstrous state, where one chain of evil extends from the executioner to the Pope. She assures the Judge that it galls her worse than physical torture to see "what a world we make," the "oppressor and the oppressed." It is true that she, her father, and her mother are three versions of the disgrace called Catholic faith. Beatrice suffers all the evils that the cruelest despotism could provide. In denying to his publisher Charles Ollier the presence of politics or religion in *The Cenci,* Shelley was assuring him—rashly—that neither the Constitutional Association nor the Society for the Suppression of Vice could bring a successful information against the printed play for sedition or seditious blasphemy. He could not deny that he had produced here one more assault on the wicked conjunction of anarchic tyranny and religion.

It is only before Beatrice begins to act, however, that she can be counted among "those who do endure" deep "wrongs for man." Only in early innocence was she, like Prometheus, "our one refuge

311

Politics in English Romantic Poetry

and defence" (*The Cenci* II.i.49, derived ironically from the Lord of the Psalms, like the ironic appeal in the same scene to "Thou, great God, / Whose image upon earth a father is," II.i.16–17). Swinburne was right to call the play *Les Cenci,* and producers are correspondingly wrong to mount the play as a spectacle hinging on physical rape. Nor is it merely a question of heritage. Satiated in all lusts and crimes but one, Count Cenci must now reach out a finger, heated in the fires of hell, to burn another soul. After the dread act, Beatrice moans:

> My brain is hurt . . .
> There creeps
> A clinging, black, contaminating mist
> About me . . .   (III.i.1,16–18)

Her father goes further:

> No, 'tis her stubborn will
> Which by its own consent shall stoop as low
> As that which drags it down.   (IV.i.10–12)

When she first said, "'Twere better not to struggle any more," she thought of her own death as the one solution; now she does consent to struggle and to stoop. She conspires to murder; she denies that she has committed a crime; she scorns her weaker accomplices; she is ruthless in her new applications of a strength that was the strength of ten. In the words of the Preface, she has been "violently thwarted from her nature." She has supplanted her father. From the records before him, Shelley has mitigated the horrors, but he has converted to "sad reality" the legend of an immaculate Beatrice. He describes "that which has been."

An actress cannot easily negotiate this transition, but the tragedy requires it. The play calls upon her not only to speak beyond all limits of decorum and memory, and not only to echo a hundred phrases from Shakespeare as if nobody ever heard or spoke them before, but also, what is most pertinent here, to show in the failures of Beatrice that "the fit return to make to the most enormous injuries is kindness and forbearance, and a resolution to convert the injurer from his dark passions by peace and love"—the way of Prometheus in the concurrent example of Shelley's "dreams of what ought to be, or may be" (SP, 275, 276). Not even in the fiendish despotism that oppressed Beatrice is violence a fit return for injury.[68]

For his last dramatic poem Shelley returned to a vision of the beautiful and the just, but a vision grounded in the actual and the contemporaneous. At the age of twenty-nine, he had an opportunity to construct a myth around an actual revolution in progress. *Hellas: A Lyrical Drama,* planned and executed almost as rapidly as Coleridge and Southey had composed and published *The Fall of Robespierre,* had a degree of daring beyond the hot topicality that it shared with their ephemeral play.[69] Robespierre, however recently dead, was safely so. The French Revolution continued, but the cycle of events reported in the play by Coleridge and Southey had come to an end with the execution of Robespierre. The uprising by Shelley's Greeks, still in its early stages, was chaotic and seemingly ineffectual. As fervently as he hoped for a Greek victory, he could not prophesy it as a military event of the near future. Nevertheless, he had practical aims in the rapidity of composition. His play was a kind of spiritual benefit for the combatant Greeks. As I hope to show from its references to Britain, it also possessed the material aim of an actor's benefit: to raise funds in a worthy cause.

For his declared model Shelley looked back to *The Persians.* Aeschylus had celebrated the defeat of Xerxes' fleet at Salamis, in the historic present of drama, eight years after the event. As part of the feigned contemporaneity, the Ghost of Darius foretells further defeat at Plataea, which in history follows a few months after Salamis. Without feigning, *Hellas* gives heightened details of current skirmishes between Greek and Turk while the future of the revolution is in strong doubt.

For performance before Greeks as victors, Aeschylus' setting of *The Persians* in a remote hamlet of the suffering enemy is decorously humble. Action reported in *Hellas* scatters geographically from Bucharest to the Sea of Crete, but the performed action occurs in Constantinople, at the seat of the Sultan's power. The immediate need for hope and aspiration, as the converse of a victor's need for humility, explains Shelley's shift from Aeschylus' peripheral place of suffering to the focal place of decisions. Setting supports theme: fear sits on the tyrant's throne.

Shelley followed *The Persians* in awarding the chief roles to the enemy. Although *Hellas* does not stir the audience to pity for the whining but dangerous enslavers of Greece, Shelley refrains from making a monster of Mahmud II. Generously, Aeschylus' chorus also is Persian; Shelley, in contrast, provides his Turks with a chorus of enslaved Greek women. Without Greeks in the cast, no lyrics of affirmation would have been possible.

Amid other parallels, there are further departures from Aeschylus, equally pointed. Aeschylus' Atossa, widow of Darius and mother of Xerxes, recounts her dream of Xerxes' defeat. When Shelley's Mahmud enters with Ahasuerus (Shelley's old friend the Wandering Jew), Mahmud has already told his dream offstage and learned that Ahasuerus has no more power of divination than sages who lack his longevity. (So much for religion; as Manfred puts it to the old abbot, "I say to thee—Retire!") The effective echo of Atossa had occurred earlier in *Hellas,* when Mahmud, in his dark despair, called Hassan's attention to the clouded crescent moon beneath a single insolent star, "Wan emblem of an empire fading now!" So memorably does the Ghost of Darius condemn Xerxes' *hybris* that Shelley can afford to make Mahmud the essence of despair; a mere allusion to Aeschylus' memorable lines suggests the evil of tyrannic pride. And the availability of *The Persians*—in fact the very existence of Aeschylus' historical subject—invites such allusion throughout *Hellas.* A semichorus sings in Mahmud's ear of how Persia was followed by "Discord, Macedon, and Rome" and "lastly thou," where *thou* can be construed interchangeably as Mahmud II or "Slavery! thou frost of the world's prime." *Hellas* traces the law by which the Turks must be driven out as the Persians were driven out.

Four messengers, in addition to Hassan, bring word of reversals that Shelley knew about from Italian newspapers, from Prince Alexander Mavrocordatos, and from insurgents allowed passage through Pisa. Mavrocordatos taught Mary Shelley Greek in return for English until 26 June 1821, when he sailed to join the battle

Shelley

(and later to become the first President of Greece). After he left, one of his cousins kept the Shelleys abreast of news and rumors. With such informants between us and the record, it is pointless to raise questions of historical accuracy in the messengers' reports to Mahmud. More to the point than historical accuracy, the drama bore the clear intent to celebrate the rising of the Greeks in such a way as to arouse English interest, English funds, and patriotic shame at the roles of such diplomats as the English ambassador at Constantinople—tools, to Shelley, of Metternich—in keeping the rest of Europe neutral:

> And now, O Victory, blush! and Empire, tremble
> When ye desert the free—   (1000–1001)

Naturally *Hellas* does not describe the barbaric slaughter then practiced at every opportunity by the Greeks. In this work Shelley tries to persuade.

When he began to write in October 1821, Byron had awakened much of the Continent, as Harold Nicolson noted in *Byron, the Last Journey,* but had not awakened London. The policy of Castlereagh, carried out through Lord Strangford, the ambassador at Constantinople, was to inhibit the Greeks in order to discourage a Russian war against Turkey. When *Hellas* appeared in February 1822, the London supporters of the Greeks were still a small band. A general change of sentiment was yet to come.

One would expect in *Hellas* allusions to other struggles for independence as a way of heightening the theme, and one finds them; but the knowing Second Messenger condemns British "oaths broke in Genoa and in Norway" for a strictly practical purpose. Castlereagh's opponents had protested for six years the ceding of Genoa to Piedmont and of Norway to Bernadotte of Sweden, both by treaties initially secret. *Hellas* argues that abandonment of Greece to the Turks will constitute a betrayal similar to these. In such defenses of independence one notices, incidentally, the shading of cosmopolitanism into nationalism. Freedom for every man becomes freedom for weak countries.

Leigh Hunt, in the "Political Examiner" of 7 October 1821, calls upon English students to raise money for the Greeks. In parallel with the argument of *Hellas,* he bases his plea chiefly on the revival of high respect for Greek literature and sculpture; he quotes *The Revolt of Islam;* he conveys news of the Greeks received through the Shelleys; and he refers scornfully to the rape of Norway. That rape was one of only two previous occasions, says Hunt, when a desire to join the battle overcame his objection to "wars and fightings" as means of solving public differences. *Hellas,* which shares several other specific details with this editorial and obviously has some of the same purposes, was written by a would-be pacifist who has now chosen to praise "wars and fightings." Pacifism turns out to have been a limiting rule of reason.

Assigned the problem of defending a rebellion, *Hellas* starts right off by recognizing the "Spirit of God" in Thermopylae, Marathon, and Philippi as well as in the continued progress of freedom through Milan, Florence, Albion, Switzerland, "far Atlantis," France, Germany, Spain, and now again in Greece. At Philippi, Freedom was like "an eagle on a promontory"; at the right hand of Destiny sits "eagle-wingèd victory." Elsewhere in the drama, too, Russia, although condemned as an eagle hovering over an entangled kite and crane, and furthermore equated with a tiger gloating over the stag at bay, is forced to share the eagle of glory with more attractive states. Given the theory that volcanic eruptions relieve the pressure and thus prevent greater ruin by earthquakes, and given its metaphoric meaning that revolution stops anarchy, then the report of the Third Messenger that Crete and Cyprus catch "from each other's veins" (a pun) both "volcano-fire and earthquake-spasm" serves as an admission, or at least as a recognition, of anarchic devastation by the Greeks.[70]

Shelley's letters show that, like the Examiner, he did not wish a Greek victory beholden to Russian strength, but *Hellas* condemns Russia not only for the exercise of power but also for her failure to use it against the infidel, when the Patriarch of Constantinople was hanged in retribution for the slaughter of Turks in the Morea. England should take no lessons from Russia, and should exchange no declarations of common concern (lines 307–311, 536–545).

Hellas also shares with Hunt's editorial an unexpectedly favorable treatment of "the philosophical part of Christianity, as distinguished

316

Shelley

from the dogmas that have hitherto been confounded with and perverted it." As often as Shelley had condemned the union of armed force and religion, the inclination of his presumed readers to support a Christian thrall against a Moslem master was too tempting to ignore. Russia's failure to avenge the archpriest in Constantinople, which Shelley would normally approve, becomes an evil in *Hellas*. Internally, too, the drama generated a more elevated role for Christianity than the author in repose could endorse. Christian truth killed Greek myth, sings the Chorus, although the author interrupts with a note to say that the truth is relative. The Chorus puts it with less offense: "Worlds on worlds are rolling ever / From creation to decay." Again, in the final prophetic lyric, although the Chorus predicts a reawakening of Saturn and Love "more bright and good . . . than One who rose," the author takes the precaution of elucidating: the "sublime human character of Jesus Christ" was deformed among men by identification with Jehovah, whose followers have in fact tortured and murdered the true followers of Christ. Partly Shelley was clarifying the position he had always held; partly he had greatly increased his esteem for Jesus; and partly he had learned to live with His disciples. This change goes hand in glove with his acceptance of violence as the means of securing independence.

The most persuasive excuse for violence in *Hellas* is its concept of Hellenism. The play frees itself from the cage of opportune rhetoric in its celebration of the Hellenic Spirit. The Chorus offers a cyclic view of history. Time, as sometimes depicted in the hand of Saturn, is the *ouroboros,* the snake with its tail in its mouth. In a Humean version of Descartes, Ahasuerus disposes of the future along with the past: "Nought is but that which feels itself to be." Thought is eternal. Empire is the collective error of perceiving man as a part of time, place, circumstance, blood, and matter. Cities, "on which Empire sleeps enthroned," all bow "their towered crests to mutability." Empire and all else that mutability rules must pass. Hellenism, which is freedom of the human spirit, breaks out of this cycle of time, space, and material nothingness. Freedom belongs to Thought, with its "quick elements" Will, Passion, Reason, and Imagination. Thought cannot die; freedom therefore is immortal.

317

As thought cannot die, eternal Necessity works through it rather than through matter.[71]

Hellenism lives on, as in "young Atlantis" (the United States), which also shows promise of reviving the material strength of ancient Rome (SP, 475:992–995). Yet the final chorus, "The world's great age begins anew," is no more limited to the United States than Hellenism is limited to Troy, Ulysses, and the Argonauts. Hellenism is the freedom to improve on Hellenic history and legend. The fourth stanza of the final chorus ("Oh, write no more the tale of Troy, / If earth Death's scroll must be!") and the last stanza ("Oh, cease! must hate and death return?") do not represent a cancellation of hope that the "world's great age begins anew." If the Greeks win independence or if the spirit of Hellenism prevails anywhere, then the new Athens, wherever it may be geographically, will be free of the blood that marked the fall of Troy and the history of Athens to date. The final chorus puts some of this in the future, some in the conditional, and some in the present tense, because the renovation of Greece is part of a shining idea universally valid, but Shelley expresses wryly, in a note, the limits of this idea when expressed as hope: "Prophecies of wars, and rumours of wars, etc., may safely be made by poet or prophet in any age, but to anticipate however darkly a period of regeneration and happiness is a more hazardous exercise of the faculty which bards possess or feign." The bard sees in the uprising of the Greeks, where it was unlooked for but is uniquely appropriate, a symptom of what may be the ultimate realization of man's continuing hope for peace. In words that conclude "The Sensitive Plant," it is a "modest creed," yet pleasant "if one considers it." Given favorable signs, the bard need not drain the urn of "bitter prophecy" to its dregs.

The two major choral hymns embody speculative hope. The work as a whole, a "mere improvise" according to Shelley's Preface, embodies a lyrical expression of his "intense sympathy" with the Greek cause, which he offers as a replacement for the prevailing policy, whereby the English "permit their own oppressors to act according to their natural sympathy with the Turkish tyrant" (SP, 446, 447).

With *Hellas* Shelley published "Lines Written on Hearing the News of the Death of Napoleon," expressing mock surprise that

Shelley

the earth still moves. Mother Earth declares that this life and death, like others, warms her: "I feed on whom I fed." The new revolutions will be better.

> 'Still alive and still bold,' shouted Earth,
> 'I grow bolder and still more bold.'
>
> (SP, 641:25–26)

Earth requires for hope only the endless renewal of the seasons. It is true that she once invested hope in Bonaparte, but she has nothing to lament in the fading of glory that was "terror and blood and gold." The energy of his spirit will pass into glories yet to come.

Shelley's strong response to the death of Keats had as one of its driving forces his partisan appraisal of one befriended by Leigh Hunt and hounded to death by Tory reviewers. *Adonais: An Elegy on the Death of John Keats,* Pisa, 1821, conveys this partisan force. The myth of Venus and Adonis, and equally Milton's *Lycidas,* with its repudiation of priesthood's blind mouths, gave Shelley's elegy license to attack all the herded wolves of the Government press in the one nameless worm whose review gored Keats. Yet political motive probably adds its bit—certainly more than identification of the poet with his protagonist adds—to the potentiality rather than accomplishment, and to the passivity, of the character Adonais. Although an early stanza of the poem celebrates Keats's great forerunner Milton, old and lonely when "The priest, the slave, and the liberticide" performed in England rites of lust and blood, even Milton is honored for suffering liberticide, not for opposing it, and the evocation of Chatterton in stanza 45, first among the "inheritors of unfulfilled renown," seems closer than Miltonic engagement to the unheroic tone of the poem. I cannot regard Shelley as suicidal, in the way that James Rieger and some other critics have regarded him, but *Adonais* is more passive in its opposition to evil, more nearly escapist in its transcendence of the earthly, more defiantly static in its idealism, than any of his earlier poems of note.

We cannot safely guess at the poet's final direction. When his boat, the *Don Juan,* sank in a storm off Viareggio in July 1822, his last major work, "The Triumph of Life," was unfinished. Since

319

we can hope for no more of it than we have, exegetic critics are right to drop the last four lines and interpret the fragment as if it were a whole. For any study of the poet's development, however, the fragment imposes great hazards.[72]

The title contains twists of irony, but how many? Life, as the juncture of time and the world, rides in imperial triumph to display his captives and slaves. The formless shape in the car of Life resembles too closely for chance the shape of Death, if "shape it might be call'd that shape had none," in *Paradise Lost*.[73] Would Shelley's usual images for triumph over death, here buried under the powerful figure of worldly life as enslaver, triumph again as the poem continued? More narrowly, does the fragment contain evidence that the car of worldly triumph is the only vehicle in which triumph can appear to a divine prophet? Had Shelley, politically and privately, lost faith in renovation?

The answers come within a vision, itself within an outer frame of sunrise on a slope of the Apennines and an inner border of trance, *déjà vu* ("I knew / That I had felt the freshness of that dawn . . . / Under the self same bough"). Within these psychic vistas, Rousseau is the Vergil who guides the poet among the sights of hell, here presented in sharper, more Dantesque images than when the Furies reviewed them for Prometheus. Rousseau himself has remained in the purgatory of root and grass, doomed like the Ancient Mariner to make his hearer a wiser and a sadder man. He tells how he came to the same vision of the triumph as our poet was envisioning when he discovered Rousseau, not a chained captive but thrown to earth. Although his experience corroborates the narrator's, he lacks the authority of Queen Mab. When asked, "And what is this? / Whose shape is that within the car? & why," he answers only out of fuller experience: "Life" (180). Denying all knowledge of "why," Rousseau suggests that he might at a later time learn from our poet (303–308).

At the point where the fragment breaks off, the narrator asks "the cripple," Rousseau: "Then, what is Life?" Only a critic overhot for certainties or grossly inattentive could believe that we have already been told, in the lines that precede this question, the ultimate answer. We have seen the shape of Life, not necessarily the ground of Life, and not with absolute certainty even "Life" as Rousseau identifies it.[74] At line 180, Adonais was still a "leprous corpse," and the "intense atom" of his spirit "quenched in a most cold repose." Rousseau may have had much yet to learn.

Since, for all we know, Shelley may have shared Rousseau's ignorance and may have gone as far as he could go in "The Triumph of Life," it is unprofitable to ask whether veils would fall, after line 547, to reveal an old acquaintance like intellectual Beauty or Love as the final reality knowable to man. It might be profitable, however, to ask how the likes of these fare in the 547 lines we have. "I was overcome," Rousseau protests, by "my own heart alone" (240–241). Among recent "spoilers spoiled," besides Napoleon, he identifies "Voltaire, Frederic, & Kant, Catherine, & Leopold, / Chained hoary anarch, demagogue & sage," as all conquered in the battle with Life. He himself abandoned the futile effort. He recognized in Dante one who told, although in "words of hate & awe," how "all things are transfigured, except Love" (476). "All that is mortal of great Plato" is chained to the triumphal car, for in him Life conquered "the heart by love" (254–258). The poem clearly distinguishes between conquered Plato and exhausted but unconquered Rousseau. We seem to have a consistent distinction also between love in the mortal heart and the immutable Love invoked in myth and wondrous story by Plato and Dante.[75]

Rousseau identifies the "mighty captives"; our own guide tells how few have escaped:

> All but the sacred few who could not tame
> Their spirits to the Conqueror, but as soon
> As they had touched the world with living flame
>
> Fled back like eagles to their native noon,
> Or those who put aside the diadem
> Of earthly thrones or gems, till the last one
>
> Were there;—for they of Athens & Jerusalem
> Were neither mid the mighty captives seen
> Nor mid the ribald crowd that followed them . . .
>   (128–136)

Notably, the "native noon" of "the sacred few" is outside this world altogether. They died young. The second group, "they of Athens

& Jerusalem," have sometimes been taken as Socrates and Jesus alone. Described in the preceding tercet as ideal versions of Byron's Cincinnatus and Washington, with the Shelleyan touch that they put away thrones and jewels "till the last one," they are more likely to include all true disciples, however few, of the two distinctive precepts, that of Athens, "Know thyself," and the second commandment pronounced by Jesus in Jerusalem, "Thou shalt love thy neighbour as thyself."

For Shelley the precept of Jerusalem has the special meaning, as we have seen it in many of his poems, of Narcissus finding his fullest self mirrored in the nymph Echo. Loving our neighbor is what the brief essay "On Love" describes as the search "to awaken in all things that are, a community with what we experience within ourselves" (SW, VI, 201).

The Athenian precept appears elsewhere in the poem, notably and explicitly when Rousseau describes those who wielded power by miter, helmet, crown, or "thought's empire over thought" (like Aristotle, Kant, and, to judge by trial lines, Sir Humphry Davy) as lacking one requisite, "to know themselves" (212). To know yourself, then, means to avoid dominion over others, thus to escape life's dominion over you, and in the effect to love your neighbor. The precept is writ large in "Sonnet: To the Republic of Benevento,"[76] assigned by Mary Shelley to 1821 and published as "Sonnet: Political Greatness":

> Man who man would be,
> Must rule the empire of himself; in it
> Must be supreme, establishing his throne
> On vanquished will, quelling the anarchy
> Of hopes and fears, being himself alone.
>
> (SP, 642:10–14)

Only a rapid reading, influenced by the title "Political Greatness" and the coincidence of Napoleon's death, would assign to this sonnet the subject of political leadership. It concerns men in numbers, now the "blind millions," "those herds whom tyranny makes tame," but capable of the happiness, majesty, fame, peace, strength, and skill in arms or arts they cannot have so long as "History is but the shadow of their shame." The negative in the octave of this sonnet,

Shelley

like the negative of "The Triumph of Life," is a way of defining the affirmative.

The sonnet ends with an ideal that is implied throughout the "Triumph." It also suggests that the saving remnant is confined to leaders only in the sense that the poet or artist or sage or citizen who puts aside all temptations, "till the last one," is automatically distinguished as a savior. A leader of the commonwealth is simply the rare good man. It may be the identification of power with conquest by Life that prevents the appearance by name of such favorites of Shelley's as Franklin, Jefferson, and Washington. The ideal that made them favorites is implied throughout "The Triumph of Life."

Shelley's last poem approaches his earlier patterns most closely in the account of Rousseau's experience with a feminine "shape all light." The context is a record of burgeoning consciousness and conscience. Hints may appear in a few sentences of Rousseau's *Confessions* and the *Nouvelle Héloïse,* but the symbols embody an idealized experience of aspiration. Conscious delight in impressions from nature began in *enfance,* in "the April prime" after the blankness of what is called infancy in English. Almost at once, "Amid the sun," appeared the shape all light, "light's severe excess" in feminine form. Rousseau knows this shape only as a fusion of inner and outer impressions, but he has lamented earlier the poor environment given to "the spark with which Heaven lit my spirit" (201). Even if the shape all light is not from Heaven, light from Heaven has somehow touched him. Either as authentication or as illusion of divinity, the feminine shape is brighter than the sun of common day (336–339, 343–352). Her tread on dancing foam is that of love, as appropriated by Shelley, in kindred passages of poetry and prose, from Plato's description of love's light tread and from celebrants, in word and pigment, of Aphrodite's birth.[77] Uncertain whether Wordsworth has had the right intimations about the child's divine origins, the envisioned Rousseau addresses the shape without metaphysical prejudice:

> If, as it doth seem,
> Thou comest from the realm without a name,
> Into this valley of perpetual dream,
> Shew whence I came and where I am, and why—
> Pass not away upon the passing stream.   (395–399)

He makes this request after her feet, moving to wondrous music, have trampled from his mind all lesser impressions.

In answer to his request, she offers him the opportunity to quench his thirst from a crystal glass "Mantling with bright Nepenthe." Whatever lexicographers of a later day may believe, Shelley, like almost every quotable writer before him, understood Nepenthe to be, not a narcotic, but an exhilarant.[78] The prophetic Spirit of the Hour in *Prometheus Unbound* foresees the day when women may freely feel and communicate emotions they were forced to hide in the days when drops of gall "Spoilt the sweet taste of the nepenthe, love" (III.iv. 163). A true nepenthe leads to joy.

Rousseau touched the cup with his lips. The first, sudden result—or event, appearing to be a result—answered his request to know where he was. The event could in no way be described as exhilarant. There burst upon his sight "a new Vision never seen before"—the chariot with its captives. Taken together, the two visions, first of the shape all light and then of the car of Life, make up the rites of initiation of one who recognizes and tries to follow an ideal. He is initiated into manhood and into a select company, but not into the "sacred few." Dawning consciousness of an ideal bestows on the supplicant—hands to him in a crystal glass—the power to see life as it is. The grim vision of Life as a blindfolded power chaining its votaries and enslaving the credulous multitude is not given either to the votaries or the multitude, but only to those like Rousseau and Shelley who have had a vision of light. Awareness of the ideal stamps out childhood innocence. It gives one a nasty view of worldly life. It does not assure the supplicant of martyrdom with the sacred few or of saintliness in age. Although the shape all light accompanied Rousseau like a "half extinguished beam" of a "light from Heaven," he joined the ghastly dance and moved among the "thickest billows of the living storm" (429, 466). He could perceive, as the chained captives could not, the phantoms of thought and impulse that soar and buzz around the procession, but he could not resist the blandishments of power in the world.

"The Triumph of Life" differs from Shelley's earlier poems by a reduction of evanescence and by prolonged attention to the multitude. Life, or at least the pageant of life, is people. Ten years have

Shelley

not transformed the poet's attitudes toward tyrants, sacrificial deliverers, or commoners reduced by slavery to a stinking mob. He will not pity "the great form" of Napoleon, whose "grasp had left the giant world so weak" that "every pigmy kicked it as it lay" (215–234). From Italy, Shelley had kept prophetic watch over English affairs, but his cosmopolitan interests were adequate to the task of keeping Castlereagh and Sidmouth, if they appear at all, nameless among the pygmies—no doubt mostly royal pygmies—who had kicked the world since 1815. The absence of recent heroes and political martyrs may be owing solely to the fragmentary state of the poem, but the new care with graphic metaphor has at last driven out the "tyrant-slaves," "Coward Chiefs," and similar epithets that the political passions of rationalism had bestowed on monarchs and their ministers.

To bring all their convictions toward the faith we call romantic, Wordsworth and Coleridge uprooted most of their political assumptions and planted anew. Shelley tended continuously his original garden. He replaced a few individual ideas, grafted promising scions, and raised hybrids to his own specifications. "His patience," Leigh Hunt said in the Preface to "The Masque of Anarchy," is "the deposit of many impatiencies." He strove much more stubbornly than the older poets to understand the subtleties of the Enlightenment. He gave ever-increasing honor to imagination, but he did not take it "as a repetition in the finite mind of the eternal act of creation in the infinite I AM" (BL, I, 202). From a program in 1812 something like that announced by Erasmus Darwin in the Preface to *The Temple of Nature,* to bring "distinctly to the imagination the beautiful and sublime images of the operations of Nature," Shelley moved in a direction at once idealistic and agnostic to employ his "passion for reforming the world," not toward "the direct enforcement of reform" or "a reasoned system on the theory of human life" (as Darwin had done), but "to familiarise the highly refined imagination of the more select classes of poetical readers with beautiful idealisms of moral excellence." Admitting man's inability to know the highest reality, Shelley tried to benefit mankind by repeated attempts to imagine it.

325

CONCLUSION

We have been considering selectively the nature, quantity, and quality of political impulses in poems of the English romantic movement.

In youth each of the major English romantic poets encountered, and each was attracted by, the intellectual emphases accumulated by liberals and libertarians in the century after Newton and Locke. This intellectual climate included a skepticism consequent upon the conflict between a deistic belief in the mathematical order of the universe and the epistemological limitation of each man's certainty to the impressions provided by his own physical senses. Other emphases included the possibility of increasing justice by limiting privilege, superstition, enthusiasm, and prejudice through exercise of reason; the right of each man to speak freely in his own interest; a cosmopolitan aspiration toward world brotherhood; and the possibilities for progress through increase of knowledge and rearrangements of government and society. Out of such ideas had come an era of political revolution.

Drawing initially upon one aspect of the heritage from Locke—the epistemological confinement of each man to his own experience—the romantic poets pursued new emphases difficult to reconcile with the ideological bases of reform and revolution. They emphasized private emotion, the individual, the particular, the local; organic growth, organic unity, imagination, symbol, and myth. They rejected

326

Conclusion

the fanciful commonwealths contrived by abstract reason and looked within the individual for powers more exciting than the routine of common sense, "the light of common day." They found inadequate any description of human association too abstract to emphasize personal affection, imaginative sympathy, and the ever-present reality of change and growth. "Reform" meant to them a return to normal development.

A notable outburst by Samuel Wilberforce against "modern liberalism" in 1837 came as much from the romantic as from the Evangelical heritage of this future bishop of Oxford: ". . . I abhor it. I think it is the Devil's creed: a heartless steam-engine, unchristian, low, sensual, utilitarian creed which would put down all that is really great and high and noble; all old remembrances and customs . . . and worship the very Devil if his horns were gold and his tail were a steam engine."[1] Coleridge had protested in behalf of the new sensibility as early as 1797: "I can contemplate nothing but parts, & parts are all *little*—!—My mind feels as if it ached to behold & know something *great*—something *one & indivisible*—and it is only in the faith of this that rocks or waterfalls, mountains or caverns give me the sense of sublimity or majesty!—But in this faith *all things* counterfeit infinity!"[2] The other romantics shared with Coleridge a distaste for self-interest, meanness, littleness, and fragmentation, all of which they ascribed to eighteenth-century rationalism.

Out of the conflict between the two sets of emphases, a romantic might embrace the politics of Edmund Burke, or some other conservative political philosophy of slow growth, as Coleridge, Wordsworth, and Southey did; he might abandon considerations of government as external to man's true concerns; he might, like Byron, find the imagination delusive; he might live with recurrent crises or continuous dilemma; he might try to create a myth of quintessential love that would communicate to the imagination what the doctrine of equality in universal brotherhood had communicated to the "lower" reason. The poetry of the major English romantics reveals that each was aware of the problem and that each was tempted toward each of the possibilities named. The difficulty of adjusting divergent political and poetic allegiances probably made politics con-

327

tinue as a more significant element in the major work of each poet than it would have been had the political and artistic principles easily harmonized.

One important conclusion implied throughout the present study is that the romantics did not recoil from a world without order. They recoiled from philosophies that attributed superficial, geometric order to a living universe that is profoundly if impalpably ordered. They hesitated when confronted with visions of volcanic revolution as the natural center of organic growth, but they were unanimous in accepting volcanoes as more natural in the life of man than Malthusian segregation into male and female workhouses. Their spiritual condition did not require that the universe continue under mathematical laws of order. In the Augustinian and Calvinistic tradition that prevailed in England—and never more than with John and Charles Wesley—all earthly matter represented evil. The aesthetic change occurring in the romantic era made the asymmetries of earth acceptable to seekers of the sublime and the sacred. The romantics accepted a corresponding asymmetry in the heart of man.

The emphases on particularity and on organic growth allowed all the romantics, whatever their domestic politics, to find something "of sublimity or majesty" in nationalism, the self-determination of a people formed by a common history. Several philosophies of the last century and a half have considered the character and consciousness of the individual as formed in great part by the circumstances, manners, and symbols of the society that environs him. Wordsworth's emphasis on solitude and elation amid the grandeur of the hills seems to belong to an analogy he formed between the shaping of the individual consciousness by nature, both internal and external, and the shaping of the social ethics of the individual through the national environment. In any event, the largest political child of the age of Wordsworth was the universal sentiment of nationalism. To the romantics, a migratory people can have no nation. Land and language are Siamese twins. As a part of a vast avalanche by which revolutionary capitalism swept away the ruins of feudalism, Shelley as well as Coleridge and Wordsworth continued to base the claims for individual dignity on agrarian economics and rural life. All three opposed the continuing erosion of agrarian values in "the active universe."

Conclusion

Nationalism was a sentiment of particularity. Love the little platoon, but guide it, without fixed cadence, toward service in the universal army of tomorrow, which is the force of lovers, of families, and next of small communities, applied through outward waves of affection. In nationalism the romantics acquired a check to the illusion, encouraged by their subjective attention to the self, that identity can be discovered in isolation from its social context. Even yet, it is difficult to see how any practical movement from dynasty and empire toward world government could avoid the intermediate process of nationalization. Distant, unknown brothers, as the romantics recognized, are ineffective abstractions.

For good or ill, nationalism has endured longer than some of the romantics' more specific enthusiasms. Their idealization of the United States, of George Washington, Thomas Jefferson, and other founding fathers, and of frontiersmen like Daniel Boone, stood in clear contrast to the idealization of the noble Indian by French writers as diverse as Jean-François Marmontel and François-René de Chateaubriand. Romantic enthusiasm for the new nation intensified the disillusionment of later writers who crossed the Atlantic to observe the expanding republic in the first decades of the Victorian era. It was in this era of disillusionment that Wordsworth composed his sonnet in denunciation of the men of Pennsylvania because they threatened to stop payment on the state bonds he had purchased in romantic good faith.

A second major assault on liberalism coincided with a reaction against the Victorians and their heirs who had embraced simultaneously liberal dogmas and romantic poetry. William Blake, because his popularity began much later than that of the other poets and because of his fierce intolerance for all worldly authority and convention, was free to become a far stronger voice than he had ever been before.

We need not deny that the English romantics were adherents of dream, revivers of myth, addicts of vision, and scholars of self in order to see why they had remained the chief guides in feeling, and even in thought, for more than a century. They were students of power, observers of the real object, believers in imaginative synthesis, assayers of an ever-renewing contract with nature to improve man's communal life, and affirmers of private yearning as a war-

329

ranted power in political action. Earnest and often fervent in their attempts to validate the unifying imagination, they shared a hope that all art carrying the breath of inspiration into verbal craftsmanship will retain a power to regenerate.

Politically, the romantics contributed most to later generations in deepening the liberal ideal. They introduced into poetry and life a sense—too variable from one poet to another to be called an idea—of imagination as the sympathetic movement from self into others. The liberal had said, To understand is to forgive—*Tout comprendre c'est tout pardonner.* The romantic said, Truly to comprehend is to imagine. Whomever you understand, you may pity, but to understand and to pity are not enough. Without imagination, you cannot love. Whom you truly imagine, you love. Not only must emotion and dream have their place in man's search for the beautiful, the good, and the true, but attention to the individual and the particular must lead to empathy with those who would otherwise appear as your foes. Negative capability is the name that Keats gave to this empathetic departure from self. Of sympathetic imagination in the sense politically applicable, Blake had less than the other major romantics. Wordsworth practiced it less successfully than he taught it to others. Even if imaginative sympathy arose, as some would say, because the romantics were disturbed men escaping from internal conflict, the ideal will have social applicability for generations yet to come.

To the romantic movement in England, politics contributed scores of minor poems. Political impulses contributed to poems both minor and great, and the best of these impulses contributed to the greatness of major romantic poems.

NOTES
INDEX

NOTES

I. INTRODUCTION

1. For recent debate on the chronology of agricultural change, see J. D. Chambers and G. E. Mingay, *Agricultural Revolution 1750–1880* (London: Batsford, 1966); Eric Kerridge, *The Agricultural Revolution* (London: Allen and Unwin, 1968).

2. Phyllis Deane, *The First Industrial Revolution* (Cambridge University Press, 1965), pp. 32, 48.

3. Helen Maria Williams, *Letters written in France in the Summer 1790, to a Friend in England* (London, 1790), pp. 14, 21, 61–62, 195, 209.

4. *A Narrative of the Events which have taken place in France,* 2nd ed. (London, 1816) p. 212.

5. It was thus an age of paradox, Hazlitt said, in its own "love of paradox and change, its dastard submission to prejudice and to the fashion of the day." See W. P. Albrecht, *Hazlitt and the Creative Imagination* (University of Kansas Press, 1965), p. 60.

6. For the major figures see Kenneth Hopkins, *Portraits in Satire* (London: Barrie, 1958).

7. *Political Poems and Songs relating to English History,* ed. Thomas Wright (London, 1859), I, 278. I have modernized the spellings.

8. Beginning "Weary way-wanderer languid and sick at heart." The motif of oppressed wanderer, to which we must return in connection with both Wordsworth and Shelley, appeared also in Southey's sonnet of 1794, "With

333

wayworn feet a Pilgrim woe-begone" (later beginning less woefully, "With many a weary step, at length I gain"); in "The Triumph of Woman," which begins "Glad as the weary traveller tempest-tost" and is explicitly associated by Southey with Mary Wollstonecraft as author of *A Vindication of the Rights of Woman;* and similarly throughout his early canon.—Southey, *Poems,* 4th ed. (London, 1801), pp. 7–28, 77, and prefatory pages.

II. THE CLIMATE

1. S. J. Pratt, *Bread, or the Poor,* 2nd ed., 1802, sig. F^1.

2. Leon Radzinowicz, *A History of English Criminal Law . . . from 1750,* I (London: Stevens; New York: Macmillan, 1948), 3–40.

3. Among many valuable studies, see Michael Roberts, *The Whig Party 1807–1812,* 2nd ed. (New York: Barnes and Noble, 1965), with bibliography, pp. 419–434; Austin Mitchell, *The Whigs in Opposition 1815–1830* (Oxford: Clarendon, 1967); Arthur Aspinall, *Lord Brougham and the Whig Party* (Manchester, 1927); Chester W. New, *The Life of Henry Brougham to 1830* (Oxford: Clarendon, 1961); M. W. Patterson, *Sir Francis Burdett and His Times (1770–1844),* 2 vols. (London: Macmillan, 1931); Elie Halévy, *England in 1815,* trans. E. I. Watkin and D. A. Barker, *The Liberal Awakening 1815–1830,* trans. E. I. Watkin (both 2nd ed., London: Benn, 1949); E. P. Thompson, *The Making of the English Working Class* (New York: Pantheon, 1964); J. Steven Watson, *The Reign of George III, 1760–1815* (Oxford: Clarendon, 1960); E. L. Woodward, *The Age of Reform 1815–1870* (Oxford: Clarendon, 1938, with revised bibliography in the corrected impression of 1949).

4. Watson, *Reign of George III,* p. 450.

5. See Woodring, "Leigh Hunt as Political Essayist," in Leigh Hunt, *Political and Occasional Essays,* ed. L. H. and C. W. Houtchens (Columbia University Press, 1962), pp. 57–60.

6. Radzinowicz, pp. 551–607.

7. See Paul Elmer More, *Shelburne Essays,* 11 vols. (New York, 1904–1921), especially Series VII (1910) and VIII (1913); Irving Babbitt, *Rousseau and Romanticism* (Boston, 1919) and *On Being Creative, and Other Essays* (Boston, 1932); T. E. Hulme, *Speculations* (London, 1924); Carl Schmitt-Dorotic, *Politische Romantik,* 2nd ed. (Munich and Leipzig, 1925); Paul Roubiczek, *The Misinterpretation of Man: Studies in European Thought of the Nineteenth Century* (London: Routledge, 1947); F. L. Lucas, *The Decline and Fall of the Romantic Ideal* (New York: Macmillan, 1936).

8. Walter Jackson Bate, *From Classic to Romantic: Premises of Taste in Eighteenth-Century England* (Harvard University Press, 1946).

9. On the "English Jacobins" see Crane Brinton, *The Political Ideas of the English Romanticists* (Oxford University Press, 1926), pp. 8–47; M. Ray Adams, *Studies in the Literary Backgrounds of English Radicalism with Special Reference to the French Revolution* (Lancaster, Penn.: Franklin and Marshall College, 1947); W. N. Hargreaves-Mawdsley, *The English Della Cruscans and Their Time, 1783–1828* (The Hague: Nijhoff, 1967).

Notes to Pages 27–40

10. "New Morality," lines 335–336, in *Poetry of the Anti-Jacobin,* ed. L. Rice-Oxley (Oxford, 1924), p. 185.

11. For an emphasis on movement from negative to positive, see two speculations by Morse Peckham, "Toward a Theory of Romanticism," *PMLA,* 66 (1951), 5–23, and "Toward a Theory of Romanticism: II. Reconsiderations," *Studies in Romanticism,* 1 (1961), 1–8. See also Peckham's *Beyond the Tragic Vision* (New York: Braziller, 1962). For one of René Wellek's many statements of the problem rejected by Lovejoy, and for a survey of recent views, see "Romanticism Re-examined," in *Romanticism Reconsidered: Selected Papers from the English Institute,* ed. Northrop Frye (Columbia University Press, 1963), pp. 107–133. The eddies of change are best set forth in M. H. Abrams, *The Mirror and the Lamp: Romantic Theory and the Critical Tradition* (Oxford University Press, 1953). For a representative study of the vitalistic impulse, see H. W. Piper, *The Active Universe: Pantheism and the Concept of Imagination in the English Romantic Poets* (London: Athlone, 1962).

12. *Brief über den Roman,* cited by Ralph Tymms, *German Romantic Literature* (London: Methuen, 1955), p. 24.

13. René Wellek, "The Concept of 'Romanticism' in Literary History," *Comparative Literature,* 1 (1949), 1–23, 147–172.

14. *Philosophie des Lebens,* Vorlesung 13 (1827), in *Sämmtliche Werke* (Vienna, 1846), XII, 318–321.

15. F. S. C. Northrop, *The Meeting of East and West: An Inquiry Concerning World Understanding* (New York: Macmillan, 1946), p. 72 and passim.

16. For possible qualifications, see Ernest Lee Tuveson, *The Imagination as a Means of Grace: Locke and the Aesthetics of Romanticism* (University of California Press, 1960), and Mary P. Mack, *Jeremy Bentham: An Odyssey of Ideas* (Columbia University Press, 1963).

17. Dove Cottage MS. 3. See Geoffrey Little, "An Incomplete Wordsworth Essay upon Moral Habits," *A Review of English Literature,* II, no. 1 (1961), p. 12.

18. For attention to a strain in Godwin that can be called Platonic, see F. E. L. Priestley, ed., *An Enquiry concerning Political Justice,* 3 vols. (University of Toronto Press, 1946).

19. For example, George H. Sabine, *A History of Political Theory* (New York: Henry Holt [1950]), p. 544; Alfred Cobban, *Edmund Burke and the Revolt against the Eighteenth Century* (London, 1929), pp. 20–21; Harold Beeley in *Coleridge: Studies by Several Hands,* ed. E. Blunden and E. L. Griggs (London, 1934), pp. 160–161.

20. For a wry view of these contradictions, see Peter Gay, *The Party of Humanity: Essays in the French Enlightenment* (New York: Knopf, 1964), p. 216.

21. Quoted by Robert Birley, *The English Jacobins from 1789 to 1802* (London, 1924), p. 49.

22. T. E. Utley and J. S. Maclure, eds., *Documents of Modern Political Thought* (Cambridge University Press, 1957), p. 242.

23. See Ludwig W. Kahn, *Social Ideals in German Literature 1770–1830* (Columbia University Press, 1938), pp. 57–59, 92–96.

24. *A New View of Society,* Everyman's Library (1949), p. 17.

25. Keats questioned the power of "consequitive reasoning" to compete with the imagination in the pursuit of truth. See *The Letters of John Keats,* ed. Hyder Edward Rollins, 2 vols. (Harvard University Press, 1958), I, 185.

26. "Byron," *Critical Miscellanies* (London, 1923), p. 152.

27. *Politics and Opinion in the Nineteenth Century* (London: Cape, 1954), pp. 51, 566.

28. See Walter Graham, "The Politics of the Greater Romantic Poets," *PMLA,* 36 (1921), 60–78.

29. *Sketches in Nineteenth Century Biography* (London: Longmans, 1930), p. 75.

30. *The Poetical Works of William Wordsworth,* ed. E. de Selincourt and Helen Darbishire, 5 vols. (Oxford: Clarendon, 1947–1954), IV, 419. Hereinafter referred to as WPW. See Harry W. Rudman, "Wordsworth and Admiral Nelson," *College English,* 15 (1953), 177–178.

31. *Inquiring Spirit: A New Presentation of Coleridge,* ed. Kathleen Coburn (New York: Pantheon, 1951), p. 321.

32. A. P. d'Entrèves, *Dante as a Political Thinker* (Oxford: Clarendon, 1952), pp. 14–20. On nationalism generally, see especially Hans Kohn, *The Idea of Nationalism: A Study in Its Origins and Background* (New York: Macmillan, 1944) and *The Age of Nationalism: The First Era of Global History* (New York: Harper, 1962), and see Chapter IV below.

33. In *The Collected Works of Samuel Taylor Coleridge,* ed. Kathleen Coburn and Bart Winer: *The Friend,* ed. Barbara E. Rooke, 2 vols. (London: Routledge, 1969), I, 292. In this section of *The Friend,* "On the Principles of Political Knowledge," Coleridge finds in national independence and growth a justification for Burke's doctrine of expediency.

34. *Poems on Affairs of State,* 6th ed. (London, 1710), I, sig. A².

35. See M. H. Abrams, "English Romanticism: The Spirit of the Age," in *Romanticism Reconsidered,* ed. Northrop Frye, pp. 26–72; Piper, *Active Universe,* pp. 49–55, 94; E. P. Thompson, *Making of the English Working-Class,* pp. 48–51, 116–120, 382–392.

36. *The Criterion Book of Modern American Verse* (New York: Criterion Books, 1956), p. 17.

III. VARIETIES OF ROMANTIC EXPERIENCE

1. I have attempted a detailed study in *Politics in the Poetry of Coleridge* (University of Wisconsin Press, 1961). On politics in the prose, see John Colmer, *Coleridge: Critic of Society* (Oxford: Clarendon, 1959); David P. Calleo, *Coleridge and the Idea of the Modern State* (Yale University Press, 1966); Alfred Cobban, *Edmund Burke and the Revolt against the Eighteenth Century* (London, 1929); Waldemar Wünsche, *Die Staatauffassung Samuel Taylor Coleridges* (Leipzig, 1934).

2. *The Complete Poetical Works of Samuel Taylor Coleridge,* ed. Ernest Hartley Coleridge, 2 vols. (Oxford: Clarendon, 1912), I, 69:5, 245:46, 247:86. This work is hereinafter designated CPW. Numerals following a colon indicate line numbers.

Notes to Pages 53–65

3. *Collected Letters of Samuel Taylor Coleridge,* ed. Earl Leslie Griggs, II (Oxford: Clarendon, 1956), 706.
4. *Biographia Literaria,* ed. J. Shawcross, 2 vols. (Oxford University Press, 1907), I, 202. This work is hereinafter designated BL.
5. For examples see Colmer, pp. 104–107; Calleo, pp. 22–25.
6. S. T. Coleridge, *On the Constitution of the Church and State, according to the Idea of Each: with Aids toward a Right Judgment on the Late Catholic Bill* (London, 1830), p. 47.
7. *The Letters of Robert Burns,* ed. J. DeLancey Ferguson, 2 vols. (Oxford: Clarendon, 1931), I, 269. For the quotations in prose that follow, see I, 107, 148, 269–271, II, 143–144.
8. *The Poems and Songs of Robert Burns,* ed. James Kinsley, 3 vols. (Oxford: Clarendon, 1968), I, 469:28. Hereinafter designated PSB.
9. William Paton Ker, *Two Essays* (Glasgow, 1918), pp. 29–30, 39–45. Reprinted in Ker, *Collected Essays,* ed. Charles Whibley (London, 1925), I, 128ff. The argument is moderated in W. P. Ker, *On Modern Literature: Lectures and Addresses,* ed. Terence Spencer and James Sutherland (Oxford: Clarendon, 1955), pp. 46–51. In PSB, I, 49ff., the "ballad" beginning "When *Guildford* good our Pilot stood" is entitled "A Fragment."
10. "The Twa Dogs: A Tale," PSB, I, 140:95–96.
11. For the parallel see Thomas Crawford, *Burns: A Study of the Poems and Songs* (Edinburgh and London: Oliver and Boyd, 1960), p. 238.
12. Beginning "You're welcome to Despots, Dumourier," it is entitled "Address to General Dumourier" in PSB, II, 680.
13. Burns, *Letters,* II, 250, 257. See PSB, II, 668–669.
14. PSB, II, 822.
15. *The Poetry and Prose of William Blake,* ed. David V. Erdman (Garden City, N.Y.: Doubleday [corr. issue, 1966]), p. 411.
16. Ibid., p. 169 (inscription to Plate 26 of *Jerusalem*).
17. By far the fullest historical exposition of these prophecies appears in David V. Erdman, *Blake: Prophet against Empire* (Princeton University Press, 1954), a work that makes possible the brevity of the present sketch. There is historical detail also in J. Bronowski, *William Blake: A Man without a Mask,* 3rd ed. (London, 1947), and a social context in Mark Schorer, *William Blake: The Politics of Vision* (New York, 1946). Northrop Frye, *Fearful Symmetry: A Study of William Blake* (Princeton University Press, 1947), treats the revolutions of Blake's day as representative cycles in the mythic life of Orc.
18. See Erdman, *Blake,* pp. 375–386 (where the name is spelled "Schofield").
19. Plate 2:18–21. On the chronology of the variant copies, see G. E. Bentley, Jr., "The Printing of Blake's *America,*" *Studies in Romanticism,* 6 (Autumn 1966), 46–57.
20. *Milton* 14:2, 23:49. These crises, or "conversions," are given special attention in Jean H. Hagstrum, " 'The Wrath of the Lamb': A Study of William Blake's Conversions," in *From Sensibility to Romanticism,* ed. F. W. Hilles and H. Bloom (Oxford University Press, 1965), pp. 311–330. To ignore the subjective fervor and torment is to make Blake a didactic prig.

Notes to Pages 66–81

21. Frye, *Fearful Symmetry*, p. 201.

22. *The Works of Thomas Love Peacock*, ed. H. F. B. Brett-Smith and C. E. Jones, 10 vols. (London: Constable, 1924–1934), IV, 51.

23. *Works*, IV, 16.

24. *Works*, IX, 187, 219. See Carl Dawson, *His Fine Wit: A Study of Thomas Love Peacock* (London: Routledge, 1970), pp. 112–117.

25. *Works*, VII, 16 ("Rhododaphne," end of Canto I).

26. See George J. Becker, "Landor's Political Purpose," *Studies in Philology*, 35 (1938), 446–455; R. H. Super, *Walter Savage Landor: A Biography* (New York University Press, 1954), *passim*.

27. *The Poetical Works of Walter Savage Landor*, ed. Stephen Wheeler (Oxford: Clarendon, 1937), II, 269, 300. On Chatham, see also Landor's *Charles James Fox: A Commentary on His Life and Character*, ed. S. Wheeler (London, 1907), pp. 20–23.

28. Ian Jack, *English Literature 1815–1832* (Oxford: Clarendon, 1963), p. 168.

29. Ibid., p. 166.

30. Howard Mumford Jones, *The Harp that Once—A Chronicle of the Life of Thomas Moore* (New York: Holt, 1937), p. 110.

31. Georg Lukács, *The Historical Novel*, trans. Hannah and Stanley Mitchell (Boston: Beacon, 1963), p. 53.

32. A few numbers of the *Albion* for Lamb's period survive in the Bath Municipal Libraries. For the epigram, see *The Letters of Charles Lamb*, ed. E. V. Lucas (London: Dent and Methuen, 1935), I, 264. Cf. "The Two Round Spaces on the Tombstone," CPW, 353–355.

33. Mario Praz, *The Hero in Eclipse in Victorian Fiction*, trans. Angus Davidson (Oxford University Press, 1956), p. 69.

34. *Letters*, ed. Lucas, II, 70, 128, 282.

35. "Letter of Elia to Robert Southey, Esquire," *The Works in Prose and Verse of Charles and Mary Lamb*, ed. Thomas Hutchinson, 2 vols. (Oxford University Press, 1908), I, 291. Southey made a brief but noble answer; see Lamb, *Letters*, II, 408.

36. H. W. Garrod, *Keats* (Oxford: Clarendon, 1926), pp. 28–45 and passim. Garrod retained his argument concerning the ruinous effect of intellectual interests in the revised edition of 1957.

37. Aileen Ward, "Keats's Sonnet, 'Nebuchadnezzar's Dream,' " *Philological Quarterly*, 34 (1955), 177–188.

38. *The Letters of John Keats 1814–1821*, ed. Hyder Edward Rollins (Harvard University Press, 1958), I, 108. The language was unchanged in the published *Poems*, 1817.

39. Douglas Bush, *John Keats: His Life and Writings* (New York: Macmillan, 1966), p. 52. With this condemnation of the poetic result, expressed with Bush's habitual trenchancy, compare the just appraisal of Keats's humanitarian sympathies, pp. 167–168.

40. Lines 140–141. I probably owe my emphasis on the brothers' way of seeing to Eve Leoff, "A Study of Keats's *Isabella*," unpubl. diss., Columbia University, 1968. I certainly owe to this work my revised respect for *Isabella* as a whole.

338

Notes to Pages 81–87

41. On the metaphor of harvest, and its relation to patriot heroes, see Walter H. Evert, *Aesthetic and Myth in the Poetry of Keats* (Princeton University Press, 1965), pp. 73–85.

42. The evidence of the transcripts has been mistaken, even by Ernest de Selincourt and others arguing for the retention of lines 187–210, as proof of cancellation by Keats rather than as evidence that Keats recognized the need for further work on this area of the poem. For the entire evidence that survives, see *The Poetical Works of John Keats,* ed. H. W. Garrod, 2nd ed. (Oxford, 1958), p. 514.

43. *The Complete Poetical Works of Thomas Hood,* ed. Walter Jerrold (Oxford University Press, 1906), p. 506.

IV. WORDSWORTH

1. *Biographia Literaria,* ed. J. Shawcross, 2 vols. (Oxford University Press, 1907), I, 56.

2. But see Geoffrey H. Hartman, "Wordsworth's *Descriptive Sketches* and the Growth of a Poet's Mind," *PMLA,* 76 (1961), 519–527, and *Wordsworth's Poetry 1787–1814* (Yale University Press, 1964), pp. 102–115. And cf. Frederick A. Pottle, *The Idiom of Poetry,* rev. ed., (Cornell University Press, 1946), pp. 109–134. The first thorough study of sources and analogues was made by Emile Legouis, *La Jeunesse de William Wordsworth, 1770–1798* (Paris, 1896); translated by J. M. Matthews, London, 1897.

3. If Wordsworth wrote the shoddy sonnet (regular, oddly enough, only in rhyme-scheme), entitled "Sonnet on Seeing Miss Helen Maria Williams Weep at a Tale of Distress" and signed "Axiologus" in the *European Magazine* for March 1787, the title may have been added arbitrarily, whether by the editor or by the schoolboy poet. The content follows the pattern of socially oriented sentimental morality, "To cheer the wand'ring wretch with hospitable light." It is not political. For the text, see *The Poetical Works of William Wordsworth,* ed. E. de Selincourt and H. Darbishire, 5 vols. (Oxford: Clarendon, 1947–1954), I, 269. (This edition will be hereafter referred to as WPW, followed by volume, page, and, after a colon, line numbers.) On the authorship, see Mark L. Reed, *Wordsworth: The Chronology of the Early Years 1770–1799* (Harvard University Press, 1967), p. 71 and note.

4. WPW, I, 84n. Wordsworth's emotions were sufficiently committed to the Revolution (and to Annette Vallon) for him to have returned secretly to France, but the evidence for such a visit has never gone beyond Carlyle's record of Wordsworth's reference to the execution of Gorsas, which occurred in October 1793. See Mary Moorman, *William Wordsworth, a Biography: The Early Years 1770–1803* (Oxford: Clarendon, 1957), pp. 238–242; Reed, p. 147 and note. The basic work is the unpublished dissertation (Harvard University, 1930) of James R. MacGillivray, "Wordsworth and His Revolutionary Acquaintances." See also H. W. Piper, *The Active Universe* (London, 1962), pp. 63–72.

5. Southey's early poems must be seen in the original volumes and newspapers; few of them survived intact in the collective editions. Even the

pacifism of "The Battle of Blenheim," in the *Morning Post* of 9 August 1798, when Nelson was pursuing French ships in the Mediterranean, has a subversive strength lost in the anthologies. Work toward recovery of the newspaper poems has been done variously by Kenneth Curry, Geoffrey Carnall, R. S. Woof, David V. Erdman, among those who have aided my searches.

6. WPW, I, 111 app. crit., here further corrected from three copies each of the editions of 1798 and 1800. On the evolution of the poems, see Enid Welsford, *Salisbury Plain: A Study in the Development of Wordsworth's Mind and Art* (Oxford: Basil Blackwell, 1966), pp. 138–141.

7. Except as noted, quotations from *The Prelude* come from the version of 1805-6 in *The Prelude; or, Growth of a Poet's Mind,* ed. Ernest de Selincourt, 2nd ed. rev. Helen Darbishire (Oxford: Clarendon, 1959).

8. *The Letters of William and Dorothy Wordsworth,* ed. Ernest de Selincourt; 2nd ed., vol. I: *The Early Years 1787–1805,* rev. Chester L. Shaver (Oxford: Clarendon, 1967), 123–124, 128.

9. For an expansion of this point, see Woodring, *Wordsworth,* corr. ed. (Harvard University Press, 1968), pp. 14–19. For a defense of the anti-Godwinian interpretations of Legouis and de Selincourt, see Welsford, *Salisbury Plain,* pp. 145–148.

10. The words, which probably refer to Hazlitt, come from the Advertisement to *Lyrical Ballads,* 1798 (WPW, II, 384). See WPW, IV, 141.

11. "*The Borderers:* Wordsworth on the Moral Frontier," *Durham University Journal,* 25 (1964), 170–183. Sharrock takes Marmaduke's good end, to which evil means are applied, to be personal; I should think the good end social enough, and in Godwin's own terms. In a lesser disagreement, where Sharrock sees the seizure of paramour by lord as part of the disruption, I should think it part of the *ancien régime* that led to disruption.

12. See O. J. Campbell and Paul Mueschke, " 'Guilt and Sorrow': A Study in the Genesis of Wordsworth's Aesthetic," *Modern Philology,* 23 (1926), 293–306; Robert Mayo, "The Contemporaneity of the *Lyrical Ballads,*" *PMLA,* 69 (1954), 486–522.

13. *Tales of the Hall,* bk. V ("Ruth"), in *Poetical Works* (London, 1834), VI, 101.

14. *Letters,* I, 315. Coleridge dictated suitable letters to Wilberforce and others; Wordsworth wrote to Fox: see British Museum MS. Add. 35, 344, foll. 142, 143.

15. Herbert Read, *The True Voice of Feeling: Studies in English Romantic Poetry* (London: Faber, 1953), p. 192.

16. For a fuller discussion of compassionate and incompassionate eyes, see June Q. Yaros, "Wordsworth's Wanderers and Workers," unpubl. diss., Columbia University, 1965.

17. *Journals of Dorothy Wordsworth,* ed. E. de Selincourt, 2 vols. (London: Macmillan, 1941), I, 123.

18. On the problem of dating the momentary experience, see Moorman, *Early Years,* pp. 124–126. For his sense of unity in the city, Wordsworth's own dating would give us 1804 rather than 1802. The importance of the question lies beyond biographical fact, in the narrative spacing of spiritual events.

19. See Ben Ross Schneider, Jr., *Wordsworth's Cambridge Education* (Cambridge University Press, 1957), pp. 11–57; F. M. Todd, *Politics and the Poet: A Study of Wordsworth* (London: Methuen, 1957), pp. 18–22.

20. See Todd, pp. 221–225; Chester L. Shaver, "Wordsworth's Vaudracour," *Times Literary Supplement*, 21 February 1958, p. 101, and "Wordsworth's Vaudracour and Wilkinson's *The Wanderer*," *Review of English Studies*, 12 (1961), 55–57.

21. X.159–176. It may be as late as 1795 that Wordsworth made his "Translation of a Celebrated Greek Song" on the celebrated assassins, published in the *Morning Post* of 13 February 1798 over the signature "Publicola" (probably sent, and possibly revised, by Coleridge). See WPW, I, 299–300; R. S. Woof, "Wordsworth's Poetry and Stuart's Newspapers, 1797–1803," *Studies in Bibliography* (Virginia), 15 (1962), 149–189, esp. pp. 164–166. Woof (p. 164) reads "Publicosa" where I read "Publicola."

22. See *Prelude*, pp. 603–607; Todd, *Politics and the Poet*, pp. 78–80; Schneider, *Wordsworth's Cambridge Education*, pp. 203–227, 239; Moorman, *Early Years*, pp. 254–278; Raymond Dexter Havens, *The Mind of a Poet: A Study of Wordsworth's Thought with Particular Reference to "The Prelude"* (Johns Hopkins Press, 1941), pp. 531–532; Herbert Lindenberger, *On Wordsworth's "Prelude"* (Princeton University Press, 1963), pp. 102–104, 225, 262–268. For Lindenberger, who sees Wordsworth as a theorist and idealist with no comprehension of the political clash of individuals in concrete situations, the details matter little.

23. For an argument that Wordsworth strengthened his disapproval of the Government, see Mary E. Burton, *The One Wordsworth* (University of North Carolina Press, 1942), pp. 67–70.

24. For the relation to Milton's Satan, see Abbie Findlay Potts, *Wordsworth's "Prelude": A Study of Its Literary Form* (Cornell University Press, 1953), pp. 321–328. On the dark places, see David Ferry, *The Limits of Mortality: An Essay on Wordsworth's Major Poems* (Wesleyan University Press, 1959), esp. pp. 128, 164; David Perkins, *The Quest for Permanence* (Harvard University Press, 1959), pp. 12–62. On Wordsworth's mathematical studies, see Havens, *Mind of a Poet*, pp. 410–411, 551–552.

25. Hans Kohn, *The Idea of Nationalism: A Study in Its Origins and Backgrounds* and *The Age of Nationalism: The First Era of Global History*, both cited in Chapter II, n. 32. For examples of the current distrust for romantic nationalism, see Ernst Cassirer, *The Myth of the State* (Yale University Press, 1946); Elie Kedourie, *Nationalism*, 2nd ed. (London: Hutchinson, 1960); Joseph Anthony Mazzeo, *Renaissance and Revolution* (New York: Pantheon, 1965), pp. 115–118.

26. The letter to Pasley is included with the tract in *Wordsworth's Tract on the Convention of Cintra*, ed. A. V. Dicey (London, 1915). For discussion, see Dicey, *The Statesmanship of Wordsworth: An Essay* (Oxford, 1917), pp. 76–90; John E. Wells, "The Story of Wordsworth's *Cintra*," *Studies in Philology*, 18 (1921), 15–76; Crane Brinton, *The Political Ideas of the English Romanticists* (London, 1926), pp. 56–60, 64; R. J. White, ed., *Political Tracts of Wordsworth, Coleridge and Shelley* (Cambridge University Press, 1953), pp. xxvii–xxxv; Mary Moorman, *William Wordsworth, a Biography: The*

Notes to Pages 119–140

Later Years 1803–1850 (Oxford: Clarendon, 1965), pp. 135–154; Woodring, *Wordsworth*, pp. 134–141. For a new text, see *The Letters of William and Dorothy Wordsworth*, ed. Ernest de Selincourt, 2nd ed., vol. II, rev. Mary Moorman (Oxford: Clarendon, 1969), 473–482. A table of variations between the MS at Dove Cottage and the letter actually sent to Pasley is promised for *Letters*, vol. III.

27. This paragraph is based on WPW, II, 280–286; III, 115–118, 125, 131, 137, 139–140, 345; V, 256, 337.

28. See, for example, the sonnet "Oxford, May 30, 1820," WPW, III, 39. For an expansion of the argument, see Woodring, "On Liberty in the Poetry of Wordsworth," *PMLA*, 70 (1955), 1033–1048.

29. R. S. Woof, troubled as others have been over the absence of the sonnet on Venice from the series in the *Morning Post*, January–September 1803, first repeats de Selincourt's date as "probably August, 1802" and then notes that the sonnet was "not certainly written by January, 1803."—"Wordsworth's Poetry and Stuart's Newspapers," p. 156 (see note 21 above). Woof, who corrects many dates and other details as given in WPW, argues persuasively that the increasing conservatism of the *Morning Post* helped determine what poems by Wordsworth were published, and when.

30. *Examiner*, 30 September, 1810, p. 610, as reprinted in Leigh Hunt, *Political and Occasional Essays*, ed. L. H. and C. W. Houtchens (Columbia University Press, 1962), p. 118.

31. I have discussed this sonnet differently, but I think not contradictorily, in *Wordsworth*, pp. 126, 169–170.

32. WPW, III, 215. On the question of Wordsworth's actual experience, see III, 495; Edith C. Batho, *The Later Wordsworth* (Cambridge, 1933), p. 142; Moorman, *Later Years*, pp. 528–530. For passages cited, see WPW, III, 181–183, 215–217, 228–229, 501, IV, 132–133; *Prelude*, X.948.

33. *Letters*, I, 373; cf. 382–383.

34. Moorman, *Later Years*, pp. 334–335.

35. *The Prose Works of William Wordsworth*, ed. A. B. Grosart, 3 vols. (London, 1876), I, 19. The surviving transcription, Dove Cottage W.W. Prose MS. 1, contains interesting variants, as on "the consuming expence of our never-ending process, the verbosity <verbose inaccuracy> of <our statute> unintellig[ib]le statutes and the perpetual contrariety in our judicial decisions."

36. WPW, V, 112, 119, 335 (*Excur.* IV.80–81, 332–350, V.669–676). The subject was made his own by Arthur O. Lovejoy, *The Great Chain of Being: A Study of the History of an Idea* (Harvard University Press, 1936).

37. For convenient summaries, see E. L. Woodward, *The Age of Reform 1815–1870* (Oxford University Press, 1949), 455–460; John Roach in *The New Cambridge Modern History*, IX, ed. C. W. Crawley (Cambridge University Press, 1965), 193–208.

38. *Thanksgiving Ode, January 18, 1816, with Other Short Pieces, Chiefly Referring to Recent Public Events* (London, 1816), p. vi. In softening both verse and prose, he deleted the "martial propensities" and abandoned the intensive "assiduous"—WPW, III, 463. If he wrote in 1816 the sonnet beginning "Emperors and Kings, how oft have temples rung / With impious thanksgiving," which urges the monarchic powers to "Be just, be grateful" (WPW, III, 151), he withheld this emollient from the public until 1827.

39. Quoted in Moorman, *Later Years,* p. 288.

40. *Poems on Occasional Subjects,* 4th ed. (Bristol, 1795), pp. 74–75. On Shelley's "progress piece" and *Peter Bell the Third,* see Chapter VI below.

41. Moorman, *Later Years,* p. 292.

42. See J. P. Pritchard, "On the Making of Wordsworth's 'Dion,'" *Studies in Philology,* 49 (1952), 66–74; Z. S. Fink, "'Dion' and Wordsworth's Political Thought," *SP,* 50 (1953), 510–514; Jane Worthington, *Wordsworth's Reading of Roman Prose* (Yale University Press, 1946), p. 17 (and cf. pp. 27–29).

43. G. T. Garratt, *Lord Brougham* (London, 1935), pp. 109–110.

44. Richard S. Ferguson, *Cumberland and Westmorland M.P's from the Restoration to the Reform Bill of 1867* (London and Carlisle, 1871), p. 228.

45. See Garratt, *Lord Brougham,* p. 125; Moorman, *Later Years,* pp. 340, 344–363 (and the works by J. E. Wells, W. W. Douglas, and John E. Jordan therein cited). In a typical reaction from the world of letters, B. W. Procter wrote to Leigh Hunt on 27 July 1826 that he had turned in his reading from law to poetry: "it sounds sweetly & pleasantly—like the nightingale to the Arabian bands—(although I do not choose to quote Mr. Wordsworth, who has been Lowthering again at the Westmorland Election)"—British Museum MS. Add. 38109, fol. 34.

46. 5 February 1833, in *The Correspondence of Henry Crabb Robinson with the Wordsworth Circle,* ed. Edith C. Morley, 2 vols. (Oxford: Clarendon, 1927), I, 233, where the spelling is "Tyrranies."

47. *The Faerie Queene* V.ii.36; WPW, IV, 129. In a parallel to processes of Wordsworth's thought, Lafayette, in the successful effort to secure Napoleon's abdication in June 1815, called upon the Chamber of Deputies to rally the French nation around the tricolor standard of 1789, "sacré de la liberté, de l'égalité et de l'ordre public." As Lafayette and Wordsworth remembered it in old age, the true meaning of fraternity had always been public order. See Etienne Charavay, *Le Général La Fayette 1757–1834: notice biographique* (Paris, 1898), p. 403n.

48. Perkins, *Wordsworth and the Poetry of Sincerity* (Harvard University Press, 1964), p. 252.

V. BYRON

1. *The Works of Lord Byron: Poetry,* ed. E. H. Coleridge, 7 vols. (London: Murray, 1898–1905, variously reprinted with corrections to 1924), I, 14. This work, the source of quotations from Byron's poetry except where noted, is hereinafter abbreviated BWP.

For biographic facts, except as indicated, I have relied on Leslie A. Marchand, *Byron: A Biography,* 3 vols. (New York: Knopf, 1957).

2. In the version of "Childish Recollections" in *Poems on Various Occasions* (BWP, I, 84 *app. crit.*).

3. For the heroes, see *The Works of Lord Byron: Letters and Journals,* ed. R. E. Prothero, 6 vols. (London: Murray, 1898–1901), II, 340. Hereinafter abbreviated LJ.

For the adage, see BWP, IV, 441 (*Marino Faliero* V.i.289), VI, 173 (*Don Juan* III.88:1); LJ, II, 319–320, III, 89. Cf. *Childe Harold* III.st.114. Byron attributes the adage to Mirabeau.

Byron in most moods would have agreed with Shakespeare's Henry VIII that "words are no deeds," but Robert Escarpit's view (*Lord Byron,* Paris: Le Cercle du Livre, 1955–1957, II, 244–245) that Byron never attempted to create a lasting work of art seems to assume the existence of an aesthetic purity that Byron could not find in the masterpieces of the past. The recent concordance, compiled by Ione Young, shows that he was sufficiently interested in the power of the word to use *word* in his poetry two hundred times and with its various inflections about four hundred and fifty times. Hugo, a purer but equally political poet, said not only that *"le mot, qu'on le sache, est un être vivant,"* but also that *"le mot, c'est le Verbe, et le Verbe c'est Dieu"* (Tristesse d'Olympio VIII.1; Les Contemplations. Réponse à un acte d'accusation VIII). Hugo had even more panache than Byron, but both believed in the word.

4. *Lord Byron's Correspondence* . . . , ed. John Murray, 2 vols. (London: Murray, 1922), II, 143, 148.

5. Walter Graham, "The Politics of the Greater Romantic Poets," *PMLA,* 36 (1921), 60–78. Previous to Graham, the force of Byron's political influence had been variously recognized by Edward Dowden, "The French Revolution and Literature," *Studies in Literature 1789–1877* (London, 1897); Albert Elmer Hancock, *The French Revolution and the English Poets: A Study in Historical Criticism* (New York, 1899); Georg Brandes, *Naturalism in Nineteenth Century English Literature,* vol. IV of *Main Currents in Nineteenth Century Literature,* trans. D. White and M. Morison, 6 vols. (London, 1906). For the standard account of Byron's political activities in England, see Dora N Raymond, *The Political Career of Lord Byron* (New York, 1924). Modern studies cannot easily convey the excitement of such contemporaries of Byron as the anonymous biographer of Lord Eldon, who refers typically to "the discussion on the Frame-work Knitters Bill, on the 27th of February 1812, ever memorable for having been the theme of an ardent burst of eloquence from Lord Byron"—*The Life, Political and Official, of John, Earl of Eldon, Late Lord Chancellor of Great Britain, &c. &c.* (London: Hunt and Clarke, 1827), p. 64.

6. So at least E. H. Coleridge (BWP, I, 356n) interpreted *English Bards,* lines 741–748. But Byron may be attacking the whole flock of warring poetasters, whatever side paid them. The passage can be so interpreted merely by taking line 745, "On 'All the Talents' vent your venal spleen," as referring to *All the Talents: A Satirical Poem,* by Polypus (E. S. Barrett), rather than to *All the Blocks, or An Antidote to "All the Talents,"* by Flagellum (W. H. Ireland). Gifford then becomes the true poet, not merely the anti-Jacobin, opposed to those who "daily scribble." An ambiguous line, "Let Monodies on Fox regale your crew," can be taken as directed against parodists rather than against monodists. Nothing in this passage, however, could have fostered an invitation to Melbourne or Holland House.

7. R. C. Dallas, *Recollections of the Life of Lord Byron* (London, 1824), p. 54. The wording is Dallas', but Byron had written in the same spirit to his solicitor, John Hanson. See LJ, I, 209–210.

8. Canto I, completed in 1811, was first published in March 1812 with Canto II, which received ten additional stanzas in 1814. Canto III, begun

in May 1816 soon after Byron's return to the Continent, appeared with Canto IV in April 1818. Robert F. Gleckner, in *Byron and the Ruins of Paradise* (Johns Hopkins Press, 1967), distinguishes the voice of the rational, libertarian, Hobhouse-like narrator, especially evident in Canto I, from the voice of the poet, who envisions "lost, fallen man in a lost, fallen world" (p. 229).

9. John Henry Newman, "Poetry, with Reference to Aristotle's Poetics," *Essays and Sketches,* ed. Charles F. Harrold, 3 vols. (New York: Longmans, 1948), I, 71.

10. BWP, II, 191, 192.

11. See E. R. Vincent, *Byron, Hobhouse, and Foscolo: New Documents in the History of a Collaboration* (Cambridge University Press, 1949), passim, on Foscolo's role.

12. *C.H.* III.36–49; IV.5–7, 20, 49, 93, 121–127.

13. See the point well made in Peter L. Thorslev, Jr., *The Byronic Hero: Types and Prototypes* (University of Minnesota Press [1962]), p. 156.

14. On Lady Oxford and other associates of this period, see David V. Erdman, "Lord Byron and the Genteel Reformers," *PMLA*, 56 (1941), 1065–1094; "Lord Byron as Rinaldo," *PMLA*, 57 (1942), 189–231.

15. *Letters of the Princess Charlotte,* ed. A. Aspinall (London: Home & Van Thal, 1949), p. 88. See also pp. 35, 50, 108, 134, 240, 241.

16. See Joseph Slater, "Byron's Hebrew Melodies," *Studies in Philology*, 49 (1952), 75–94. Poems on the Israelite bondage had been common enough. A series appeared in the *Morning Post* in 1798, e.g. "The Passage of the Red Sea," 8 October. To say that the Israelites in the "Hebrew Melodies" are an analogue for the Irish, Polish, Italian, Greek, and other peoples undergoing national travail in Byron's day is not to say that his Israelites do not represent, in a different perspective, all mankind suffering from a loss of Eden, as argued in Leslie A. Marchand, *Byron's Poetry: A Critical Introduction* (Boston: Houghton Mifflin, 1965), p. 134, and Gleckner, *Byron and the Ruins of Paradise,* pp. 204–213.

17. See Wilfred S. Dowden, "Byron and the Austrian Censorship," *Keats-Shelley Journal,* 4 (1955), 67–75. For the best study of the relationships between Byron's attitudes toward Dante and Tasso and his political activities in Italy, see Giovanna Foà, *Lord Byron, poeta e carbonaro: studio critico-storico* (Florence: La Nuova Italia, 1935), which can be supplemented with additional facts made available in Iris Origo, *The Last Attachment* (New York: Scribner's, 1949).

18. Byron's note to "The Waltz," line 21 (BWP, I, 484): "'Saviour of the world,' quotha!—it were to be wished that he, or any one else, could save a corner of it—his country. . . . I suppose next year he will be entitled the 'Virgin Mary;' if so, Lord George Gordon himself would have nothing to object to such liberal bastards of our Lady of Babylon."

19. BWP, III, 434. Several critics have followed E. H. Coleridge (IV, 110 n.3) in taking these poems and the lyric on "The Captive Usurper" at *Manfred* II.ii.16 as predictions of Napoleon's escape to fight still again, but the Voice on the Jungfrau belongs to a past for which Napoleon's first escape is a prediction, similar to the dire prediction in *Marino Faliero*

Notes to Pages 187–196

(V.iii.49) that a "bastard Attila" will ruin Venice. Byron was not beyond threatening his countrymen with the Bogeyman, nor was he incapable of hoping that his "pagod" would rise, but I think that he relies in these passages on the spirit of liberty rather than on Napoleon the individual. Of course his Tory foes found him sincere in his heinous jacobinism and false in the appeal to "equal laws"; see the *Champion,* 14 April 1816, pp. 113–114.

20. Fairholt collection of pamphlets on the Queen's trial, British Museum 1852.b.9.

21. V.i.146–149; BWP, V, 187. The Austrian anarch, officially Francis I, always connotes Metternich as well. The idea of a despot who creates such social chaos that he is less a "monarch" than an "anarch" has seemed distinctively Shelleyan, but it is first anticipated in Byron's "Epistle to a Friend" of 11 October 1811, wherein he threatens to become

> One, who in stern Ambition's pride,
> Perchance not blood shall turn aside;
> One ranked in some recording page
> With the worst anarchs of the age . . .
>
> (BWP, III, 30)

The idea is full-blown in Byron's "Imperial Anarchs" of *Childe Harold* II.45:8.

22. Byron in Venice had differed from Sardanapalus by tempering his dissipations with hard writing, but the question is not what he did, but how he regarded his conduct. Effete Sardanapalus has kinsmen in the patrician Leoni of *Marino Faliero,* who eulogizes the soft life (IV.i.1–112), and Leoni's protégé Bertram, who opposes brawling and ungrateful rebellion (III.ii.74; IV.i.160ff.). Jacopo Faliero's gentleness is not made blameworthy, but his lines on the pleasures of swimming are similar in dramatic purpose, position, and tone to Sardanapalus' lines on the beauty of stars (II.i.252–269). Byron's uneasiness over sensitivity and lassitude continues in his portrait of the defiant Christian, in *The Island.*

23. *Marino Faliero* IV.ii.138, 241; V.i.430; *The Two Foscari* III.i.10–14.

24. "The Irish Avatar," BWP, IV, 557, st. 8. So steadily were Byron and the Hunts striking at Castlereagh and the King that publication of "The Irish Avatar" in the *Examiner*—partially on 21 April 1822, pp. 252–253, and in full, except for a few blanks (teased into clear identifications by footnotes) on 28 July 1822, pp. 473–474—went unnoticed by Byron's editors and collectors for eighty years. Although there are a few exceptions to the rule that every unique item in T. J. Wise's Ashley collection is a fake, the copy of "The Irish Avatar" reportedly printed by Moore in Paris on 19 September 1821 and acquired by H. Buxton Forman from "one Noble (*lucus a non lucendo,* for he was a grubby fellow)," now Ashley 2696 in the British Museum, is decidedly not an exception. See Forman's fumbling article, "Some Byron Crumbs: 'The Irish Avatar' Again," *Athenaeum,* 26 June 1909, pp. 756–757.

25. The epithets echo King Lear's self-description, "A poor, infirm, weak, and despis'd old man," by way of the opening of Shelley's "Sonnet: England in 1819": "An old, mad, blind, despised, and dying king."

26. The fine was one element in a morass of bad feeling between Byron

and the Hunts. For a review of the facts, see William H. Marshall, *Byron, Shelley, Hunt and "The Liberal"* (University of Pennsylvania Press [1960]).

27. "The Two Eternities: An Essay on Byron," in *The Burning Oracle* (Oxford University Press, 1939), reprinted in anthologies of criticism, and by G. Wilson Knight himself as "Byron: the Poetry," *Poets of Action* (London: Methuen, 1967), pp. 179–265.

28. So completely has *Don Juan* become to us Byron's one great "modern" poem that Andred Rutherford, in his finely balanced *Byron: A Critical Study* (Edinburgh, 1961), perversely misinterprets Byron's own judgments of the poem and sanctifies our own. Of many recent studies, my discussion has drawn particularly on Elizabeth French Boyd, *Byron's Don Juan: A Critical Study* (Rutgers University Press, 1945); Truman Guy Steffan, *The Making of a Masterpiece,* vol. I in *Byron's Don Juan,* ed. T. G. Steffan and W. W. Pratt, 4 vols. (University of Texas Press, 1957); George M. Ridenour, *The Style of Don Juan* (Yale University Press, 1960); E. E. Bostetter, *The Romantic Ventriloquists* (University of Washington Press, 1963); Brian Wilkie, *Romantic Poets and Epic Tradition* (University of Wisconsin Press, 1965); Leslie A. Marchand, *Byron's Poetry: A Critical Introduction* (Boston: Houghton Mifflin, 1965); Alvin B. Kernan, *The Plot of Satire* (Yale University Press, 1965). Although it appeared too late to influence the present chapter, the most balanced study so far is provided by M. K. Joseph, *Byron the Poet* (London: Gollancz, 1966).

29. *Byron's Don Juan,* ed. Steffan and Pratt, II, 150–155, 162 (version of *D.J.* II.10:8, censored by Murray). This edition is followed for all quotations from *Don Juan,* except as noted. The roman numeral refers to the canto; the numeral after a period, to the stanza; a numeral after a colon, to the line in the stanza.

30. See Karl Kroeber, *Romantic Narrative Art* (University of Wisconsin Press, 1960), pp. 148–167.

31. *The Letters of Percy Bysshe Shelley,* ed. Frederick L. Jones, 2 vols. (Oxford: Clarendon, 1964), II, 193. Hereafter designated as SL.

32. I am grateful to Mr. Eugene P. Sheehy of the Columbia University libraries for acquiring, from the Biblioteca Estense di Modena, microfilm of *Galignani's Messenger* for July–November 1821 and 5–8 April 1822.

33. *The Letters of Thomas Moore,* ed. Wilfred S. Dowden, 2 vols. (Oxford: Clarendon, 1964), II, 511.

34. *Don Juan* VIII.61–67. On John Kyrle, the Man of Ross, the civilized English exemplar of philanthropic rusticity, see Alexander Pope, *Moral Essays* III.249–298, and Coleridge's lines beginning "Richer than Miser o'er his countless hoards" (CPW, 57–58).

35. *Gentleman's Magazine,* August 1822, pp. 105–106. See also July, pp. 70–71; London *Times,* 9 July 1822, p. 3; *Examiner,* 14 July 1822, p. 443 (quoting the *Times*); 21 July 1822, p. 459 (quoting the *Traveller*).

36. Explanation of "the revolutionary stork" may begin with a letter written by Shelley to Peacock from Rome, 6 April 1819: "The Emperor of Austria is here, & Maria Louisa is coming. On the journey thro the other cities of Italy she was greeted with loud acclamations, & vivas of Napoleon. Idiots & slaves! like the frogs in the fable because they are discontented with the log they call upon the Stork who devours them" (SL, II, 93). To this

fable can be referred the allusions to King Log and King Stork in political poems of the Commonwealth and Restoration—see *Poems on Affairs of State: Augustan Satirical Verse*, vol. II (1678–1681), ed. Elias F. Mengel, Jr. (Yale University Press, 1965), 342–343, 485n. In William Collins' "Ode to Liberty," however, the stork of line 57 is sacred to the liberties of Holland, as explained by Collins himself. Just as an angel announced to Mary the coming of Christ, so the stork, as harbinger of the spring, announces new birth. Medieval bestiaries declared the stork capable of migrating across the ocean; this ability has an obvious value for new birth in international politics. Thomas Day's "Stanzas written on the Failure of the Application for an Equal Representation in Parliament," published in the *Cambridge Intelligencer* of 7 September 1793 as "The Disgusted Patriot," applies the converse of the emblem of revolutionary hope:

> When faithless Senates venally betray,
>
> . . . .
>
> In vain the task to rouse my country's ire,
> And imp once more the stork's dejected wings . . .

Byron combines the revolutionary emblem with a joke on the ambitious logs of the Holy Alliance.

37. This passage is one of two in *The Age of Bronze* praised by an otherwise chilly reviewer in Thomas Wooler's radical *Black Dwarf* for 2 April 1823 (10:465–470). Besides quoting the passage at length, the reviewer repeated three times in his own text the phrase "rent—rent—rent."

38. The reviewer in the *Monthly Review*, n.s. 101 (July 1823), 316–319, boasted that he had examined and reviewed not only both of Byron's sources and further sources modifying Byron's partial information, but also a poem by Mary Russell Mitford based on later information than Byron's. The reviewer of Miss Mitford's *Christina, the Maid of the South Seas*, in the *Monthly*, n.s. 65 (June 1811), 249–256, had then thought that Christian "committed suicide in a fit of remorse for his ingratitude to Captain Bligh." The important point is of course not that E. H. Coleridge was wrong in saying that Byron's reviewers had not heard of Miss Mitford's poem, but that Byron knew neither of Christian and his comrades' settlement on Pitcairn Island nor of the transformation then commencing in Bligh's reputation.

VI. SHELLEY

1. Peter Gay, *The Enlightenment: An Interpretation*, vol. I: *The Rise of Modern Paganism* (New York: Knopf, 1966), p. 3.

2. *The Letters of Percy Bysshe Shelley*, ed. Frederick L. Jones (2 vols., Oxford: Clarendon, 1964), I, 202. Cf. 175, 184. This edition is hereinafter designated SL. All other prose, designated SW, is quoted from *The Complete Works of Percy Bysshe Shelley*, ed. Roger Ingpen and Walter E. Peck (London: Benn, 1926–1930), vols. V–VII.

3. William Godwin, *The Enquirer: Reflections on Education, Manners, and Literature, in a Series of Essays* (London, 1797), pp. x, 173–175, 214.

Notes to Pages 234–239

Shelley, who ordered a copy of *The Enquirer* from Wales at Christmas, 1812, had recommended it to Elizabeth Hitchener in 1811 as "very good," the first of Godwin's works to be read in the pursuit of "truth, that introducer of Virtue to Usefulness" (SL, I, 195, 345).

4. *The Complete Poetical Works of Percy Bysshe Shelley,* ed. Thomas Hutchinson (Oxford University Press, 1952), p. 849:16. Unless otherwise indicated, all quotations from Shelley's poetry come from this edition, hereafter designated as SP, followed by page number and, after a colon, line number.

5. F. W. Bateson, *English Poetry: A Critical Introduction* (London: Longmans, 1950), p. 217; 2nd ed. (1966), pp. 151–152.

6. *Criticisms on the Rolliad.* Part the Second (London, 1970), p. 113; *The Rolliad,* 22nd ed. (London, 1812), p. 212. On Margaret Nicholson (but not in connection with *The Rolliad*) see *DNB* and *Shelley and His Circle 1773–1822,* ed. Kenneth Neill Cameron (Harvard University Press, 1961), I, 34–38, 88–89. This work is designated below as *Shelley Circle.*

7. T. J. Hogg, who in later years was as inaccurate as he dared be about his associations with the wild Shelleys, said of the "puling trash" of this first poem: "The MS. had been confided to Shelley by some rhymester of the day, and it was put forth in this shape to astonish a weak mind; but principally to captivate the admirers of philosophic poetry by the manifest incongruity of disallowing all war, even the most just, and then turning sharp round and recommending the dagger of the assassin as the best cure for all evils, and the sure passport to a lady's favour." *The Life of Shelley,* in *The Life of Percy Bysshe Shelley,* ed. Humbert Wolfe (London: Dent, 1933), I, 161–162. As even Hogg was capable of the truth, Shelley may conceivably have begun with the MS of "some rhymester"; but Hogg's disclaimers of political malice in the publication must be disallowed.

8. *The Esdaile Notebook: A Volume of Early Poems by Percy Bysshe Shelley,* ed. Kenneth Neill Cameron (New York: Knopf, 1964), pp. 41:11, 42–45, 40:10, 44:1–2. This edition, designated EN and used for quotations, has been collated with *The Esdaile Poems: Early Minor Poems from the 'Esdaile Notebook,'* ed. Neville Rogers (Oxford: Clarendon, 1966).

9. SP, 881–882; EN, pp. 161–162, 284–287.

10. Rogers, *Esdaile Poems,* p. 12, acknowledges the difficulty by dating the poem "?1805–10," but the oddity remains even if we assume the origin of the stanzas to be a task assigned at Eton.

11. Cameron (EN, 264–266) prefers the expedition of 1807, but several details suggest the earlier battle. The "hostile flags on Egypt's strand unfurled" (138:174), the "hostile myriads" clashing, would be appropriate to the French and British in 1801, but hardly to the lesser numbers in 1807. As the Turks had ruled in Egypt since 1517, the "Genius of the south" could not have been surprised to find their flag there in 1807, when both the Mamelukes and the "nationalist" Mehemet Ali (by birth Albanian) fought with the Turks against the British. The "victor's steel-clad brow," "flushed by conquest's crimson glow," scarcely suggests, despite a "secret dread," the defeat by Mehemet Ali at Rosetta (143:307–309). The attack on slavery (138:169) would have lost much of its force after the abolition of the slave trade

Notes to Pages 239–243

in 1807. There is still stronger evidence. Although the expedition of 1807 aimed to stop the influence of the French Ambassador Sébastiani in the Porte, Shelley's sarcastic paraphrase of popular attitudes toward Napoleon has a much more direct point with reference to the battle of 1801:

> Say, is not he the Tyrant of the World
> And are not we the injured and the brave?
> Unmoved shall we behold his flag unfurled,
> Flouting with impious Wing Religion's grave,
> Triumphant gleaming o'er the passive wave . . .?
> (EN, 134:72–76)

Cameron takes the Turks as more "impious" than the French; Shelley might have taken them so, too: the whole point is that the Anglican charge of impiety against the Revolutionists and their successor Bonaparte is a dastardly abuse of Virtue (143:295) for the promotion of war. "Religion," says Henry, "sanctifies the cause" (134:67). Wherever there is vengeance, the Esdaile poems answer again and again, religion usually is the cause.

Professor Cameron gives an excellent account of the passage in which Nature pierces Henry with a pang of sorrow, but surely it is a mistake to take Louisa's acquiescence after protest ("Go . . mingle in thy country's battle tide . . .") as evidence that she, too, is "obsessed by chauvinistic concepts" (EN, 262). She is defeated by the chauvinism of others, by her lover's thirst for glory, and by her love.

The sentiments are those of Shelley from 1809 on, but the poem is either a borrowing or a historical re-creation, or both.

12. On the fragment and its authorship, see EN, pp. 127, 255–256; Rogers, *Esdaile Poems,* pp. xxiii and note, 114–115; *Shelley Circle,* II, 700–705; SL, I, 41–43; and note 16 below.

13. Geoffrey Carnall, *Robert Southey and His Age: The Development of a Conservative Mind* (Oxford: Clarendon, 1960), pp. 82, 94; *New Letters of Robert Southey,* ed. Kenneth Curry, 2 vols. (Columbia University Press, 1965), I, 458, 462.

14. SP, 864:52. Shelley probably found Ravaillac's story in the Abbé Augustin Barruel's *Mémoires pour servir à l'histoire du Jacobinisme,* of which Shelley owned the translation by R. Clifford, *Memoirs Illustrating the History of Jacobinism,* 4 vols. (London, 1797–1798). Barruel's work, designed as a Christian and monarchist exposure of Voltaire, the Encyclopedists, Freemasons, the Illuminati, Condorcet, and others in the "Club d'Holbach," ironically provided Shelley, through its copious quotations, an arsenal of objections to monarchy and priestcraft. See SL, I, 264, II, 469, and Walter Peck, "Shelley and the Abbé Barruel," *PMLA,* 36 (1921), 347–353.

15. EN, 120. In Rogers, *Esdaile Poems,* p. 72, the last line reads: "Where the rank serpent Interest feeds!"

16. EN, 128; SP, 869–870; SL, I, 38–39; *Shelley Circle,* II, 687–694. The three stanzas in the Esdaile book are dated 1809, but it is to be noted that they follow immediately the stanzas said to be "suggested by the cowardly and infamous bombardment of Copenhagen"; that both sets are in a tetrameter version of rhyme royal, with feminine endings; that versions of the two sets

were sent to Hogg within one week; that the order and content of the stanzas sent to Hogg concern British crimes throughout the world, not just in Denmark; that Shelley told Hogg in both letters that the quoted stanzas were by Elizabeth; and that his remarks may be taken in combination to mean (1) he has submitted a long poem to the Oxford bookseller John Munday for publication, (2) "there is some of Eliza's in it," (3) "I have something to add to it," and (4) "These are Eliza's." (See SL, I, 42–43.) Roger Ingpen and F. L. Jones, as well as Cameron (*The Young Shelley* [see note 17 below], p. 50), identify the planned poem with a lost work, *A Poetical Essay on the Existing State of Things*, advertised to be sold in aid of Peter Finnerty, imprisoned for protesting the disaster of the Walcheren expedition. Although all editors have agreed to suspect Shelley of deceiving Hogg by attributing some of the stanzas to Elizabeth, none has suggested that the quoted stanzas themselves belong to the long poem intended for publication. It seems at least possible that the stanzas so belong.

17. See Kenneth Neill Cameron, *The Young Shelley: Genesis of a Radical* (New York: Macmillan, 1950), pp. 36–51, 85–88, 109 111; Roger Ingpen, *Shelley in England* (London, 1917), pp. 11, 257–259, 344–349, 360–366, 403–405. For brevity, see Newman Ivey White, *Portrait of Shelley* (New York: Knopf, 1945), pp. 4, 31, 58; Edmund Blunden, *Shelley: A Life Story* (New York: Viking, 1947), pp. 26, 65. The standard life is N. I. White, *Shelley* (corr. ed., 2 vols., London: Secker and Warburg, 1947).

For a general survey of Shelley's political thought, with emphasis on episodes, ideals, lessons, and rituals from the French Revolution, see Gerald McNiece, *Shelley and the Revolutionary Idea* (Harvard University Press, 1969).

18. *Hours in a Library* (London, 1892), II, 77–78.

19. See Cameron, *Young Shelley*, pp. 187–191; H. M. Dowling, *Notes and Queries*, 199 (1954), 306 309, 391–395, 532–535; 200 (1955), 119–123, 540–542; and a modified summary by Dowling in *Keats-Shelley Memorial Bulletin*, 12 (1961), 28–36; Elisabeth Beazley, *Madocks and the Wonder of Wales* (London: Faber, 1967), pp. 190 197, 259–262.

20. See A. M. D. Hughes, *The Nascent Mind of Shelley* (Oxford: Clarendon, 1947), p. 156.

21. Cf. John Plamenatz, *Man and Society* (New York: McGraw-Hill, 1963), II, 426.

22. SP, 808. See the discussion in Earl R. Wasserman, *Shelley's "Prometheus Unbound": A Critical Reading* (Johns Hopkins Press, 1965), pp. 41–47.

23. On the vitalism, see the discussion of *Queen Mab* IV.139–152 in H. W. Piper, *The Active Universe: Pantheism and the Concept of Imagination in the English Romantic Poets* (London: Athlone, 1962), pp. 165–170.

24. The indebtedness to Byron's "Imprecation" was noted by C. D. Locock, ed., *The Poems of Percy Bysshe Shelley*, 2 vols. (London [1911]), II, 494. This is the curse in 'Manfred,'" I.i.192–261, praised by Shelley in a letter to Byron, 17 April 1821 (SL, II, 283).

25. See Southey, *New Letters*, II, 150n, 333; Jack Simmons, *Southey* (London: Collins, 1945), pp. 158–162. In fact, Eldon applied his principle

of intent to corrupt without respect of party. An anonymous biographer wrote in 1827: "Thus has Lord Eldon, by a most unconstitutional and mischievous stretch of the power of the court, decided a question, which, to say the least of it, was very doubtful, and which, from its great importance, should have been determined only after solemn argument, and that too by the *regular* tribunal, namely, that the statute of the 8th of Anne, the great charter of literary rights, does not extend its protection to works of an immoral tendency." *The Life, Political and Official, of John, Earl of Eldon, Late Chancellor of Great Britain, &c. &c.* (London: Hunt and Clarke, 1827), p. 77.

26. *The Revolt of Islam,* 466–468, 784–792, 1540–1548, 1686–1690. See especially G. M. Matthews, "A Volcano's Voice in Shelley," *ELH,* 24 (1957), 191–228.

27. This sequence of thought is proposed by Rogers, *Shelley at Work,* p. 33. Although finding Platonism more often than it is present and ignoring Holbach, who is central, Rogers notes the possible importance of Lucretius as gadfly to Shelley's thought. See also Ross Greig Woodman, *The Apocalyptic Vision in the Poetry of Shelley* (University of Toronto Press, 1964), pp. 88–89.

28. Reluctantly I omit peripheral poems: *Rosalind and Helen* is a brief, oddly naturalistic, and confessional appendage of *The Revolt of Islam. Julian and Maddalo,* despite its apparent evocations of Tasso as a martyred hero of liberty and its explorations beyond the portrait of Byron into the psychology of an aristocratic liberal, is equally confessional.

29. See David V. Erdman, *Blake: Prophet against Empire* (Princeton University Press, 1954), pp. 197–206; M. Dorothy George, *English Political Caricature to 1792* (Oxford: Clarendon, 1959), p. 217, Pl. 91; Draper Hill, *Mr. Gillray, the Carciaturist: A Biography* (London: Phiadon, 1965), p. 45, Pl. 44. The caricaturists aided such passages as Shelley's on Sin and Death in Padua by intensifying the association of Milton and politics in the public mind. See the illustration on page 260 of the present work, with the description on page xvi.

30. See the illustrated argument of Johnstone Parr, "Shelley's *Ozymandias,*" *Keats-Shelley Journal,* 6 (1957), 31–35; cf. H. M. Richmond, "*Ozymandias* and the Travelers," ibid. 11 (1962), 65–71.

For Shelley's Ozymandias as "a Godwinian monarch, corrupted by the effects of 'an evil education,'" see Burton R. Pollin, "Godwin's *Mandeville* in Poems of Shelley," *Keats-Shelley Memorial Bulletin,* no. 19 (1968), pp. 37–39.

31. Surviving records suggest that *Queen Mab* was more widely distributed than the poems for plain men; see Newman Ivey White, *The Unextinguished Hearth: Shelley and His Contemporary Critics* (Duke University Press, 1938), pp. 20, 52, 95–98; White, *Shelley,* II, 304, 404–410, *Portrait of Shelley,* pp. 472–474, 477–478; Sylva Norman, *Flight of the Skylark: The Development of Shelley's Reputation* (London: Reinhardt, 1954), pp. 149–153, 167; H. Buxton Forman, "The Vicissitudes of Shelley's *Queen Mab;* A Chapter in the History of Reform," printed for private circulation in 1887 and in *The Shelley Society's Publications,* 1st Series, No. 1 (1888), pp. 19–35; Crane Brinton, *Political Ideas of the English Romanticists,* p. 187.

Notes to Pages 264–272

Richard Carlile and William Clarke (of 201 Strand) were among the early pirates. Officially Shelley tried to stop publication and disclaimed respect for the early poem, but he certainly did not turn against Carlile, he coveted a copy of Clarke's edition, and he wrote to John Gisborne: "For the sake of a dignified appearance however, & really because I wish to protest against all the bad poetry in it, I have given orders to say that it is all done against my desire. and have directed an attorney to apply to Chancery for an injunction, which he will not get." SL, II, 301.

Counteraction is epitomized in the banner, "Queen Mab or Killing no Murder," held by the army of the Devil in I. R. Cruikshank's caricature of 1821, *The Revolutionary Association,* No. 14194 in M. Dorothy George, *Catalogue of Political and Personal Satires . . . in the British Museum, X* (London: British Museum, 1952), 225–227.

On the audience for the poems for plain men, see R. K. Webb, *The British Working Class Reader, 1790–1848: Literacy and Social Tension* (London: Allen and Unwin, 1955).

To illustrate Shelley's continuing influence, we can take a sample that has the statistical virtue of being random, for an anthology of Chartist literature published in Moscow in 1956, *Antologiya Chartistskoi Literatur'i,* ed. Yu. V. Kovalev, shows a near-worship of Shelley's name. The verse, which sometimes echoes Moore and Byron, often strikes a note from Shelley, as in W. S. V. Sankey's "Men of England, ye are slaves" and "Working men of every clime"; Ernest Jones's "Who bids us backward—laggards, stay!" (including the line "While you were many, we were few"); and probably W. J. Linton's "The Gathering of the People: A Storm-Song," beginning "Gather ye silently, / Even as the snow / Heapeth the avalanche: / Gather ye so!" (pp. 76, 77, 150, 188). With Linton's poem, cf. *Prometheus Unbound* II.iii.36–42.

Kovalev's introduction is translated as "The Literature of Chartism," *Victorian Studies,* 2 (1958), 117–138.

32. SW, V, 272. Richard Carlile reprinted the "Declaration of Rights" in the *Republican* for 24 September 1819 (pp. 75–78).

33. See E. P. Thompson, *The Making of the English Working Class* (New York: Pantheon, 1964), pp. 160, 624.

34. Thompson, pp. 485–494, 650–669; Elie Halévy, The *Liberal Awakening 1815–1830* (vol. II of *A History of the English People in the Nineteenth Century,* rev. ed., London: Benn, 1949), pp. 28–29 (based on J. L. and Barbara Hammond, *The Skilled Labourer,* London, 1919, ch. XII). I find half my points about "England in 1819" also made by G. M. Matthews, ed., *Shelley: Selected Poems and Prose* (Oxford University Press, 1964), p. 201. Matthews shows by reference to *An Address to the People on the Death of Princess Charlotte,* 1817, that the "glorious Phantom" of line 13 is "the Spirit of Liberty."

35. E.g., Kenneth Hopkins, *Portraits in Satire* (London, 1958), pp. 272–273.

36. See N. I. White, "Shelley's Swell-Foot the Tyrant in Relation to Contemporary Political Satires," *PMLA,* 36 (1921), 332–346; *Examiner,* 20 Aug. 1820, p. 540, on "the Rat," or "Mouse Powell"; and, as always for historical detail, M. Dorothy George's catalogue of satires (see notes 29 and 31 above).

37. E.g., W. J. Fox, *The Duties of Christians toward Deists: A Sermon*

353

Notes to Pages 272–277

. . . *Sunday, October 24, 1819, on Occasion of the Recent Prosecution of Mr. Carlile, for the Re-publication of Paine's Age of Reason* (London, 1819), p. vii: "To try by a Jury, to hang a felon, are parts of the Common Law, which we derive from the customs of our Gothic ancestors." For the relation to "Whig aesthetics," see Samuel Kliger, *The Goths in England* (Harvard University Press, 1952).

38. In the spirit of *Swellfoot,* "Ch. FitzPaine" treated the royal command that bishops attend "the trial, as it is called, of the Queen" under the ironic title "Plot to Degrade the Bench of Bishops," *Examiner,* 1 Oct. 1820, pp. 626–627.

39. On the type, which includes Byron's "Prophecy of Dante," see R. H. Griffith, "The Progress Pieces of the Eighteenth Century," *Texas Review,* 5 (1920), 218–233; R. A. Aubin, "A Note on the Eighteenth-Century Progress Pieces," *Modern Language Notes,* 49 (1934), 405–407.

40. Milton Wilson, *Shelley's Later Poetry: A Study of His Prophetic Imagination* (Columbia University Press, 1959), pp. 196–203. For detailed notes on the poem, see Shelley, *Poems Published in 1820,* ed. A. M. D. Hughes, 2nd ed. (Oxford: Clarendon, 1957), pp. 224–229.

41. For a compact summary of the idealized history in the "Ode to Liberty," including identification of the medieval communes that made possible the greatness of Italian art, see Donald H. Reiman, *Percy Bysshe Shelley* (New York: Twayne, 1969), p. 99.

42. Since the passage is little known, and since it provides an essential and thorough gloss to "Ode to the West Wind," I give Cythna's words from *The Revolt of Islam,* Canto IX:

xxi

'The blasts of Autumn drive the wingèd seeds
Over the earth,—next come the snows, and rain,
And frosts, and storms, which dreary Winter leads
Out of his Scythian cave, a savage train;
Behold! Spring sweeps over the world again,
Shedding soft dews from her ethereal wings;
Flowers on the mountains, fruits over the plain,
And music on the waves and woods she flings,
And love on all that lives, and calm on lifeless things.

xxii

'O Spring, of hope, and love, and youth, and gladness
Wind-wingèd emblem! brightest, best and fairest!
Whence comest thou, when, with dark Winter's sadness
The tears that fade in sunny smiles thou sharest?
Sister of joy, thou art the child who wearest
Thy mother's dying smile, tender and sweet;
Thy mother Autumn, for whose grave thou bearest
Fresh flowers, and beams like flowers, with gentle feet,
Disturbing not the leaves which are her winding-sheet.

354

xxiii

'Virtue, and Hope, and Love, like light and Heaven,
Surround the world.—We are their chosen slaves.
Has not the whirlwind of our spirit driven
Truth's deathless germs to thought's remotest caves?
Lo, Winter comes!—the grief of many graves,
The frost of death, the tempest of the sword,
The flood of tyranny, whose sanguine waves
Stagnate like ice at Faith the enchanter's word,
And bind all human hearts in its repose abhorred.

xxiv

'The seeds are sleeping in the soil: meanwhile
The Tyrant peoples dungeons with his prey,
Pale victims on the guarded scaffold smile
Because they cannot speak; and, day by day,
The moon of wasting Science wanes away
Among her stars, and in that darkness vast
The sons of earth to their foul idols pray,
And gray Priests triumph, and like blight or blast
A shade of selfish care o'er human looks is cast.

xxv

'This is the winter of the world;—and here
We die, even as the winds of Autumn fade,
Expiring in the frore and foggy air.—
Behold! Spring comes, though we must pass, who made
The promise of its birth,—even as the shade
Which from our death, as from a mountain, flings
The future, a broad sunrise; thus arrayed
As with the plumes of overshadowing wings,
From its dark gulf of chains, Earth like an eagle springs.

(SP, 127–128)

43. Shelley's own note reads: "The phenomenon alluded to at the conclusion of the third stanza is well known to naturalists. The vegetation at the bottom of the sea, of rivers, and of lakes, sympathizes with that of the land in the change of seasons, and is consequently influenced by the winds which announce it" (SP, 577n).

44. A. J. Grant and Harold Temperley, *Europe in the Nineteenth and Twentieth Centuries (1789–1939)* (London: Longmans, 1948), p. 203.

45. *Queen Mab* VI.40–46 and Shelley's note to VIII.211 (SP, 826). See also pp. 247–249 above and Wasserman, *Shelley's "Prometheus Unbound,"* pp. 41–47.

46. Critics have seldom noted that the poet expects "a deep autumnal tone, / Sweet though in sadness" (SP, 579:60–61). An exception is Harold Bloom, *The Visionary Company: A Reading of English Romantic Poetry* (Garden City, N.Y.: Doubleday, 1961), p. 293, but Professor Bloom takes as the theme "the possibility of breaking out of cycle" (p. 289). Neville Rogers, *Shelley at Work: A Critical Inquiry* (Oxford: Clarendon, 1956), pp. 26–27, supports a similarly optimistic reading by appeal to the symbol of New Birth, an association of spring with a regeneration of thought. Admittedly, too, a serpent of eternity even more common than the *ouroboros* enjoys renewal as it seasonally sheds its skin (see *Hellas*, 1060–1063). All this still leaves us with a worthwhile revolution that must give way to another cycle in what is at best a spiral, even if one tries to destroy the problem by equating all cycles with the permanence of stars, as does Hélène Lemaître, *Shelley: Poète des Eléments* (Paris: Didier, 1962), pp. 275–306. On the cycle and revolution, see I. J. Kapstein, "The Symbolism of the Wind and the Leaves in Shelley's 'Ode to the West Wind,'" *PMLA*, 51 (1936), 1069–1079.

The disadvantages of taking Shelley's impulse as religious in the sense of the individual's relation to God can be seen in a clause of Bloom's larger, more valuable discussion of the poet in an earlier book. "By now it ought to be evident," he wrote, "that the thorns of life have nothing to do with Lord Chancellors, quarterly reviewers, despotic fathers, etc." *Shelley's Mythmaking* (Yale University Press, 1959), p. 85. In my view, the thorns of life have everything to do with these, in at least the three senses that the poet's experience is representative, that he bleeds through relapse of love (a failure in himself to unify love and wisdom, as *Prometheus Unbound* explains concerning unnecessary pain from thorns), and the largest sense that thorns belong to "unawakened earth" and man benightmared. When all the poem is seen as leading to the final section, then "the thorns of life" include very definitely such corruptions of government as the Earl of Eldon's performance in the role of Lord Chancellor.

47. All quotations are from SP, but I have made extensive use of *Shelley's "Prometheus Unbound": A Variorum Edition,* ed. Lawrence John Zillman (University of Washington Press, 1959). Of works listed and utilized by Zillman, I am indebted most to Carlos Baker, Kenneth Neill Cameron, Douglas Bush, G. M. Matthews, Arthur Clutton-Brock, and the socially oriented interpretations transmitted through John Todhunter and Henry S. Salt. On particular images, P. H. Butter, C. E. Pulos, and Neville Rogers have been especially valuable. Of works subsequent to Zillman's edition, my obligations are greatest to Milton Wilson, *Shelley's Later Poetry;* Glenn O'Malley, *Shelley and Synesthesia* (Northwestern University Press, 1964); Wasserman, *Shelley's "Prometheus Unbound";* Woodman, *The Apocalyptic Vision in the Poetry of Shelley;* Bloom, *Shelley's Mythmaking* and *The Visionary Company* (New York: Doubleday, 1961). From Wasserman, Woodman, and Bloom I have learned in admiration mixed with frequent dissent. For a repository of information about the text of the poem, but not as a definitive text to be followed, see *Shelley's "Prometheus Unbound": The Text and the Drafts,* ed. Lawrence John Zillman (Yale University Press, 1968).

48. In *A Philosophical View of Reform* Shelley designated as a unit the sorry period from Robespierre to Louis XVIII.

Notes to Pages 281–302

49. This is the usual interpretation, certainly Shelley's, of the "Priestley riots." For doubts on the ideological clarity of the event, see E. P. Thompson, *Making of the English Working Class,* pp. 26–27, 74, 78.

50. Of the criminals and their environment, Shelley observed to Peacock: "It is the emblem of Italy: moral degradation contrasted with the glory of nature & the arts." SL, II, 93–94.

51. SW, VII, 124.

52. Woodman, *Apocalyptic Vision,* p. 149.

53. SW, VII, 137. For a stringent treatment of the Platonic One in the *Defence,* see Earl R. Wasserman, "Shelley's Last Poetics: A Reconsideration," in *From Sensibility to Romanticism: Essays Presented to Frederick A Pottle,* ed. F. W. Hilles and Harold Bloom (Oxford University Press, 1965), pp. 487–511.

54. Presumably Shelley gave some consideration to the customary confusion between Demogorgon and the more firmly established Demiourgos, creator of all things. Robert Hartley has called my attention to the association of the Demiourgos with the *ouroboros,* which encircles all spiritual and material things, in Sir William Drummond's *Essay on a Punic Inscription* (London, 1810), pp. 78, 99–100. Shelley ordered this work near the end of 1812 (SL, I, 345). At II.iii.97 and elsewhere in *Prometheus Unbound* he links Demogorgon with the "snake-like Doom" beneath his throne.

55. "Shelley and Malthus," *PMLA,* 67 (1952), 113–124.

56. III.i.3, 18–24. For "The Jeremiah of a fruitful age, / Who taught in vain, that a prolific nation / Would perish through excess of population . . . ," see James Lawrence, "The Bosom Friend," a work of 1791 expanded in *The Etonian out of Bounds* (London, 1828), p. 95.

57. Notice that the full passage, in which Prometheus seems to speak of a hasty expression of words in a brief period of blinding grief, gives no sense of the summit of conversion assigned to its first four words by critics:

> It doth repent me: words are quick and vain;
> Grief for awhile is blind, and so was mine.
> I wish no living thing to suffer pain. (I. 303–305)

58. *Shelley's Prose; or, The Trumpet of a Prophecy,* ed. David Lee Clark, corr. ed. (University of New Mexico Press, 1966), p. 10.

59. Wasserman, *Shelley's "Prometheus Unbound,"* pp. 24–34 and passim.

60. I have been helped here by Bloom, *Shelley's Mythmaking,* p. 104.

61. The most difficult lines, for this suggested interpretation as for earlier interpretations, are I.192–194, spoken by The Earth:

> The Magus Zoroaster, my dead child,
> Met his own image walking in the garden.
> That apparition, sole of men, he saw.

If a phantasm lives unconsciously in a man's conscience as a motive and its consequence, perhaps Zoroaster is supposed sole among men in outfacing within his conscience a force of evil from Ahriman equal to the force of good from Mazda.

62. Along with the priesthood and soldiery in pre-Revolutionary France,

A Philosophical View of Reform denounces "fountains of literature poisoned by the spirit and the form of monarchy" (SW, VII, 13). Shelley specifically exempted Montesquieu and Rousseau, and apparently was about to exempt others, from his general condemnation of French literature, which conforms in spirit with Wordsworth's and Coleridge's condemnations.

Except for an understandable difficulty with the tenses, the key passages of the speech that originally closed the drama, III.iv.106–121, 164–179, are invaluably explicated by Donald H. Reiman, "Roman Scenes in *Prometheus Unbound* III.iv," *Philological Quarterly,* 46 (1967), 69–78.

63. SW, VII, 42. "That equality in possessions which Jesus Christ so passionately taught is a moral rather than a political truth and is such as social institutions cannot without mischief inflexibly secure."

64. Darwin, *The Temple of Nature,* IV, 450, pertinently quoted by Desmond King-Hele, "The Influence of Erasmus Darwin on Shelley," *Keats-Shelley Memorial Bulletin,* 13 (1962), 31, and *Erasmus Darwin* (New York: Scribners, 1963), p. 91.

65. On the tenets, see J. B. Bury, *The Idea of Progress: An Inquiry into Its Origin and Growth* (London, 1921); Plamenatz, I, 364ff., II, 409–457; Morris Ginsberg, *The Idea of Progress: A Revaluation* (Boston: Beacon, 1953); Joseph Anthony Mazzeo, *Renaissance and Revolution* (New York: Pantheon, 1965), pp. 275–336; Jerome Hamilton Buckley, *The Triumph of Time* (Harvard University Press, 1966).

66. SW, VII, 227. For the complete essay, with previous expurgations restored, see Clark, pp. 216–223, or James A. Notopoulos, *The Platonism of Shelley* (Duke University Press, 1949), pp. 375–413.

67. In this and the following paragraphs, I quote from SW, VII, 41, 52, 46, 11, 334, 30 ,161, 111, 47.

68. The abortive *Charles the First,* which Shelley began in 1818 and never totally abandoned, is another attempt to record "that which has been." The extant scenes embody a considerable effort to analyze a crisis in history without forcing the contemporary parallels. Yet the central scene of the fragment concerns the King's utilization of two unbending men, Archbishop Laud, with his prelates that weep crocodile tears like Eldon's—"For, when they cannot kill, they whine and weep" (SP, 491:110)—and Thomas Wentworth, Earl of Strafford, ordered to "stick not even at questionable means" in order to quiet the distempers of the North and of London. Strafford, like Castlereagh, has been the appointed ruler in Ireland. He is to fill the royal coffers by taxation, fines, confiscations, and "a forced loan from the refractory city." The Shakespearean clown Archy, with his reference to Gonzalo's commonwealth in *The Tempest* and his prophecy of "congregated lightning," performs the gadfly's role like Hone or Carlile crying for an annual Parliament as an alternative to revolution (SP, 497–502:199, 282, 361, 412). The biblical, apocalyptic allusions of Shelley's Citizens to "the Babylonian woman," to acquaintance with the "worm of Nile" through bondage in Egypt, and to "papists, atheists, tyrants, and apostates" barring the road to the New Jerusalem are not even as different as Shelley may have thought from language of Dissenters in 1818.

His persistent analogy of seasonal and historical oscillation appears early

Notes to Pages 313–320

in the first scene. Responding to a Youth eager to find good in the hour and in all men of the time, the Second Citizen asks impatiently:

> Canst thou discern
> The signs of seasons, yet perceive no hint
> Of change in that stage-scene in which thou art
> Not a spectator but an actor? (SP, 489:33–36)

In the interval between the two Golden Ages of past and future, while our earth rocks into the extremes of summer and winter, youth must learn to recognize the foretokens of the west wind that destroys in order to preserve. A youth of 1818 would be equally naive with the Youth of 1640 if he saw in the patentees and monopolists only the glorious pageant where a sage citizen could see "the pomp that strips the houseless orphan" (SP, 492:154). Shelley found parallels with his own time in 1640 because he looked to 1640 for warnings to his own day against the causes of revolution.

69. See Woodring, *Politics in the Poetry of Coleridge*, pp. 194–198.

70. Lines 588–589. Part of this acceptance of violence is simply the theory that "Revenge and Wrong bring forth their kind . . ." (729). In his edition of the poems (London, 1911, II, 471) C. D. Locock found it strange that a "Voice without," obviously hostile to the Greeks, should be invoked in later stages of the play to assure the future shelter of a Greek semichorus. But the Voice speaks for the self-destructive pride of empire. Health for the Greeks must wait on the other side of the self-inflicted ruin. Not only *Hellas,* but also *Prometheus Unbound,* is much concerned with the principle of imperial self-destruction.

71. SP, 470–471:763–806. For a time I was inclined to take Mahmud's expressions of fatalism, as at SP, 467:642–647, and a Semichorus' assignment of ruin and renovation to Destiny, the world's "eyeless charioteer" (469:711), as signs of a break in Shelley's doctrine of Necessity. Necessity is taken as equivalent in this poem to "oriental fatalism" by Douglas Bush, *Mythology and the Romantic Tradition in English Poetry* (Harvard University Press, 1937), p. 163. On such matters Bush is seldom wrong, and he goes on to read the conclusion of the poem as the fading of a "radiant mirage" (p. 165). But I now conclude, first, that Mahmud's repeated expressions concerning "the omnipotent hour to which are yoked" all men and things (457:189) belong to his own character, and second, that the choruses, who protest too much in their search to excuse the expediency of resistance, offer aspects, however inconsistent, of the Shelleyan insistence that apparent retribution is actually inevitable self-destruction: "Revenge and Wrong bring forth their kind . . ." (469:729).

72. The text followed is that in Donald H. Reiman, *Shelley's "The Triumph of Life": A Critical Study Based on a Text Newly Edited from the Bodleian Manuscript* (University of Illinois Press, 1965). I am greatly indebted also to the general lines of Professor Reiman's interpretation.

73. *Paradise Lost* II.666–673. See Reiman, pp. 29–31. Application of the passage to George IV was already notorious when Brougham quoted it at the trial of Caroline: ". . . what seem'd his head / The likeness of a Kingly Crown had on."

74. The posing of the second question, "Then, what is Life?" (544), also provides evidence that Rousseau had identified as "Life," not the chariot, but either specifically the shape within or generally the whole of "this sad pageantry" (176).

75. Lines 256–259, "That star that ruled his doom was far too fair," etc., must allude to Plato's love of the boy Aster (see the epigraph to *Adonais* and Shelley's translation, SP, 430, 720); but Shelley would recognize and accept pederasty as the outlet for "sentimental love" in Socrates equally with Plato. As he says of sexual relief in the essay on the manners of the Greeks, "The act itself is nothing" (Clark, pp. 220–221). The operative force of line 256 lies in the astrological metaphor for Necessity. We can expect Shelley to condemn only what he could regard as the consequences of Plato's love. He would not have condemned a sentimental attachment between Jupiter and Thetis. Plato "Expiates the joy & woe his master knew not" (255). Socrates was ruled by a star "where the Eternal are" (SP, 444:495), not one in the dance of life.

In the interpretation of line 256, and in his belief that the completed poem might have presented a victory of the better over the worse, but not in his insistence on an all-pervasive Platonic idealism, I am in agreement with Neville Rogers, ed., Percy Bysshe Shelley, *Selected Poetry* (Boston: Houghton Mifflin, 1968), pp. 460–466.

76. Concerning the reference to "the Republic of Benevento," George E. Woodberry was brief: "No explanation of the title has been found." *The Shelley Notebook in the Harvard College Library* (Cambridge, Mass., 1929), p. 15. Benevento was one of the centers of the uprising of the Carbonari against Ferdinand of Naples in July 1820, when that weak but treacherous king publicly accepted a constitutional government and fled, to await reconquest by the Austrians early in 1821. Couriers would have brought much secret news and rumor to the Shelleys in Livorno, as Pietro Gamba and others did to Byron in Ravenna. Mary Shelley commented on the revolution immediately, 19 July 1820: "Thirty years ago was the era for Republics, and they all fell. This is the era for *constitutions*" (SL, II, 217). Three days later, even closer to the spirit of Shelley's sonnet, Byron wrote to Murray: "The Neapolitans are not worth a curse, and will be beaten if it comes to fighting . . ." (LJ, V, 57). Possibly Shelley's conversations with Byron and Gamba in August 1821 helped inspire the sonnet. See Iris Origo, *The Last Attachment* . . . (New York: Scribners, 1949), pp. 201–203, 224–227, 270; Oreste Dito, *Massoneria, Carboneria ed altre società segrete nella storia del Risorgimento italiano* (Turin, 1905), pp. 239–273; R. M. Johnston, *The Napoleonic Empire in Southern Italy and the Rise of the Secret Societies,* 2 vols. (London, 1904), II, 69–102, on Benevento, II, 77.

77. Reiman, pp. 62–73, equates the shape with the fatal "veilèd maid" envisioned by the Poet in "Alastor"; my point is that the attributes of the shape make her imply the true Intellectual Beauty beyond. If she is not divine, Asia is the divinity she is not, the divinity Rousseau mistook her for. It is conceivable but unlikely that Shelley deliberately cancels in her everything he had previously said of Love; in other words, unlikely that Rousseau was wrong to believe in "the spark with which Heaven lit" his

Notes to Pages 324–327

spirit, with the corollary that the author of *Prometheus Unbound* was wrong to believe that "beautiful idealisms of moral excellence" do more good than harm. It is to be noted that the shape is linked by simile with the constancy of stars, in the form of Venus unseen but present throughout the day (416–419; see Reiman, pp. 12, 16–17, 68–69).

78. The connotation of *nepenthe* in Shelley's poetry and in his day strikes forcibly in John Howard Payne's report of Mary Shelley's response when he proposed to replace the drowned Shelley as her husband: "Having once tasted Nepenthe, what is there left for me to hope for?" *The Romance of Mary W. Shelley, John Howard Payne, and Washington Irving,* ed. F. B. Sanborn (Boston, 1907), p. 61. In the common usage confirmed by all the examples in the *Oxford English Dictionary* (although not in the modern definitions being illustrated), the hero of R. P. Ward's *Tremaine* passed into anxiety when he found that Euphemia loved another, whereupon "a cup filled with Nepenthe seemed dashed from his lips" (2nd ed., London, 1825, I, 40). Paolo Manuzio's edition of Ambrogio Calepino's *Dictionarium,* citing Pliny 21.21, as my colleague William Nelson has kindly called to my attention, begins the definition of *nepentes:* "herbae genus, quae vino iniecta animi hilaritatem inducit."

Shelley's lines do not say that Rousseau drank, but neither do they say that the cup was dashed from his lips; in the absence of this or a similar dramatic emphasis, we must assume that he drank when he "Touched with faint lips the cup she raised, / And suddenly my brain became as sand" (404–405). We may assume also that the "crystal glass" and "cup" are one. But we may not assume that the Nepenthe acted like a narcotic.

CONCLUSION

1. Samuel Wilberforce to Charles Anderson, August 21, 1837, Bodleian MS c.191, quoted in David Newsome, *The Wilberforces and Henry Manning* (Harvard University Press, 1966), p. 7.

2. *Collected Letters of Samuel Taylor Coleridge,* ed. Earl Leslie Griggs (Oxford: Clarendon, 1956), I, 349.

361

INDEX

363

Index

Index

Index

Byron, poems of (*continued*)
Two Foscari, The, 182, 183,
186–187, 188, 190
"Vision of Belshazzar," 174
Vision of Judgment, The, 171, 182,
192–199, 214, 218, 241
Waltz, The, 165, 170, 206, 218
"We sate down and wept by the
waters," 174
Werner, 152, 209, 226
"Wild Gazelle, The," 174
"Windsor Poetics," 171

Cabanis, Georges, 248
Caesar, Julius, 152, 214, 216, 226
Calvert, Raisley, 90
Calvin, John, 41, 65, 328
Cambridge: and republican theory,
21; a republic, 107; and Foxite
liberalism, 86, 148; impaired
Wordsworth's imagination, 102,
104, 107, 109; mentioned, 49, 150,
163, 190
Campanella, Tommaso, 127
Campbell, Thomas, 70, 71, 150, 173
Canning, George: Foreign Secretary,
44, 211, 217, 218; *Anti-Jacobin,*
10–11, 67, 154
Cap of Liberty, 18
Capital punishment, 24; Byron on,
170; Wordsworth on, 24
Capitalism, 80, 134
Carbonari, 127, 182, 185, 360 (n.
76)
Caricatures ("public prints"), 7, 14;
as parody, 194, 260; inconography
for verse satire, 16, 18, 218, 241,
269, 270
Carlile, Mary Ann, 270
Carlile, Richard: radical, 21, 209,
282; freethinker, 17, 212; disciple
of Paine, 242; on spies, 265; imprisoned, 209, 270
Carlisle, Frederick Howard, 5th Earl
of, 155
Carlyle, Thomas, 40, 116
Caroline, Princess of Wales, 269;
marital troubles, 17, 23, 269; popular support, 187, 205, 270; trial,
17, 194, 209, 268–272; vulgarity,
184; death, 206; and Byron, 168,
270; and Hone, 194; and Lamb,
75, 76; and Shelley, 268–272

Cartwright, John, Major, 17, 168
Cary, Henry Francis, 23
Cassirer, Ernst, 100
Cassius, Gaius, 152
Casti, Giambattista, 200
Castlereagh, Robert Stewart, Vis-
count, 17, 195, 197, 209; Foreign
Secretary, 17; and Holy Alliance,
23, 211, 315; in Ireland, 197, 209;
and Greece, 315; and civil liberties,
21, 195, 265, 269, 285; unre-
sponsive, 24; a tool, 197, 286; as
Murder, 265–266; suicide of, 209,
217; mentioned, 9, 171, 178, 230,
271, 325
Catherine the Great, 202, 216, 321
Catholic Emancipation, 24, 55, 130,
168, 195, 244
Catholicism, 131, 236, 311; *see also*
Irish Catholics
Cervantes, Miguel de, 152, 202
Ceylon, 80
Chain of being, 134, 135
Champion, 76, 124, 170
Charles I, 11, 171
Charles XII (of Sweden), 180, 216
Charlotte Augusta, Princess, 23, 169,
172
Chartism, 7, 263
Chartreuse, Grande, 86, 92, 103–104
Chateaubriand, François René,
Vicomte de, 9, 217, 329
Chatham, William Pitt, 1st Earl of,
56, 150
Chatterton, Thomas, 33, 128, 319
Chaucer, Geoffrey, 10
Chesterton, G. K., 222
Christian, Fletcher, 222–226
Christianity: as romantic conserva-
tism, 26, for Coleridge, 53, for
Wordsworth, 137; and Blake's "in-
nocence," 60; forgiveness, 63;
Byron's universalism, 197; Shelley's
resentment of, 232, 247; oppressive,
248, 258, 273, 285; redemptive,
309; "philosophical," 316–317
Church of England: status quo, 20,
131, 281; bastion, 139, 145; national trust, 55; refuge, 131–132;
and popular education, 137; tithes,
208, 209, 221; victim of landlords,
220, 222
Churchill, Charles, 75, 153

366

Index

Index

Dandolo, Enrico, Doge, 177
Daniel, Samuel, 140
D'Annunzio, Gabriele, 41
Dante Alighieri, 278; hero of liberty, 23, 152, 161, 175, 176, 281, of love, 321; and nationalism, 45, 175; demonic, 188; comprehensive, 278; mentioned, 101, 179, 221, 303, 320
Darwin, Erasmus: "Jacobin," 27, 68, 154, 325; expository verse, 42, 106, 242, 325; tinsel, 153; addresses imagination, 325; evolutionist, 67, 306
Daumier, Honoré, 94
Davy, Sir Humphry, 11, 322
Delacroix, Eugène, 27, 174, 228
Della Cruscans, 27, 154
Demagogues, 130, 149, 321
Democracy, 6, 33, 96, 115, 145, 211
Democratic idea, 77, 94, 96–98, 107, 202
Demosthenes, 216
Denmark, 44, 139, 165, 239
De Quincey, Thomas: on acceleration, 2; depreciates understanding, 32; and Wordsworth, 118, 143, 244
Descartes, René, 32, 310, 317
Devonshire, Georgiana, Duchess of, 16
Dickens, Charles, 203, 222
Diderot, Denis, 37
Dilke, Charles, 81
Diodorus Siculus, 187, 188
Diogenes, 217, 221
Disraeli, Benjamin, 10, 20, 147
D'Israeli, Isaac, 160
Dominion, 166, 288, 322
Drummond, Sir William, 289
Dryden, John, 47, 153, 222
Du Guesclin, Bertrand, 216
Dumouriez, Charles François, General, 58
Dundas, see Melville
Duty, 36, 129, 222, 296

Eagles: Roman, 177; Napoleonic, 9, 142, 177, 179, 215; strength of liberty, 176–177, 190, 223, 316; rational hope, 153; power, 321; force, 255, 256; predator, 316
Eaton, Daniel Isaac, 244
Economics, 4, 95, 113, 204, 206–209; see also Paper money, Taxation

Edgeworth, Maria and Richard, 137
Edinburgh Review, 16, 117, 148, 205
Education, popular, 17, 136–138, 144
Edward I, 264
Edward III, 60, 62
Edwards, Jonathan, 51
Egoism, 8, 42, 125, 156, 163, 329
Egypt, 215, 238–239; battle of Nile, 14
Eldon, John Scott, Lord, 17; Lord Chancellor, 17, 302; and civil liberties, 21, 195, 285; rulings on literature, 209, 253, 351–352 (n. 25); as Fraud, 170, 265; tearful, 266
Elgin, Thomas Bruce, 7th Earl of, 165
Eliot, George (Mary Anne Evans), 256
Eliot, T. S., 25, 167
Elizabeth I, 131, 253
Ellenborough, Edward Law, Baron, 17, 194, 195, 302
Elliott, Ebenezer, 84
Ellis, George, 154
Emerson, Ralph Waldo, 304
Emigration, 136
Emmet, Robert, 71, 237
Emotion, 27, 39, 40, 119, 126
Empedocles, 67
Empiricism, 32–35; stresses the individual, 8; as contracted vision, 65; in romantic poetry, 37–38, 47, 94, 156, 275, 310
Enclosure, 2, 15, 88
Energy: a romantic emphasis, 27, 39, 162, 179; divine, 8, 62; unifying, 63; and will, 43; and revolution, 61; amoral, 113, 162; and Napoleon, 5, 27
Enlightenment, 37, 38, 41, 153, 232–233; certitude, 75; self-interest, 38, 106; *bon sens,* 37; program of freedom, 232; natural goodness, 41; conquest over Nature, 77, 306–307; systematization, 75, 106; divorced understanding from love, 307; reaction against, 28–39, 75, 106, 325; seduction by, 82, 102, 109–110; stabilizing, 161–162; Encylopedists, 37, 287; in Scotland, 56, 75
Equality, 303; Christian, 41; democratic, 33; requires justice, 36; in reason, 34, 41; in imagination and

368

Index

Index

370

Index

Index

Index

Index

Index

Index

377

Index

Index

Index

112; as sentiment, 154; and society, 112, 234

Tacitus, 259
Tasso, Torquato, 152, 160–161, 163, 175–176, 178
Taxation, 207, 208, 209; and War, 15; and Allies, 18; and royal mistresses, 196; and National Debt, 207, 208, 266, 271; poor rates, 21, 208; "Taxes on Knowledge," 17, 18, 21, 48
Taylor, Jeremy, 77
Tennyson, Alfred, Lord, 7, 143
Thackeray, William Makepeace, 140
Thelwall, John, 37, 43, 51, 106, 134
Themistocles, 167
Thermopylae, 167, 227, 316
Thomson, James, 44, 106, 164
Thucydides, 152
Thurlow, Edward, 1st Baron, 171, 259
Thurlow, Edward, 2nd Baron, 171
Tiberius, 190
Times (London), 19, 206
Titans: large-scale humanity, 83; noble leaders, 162, 176, 179, including the self-destructive, 178, 216; defiant outlaws, 168; as analogy in *Childe Harold,* 156; *see also* Heroes, Leaders, Prometheus
Tolerance, 33, 75, 256, 266
Tooke, John Horne, 19, 194
Toussaint L'Ouverture, 120–121
Transcendentalism, 6, 53, 117
Treasonable Practices Act, 19, 21
Tremadoc, Wales, 245
Turgot, Anne Robert Jacques, Baron de l'Aulne, 97, 216
Turks, 166–167; and Napoleon, 14; Ottoman Empire, 122; and Sobieski, 123; Greek enemy, 166, 210, 227, 313–315, 318; and English ministers, 318; as Islam, 255; Turkish tales, 166–168, 175, 223, 224
Tuscany, 191
Twain, Mark (Samuel Clemens), 72
Tyrannicide, 69; recommended, 69, 152, 183, 226, 241; Wordsworth tempted to, 93, 109; and Glory, 243; and fraternity, 306; as ritual magic, 244; in *The Cenci,* 311–313
Tyranny, 69, 173–174; created by slaves, 44, 188, 191, and tyrant-

Tyranny (*continued*)
slaves, 236, 238, 241, 256, 278, 287, 289, 291, 311, 326; removable, 62, 136; self-destroying, 292, 293, 295; governmental, 62, 255, 279, 311–313; monarchic, 78, 216, 235–243; under George III, 194–195; democratic, 145; intellectual, 61, 212; of luxury, 187; as measurement, 61; as frost, 277, 279, 287; begets anarchy, 259, 265–268; *see also* "Anarch," Jehovah, Nimrod
Tyrol, 120, 126
Tyrwhitt, Sir Thomas, 172

Understanding, 32, 34, 43
Unionization, 19, 24, 147
United Irishmen, 130
United States, *see* America
Utilitarianism, 37–39, 233; unromantic, 54, 95–96, 134, 304; "steam-engine" creed, 327; narrow vision, 99; and self-interest, 4, 285; in tales for children, 106; *Westminster Review* as organ of, 67; Peacock and, 68; Scott and, 73; *see also* Bentham, Paley, Priestley

Vallon, Annette, 86, 108, 116, 128
Vane, Sir Henry, 8, 116
Vegetarianism, 247–248
Venice: commonwealth, 121–122, 179; oligarchic, 122, 182–187; enslaved, 126, 160, 164, 177, 261; decay of tradition, 160–161; Castlereagh and, 197
Vergil, 150, 218, 297, 320
Verona, Congress of, 210, 214–220
Violence, 89, 166, 267; an evil, 89, 92–93, 258, 291; from accumulated grievance, 93, 263, 311–313; revolutionary, 130, 234, 263, 305, 310, 317; mob, 21, 267, 272–273; of militia, 267, 273; and devastation by Greeks, 316, 317; *see also* Frame-breaking, Peterloo, Revolution, Tyrannicide, War
Volcanoes: instrument of God, 140; sublime, 215; Titanic, 223; inspirational, 267, 295; revolutionary, 256, 267, 277, 328; prevent earthquakes, 277, 291, 316

Index

Volney, Constantin François, Comte de, 250; reformist, 90, 302; millenarian, 236; on general assembly, 257; on dissent of sects, 258

Voltaire (François Marie Arouet): iconoclast, 162, 287; skeptic, 189; easy deism of, 197; spoiler spoiled, 178, 321; and Byron, 162, 180, 216; and Shelley, 287, 321; Wordsworth's distate for, 116; mentioned, 157; *Candide*, 203

Vowles, S., 270

Wagram, battle of, 238
Walcheren expedition, 69, 197
Wallace, Sir William, 73
Wanderers, 92–93, 237; oppressed, 10–11, 86–88, 113, 237; in expiation, 92–93; ennobled, 132
War: and established institutions, 220, 248; and repression, 10, 61, 88, 236; against Liberty, 109; justified if for Liberty, 119, 140, 210; carnage, 172, 210, 213, 231; madness, 295, 318; divine carnage, 140, 141, 268; self-defeating, 65; paralyzes choice, 157; and taxation, 15, 18
Warton, Joseph, 33
Warton, Thomas, 33
Washington, George: hero of liberty, 6, 67, 152, 179, 193, 194, 201, 329; defeated George III, 62, 201; ruled and retired, 177, 178, 186, 216, 322; mentioned, 196, 214, 229, 323
Waterloo: final defeat of Napoleon, 140, 157, 170; slaughter, 210; Holy Alliance as beneficiary of, 178; monuments to, 124, 140, 218; and economic change, 21; mentioned, 161
Watson, Dr. James, of Spa Fields riots, 209
Watson, James, weaver, 19
Watteau, Jean Antoine, 27
Watts, Isaac, 60
"Wealth of nations," 38, 113, 135
Wellek, René, 29, 53
Wellington, Arthur Wellesley, 1st Duke of, 20; honors and loot, 20, 207, 218, 219, 221; hero manqué, 124–125, 142; condemned by poets, 202, 209, 238; at Cintra, 20, 124, 158; on night before Quatrebras,

Wellington (*continued*)
164; at Waterloo, 178, 179; in India, 209; at Verona, 210, 220; Tennyson on, 143; mentioned, 215
Wesley, Charles, 60, 106, 328
Wesley, John, 18, 60, 106, 194, 328
Westminster Review, 67
Westmorland Gazette, 144
Whigs, 16–17; Foxite, 16, 130, 148; Grenvillite, 16, 168, 206; independent, 16–17, 205; moderate (landed, Holland House), 16, 149, 154, 165, 206; Radical, 17, 168, 205; Reform, 16, 57; somnolent, 243–244; and liberty, 120, 187; and commerce, 122; Burke and, 50; Byron and, 148, 149, 154, 155, 165, 168; Campbell as, 70; George IV and, 169, 210; Hobhouse and, 185, 226; Moore as, 70–71
Whitbread, Samuel, 17, 148
Wilberforce, Samuel, Bishop, 327
Wilberforce, William, 210
Wilde, Oscar, 41
Wilkes, John, 193, 194
Will, belief in, 43–44
Williams, Helen Maria, 3, 86, 258, 339 (n. 3)
Winscom, Jane Cave, 141
Wolcot, John ("Peter Pindar"), 75, 165, 268
Wollstonecraft, Mary, 249, 252, 302
Wooler, Thomas J., 17, 21, 209, 242, 265
Wordsworth, Christopher (1774–1846), 131, 137
Wordsworth, Dorothy, 90, 100, 102, 128, 143
Wordsworth, John (1772–1805), 129, 131, 142
Wordsworth, Mary Hutchinson, 116
Wordsworth, William, 5–47 *passim*, 85–147; particularity in, 38, 94, 98–99, 127, 156, 255; and metaphysics, 74; and Roman virtue, 44, 77, 119, 155, 239; on Venice, 121, 161; patriot, 162; and Reform Bill, 144, 227; sanguinary, 273; chilled, 199, 252; fluidity of, 274; in intellectual crisis, 325; and sympathy, 330; Byron and, 154, 163, 198; Keats and, 78, 81; Lamb and, 74, 75, 76; parodied by Pea-

383

Index

Index